In the Saddle

Dr. Dave Smith

In the Saddle

Faithful Life Publishers & Printers
North Fort Myers, FL 33903

FaithfulLifePublishers.com
info@FaithfulLifePublishers.com
888.720.0950

Cover design: Dannah Bottrell
Editing: Letha Johnson & Jodi Raasch

For additional copies contact:
Saddle Up Ministries
P. O. Box 527
Lancaster, KY 40444
saddleupmin@gmail.com

Scripture quotations are from the King James Version

Published in the United States of America.

25 24 23 22   1 2 3 4 5

Foreword

There are many devotional books and booklets available to us. Devotional books are a tremendous tool to help many have direction in their daily devotions and their personal walk with God.

To me, what makes a devotional book a good and helpful resource is when the author or compiler of that book has a personal walk with God that is evident in their life. That is the case with this book In the Saddle. Brother Dave Smith is a man who not only walks with the Lord, he has done so for many, many years and it is evident in his life. The evidence of his walk with the Lord in the prayers that have been answered, the goals that have been reached, a marriage of fifty years, success as a soul winner and one who mentors his converts as well as the success in the area of leadership in his life. His wife, children and grandchildren admire him and those who have worked for him respect him. I am pleased to recommend to you this devotional booklet to assist you in not only following Brother Smith's devotional life but to develop your own as you learn from Brother Dave Smith.

— Pastor Jeffrey J. Fugate

Acknowledgments

Thank you to all the summer staff that we have served the Lord together with throughout the years. Many of you have suggested that I put into print the daily devotions that were given each morning and at the morning flagpole. Thank you to many from the Life Builders Sunday School Class that I sent devotions to in an attempt to be of an encouragement to in your walk with God. All of you were an encouragement to me to begin putting together this book.

I want to thank my children and their mates, my grandchildren and especially my granddaughter, Dannah Bottrell, who designed the cover and kept up with me in all of the organizing, correcting, layout and endless hours of work, to make this book possible. Each of you have encouraged me on.

Thanks goes to Letha Johnson and Jodi Raasch for the tedious job of reading, correcting, and proofing every devotional. Miss Jodi was able to put up with my country homespun writing and not lose the tenor of what I was trying to say. This work could never have made it to the printer without you.

A special thanks to Mrs. Robert Steffen who faithfully posted every rough draft I wrote for our Life Builders Sunday School class. You were faithful every day and an encouragement to keep going.

I want to thank Bro. William Davis and his staff for preparing this work for the printer and for encouraging me to have the devotions in print.

Thank you to my pastor who has given me the opportunity to serve the Lord at Clays Mill Baptist Church and to have the privilege to direct Circle C Baptist Ranch, and to teach the Life Builders Sunday School Class. It was under Pastor Fugate's leadership, vision and faith that Circle C Baptist Ranch came into existence.

Dedication

I dedicate this book to my wife, Shonna Jo Smith, who has stood faithfully by my side since May 22, 1971. Your love for the Lord, dedication to the Lord, servant's heart, faithfulness in being a student of the Word, has inspired me to write this book. You have pushed on when others would have quit. You have served and labored in pain that many could not bear, and most would have said, I quit. Your love for souls and your desire to see people go on for the Lord has motivated me. You have been the greatest intercessor of my life.

Thank you, honey, for being you and believing in me, loving me. You are my help meet from the Lord.

Thank you for the years we have served our KING together.

Genesis 1-3   Psalm 1   Proverbs 1   Matthew 1-2

A New Year in God's Word

Good morning! We now begin a New Year in life as well as a New Year in reading through the Word of God. Now for over sixty-eight years I have been on this earth, and I want to give testimony for God and to God that His Word is truth and has been forever and will last forever, and on the very first day of the year may we make God's Word a fresh final authority in our lives. As I began reading this morning in Genesis 1-3, I began to mark God's authority that is recorded. Please bear with me and just watch; "God said, God called, God divided, God saw, God made, God set, God created, God blessed, God ended, God formed, God planted, God took, God commanded, God caused, God doth know, God walking, and God make." In every area of our lives and in every decision that we make, let us put God in the foremost spot as our first and final authority.

I turned and began reading in Matthew 1 and down to verse 23, "Behold, a virgin shall be with child, and shall bring forth a son, and they shall call his name Emmanuel, which being interpreted is, God with us." No one or nothing but God can allow a woman to be with child without man; only God. God brought God to us as Jesus the Son of God because He is God. AMEN! In Psalm 1:1, "Blessed is the man that walketh not in the counsel of the ungodly." Start today and allow God every day to be your foremost guide, counselor, decision maker, leader and final authority.

As an older man, I seek counsel of others whom I respect and admire, but my final authority is God. When I go to man for counsel, I take that counsel to God in prayer, and I evaluate it through the eyes of the Bible. I hunger to grow in every area of my life, and I have made enough wrong decisions and mistakes. Today is the beginning of a New Year. May

I encourage you to seek God's wisdom and guidance. Proverbs 1:2, "To know wisdom and instruction; to perceive the words of understanding." Do not let pride, fear, selfishness, lack of confidence, worldliness, sin of any kind get in front of what God says. Proverbs 1:5, "A wise man will hear, and will increase learning; and a man of understanding shall attain unto wise counsels." Seek the Lord today and every day. Put God and His Word first place. Do not let emotions, this world or anything get in front of God. He is and He always will be God. I am beginning this New Year with you. Let us walk with God through His Word and grow in Him. Happy New Year!

Seek God's wisdom and guidance every day of this new year.

January 2

Genesis 4-6   Psalm 2   Proverbs 2   Matthew 3-4

Lesson from the Otters

Good morning! One of the neighbors stopped me the other day and asked if I had seen any otters by the ponds, and we began to talk. Over a year ago he had stocked one of the brand-new ponds with some fish and they fed them every day until they reached a good size. I said to him that I had not, and asked him why he was asking. He told me that all of the fish were gone in one pond, and he had found tracks by another pond. He said the otters were eating all the fish. How did those otters find the new pond? Just like every animal of the forest, they were given an instinct by God. Genesis 5:1-2, "This is the book of the generations of Adam. In the day that God created man, in the likeness of God made he him; Male and female created he them." Inside of all creation God created a consciousness of Him and how we are to be. We read in Genesis 5:22 how Enoch walked with God. In Genesis 6:9, "and Noah walked with God." Matthew 4:4, "It is written, Man shall not live by bread alone, but by every word that proceedeth out of the mouth of God." All of God's creation were created to be dependent on God.

Those otters do not go to a grocery store, a clothing store, or even seek a medical doctor. They exist and survive because of God. I am not against going to any of the above. My point is that you and I were created to have an understanding and dependency on God. We have just started this new year and it is vitally important for us to daily go to God, seek His face, spend time in His Word, spend time with Him in prayer. To learn of Him, love Him and understand the importance of serving Him. Matthew 4:19, "Follow me, and I will make you fishers of men." Matthew 4:22, "And they immediately left the ship and their father, and followed him." There were no announcements made that there was a new pond and new fish. The otters are a perfect picture of living as they were created by God, to be dependent on how God created them. I do not know or totally understand how it all works, but I know that if man will submit to following God, He will bless and use man. Psalm 2:12, "Blessed are all they that put their trust in him." The otters will not come to the ponds where there is a lot of human traffic, but they come and feed at the ponds that are far away.

Reading, studying, learning God's Word will bring guidance in all areas of our lives. That is why being under sound Biblical teaching and preaching and learning principles to live by is a must. Proverbs 2:11, "Discretion shall preserve thee, understanding shall keep thee." Those otters have more common sense and understanding of God than many a man and woman that were created in the very image of God. Something to think about.

All of God's creation were created to be dependent on God.

January 3

Genesis 7-9   Psalm 3   Proverbs 3   Matthew 5

Keep Learning

Good morning! Many years ago, I came across a little piece of wood that was made to sit on a desk. I have read the quote, taught the quote and reminded myself of the quote hundreds of times. The quote says, "When a man ceases to learn, he ceases to lead." I find myself forgetting sometimes and I will stop myself and speak to the Lord and ask Him to help me remember whatever it is that I have forgotten. It has been often said that we will forget more than we have learned. I hunger to remember what is important that will help me in my relationship and service for the Lord.

In Genesis 7-9 this morning we learned so much, but may I put an emphasis on just some short statements by God to Noah that could help us today. Genesis 7:1, "Come," Genesis 7:5, "Noah did," Genesis 7:16, "the Lord shut him in," Genesis 8:1, "God remembered Noah," Genesis 8:16, "Go forth," Genesis 8:20, "Noah builded an altar," and in Genesis 8:22, "shall not cease." God was leading and teaching Noah every step to take, follow, and obey. In Matthew 5:2, we read, "And he opened his mouth, and taught them." Life is full of listening, learning and obeying. This should be the pattern for our walk with the Lord. As we read His Word, we listen to the Holy Spirit and learn and apply the Biblical principles in every area and every day of our lives. Proverbs 3:1, "My son, forget not my law; but let thine heart keep my commandments." This morning before I go to church to work, I will feed the dogs and check on the horses and buildings. The horses, young and old, will wait to see if I will bring grain along with their hay. The smartest horse out of the group will stand at the fence and watch the house almost every morning, waiting for me to come. The dogs wait at the back door and the oldest dog will be the first to sit down and wait for the treat that I will give while the younger dog is running back and forth all excited. It is amazing how the older animals have the patience and more obedience.

Learn from the Word of God daily and be patient to wait upon God. Psalm 3:3, "But thou, O Lord, art a shield for me; my glory and the lifter up of mine head." Genesis 7:5, "And Noah did according unto all that the Lord commanded him." May that be said about us today.

Life if full of listening, learning and obeying,
and should be our pattern in walking with God.

Genesis 10-12   Psalm 4   Proverbs 4   Matthew 6-7

The Perfect Place

Good morning! May I start our thoughts this morning from our Bible reading by asking a couple of questions? Do we know the will of God, are we serving in the will of God, and are we enjoying the blessings of God in His will? Please note that I used the word "we" several times, so that I am not pointing a finger. Also please note that when we point a finger, there are three pointing back at us. We must constantly remind ourselves that God saved our soul not just to redeem us, but to be in His will and serving. Many a person will live in confusion and miss the joy of the Lord because of not being in the will of God.

We read in Genesis 12:1-3, three different phrases; "I will shew," "I will make," "I will bless." God wants to shew each of us His will but that takes submission when we spend time in prayer with God. God wants to "make" us which causes us to be separated from this world and that often brings us to a time of seeking God through fasting. The blessings of God will only come as we decide that we are going to serve Him where we are, however, we can, and that causes us to take a great step of faith. Matthew 6:33, "But seek ye first the kingdom of God, and his righteousness; and all these things shall be added unto you." Matthew 7:24, "Therefore whosoever heareth these sayings of mine, and doeth them, I will liken him unto a wise man, which built his house upon a rock." The will of God is the perfect place for the child of God. Proverbs 5:7, "Hear me now therefore, O ye children, and depart not from the words of my mouth." Many a person has quit serving the Lord, quit church, lost their joy, lost their peace, all because they quit living in the will of God. Our daily plea to God should be Psalm 5:8, "Lead me, O Lord, in thy righteousness because of mine enemies; make thy way straight before my face." The will of God is the perfect place to live, serve and be blessed.

There is a lot to think about today, so let us make it very simple. God desires to "shew" us His will and He will "make" us to be what we need to be, so that He can "bless" us with His great blessings. Yield to Him today and tell Him that you want to live in His will, and then seek Him and serve Him. Enjoy His will today.

The will of God is the perfect place for the child of God.

January 5

Genesis 13-15   Psalm 5   Proverbs 5   Matthew 8-9

Growing in Faith

Good morning! As I was reading this morning, I could hear our daughter say, "I am scared, Daddy," as I was attempting to teach her how to ride a bicycle. Our daughter is grown now, is a mother and a pastor's wife but some things will never leave your mind. A preacher friend of mine had three daughters and the youngest came to him one day and said, "Daddy, how come the children of Israel never grow up?" The pastor said, what do you mean? She said, "Daddy, in the Bible, God always calls them the children of Israel."

So often I look at myself and feel I am still a child in my walk with God. There have been times I have questioned my faith or had doubts. Our reading today is like a father looking at his child, helping us to grow, mature and get stronger in our faith in God. Genesis 15:1, "Fear not, Abram: I am thy shield, and thy exceeding great reward." Genesis 15:6, "And he believed in the Lord." Helping our little girl learn to ride a bicycle for the first time was an eventful day. "Daddy, I can't; Yes, you can. Help me, Daddy, I am doing it, Daddy." Matthew 8:26, Why are ye fearful, O ye of little faith?" Matthew 9:2, "and Jesus seeing their faith said unto the sick of the palsy; Son, be of good cheer; thy sins be forgiven thee." Matthew 9:22, "thy faith hath made thee whole." Matthew 9:29, "According to your faith be it unto you." May our faith in the Lord be growing each day.

Our daughter is a long way from learning to ride a bicycle. We were just talking a couple of weeks ago about the first time she rappelled down a building. Her fear of falling on a bicycle left her when she began to learn, listen and follow instructions. May our faith grow as we learn to listen to God and follow His instructions. Proverbs 5:7, "Hear me now therefore, O ye children, and depart not from the words of my mouth." When our little girl rode her bicycle by herself there was a great big smile and joy in her heart. Psalm 5:11, "But let all those that put their trust in thee rejoice." How is your faith in God today? Are you listening and learning more about Him so that you can have greater trust in Him? Faith causes me to lean on and depend on God. It was our faith in God and His Word and His forgiveness of our sins that was the first step in you and I getting saved. Let that faith grow and rejoice in a life in Christ.

Growing in our faith will cause us to have greater trust in God.

January 6

Genesis 16-17   Psalm 6   Proverbs 6   Matthew 10

Hungry for God

Good morning! As Mrs. Smith and I were driving home from church, she looked at me and said, what do you enjoy for Sunday noon meal? I have been blessed with a wife that is a great cook. She loves to cook and I love to eat. I named off several meals that I enjoy and then I said to her, there is nothing that you fix that I do not enjoy. Every meal is great, and I love her trying new recipes. When I was growing up, we basically ate things that we grew in the garden, and we ate the meat that we raised or hunted. No fancy meals, no foreign foods. You could say I was raised on meat and potatoes, farm fresh eggs and Jersey cow milk and butter. I am not complaining, but I have learned to enjoy foods from around the world that you would not find in a little farm town in Missouri.

I have so many notes from my reading today, but the note that I keep dwelling on is Genesis 17:1, "And when Abram was ninety years old and nine, the Lord appeared to Abram, and said unto him, I am the Almighty God; walk before me and be thou perfect." Ninety-nine years old and God has a plan for him. Ninety-nine years old and God wants to use him. Ninety-nine years old and God is not done with him. Ninety-nine years old and God brings our attention to him. If you are in your teens, twenties, thirties, forties, fifties, and on up, please stop and take note. God is not done with us until we breathe our last breath and God wants us to know that in the later years of our life, we are to be even a greater example of a life in Christ that has walked with God. The two words "Almighty God," are the words "El Shaddai," meaning "Strength-giver and Satisfier." Sometimes we get our strength in everything else but God. Sometimes we look to the things of this world to satisfy us instead of God.

Every meal my wife has made for me has satisfied me. I am not looking for a new wife to make a new meal. We look too often to our family to be our strength and you are reading words from a man that loves his family more than words could ever tell, but listen to the words of Matthew 10:37, "He that loveth father or mother more than me is not worthy of me: and he that loveth son or daughter more than me is not worthy of me." I am to learn from my parents. Proverbs 6:20, "My son, keep thy father's commandment, and forsake not the law of thy mother." My God hungers to walk with me, teach me, give me His power and wisdom. Talk with Him continually, get your strength from Him. Psalm 6:9, "The Lord hath heard my supplication; the Lord will receive my prayer." Every meal my wife prepares satisfies me, but I get hungry for the next meal. When I allow the Lord to feed me, I am satisfied and strengthened more than any food that I can eat. Let Him be the "Almighty God" He is today.

When God feeds us, we are strengthened and satisfied more than any food.

January 7

    Genesis 18-19   Psalm 7   Proverbs 7   Matthew 11

Keep Looking Forward

Good morning! If we were asked the simple question, "Is anything too hard for the Lord?," as we read in Genesis 18:14, we would all answer with a quick, no. All of us have had times that we would say we could see no way that things are going to work out. To some, victory over a sin seems impossible. To some, a victory in a marriage relationship seems impossible. To some, finding a mate that meets the list of prayer requests seems impossible. Many times I have had to tell myself that nothing is impossible with God.

We must start by reading the words of Genesis 19:17, "look not behind thee." The city of Sodom and Gomorrah was going to be destroyed because of the wickedness of sin, and the angel of the Lord told Lot, his wife, and daughters to not look back. We know from the reading that Lot's wife looked back "and she became a pillar of salt." My heart breaks whenever a person turns back to their sin. We read the words, "Is any thing too hard for the Lord?," and yet we turn back to sin that destroys. We read this morning about coming to God and getting our strength from Him in Matthew 11:28-29, "Come unto me, all ye that labour and are heavy laden, and I will give you rest. Take my yoke upon you, and learn of me, for I am meek and lowly in heart: and ye shall find rest unto your souls."

As I was reading this morning, I wrote this statement, God cannot take me where I need to go if I keep looking back. Proverbs 7:1, "keep my words." Proverbs 7:2, "keep my commandments." God can do anything, so we need to keep looking forward and not turn back. Keep your eyes on the Lord and let Him give you strength every step. We will not get the strength and faith we need if we look back and if we look too far ahead, so take one step at a time and keep your eyes on the Lord. Psalm 7:1, "O Lord my God, in thee do I put my trust." Have you prayed and there is no answer? Keep telling yourself there is nothing too hard for the Lord. You had victory over sin and you turned back. Confess, forsake the sin and keep moving forward with Christ. Dwell on the promise that nothing is too hard for God. My brother and sister, keep looking forward and have a blessed day.

God cannot take us where we need to go if we keep looking back.

January 8

Genesis 20-22   Psalm 8   Proverbs 8   Matthew 12

In Your Place

Good morning! My daily prayer is that everyone that takes the time to read these simple devotions are seeing the life in the living Words of

God. Too often we do not see the importance of taking the time to daily read the Word of God and spend time meditating on His Word. As I read today, there was one word that kept drawing my attention and that word is "place." We too often only see ourselves and we do not see the importance of being in our "place" where God would have us to be.

Genesis 22:3, "went unto the place," Genesis 22:4, "saw the place," Genesis 22:9, "came to the place," Genesis 22:14, "that place." I turned to Matthew 12 and read down to verse 6, "in this place." I then turned to Proverbs 8:2, speaking of wisdom; "She standeth in the top of high places, by the way in the places of the paths." Places we should be, places that we can serve, places where we will be taught, places where we have responsibility, places where we meet friends, places that we build relationships, places of encouragement, places that God speaks to us. I could go on and on about the importance of always being in our place when it comes to God speaking to us and teaching us. Proverbs 8:34, "Blessed is the man that heareth me, watching daily at my gates, waiting at the posts of my doors."

Do not think that you are not important so there is no need to be in your place. It is not about us; it is about being in the right place so that God can speak to us and we can grow in our walk with Him. Psalm 8:4, "What is man, that thou art mindful of him? And the son of man, that thou visitest him?" God wants to speak, so we need to be in the right "place." Always be in your "place," even if you think you do not have a "place," because God wants to speak to you in your "place." Always be in the right "place." Church is always the "place" to be when the doors are open.

We must always be in our place so God can speak
to us and we can grow in Him.

January 9

Genesis 23-24   Psalm 9   Proverbs 9   Matthew 13

Headed in the Right Direction

Good morning! The Christian life has a path to be walked, a road to be followed, a destination to arrive at. The right path, the right road and the right destination is the will of God. We speak much about the will of God and yet we spend little time making sure we stay in the will of God. To some, the will of God is what makes them happy; to others the will of God is when things seem to work out. To God, the will of God is following a path, a road that leads us through a journey that God has for us to become more like Him and to be used as He sees fit. I do want to reassure you that the will of God brings peace, happiness and a joy that is beyond what we think.

In Genesis 24, Abraham sends his servant on a journey to find a bride for his son Isaac. It would seem from our side to be an impossible task and yet there are some things that can be observed that can help each of us who desire to be in the will of God. Genesis 24:11, "at the time," "even the time." Finding the will of God is learning and waiting for God's timing. You see, before a child can run, they need to learn to walk and before that they need to learn to crawl, and before that they will need to learn to roll over. Genesis 24:27, "I being in the way, the Lord led me." We must stay patiently waiting and learning until the Lord is ready to show us His next step. Years ago, Mrs. Smith and I were traveling in Canada where I had preached in a couple of churches, and we were making our journey back to the States. We were in the state of Michigan and heading north to where I was to preach. We enjoyed the drive through the tall pines, and we found ourselves lost where there were no road markings or signs that would let us know what road we were on. In our vehicle was a compass and I told my wife that I knew the main road was east of where we were, and we needed to keep heading east. Sure enough, we made it to the road we needed to get on because we kept following in the direction that we knew we needed to be going.

We need to keep heading in the direction that we know we need to be going. Faithful church attendance, daily Bible reading, continuing in prayer, soul winning, tithing, separation unto God, seeking counsel; staying in a direction that God can lead us. Genesis 24:40, "The Lord, before whom I walk, will send his angel with thee, and prosper thy way." Matthew 13:16, "But blessed are your eyes, for they see: and your ears, for they hear." We needed to keep going east. I had to depend on what the compass was telling us. Proverbs 9:6, "go in the way of understanding." At every turn or crossroads, we kept heading east. Sometimes it would seem in the depth of the forest that we could not see where the sun was, so we kept our eyes on the compass and kept going east. Psalm 9:10, "And they that know thy name will put their trust in thee: for thou, Lord, hast not forsaken them that seek thee." We found the road and we made it to the next meeting in plenty of time. Let the Word of God be the compass that you and I need to be in the will of God, stay focused on the direction you need to go. While you are traveling in the right direction, just enjoy the journey.

With the Word of God as your compass,
stay focused on the direction you need to go.

January 10

Genesis 25-26 Psalm 10 Proverbs 10 Matthew 14

Give Him Your All

Good morning! I have decided that getting old has its positives. Now, there are some negatives, but we will not discuss them, such as hair loss, forgetfulness, tiredness, and that is enough. There is something that comes with years, and I am very thankful for those things. Experience, wonderful memories, joy of watching children grow and serve the Lord, grandchildren and watching them listen, learn and live as they have been taught by their parents, seeing your children and grandchildren serve the Lord together.

In Genesis 25:5, "And Abraham gave all that he had unto Isaac." The words "gave all that he had," spoke to me this morning. I do not want to come to the day that my life is ending, and I realize I could have given more. We need to give all that we have to the Lord so that He can use everything that He has blessed us with. I can remember a coach saying, "Give it all you have because when the game is over and you look back, you will regret not giving your all." In Matthew 14:16, the crowd had come to see Jesus and it was the end of the day and the disciples told Jesus that the people needed to be sent away. Jesus said, "They need not depart; give ye them to eat." Matthew 14:20, "And they did all eat, and were filled: and they took up of the fragments that remained twelve baskets full." What we see and what God sees is not always the right thing to see. My brother and sister, give all that you have in your service for the Lord. Give your life and be a blessing to others. Give beyond your tithe and see the needs of others. Proverbs 10:11, "The mouth of a righteous man is a well of life:." Give all you have so God can give you more. Give all you can so that others can be blessed. Psalm 10:4, "The wicked, through the pride of his countenance, will not seek after God." God has blessed us with so much; let us decide to give all we have.

Years ago, my wife was given a couple of dozen eggs. We were getting ready to travel to a preaching meeting and she gave the eggs away that we had left to someone in need. We went to the meeting and a lady gave my wife some eggs. We have laughed many a times because we went several weeks and everywhere that we went my wife was given eggs. My daughter, when growing up, was often given dresses and she would tell us that she was getting so many dresses, so we suggested she give some away and guess what happened? She was given more. Give what you have to give. Your voice, your service, your finances, your prayers, your encouragement to someone else. "And Abraham gave all that he had." The saddest people are the most selfish people. Decide today you are going to look for someone that you can help, serve and give a portion of yourself for the Lord.

Give what you have so God can give you more and others will be blessed.

January 11

Genesis 27-28   Psalm 11   Proverbs 11   Matthew 15

Are You for Real?

Good morning! I love going to livestock sales. I love to be around the animals, and I love to hear an auctioneer. Years back we had a horse that I had bought for Mrs. Smith. This horse was a beautiful paint, very smooth to ride, but had an unpredictable personality. One day this horse would be as calm as can be and the next day she would be jumpy and very disobedient. You never knew. Mrs. Smith actually got very hurt because of my stubbornness in trying to make this horse settle down. That is another story that I would not like to return to. My son and I loaded that horse up and took it to the horse sale. I knew if I saddled the horse and rode her into the sale ring, she would sell for more money than if she just got led into the ring. When we unloaded her from the trailer, she was jumpy, nervous and would not settle down. I made the decision just to have her led in to the sale ring instead of me riding her. When it came time for her to come through to be sold, she was led into the ring and seemed as gentle as can be and she stood so beautifully. I thought to myself, you little brat, if I had ridden you in you would have sold for a better price.

In Genesis 27:18 we see Jacob covering himself to deceive his father Isaac to get his father's blessing that was to really go to Esau. We read in verse 18 Isaac's words, "who art thou;" and in verse 24, "Art thou my very son Esau?" If God asked us today, "who art thou?," who are we? I am not talking about a name, I am speaking in our hearts, who are we? Are we the same in public as we are in private? Are we the same in front of Christians as we are in front of lost people? Are we the same on Sunday as we are on Monday? I did not tell you the name of the horse that we sold, I just told you of the actions of the horse. Matthew 15:8 "This people draweth nigh unto me with their mouth, and honoureth me with their lips; but their heart is far from me." As we look in the mirror, we only see the outside, but what is our heart really like? Proverbs 11:3, "The integrity of the upright shall guide them: but the perverseness of transgressors shall destroy them." We must be honest with ourselves and honest with God. Psalm 11:3, "If the foundations be destroyed, what can the righteous do?" As I read this verse, I thought about us being honest with ourselves because honesty is the foundation of who we really are. Jacob lied and deceived his father. Genesis 27:36, "Is not he rightly named Jacob? For he hath supplanted me these two times."

Let us be real with God and then we can grow and get our life on the right track and stay on the right track. We must be truthful to ourselves so that we can deal with the reality of sin in our lives. Mrs. Smith's horse that we sold was beautiful, but she could not be trusted, and if she could not be trusted, she could not be safe for others to ride. We need to ask ourselves today, how does God really see us? Am I who I say I am?

We must be real with God to stay on the right track in life.

Genesis 29-30   Psalm 12   Proverbs 12   Matthew 16-17

What Have You Learned?

Good morning! Life is full of lessons to learn. Sometimes the lessons are tough to learn because of our lack of wanting to change or lack of a desire to grow. I try to tell myself every day, God always knows best, and I need to stay out of the road and just learn the lesson. A car was just setting on our lane by the activity field here at the camp. Mrs. Smith was washing dishes and she let me know there was a car that had been stopped out there quite a long time. I drove my truck out to see what was going on and it was a neighbor trying to find a good signal on their cellular phone. As we howdied for a few moments they then asked me what I had learned from a situation that is affecting us in this end of the county. What had I learned from this situation?

In our reading today in Genesis 29 and 30 there are fourteen years that passed, and we read in Genesis 30:22-23, "And God remembered Rachel, and God hearkened to her and opened her womb. And she conceived, and bare a son; and said, God hath taken away my reproach." As we read on in verse 25, Jacob says, "that I may go unto mine own place, and to my country." Fourteen years of waiting, and what lessons were learned? I feel the most difficult lessons for all of us are total dependence on God and patience. Praying and believing and waiting. As I looked at my neighbor, I said the situation has brought us to pray and wait on God. I cannot fix it, but God can.

What has God been trying to teach you? Has your patience with God run short? Matthew 16:24, "If any man will come after me, let him deny himself, and take up his cross, and follow me." Are we in full control of our lives, or is God? Matthew 16:25, "For whosoever will save his life shall lose it: and whosoever will lose his life for my sake shall find it." Each day there is something to learn and learning could mean changing. Proverbs 12:15, "The way of a fool is right in his own eyes: but he that hearkeneth unto counsel is wise." I have learned that I cannot change anyone but God's principles taught can change anyone if they are willing to learn. Psalm 12:6, "The words of the Lord are pure words: as silver tried in a furnace of earth purified seven times." As I looked at the neighbor to give them the answer about something that I personally cannot fix, I was convicted to always be in a place to look to God and patiently wait on God. My heart breaks for those that could grow in Christ, but I cannot force anyone to get past themselves. Thank God we can take our burdens and situations to God in prayer. Be patient with your situation, take it to the Lord and leave it with Him. He has not forgotten you and for sure He will never forsake us.

We cannot change anyone, but God's principles can
if they are willing to learn.

January 13

Genesis 31-32   Psalm 13   Proverbs 13   Matthew 18

Getting Past Our Past

Good morning! Psalm 13:6, "I will sing unto the Lord, because he hath dealt bountifully with me." Those words, "he hath dealt" echoed a lot of memories in my mind today. If you have lived very long, the mistakes you have made seem to rise up in front of you at times. Even though God's grace is always sufficient, there seems to be that sadness of asking, why did I let that happen?

Years ago, when our son was just a little fellow, he would go with me and I began working with him in teaching him how to use a firearm, and at that time it was a 22 rifle. We would set up targets and I would take him to the woods to hunt squirrels and rabbits. The day came that we purchased for him his very own BB rifle. He was so proud and so excited. We warned him not to shoot at birds or anything that was not to be hunted. I will never forget the day that he shot a red winged black bird. His heart broke, our hearts were so sad and I told him that if he ever shot anything that he was not supposed to, that I would take his rifle away. The tears were shed and he lost the use of his rifle. The day came that I gave him the rifle back, but I also took the time to ask what he had learned. We purchased more guns for him throughout the years. He hunts every year now and he now takes his sons hunting and he has purchased them rifles to learn how to use and to enjoy.

God's love, mercy and grace to us are beyond description to me. His forgiveness of our sins is there at any time. We are not worthy but it is there. As my heart broke that day over disobedience and disappointment, my belief in him and my love for him never wavered. Too many Christians live in defeat and cannot get past a sin to enjoy the love of Christ. I know we are not worthy. Genesis 32:10, "I am not worthy of the least of all the mercies, and of all the truth." Matthew 18:27, "forgave him the debt." I have a picture of my son with his sons, and them hunting together. We got past the wrong and have gone on. Okay, maybe something has happened in your past; get past the past. Learn and go on. Proverbs 13:6, "Righteousness keepeth him that is upright in the way: but wickedness overthroweth the sinner." When we confess, forsake and learn from our sin, we can go on with a victorious life. That day I had to take away his very first rifle was the day of beginning to learn responsibility and accountability of a firearm. Our son has gone on and lives to hunt and enjoy the outdoors. What from your past is stopping you today? Confess it to God, learn from it and go on for Christ. The Psalmist wrote, "How long wilt thou forget me, O Lord? For ever? How long wilt thou hide thy face from me?" The relationship with God is there when we face our sin, ask forgiveness of sin, forsake sin and live victoriously in Christ. The lesson learned from a little bird has lasted a life time. I have not asked, but I have a feeling that our son told that same story to his sons. Live with joy in Christ today.

When we confess, forsake and learn from our sin,
we can go on with a victorious life.

January 14

Genesis 33-35   Psalm 14   Proverbs 14   Matthew 19

The Importance of Church

Good morning! The day after Christmas in 1963 my father moved our family from Missouri to Iowa. That was a Christmas that carried with it a lot of emotion for all of us. We were leaving the area where most all of our family lived and going to a new place where I knew no one. My father found a church that had a bus we could ride. Every Sunday my mother, sister, brother and me rode that old bus. Church has always been a special place for me. Going to church has been the center of my life.

As I read in Genesis 35:1, "And God said unto Jacob, Arise, go up to Bethel." "Bethel" means the house of God. We read on in Genesis 35:3, "And let us arise, and go up to Bethel." Every time I go to church, I hunger for God to speak to me. Church is not a place for entertainment. Church is the place to meet with the Lord and to meet together with His people. Church is a place for the lost to be saved. Church is a place for us to find God's direction for our lives. God is all around us but church is a place that God has established for us to gather to meet with Him. Genesis 35:15, "And Jacob called the name of the place where God spake with him, Bethel." Do not put other things before you when it is time to be in church. This world has now put itself in front of God by scheduling all kinds of things when the church doors are open. When I was a boy, all the stores were closed on Sundays and no athletic events were ever scheduled on Wednesdays because of church. I am afraid many Christians have learned how to go on in life without the church or God's house being the center focus. Proverbs 14:12, "There is a way which seemeth right unto a man, but the end thereof are the ways of death." Proverbs 14:14, "The backslider in heart shall be filled with his own ways." There are times of sickness but even in times that we go on vacation or visit friends and relatives, it is very important to be in church. Buildings now do not even look like a church, they look more like a business or social hall. Psalm 14:2, "The Lord looked down from heaven upon the children of men, to see if there were any that did understand, and seek God."

Stay in church. Raise your family in church. Be faithful to church. With the things of the world being so busy, make sure church is at the top of the list. Matthew 19:26, "With men this is impossible; but with God all things are possible." Jesus Christ is the corner stone of the church and it is not a building but it is a place to meet with God. Church is not about the people; it is about a meeting with the Lord. I will be seeing you in church.

Church should be the center of our life and at the top of our list.

January 15

Genesis 36-38   Psalm 15   Proverbs 15   Matthew 20

The Greatest Servant

Good morning! There will be days that we read our Bible and maybe things do not speak to us the way we need, or the Bible does not seem to be clear. I encourage you to not stop but keep reading. So many of us have gone to the doctor and the doctor says, I am not sure what is going on, so we will need to continue with some more tests. Or the doctor gives us some medicine and it does not help our condition, but he says to give the medicine some time to work.

The Bible is for our guidance, strength, encouragement, comfort and much more. In Genesis 37:13, Joseph said, "Here am I." It seems as the trials began for Joseph, that things kept getting worse, but we know God had a plan. In Genesis 38:25, in the middle of the verse is the word "Discern." It is like we need to stop, think, understand, evaluate. As we read on in Matthew 20, we see the story of a master hiring labourers and they all agree for an amount of income to do the work until it is payday. Matthew 20:4, "whatsoever is right I will give you." And then we learn the importance of being a servant and how Jesus came to be the least. Matthew 20:28, "Even as the Son of man came not to be ministered unto, but to minister, and to give his life a ransom for many." Proverbs 15:33, "before honour is humility." When Joseph said, "Here am I," the true meaning of whatever God wants was just beginning. Psalm 15:4-5, "he honoureth them that fear the Lord. He that sweareth to his own hurt, and changeth not. He that putteth not out his money to usury, nor taketh reward against the innocent. He that doeth these shall never be moved."

The most important lesson from today's reading that all of us can learn is God wants to use us and we need to allow God to do whatever, whenever and however He wants. Yes, sometimes it is very hard but remember Matthew 20:26, "whosoever will be great among you, let him be your minister." That word "minister" means servant. Enjoy serving today and be blessed by the greatest Servant.

Jesus is our greatest example of serving and ministering to others.

January 16

Genesis 39-40   Psalm 16   Proverbs 16   Matthew 21

God's Outstretched Hand

Good morning! I knelt down and reached out my hand to shake the hand of a little boy. This little fellow smiled at me and reached out his hand. There was a time not too long ago that I would kneel down and reach out my hand and call the little fellow by name and he would get real close to his parents and they would have to say, shake Bro Smith's hand. The little fellow would not take my hand, and then he did reluctantly and now we can meet and I will kneel down and call his name and he will walk over to me and shake my hand.

As God desires to walk with us and fellowship with us, is there a fear of not knowing God or not knowing how to respond to God? Genesis 39:21, "But the Lord was with Joseph, and shewed him mercy, and gave him favour." Joseph had learned to hear the voice of God, listen to God's voice and respond to God's voice. That is why in trials there was a peace and comfort in Joseph. Matthew 21:21, "If ye have faith, and doubt not." It seems so easy when we read it, but the problem having the faith is the lack of a relationship with God. The more I worked to greet the little boy, the more he became familiar with my voice, my words and my outstretched hand. Proverbs 16:3, "Commit thy works unto the Lord, and thy thoughts shall be established." God is always there for us and His hand is reached out to be there for our every need. The problem is not God, it is us. Psalm 16:8, "I have set the Lord always before me: because he is at my right hand, I shall not be moved." God is always ready to show me His ways and the path I should go, the problem is I am sometimes afraid to reach out and take His hand to lead me. Psalm 16:11, "Thou wilt shew me the path of life: in thy presence is fullness of joy; and thy right hand there are pleasures for evermore."

How my heart is blessed when I now reach out my hand to this little fellow and I not only get a handshake, but a smile and I even get a hug. Take the hand of the Lord, let Him lead and love you today. By the way, learn to stop and speak to children; they are the next generation. They need us and we need them.

God is always there for us and His hand is reached out for our every need.

January 17

Genesis 41-42   Psalm 17   Proverbs 17   Matthew 22

Will We Ever Learn?

Good morning! My parents and grandparents have been gone many years, but I often will be reminded of statements that they made. There are times that I wish I could turn time back and say to them, I am so sorry. This morning as I was reading in Genesis 41:9, "I do remember my faults this day." And then as we read farther down in the chapter, Joseph had two sons and he named one Manasseh, which means "forgetting," and we read in Genesis 41:52, "For God hath made me forget all my toil." There are things of the past we do forget and things we remember that can help us.

I remember my parents having to say to me, "David Lynn, will you ever learn?" How thankful I am for my parents stressing to me the importance of learning. Not just academic, but lessons for life. Honesty with self, our situations, and others will help us to grow. In Genesis 42:11, 19, 31, 33, and 34, Joseph asked and his brothers stated the words "true men." Oh, that we would learn lessons to make us "true" with ourselves and with God. Matthew 22:14, "For many are called, but few are chosen." Salvation is for all, but all will not accept Christ's free gift of salvation. We need to learn our lessons of being honest with ourselves. Proverbs 17:10, "A reproof entereth more into a wise man than an hundred stripes into a fool." I hear those words again, "David Lynn, when will you ever learn?." I hear those same words from my Lord as there are times I have to go through a trial just to learn a lesson.

I will see my parents again, but may I learn the spiritual lessons for the day I will see my Lord. Psalm 17:15, "I will behold thy face in righteousness: I shall be satisfied, when I awake, with thy likeness." May it be said of us today, I learned my lesson and I learned it well.

We need to learn the lesson of being honest with ourselves.

January 18

Genesis 43-45   Psalm 18:1-15   Proverbs 18   Matthew 23

What is Your Real Reason?

Good morning! As I was reading my Bible this morning, I stopped and began to ask myself why different people come to church. There are many reasons, but what should the real reason be? Psalm 18:1, "I will love thee, O Lord, my strength." Do we go to church for our love for God? Proverbs 18:2, "A fool hath no delight in understanding, but that his heart may discover itself." Do we go to church for personal gain from others? Matthew 23:11, "But he that is greatest among you shall be your servant." Do we go to church that we may learn how to serve others, or do we come to be served? Genesis 45:5, "God did send me before you to preserve life." Do we go to church to learn how we can preserve for another generation what God has done and is doing for us and to give testimony of and for God?

Joseph, from the very beginning of his life, saw that God had a purpose for him. Even in trials and discouragements, when seemingly all had forgotten about him, he stayed faithful to the Lord. His life was an example of constantly focusing on God's purpose. Genesis 45:7, "And God sent me before you to preserve you a posterity in the earth." God is looking for servants that have a love for God, vision for being in the will of God, and a heart to serve God. As Joseph looked at his brothers and revealed himself, he said, "So now it was not you that sent me hither, but God."

May we begin each day with a Psalm 18:1 attitude and especially when we go to the house of God, "I will love thee, O Lord, my strength." Love Him, learn of Him, trust Him, stand for Him, yield to Him, serve Him. Have a blessed day walking with the Lord.

Joseph's life was an example of constantly focusing on God's purpose.

January 19

Genesis 46-48   Psalm 18:16-36   Proverbs 19   Matthew 24

Faithful and Wise Servant

Good morning! As I type this morning, there is a window that is to my right and even though it is dark, cold and windy outside, there are two dogs that lay by that window every morning. Last night as Mrs. Smith and I called it a day, there was barking from the dogs and it was right outside our bedroom window. Yesterday I had to get hay for the horses and as I went to the barn to get the tractor, the dogs were right by my side. I store the large round bales at the back of the camp, and as I drove the tractor to get the hay, the dogs ran right along the side of the tractor.

As I read the Bible this morning, one word kept showing up from the Old Testament, New Testament and Proverbs and the principle was in the Psalms. That word is "servant." This word means submission, to show respect, submitting myself to serve. The dogs cannot do the work but they are submitting themselves to be with their master. Genesis 46:34, Joseph told his father and brothers to identify themselves as "Thy servants" before Pharaoh. The word "servants" was used six times in two chapters of Genesis. Matthew 24 is teaching the parable of the fig tree and in verse 45, "Who then is a faithful and wise servant," and again in verse 46, "Blessed is that servant, whom his lord when he cometh shall find so doing." The joy of a marriage, home, friendship, ministry, business is when all that have a part are learning to serve each other. Proverbs 19:10, "Delight is not seemly for a fool; much less for a servant to have rule over princes."

It would be wonderful to face the Lord on the day of seeing Him face to face and to be able to say, "For I have kept the ways of the Lord, and have not wickedly departed from my God." (Psalm 18:20). The greatest servant of all was Jesus and His example is perfect. May we choose today to be a servant and not to be the one served. Are we demanding of others or is our attitude that of, what can I do? Have a blessed day being a servant to the needs of others.

The greatest servant of all was Jesus and His example is perfect.

January 20

Genesis 49-50   Psalm 18:37-50   Proverbs 20   Matthew 25

Keep Your Blinders On

Good morning! When I was a very young man, and that was a long time ago, I can remember the first time I saw a team of horses with blinders on them. I asked my grandfather why the horses had part of their eyes covered. He said it was so they could only see where they were going and not get distracted by what was at their side.

As Jacob has died and Joseph's brothers are now concerned what will happen to them, we read in Genesis 50:19, "Fear not: for am I in the place of God?" How powerful are the words of Joseph in Genesis 50:20, "But as for you, ye thought evil against me; but God meant it unto good, to bring to pass as it is this day, to save much people alive." The entire family of Jacob was safe because God was in control. Grandad told me it is a must, especially with a young horse that is learning to keep its eyes focused on where it is going and not be pulling the wrong direction. We need to keep our eyes on God and His purpose for us, even in trials. We need to be watching to see where we need to be going and what we need to be doing. Too many Christians get sidetracked and miss the purpose of God for their lives. Matthew 25:13, "Watch therefore, for ye know neither the day nor the hour wherein the Son of man cometh." Joseph could have allowed his hurt to become vengeance, but he kept his eyes on going in the right direction and desiring to be in God's will. Psalm 18:47, "It is God that avengeth me, and subdueth the people under me." Keep your eyes on the Lord, and wait on Him. Proverbs 20:4, "The sluggard will not plow by reason of the cold; therefore shall he beg in harvest, and have nothing."

The blinders on the horse never hurt the horse; it just kept them focused on learning and pulling and going in the right direction. Do not let this world and its temptations mislead you, do not let your eyes focus on what God is doing in the lives of others. We need to keep the spiritual blinders on our eyes and keep our eyes focused on God and what He is doing in and through us. I remember going and watching teams of four, six, eight and more hooked up and pulling together. They all were listening to the driver, focused on pulling the load and heading in the same direction. It is time for us and God to be on the same team and going in the same direction. When the horses pull together and they are listening to the commands of the driver, the load is easier to pull. We must keep our eyes on God's will and keep listening to His voice. May it be a truth in our lives today, "for am I in the place of God?." I am not God, but I am doing His will in His strength, with Him.

We need to keep our spiritual blinders on and stay focused on God.

January 21

Exodus 1-3   Psalm 19   Proverbs 21   Matthew 26

Watch and Pray

G ood morning! Exodus 1:8, "Now there arose up a new king over Egypt, which knew not Joseph." I read those words several times this morning and tried to imagine in my heart the feeling of those people that will soon be under bondage of the taskmasters. Life had been good and settled. They were enjoying peace and blessings, and now life is taking a tumble. Pharaoh wants to have all the male children killed and yet we read in Exodus 1:17, "But the midwives feared God, and did not as the king of Egypt commanded them, but saved the men children alive."

The world is changing and turning from God. The freedoms, principles, ways of life that generations have enjoyed and have been guidelines for future generations are seemingly being taken from us. Scripture is being fulfilled and we must stay faithful. The children of God began to cry out and God heard their cry. May we not lose focus of a world without Christ and may we not shut ourselves away from the need all around us. Proverbs 21:13, "Whoso stoppeth his ears at the cry of the poor, he also shall cry himself, but shall not be heard." May we see sin in our lives and confess and forsake it so that we may have the power and presence of God and His blessings. Psalm 19:12, "Who can understand his errors? Cleanse thou me from secret faults." Psalm 19:13, "Keep back thy servant also from presumptuous sins; let them not have dominion over me:." That word "presumptuous" means willful, without yielding to reason.

Christian brother and sister, we must stay right with God. In Matthew 26:41, before Jesus was betrayed, He asked his disciples to "Watch and pray that ye enter not into temptation:." We need to live in the strength and power of "I AM." Moses asked God, "who shall I say sent me?" Exodus 3:14, "And God said unto Moses, I AM THAT I AM: and he said, Thus shalt thou say unto the children of Israel, I AM hath sent me unto you." May I remind us all today, "I AM" is still "I AM."

We need to live in the strength and power of "I AM."

Exodus 4-6   Psalm 20   Proverbs 22   Matthew 27

What's in Your Hand?

Good morning! As of this writing, it was thirty-eight years ago that we as a family stepped out by faith in the camping ministry. Throughout the years we have seen the Lord do so very much and it is beyond what we could ever write and talk about. As I read this morning in Exodus 4:2, God said to Moses, "What is that in thine hand?" I learned over sixty years ago that God wants to use each of us in a special way, and most of us will never see this side of Heaven how God does use us. Quit looking for what you think He can use about you and use what is in your hand. God has a plan for each of us and we work to try to fit in to God's plan instead of just walking with Him and allowing Him to use us the way He sees fit. Just be you and walk as close to God as you can in every area of your life. In Exodus 6:2, God told Moses "I am the Lord." In just the sixth chapter of Exodus we read the word "I," meaning God, twenty-one times. Fourteen times we read the words, "I am" and "I will."

I remember the day in the early years of camping, we needed gravel for the road. We had been loaned an old pickup truck to use and I headed down the road a mile and a half to the gravel pit. I weighed the pickup and went and shoveled gravel onto the truck and came back on the scale. When I paid for the load, the man asked who I was and I told him about us just moving to the old vacant camp and we were living in an old house trailer there. I hauled a couple of more loads and he said to me, "we have been watching and thinking about what you are doing, and we would like to give you all the rock free today that you can haul, and we are going to use our end loader to do all the loading so you do not have to shovel it in yourself." Glory be to the KING!! The "I am" heard our plea, and He said "I will" provide. That day my seven-year old son and I hauled free gravel until they closed that night. I used what I had in my hand.

In Matthew 27:54 at the cross of Calvary, the guard standing there said, "Truly this was the Son of God." Proverbs 22:19, "That thy trust may

" What is in your hand that God wants to use so that He ... e is the "I am"? Psalm 20:7, "Some trust in chariots, and ... but we will remember the name of the Lord our God." The ... to your prayers could be in something that you have, but you are not using what you have. Let the "I am" have it and the "I will" will use it. At the end of the day, we were all tired and worn out but the "I am" made Himself very real to us that day and He is more real to us today than I can even begin to tell you. "What is that in thine hand"?

Just be you and walk as close to God as you can in every area of your life.

January 23

Exodus 7-8   Psalm 21   Proverbs 23   Matthew 28

Don't Be a Charlatan

Good morning! Have you ever asked yourself the question, is it real or not? Is God in this or not? As we sometimes struggle to walk the Christian life, there are times that we ask ourselves, is this real or not? Moses and Aaron were commissioned by God to go to Pharaoh and ask to "Let my people go, that they may serve me," (Exodus 7:16). Time and again "the magicians of Egypt, they also did in like manner with their enchantments," (Exodus 7:11). The first two plagues of turning water to blood, and the frogs did not phase the magicians and then when dust turned to lice the magicians said in Exodus 8:19, "This is the finger of God."

How we live and what we do and who we are is so important. One day a piece of equipment broke as I was working at the camp and I had to have some welding done. I contacted a business that I hoped could help me. The older man that owned the business came and looked at the piece of equipment, talked with me for a while and then said he could repair it for me but I would need to bring it to his shop. I took the broken equipment to his shop and a couple of days later I went back to pay for the work and pick up the equipment. As I approached the owner of the business to thank him and pay him, he got real close to my face and said, "I know a charlatan when I see one and you are not one." He turned and walked away and followed him. He stopped and turned around and said, "No charge, glad to meet an honest man." I learned later he had been hurt by many Christians and was owed much money for work he did. Others Christians thought since he was a Christian, he could do work for them for free.

Pharaoh lied time and again. Christian friend, are you real with yourself, others and God? Matthew 28:17, "And when they saw him they worshipped him: but some doubted." We must be honest and truthful. We lose our testimony because we do not live who we say we are. Proverbs 23:3, "Be not desirous of his dainties: for they are deceitful meat." The world paints a false picture and too many Christians are deceived. Psalm 21:7, "For the king trusteth in the LORD, and through the mercy of the most High he shall not be moved." We must live by principle in everything we do and say. Our purpose for the Lord will be strengthened when we on purpose live by Godly principles. I will never forget that old man's eyes as he looked into mine and said, "I know a charlatan when I see one, and you are not one." I got in my truck and prayed, Father, please let me always be true. Live for God and be a true testimony of what a true Christian is.

We lose our testimony because we do not live who we say we are.

January 24

Exodus 9-11   Psalm 22:1-21   Proverbs 24   Mark 1

Moving Forward Straightway

Good morning! In Exodus 9:1, 9:13 and in 10:3, it is written, "Let my people go, that they may serve me." Pharaoh's heart continued to be hardened and Moses heard the voice of God say, "And in very deed for this cause have I raised thee up, for to shew in thee my power; and that my name may be declared throughout all the earth." Jesus told Simon and Andrew, "Come ye after me, and I will make you to become fishers of men." (Mark 1:17). There was no hesitation, there was not a second thought, there was obedience to the voice of God. "And straightway they forsook followed him." (Mark 1:18). The word "straightway," means thout delay and without loss of time.

..n assistant pastor, youth pastor, and bus director and my wife ..1 believed we needed to set our roots in the place we were serving the Lord. My wife was a school teacher in our Christian school. We purchased an older home and were remodeling this home. God was providing in a miraculous way. We were excited and we were almost done. Earlier in the summer we had taken our juniors and teens from our church to a camp that we had rented and joined together with two other churches. To make a long story short, that camp had been run down and was no longer used and was purchased by some deacons in a church. The pastor asked me if I would at all be interested in praying about coming and directing the camp. I love the outdoors, camping, hiking, hunting and years earlier I had worked a summer on a camp staff before Mrs. Smith and I were married. My heart was stirred to be asked. There was no salary offer, no benefits, no housing, no promises of any kind. This step would be a total step of faith. I prayed, my wife and I prayed, we prayed with our children. We left it with the Lord. In my personal prayers I asked the Lord to work in Mrs. Smith's heart and that she would come to me and let me know she was ready to take the step of faith. I hungered for unity with God and unity with my wife. As I was hanging the last new cabinet in our kitchen, Mrs. Smith came in and she said, I know God has prepared you to go into the camping ministry and I want you to know that I am ready to go also. That was 1981, and the rest is history.

Psalm 22:19, "But be not thou far from me, O LORD: O my strength, haste thee to help me." Many have come and gone, and God has always been faithful to lead. Proverbs 24:21, "My son, fear thou the LORD and the king, and meddle not with them that are given to change." What is God leading you to do for Him? He is faithful. Follow Him "straightway." Give Him your all and move forward "straightway." Mrs. Smith and I only wish we had another life to live for God.

Give God your all, follow Him and move forward straightway.

Exodus 12-13   Psalm 22:22-31   Proverbs 25   Mark 2

Setting the Example

Good morning! As I left the camp a couple of mornings ago and was driving on my way to the church, four deer jumped out in front of me, and I had to slam on the brakes of the truck. As I sat there, I noticed that the smallest deer was first and each deer thereafter was larger than the one before. As I continued on, I thought about what I saw. Did the younger run ahead or was the younger told to go ahead? Why was not the younger following the older more mature? Was the younger less cautious of danger and the older, more mature ones more cautious?

Our reading in Exodus chapters 12 and 13 teach us about each home taking a male lamb and sacrificing it; taking the blood and putting it on the door post so when the death angel passes, there will be safety and no death for that home. We read in Exodus 13:8, "And thou shalt shew thy son in that day, saying, This is done because of that which the LORD did unto me when I came forth out of Egypt." Each generation is to be teaching the next. That day when I saw the four deer, I thought about preparing another generation. I could have hit any of the deer but I noticed the largest was the most cautious. I am constantly reminded that we must be teaching. Mark 2:14, "And as he passed by, he saw Levi the son of Alphaeus sitting at the receipt of custom, and said unto him, Follow me, And he arose and followed him." Is the generation behind us seeing a tender heart in us for the things of the Lord? Do they see us reading our Bibles and winning souls to Christ? Are we setting the example of a life given to serve Christ? Psalm 22:23, "Ye that fear the LORD, praise him; all ye the seed of Jacob, glorify him; and fear him, all ye seed of Israel." May our life, lips and legacy leave an example of living for Christ. Proverbs 25:16, "Hast thou found honey? Eat so much as is sufficient for thee, lest thou be filled therewith, and vomit it."

Many have been excited in the beginning with their walk with God and have turned cold, lazy and unmoved for God in the later years. As I watched the deer cross, my heart was so convicted to be the example, teach the example and live the example for Christ. On up the hill the deer went and I thanked the Lord for the lesson He taught me that morning. The example we set will most often be the example that will be learned.

Are we setting the example of a life given to serve Christ?

January 26

Exodus 14-15   Psalm 23   Proverbs 26   Mark 3

Building Unity

Good morning! After I finished reading in the Old Testament this morning, I wrote in my notes: When we pray and seek Him, He will hear and He will answer. He will not answer if there is some sin between us and Him. Moses told the people, "Fear ye not, stand still, and see the salvation of the LORD, which He will shew to you to day:"(Exodus 14:13). When we fear not getting an answer from God, we have allowed doubt in God to enter. The people only saw that the enemy was coming toward them, and then Exodus 14:31, "And Israel saw that great work which the LORD did upon the Egyptians: and the people feared the LORD, and believed the LORD, and his servant Moses."

Whatever it is in our life that we fear most is what will keep us from the full blessing of God. Most of the time it is pride because none of us want to be wrong and we do not want to fail. When we take a step of faith, we must not doubt. Doubt will keep us from seeing the hand of God because we do not want to fail. This doubt brings division and when there is division between us and God, we will fail. Mark 3:24-25, "And if a kingdom be divided against itself, that kingdom cannot stand. And if a house be divided against itself, that house cannot stand." Homes are split because of a lack of unity. A husband must build unity, a wife must build unity and children must build unity. We cannot be in the will of God and be in strife. Dictators take no time to build unity, they just demand obedience. Proverbs 26:21, "As coals are to burning coals, and wood to fire; so is a contentious man to kindle strife." Peace comes from unity with God. Psalm 23:1, "The LORD is my shepherd; I shall not want." We can go forward when we are going the same direction.

How is your home? How is your workplace? Are you working to build unity? Husbands and wives, be on the same page. The disobedience of children could be coming from a lack of unity in parents. Unity brings peace and peace brings joy and God's blessings.

We can go forward when we are going the same direction.

January 27

Exodus 16-18   Psalm 24   Proverbs 27   Mark 4

Look, Listen, Apply

Good morning! Several weeks back I saw a farmer doing some fall plowing, turning the field over so that when spring comes the soil may be prepared and planted. Before our forefathers came to settle our country, we know that many different tribes of Indians roamed this country. If I have time when a field is plowed, I take a walk and see if there are any arrowheads, or spear points, etc. There is a neighbor that has quite a collection just from looking at the freshly plowed ground.

In Psalm 24:7 and 9 we read "Lift up your heads." I do not want to be a Christian that passes by what I need to be learning just like when I look for artifacts from freshly plowed ground. The children of Israel were never satisfied and seemed to constantly complain. In Exodus 17:7, "Is the LORD among us, or not?" God hungers for us to grow, but we have to have an open heart and mind to learn, see and receive. Mark 4:24, "with what measure ye mete, it shall be measured to you: and unto you that hear shall more be given." The neighbor that has dozens of arrowheads and artifacts had to look to find them. If we are going to grow in Christ, we have to look, listen and apply. Too many get offended instead of having an attitude of knowing someone loves them enough to tell them the truth and help them to grow. Proverbs 27:17, "Iron sharpeneth iron; so a man sharpeneth the countenance of his friend." You have to be looking to find the artifacts. You have to be reading the Word of God, listening to the Word being taught and have an open heart to accept the truth to receive from God that which will help us to grow in the Lord. "Lift up your heads." "And thou shalt teach them ordinances and laws, and shalt shew them the way wherein they must walk, and the work that they must do." (Exodus 18:20).

Almost every spring when the ground is worked and the spring rains come, you can find some type of stone that was shaped and used by generations past, but you have to look. Keep looking up and see what the Lord has for you today.

We must have an open heart and mind to learn,
see and receive the Word of God.

January 28

Exodus 19-20   Psalm 25   Proverbs 28   Mark 5

Living by Principle

Good morning! The longer I live and the older I get, the more importance I see in living by principle in everything we do. Principle is so lacking in this day and age we live. God directs us by principle and God's principles never change. In Exodus 19:3, "And Moses went up unto God, and the LORD called unto him out of the mountain." As I read that verse this morning, I thought about how people bring God down to their level instead of going up to God and where He is. As I read on further I read, "And the LORD said unto Moses, Go unto the people, and sanctify them to day and to morrow, and let them wash their clothes." (Exodus 19:10). What was so important about washing their clothes? They were being prepared to meet God, to hear God and to be guided by God. That is why mom said to me, "Those are your Sunday clothes and you need to look your best when you go to church." I did not have expensive clothes; I just wore the best I had and it was always clean and pressed and my shoes were always polished.

As I continued reading this morning I read, "And thou shalt set bounds unto the people" (Exodus 19:12). God has guidelines for us. In Exodus 20 we read the Ten Commandments that the people were taught. Church is not a social gathering, a party, a banquet, an athletic event or a concert; it is God's house and we should come to meet God, praise God, learn more of God and desire to go out and share about God. In Mark 5:18, after "Legion" was saved, he cleaned up and headed to where Jesus was; "And when he was come into the ship, he that had been possessed with the devil prayed him that he might be with him." He wanted to be with Jesus, not make excuse why he cannot come to church. Proverbs 28:5, "they that seek the LORD understand all things." A right heart is a heart that will be drawn to the love and fellowship of God. How is your attitude this morning? Psalm 25:1, "Unto thee, O LORD, do I lift up my soul." Psalm 25:4-5, "Shew me thy ways O LORD; teach me thy paths, Lead me in truth, and teach me." Our pride, stubbornness, laziness, sin, sin, sin, will lead us and keep us away from God, but a meek and humble spirit will want to seek HIM. Psalm 25:9, "The meek will he guide in judgment: and the meek will he teach his way."

I can hear mom now, "Are your Sunday clothes ready, have you shined your shoes?" Now you will hear at our house, "Honey, what are you wearing today?" We are a team serving God and we want to match. I love going to church to meet the family of God and to learn of God so that I can live for God. Oh, it hurts when my sins are preached about, but it draws me closer to God. See you in church.

A right heart is a heart that will be drawn to the love and fellowship of God.

January 29

Exodus 21-22   Psalm 26   Proverbs 29   Mark 6

Stand Faithful

Good morning! I praise the Lord daily that I have the opportunity to live for Him and to serve Him. I am not talking about being a preacher, I am talking about my sins being forgiven, Jesus paying the price by shedding His blood and the gift that God has given to me of eternal life. Oh, that man would hear, accept and live for God. This world that we live in has refused the love of God, but that cannot stop us. The guidelines of God have been thrown out, but that cannot stop us in telling the truth, teaching the truth and living the truth.

God told His people and it is recorded for us, "He that smiteth a man, so that he die, shall surely be put to death." (Exodus 21:12). "Eye for eye, tooth for tooth, hand for hand, foot for foot," (Exodus 21:24). Three times in Exodus 22 we read, "he shall make restitution." God's guideline then and yet today is, "And ye shall be holy men unto me" (Exodus 22:31). The call is for us to continue going out and telling the truth as the Lord Jesus sent them out. "And he called unto him the twelve, and began to send them forth by two and two" (Mark 6:7). Their message was, "And they went out, and preached that men should repent" (Mark 6:12). The anger and hatred in this world is living proof of Proverbs 29:2, "When the righteous are in authority, the people rejoice: but when the wicked beareth rule, the people mourn."

May we stop right now and make a fresh commitment to the Lord that we will live in truth, teach truth and pray that the truth of God and salvation for all men will go forth around the world. Stand faithful, my brother and sister in the Lord. Jesus is coming again. "I have trusted also in the LORD; therefore I shall not slide" (Psalm 26:1). Walk in truth today as we read in Psalm 26:3, "I have walked in thy truth." Oh, that revival fires would burn through the hearts of saints sold out for God. May we pray for revival in our own hearts and burn so that others see us shine for the Lord. The Lord bless you today. Keep looking to Jesus.

Stand faithful in the Lord. Jesus is coming again.

Exodus 23-24   Psalm 27   Proverbs 30   Mark 7

A Day of Rest

Good morning! It was Sunday afternoon, a very beautiful peaceful day in the mountains. The sky was a bright blue, the sun was shining, I could hear the water flowing down the creek and I thought it would be a perfect time for a horse ride. A time to relax and enjoy the beauty of the great outdoors. Sunday dinner was over and everyone was taking a nap before having to leave for Sunday evening church. The horses were in the corral and standing ever so peacefully. I enjoyed riding a horse named Sony. I got his saddle, blanket and bridle; took a lead rope and went out and got him, brought him back and was brushing him down to enjoy a Sunday afternoon ride and I heard a voice. "Hey Dave, what are you doing?" It was one of the married men that worked on the Ranch and was like a foreman. I told him I was going for a short ride and he said, "We do not ride on Sundays, we all rest." As I read Exodus 23:12, "Six days thou shalt do thy work, and on the seventh day thou shalt rest, that thine ox and thine ass may rest, and the son of thy handmaiden, and the stranger, may be refreshed." I learned from that day forward; all of God's creation need a day of rest. I did not ride that day, and I thought about all that needs to be learned from the Word of God.

"And the LORD said unto Moses, Come up to me into the mount, and be there: and I will give thee tables of stone, and a law, and commandments which I have written; that thou mayest teach them." (Exodus 24:12). Man has gone so far from what God's Word teaches us. "This people honoureth me with their lips, but their heart is far from me." (Mark 7:6). We are more interested in what we want to do than what God's Word teaches us to do and to be. Mark 7:9, "Full well ye reject the commandment of God, that ye may keep your own tradition." Oh, that we would read, learn, meditate and live the Word of God. Proverbs 30:5, "Every word of God is pure: he is a shield unto them that put their trust in him." May our desire be to learn the Word of God so that we can please God with our lives.

I remember many years ago a quote I heard, "Your talk talks but your walk talks louder than your talk talks." "Teach me thy way, O LORD, and lead me in a plain path, because of mine enemies." (Psalm 27:11). We need God's Word in every area of our lives. Be open to learn and live what God says. From that day to this, I have never ridden a horse or mule on a Sunday. If the animals need a day of rest, how about you and I rest and be obedient to God and His Word? Something to think about.

May our desire be to learn the Word of God
so that we can please God with our lives.

January 31

Exodus 25-26   Psalm 28   Proverbs 31   Mark 8

The Priority of Church

Good morning! I love driving and seeing small little country towns. When you approach many of these little towns, there will be a mill with tall silos to hold the grain of the area farmers until the grain can be shipped to market, and usually you can see the steeple of a church. Often, I have observed that the church is usually at the end of Main Street. Here at the camp we will someday have a chapel at the end of Main Street. This chapel will be the focal point as you approach the area we call "cowboy town."

God spoke to Moses in our reading this morning to build a sanctuary. Exodus 25:8, "And let them make me a sanctuary; that I may dwell among them." On down in Exodus 25:22 we read, "And there I will meet with thee, and I will commune with thee." The church in the wilderness and the buildings today are much different but the place to meet with the Lord is what I want to think about today. God established a place for Him and we know today through the wonderful gift of salvation that God dwells in our hearts in His Spirit, but He still has established the importance of a place for His people to come together to worship Him, learn of Him and to go out and serve Him. Mark 8:12 asks an interesting question, "Why doth this generation seek after a sign?" We now see church as places of entertainment, social gatherings, athletic events, etc., instead of a place to meet with God. I think it is high time to understand that the church building is yes, a building, but it is a gathering place for people to come and learn of and about God. It needs to be told that the house of God is a place of worship. Proverbs 31:8, "Open thy mouth for the dumb in the cause of all such as are appointed to destruction." People are stepping out into eternity without God and the house of God is empty of the power of God and the presence of God's people.

There needs to be a revival of teachings on the attendance of church and the hearing of a message from God. Not an emotional time of singing and a comforting story but old-fashioned sin-naming preaching. We need to come to God for our strength. Church attendance needs to be a priority. Psalm 28:7, "The LORD is my strength and my shield; my heart trusted in him, and I am helped: therefore my heart greatly rejoiceth; and with my song will I praise him." Have we forgotten the importance of attending church or have we put everything and excuse ahead of being in church? Is a ball game, a family event, a vacation, etc. of greater value than a time with God and His people singing Psalms and hymns and listening to the Word of God taught? I pray not. I love going to church and being with God and God's people and seeing us sinners walk the aisle. I said us, that means me too. See you in church.

There needs to be a revival of teachings on the attendance of church.

Exodus 27-28   Psalm 29   Proverbs 1   Mark 9

The Greatest Source

Good morning! Last night before I left my office at the church, my granddaughter asked me for any books that I might have that would help her with a paper she needs to write for one of her college classes. I loaned her two books that I thought would be of help and then I stood and looked at the books that I have accumulated throughout the years. As I got into my truck to head home, my mind was on the books. Those books are of little value unless I read and apply what I read.

The Bible is our foundation, it is our source to learn of God. The Bible is the living Word of God, for God to speak to us, to guide us, to teach us, etc. The day that we trusted Christ, the Holy Spirit of God came in and will never leave us. In Exodus 27:20, "that they bring thee pure oil olive beaten for the light, to cause the lamp to burn always." This is a picture of the Holy Spirit continually being a light within us to guide us. In Mark 9:7, "This is my beloved Son: hear him." Those words "hear him," have echoed in my heart this morning. God wants to speak to us. Proverbs 1:23, "Turn you at my reproof: behold, I will pour out my spirit unto you, I will make known my words unto you."

As my granddaughter wanted some sources to help her write her paper, I thought of the living source of the Holy Spirit that wants to guide me, teach me, prepare me, lead me every step of my life and yet we so often never go to our Source within. In Psalm 29, we read six times the phrase, "The voice of the LORD." Oh, that today we would go to the Source that dwells as a lamp that never goes out, the Holy Spirit, and may we allow the living Word of God, the Bible, to be our source of guidance and strength. Take time as you read the Bible, memorize verses that will encourage and strengthen you. We hold the greatest source in our hearts and in our hands, the Bible, God's Word. Let the lamp of God, the Holy Spirit that will never go out, guide you and lead you. Listen to the Holy Spirit. God will never lead us in a wrong direction.

The living Word of God is our source of guidance and comfort.

February 2

Exodus 29-30   Psalm 30   Proverbs 2   Mark 10

Top Priority

Good morning! Can I begin our day with a question? What is the first priority of each day? After getting ourselves awake, is the first thing we do to take time to meet with the Lord? Get your cup of coffee, throw some cold water on your face, grab your Bible and spend time with the Lord. Just think, we would not be alive if God did not give us life. I love the time each morning that I spend talking with my wife. What about spending time talking with God?

In Exodus 29 and 30 this morning we are reading about the order of worship that God is teaching the children of Israel. They are in the beginning stages of organizing the worship of God. Exodus 29:38, we read the sacrifices are to be done "day by day continually." Jesus came and was that sacrifice for all mankind. Our LORD does expect us to spend daily time with HIM. Jesus came and gave His life that all men might be saved, and He also came to leave us an example of serving others. Mark 10:45, "For even the Son of man came not to be ministered unto, but to minister, and to give his life a ransom for many."

Each week I hear so many excuses why people have other things to do instead of coming to church. When I hear the excuse, I often wonder what they would do if they got seriously sick or a loved one was on their death bed. Would there then be time for God? The Psalmist wrote in Psalm 30:2, "O LORD my God, I cried unto thee, and thou hast healed me." The horses know where the water, hay and feed is, the dogs know where their water and feed is, even the birds fly out of the forest each morning to the feeders because they know where the sunflower seeds are. How about you and me? Our strength should be in the Lord and spending time with Him in prayer and in His Word every day. Proverbs 2:10-11, "When wisdom entereth into thine heart, and knowledge is pleasant unto thy soul; Discretion shall preserve thee, understanding shall keep thee." Take time daily for God. Read of Him, learn of Him, walk with Him. Life would take on a different outlook if we would spend daily time with God and His Word. God hungers to be our strength, our guidance, our Lord. Make it a priority each day to spend time with the Lord before each day begins. Listen to God say those words again, "day by day continually." Spend daily time with God.

Make it a priority each day to spend time with the Lord before the day begins.

February 3

Exodus 31-33   Psalm 31   Proverbs 3   Mark 11

He is Still in Control

Good morning! Truly every morning that we awake is a good morning. It is another day to live, to see the hand of God, to talk with Him, to ask for His wisdom and guidance. Let me just begin with saying, do not give up and especially do not give up on God. Sometimes we go through a trial and we do not see, hear or understand why God does not do something. I must constantly remind myself that my timetable is not always God's timetable.

In Exodus 32 we read how Moses is with God and receiving the law and Moses' return to the people is delayed and their patience is gone. They cry out to Aaron and the golden calf is made. "And when the people saw that Moses delayed to come down out of the mount, the people gathered themselves together unto Aaron, and said unto him, Up, make us gods, which shall go before us" (Exodus 32:1). With God, it is never too late. Last week, day after day, I met with families and individuals for whom it seemed things were falling apart. I kept begging the Lord for wisdom and guidance. I stood on a doorstep, asking God once again for wisdom and I looked down and saw some new flowers breaking the ground from bulbs that had been planted. I stared at the green breaking through the ground and it was like God said to me, I am in control and I always know what is going on. I thanked the Lord for His grace and His love and His guiding hand. I went inside, listened, prayed, shared verses of hope from the Bible, and at the end of the day there was a light of hope and direction for this family. Exodus 33:13, "Now therefore, I pray thee, if I have found grace in thy sight, shew me now thy way, that I may know thee, that I may find grace in thy sight." Through God's gift of His Son, we have the grace of God. We need to live for God and realize He is in control. Mark 11:24, "when ye pray, believe." Proverbs 3:1, "My son forget not my law; but let thine heart keep my commandments." Psalm 31:1, "In thee, O LORD, do I put my trust." With God, it is never the end. Step back, trust Him, let God lead the way.

As I looked down at the soil, I saw more and more new flowers coming through what seemed to be nothing but plain old dirt. God will soon break through in every situation that we feel is hopeless. Psalm 31:23, "O love the LORD, all ye his saints: for the LORD preserveth the faithful, and plentifully rewardeth the proud doer." Exodus 32:26, "Who is on the LORD's side? Let him come unto me."

With God, it is never the end. Step back, trust Him, let God lead the way.

February 4

Exodus 34-35   Psalm 32   Proverbs 4   Mark 12

Early Morning Meeting

Good morning! I am constantly amazed at the animal kingdom around us. Early each morning, all the animals, from horses, dogs, birds, and others that I do not see, will make their way to where they are fed and watered. As we have been reading in the book of Exodus, we now see that

God calls Moses back to the mount to give the law on the second set of stones. As I read in Exodus 34:2, I noticed when God told Moses to come, "And be ready in the morning, and come up in the morning unto mount Sinai, and present thyself there to me in the top of the mount." Exodus 34:3 states "And no man shall come up with thee."

It is very evident that God wants to meet with us the first thing daily and that He wants a private meeting early in the morning. Do not let your day begin without the Lord. Too many get with the Lord when the distractions of the day have already begun. I wonder if Moses ever said to God, God, I am not a morning person, or God, I need to sleep in a little today. Exodus 34:4, "Moses rose up early in the morning, and went up unto mount Sinai." The animals come early to be fed and watered. Why does not man come to God early the first thing? I think the reason is our heart does not have an urgency to get the strength needed for the day from God and our priority is not to focus on what God wants. Exodus 35:21, "And they came, every one whose heart stirred him up, and every one whom his spirit made willing." As Jesus observed the widow woman cast in her "two mites" He said, she did this because of "her want." I need to check my "wanter" daily. Proverbs 4:18 taught us this morning that "the path of the just is as the shining light, that shineth more and more unto the perfect day." Psalm 32:6 taught us that "every one that is godly pray unto thee in a time when thou mayest be found."

God told Moses, and I believe He teaches us, to meet Him early each day. It is still dark, but I have some animals that need to be fed early in the morning. Have a blessed day.

God wants a private meeting with us first thing every morning.

February 5

Exodus 36-38   Psalm 33   Proverbs 5   Mark 13

You Matter

Good morning! Do not ever feel that you do not matter. Do not ever feel like what you are doing no one knows or cares about. Please do not ever feel like you are not important. Even though I type these statements this morning, our flesh is weak and all of us have had these feelings. I want you to know this very morning that our LORD sees and knows all. Proverbs 5:21, "For the ways of man are before the eyes of the LORD, and he pondereth all his goings." God sees all. Psalm 33:13, "The LORD looketh from heaven; he beholdeth all the sons of men." God not only sees but He knows all that we do, even when no one else sees or knows. Psalm 33:15, "he considereth all their works."

Our Old Testament reading this morning had us reading three chapters having to do with the construction of the Tabernacle and all of the items inside and out. In Exodus 36:1, "Then wrought Bezaleel and Aholiab, and every wise hearted man, in whom the LORD put wisdom and understanding to know how to work all manner of work for the service of the sanctuary." These men were not prophets or great men of power. They were men of labor and skilled with their hands and minds. They were not great orators or great soldiers or kings. Many times in these three Old Testament chapters, we read the words, "And he made." In Matthew 13, Jesus is meeting with His disciples and four times at the end of the chapter we read the word "watch." This "watch" is there for us to keep our eyes on the return of the LORD. We have our eyes so often on what is seemingly the greatness of men and yet today in our reading, God is letting us know that He sees all that man does and is.

Two men were the leaders in building the Tabernacle and yet they never were great men of leadership in the eyes of man, but in the eyes of God they were great men that He used. Know today that God sees all. May He be the focal point for us in what we do. May we seek to please Him and Him alone. In God's eyes, if you are faithful and doing what you can and looking for more you can do, you are great in the eyes of God. Keep watching, for He is watching. Be ready, keep working and serving. There is a work to do, let us be the doers.

If you are faithful and doing what you can,
you are great in the eyes of God.

February 6

Exodus 39-40   Psalm 34   Proverbs 6   Mark 14

Is It I?

Good morning! May we ask ourselves a question each time we go to read the Bible, listen to a message being preached or just make this question a continual practice in our daily lives? Ask yourself the question, "Is it I"? In Mark 14:19, Jesus told them He would be betrayed and each one of the disciples asked, "Is it I"?

As I read in Exodus 40:4, "set in order the things that are to be set in order," my mind went to many areas of my life, and I asked myself the question, are all things in my life spiritually "set in order"? Proverbs 6:3, we read the words, "go, humble thyself." In Psalm 34:2 we read, "the humble shall hear thereof, and be glad." It takes a humble spirit to "set things in order" spiritually in our lives and it takes a continual evaluation of looking at the details in our walk with God. As I held the Scriptures this morning and as I knelt to pray, I asked the Lord to speak to me, show me, guide me, cleanse me. The world we live in is going the opposite way of God and we must be under a constant searching of our hearts to keep it in tune with God. I imagine as the disciples sat together and Jesus said, "One of you which eateth with me shall betray me," there was a haunting quietness and their hearts came under a great conviction. That conviction should bring us closer to the Saviour. I cannot be the judge in anyone's life except my own.

May we hunger today and every day to keep things "in order" with God. When we are convicted of sin, we need to humble ourselves and say "Is it I?." To have things in order with God is to keep the relationship with God "in order." The world is continually getting farther away from God and that is why we must continually walk with God to keep our lives "in order" with God and His will. As you and I go about this day, may we "set in order the things that are to be set in order."

When we are convicted of sin, we need to humble ourselves and say "Is it I?"

Leviticus 1-3   Psalm 35:1-16   Proverbs 7   Mark 15

White as Snow

Good morning! As I walked out to the stir the coals in the wood stove and to put wood in the stove to warm the house, I looked outside and a white blanket of snow had covered everything. It is beautiful, still, peaceful and comforting. I got the fire going, started the coffee and began part of my prayer time. When I had finished the first part of my prayer time and before I began to read, I went outside and enjoyed the beauty and the peacefulness.

As I began reading in Leviticus chapter one, I read to verse 8 and thought of the word "fire" and know it speaks of God's holiness. In verse 9 I read "sweet savour" and thought of the love and devotion of Christ toward God the Father. On down to chapter 2 and verse 1 the words "fine flour" speaks of the perfection and balance of the character of Christ. As I turned to Mark 15:13, I read those evil words, "And they cried out again, crucify him." I got up from my reading and went outside and looked at the snow and thought how Jesus shed His blood that day and my sins were washed away and in the sight of God, I have been washed as white as snow. The challenge this morning of a father to a son is in Proverbs 7:1, "My son, keep my words, and lay up my commandments with thee."

Jesus is our Redeemer, our Saviour, our Lord, our KING. May we live for Him, stand for Him and serve Him. Psalm 35:9, "And my soul shall be joyful in the LORD: it shall rejoice in his salvation." The snow will soon melt but the blood of Jesus that He shed shall wash all sins away. He is holy, He is perfection, He is my Saviour. Praise Him today with everything you have. Lord bless you today.

In the sight of God, we are washed as white as snow by the blood Jesus shed.

February 8

Leviticus 4-5   Psalm 35:17-28   Proverbs 8   Mark 16

Interceding for Us

Good morning! We have been given another day. What we do with this day will be determined by our priorities. I know there are the everyday activities but what should be the priorities of every Christian? We had no hope had it not been for Christ. As we are reading today in Exodus chapters 4 and 5, we see the words "sin offering" in 4:3, which means Christ was laden with our sins. Wow, all the sins of this world have been laid on Christ! As we read on in 5:6, "trespass offering," which shows the injury that sin does. Take time this morning to think about Christ.

Proverbs 8:23 tells us Christ was "set up" before the earth. "I was set up from everlasting, from the beginning, or ever the earth was." As we read this morning in Mark 16, where Christ is risen and the angel said in verse 6, "he is risen; he is not here." Then we receive the commission that has been given to all that have trusted Christ as their Saviour in Mark 16:15, "Go ye into all the world, and preach the gospel to every creature." Each of us have received a calling from God and should be busy serving the Lord in every way that we can. Proverbs 8:4, "Unto you, O men, I call: and my voice is to the sons of man." Oh, how blessed to know that we are not alone in our service and in our life for Christ. Mark 16:19, "So then after the Lord had spoken unto them, he was received up into heaven, and sat on the right hand of God." Christ is interceding continually for you and me. Christ loves us, died for us, shed His blood for us, took the shame for us, felt the pain for us, conquered death for us and is now at the right hand of the Father for us. Christ is the "sin offering" and the "trespass offering." Live for Him.

As a child runs to their parents for protection, as a young calf will cry out for their mother and, even more, as a cow will constantly cry for their calf when the calf is lost or taken away, today and every day Christ is speaking to the Father for us. May we cry out to a lost world with the greatest plea man can hear, JESUS SAVES!

Christ is interceding continually for you and me.

Leviticus 6-7   Psalm 36   Proverbs 9   Luke 1

God's Continual Presence

Good morning! During the fall, winter and into the early spring months, we heat our home with an airtight wood heater. We have a heat pump for our heat and air, but Mrs. Smith and I enjoy the wood heat when the weather is chilly and cold. I read this morning in Leviticus 6:13, "The fire shall ever be burning upon the altar; it shall never go out." Mrs. Smith never complains, but heating with the wood takes a lot of work. I cut the wood, split the wood, stack the wood and bring it to the house to burn. I try not to make a mess of tracking wood chips and dust from cleaning out the ashes, but I know I make extra work for her. We enjoy the warmth, watching the fire, relaxing by the fire, etc. Almost all our married life we have enjoyed wood heat. I do not think about the work, I just enjoy the results.

Do you enjoy the presence of God, the answered prayers, comfort of His Word, the fellowship of the Holy Spirit, His encouragement in trials, His leading in your life? God is the "ever burning fire." His presence is always with us. Luke 1:50, "And his mercy is on them that fear him from generation to generation." Psalm 36:10, "O continue thy loving kindness unto them that know thee; and thy righteousness to the upright in heart." It takes work to keep the fire burning, but the results are far greater. The world tries to lead us away, the temptations of the flesh are constantly bombarding us. Proverbs 9:6, "Forsake the foolish, and live; and go in the way of understanding."

Thank the Lord that His presence is ever with us. Leviticus 6:13, "it shall never go out." Let His fire burn within you today as you and I serve Him. It takes work to walk with God, but the results are a warm comforting blessing beyond description. Enjoy the fire today.

It takes work to walk with God, but the blessings are beyond description.

February 10

Leviticus 8-10   Psalm 37:1-22   Proverbs 10   Luke 2

Strange Fire

Good morning! Back in November I was given a box of pictures from my brother. This box contained pictures of me, saved by my mother. As I took the time and went through the pictures with two of my grandsons, they kept saying, "Is this you, Papa? Is this you?" Yes, the pictures were me at different ages with different people.

All of us who have been saved are different, but it is the same blood that washed our sins away and the same Saviour that died for us. This world that we live in says there are many ways to worship God and that is a false statement. In Leviticus 8:6, "And Moses brought Aaron and his sons, and washed them with water." God instructed Moses in every area how the worship of God should be done. This washing by Moses is a picture of the Holy Spirit washing us clean with the blood of Jesus. We read in Leviticus 10:1, "And Nadab and Abihu, the sons of Aaron, took either of them his censer, and put fire therein, and put incense thereon, and offered strange fire before the LORD, which he commanded them not." It was what they wanted to do and it was "strange," not right. Leviticus 10:10, "And that ye may put difference between holy and unholy and between unclean and clean." God sent His Son to be the Saviour of the world and we must come to Christ, not bring Christ down to us sinners. Luke 2:11, "For unto you is born this day in the city of David a Saviour, which is Christ the Lord."

This world and its religious practices are using "strange fire" and we need to be very careful of it. Proverbs 10:9, "He that walketh uprightly walketh surely: but he that perverteth his ways shall be known." Proverbs 10:29, "The way of the LORD is strength to the upright: but destruction shall be to the workers of iniquity." We should be thankful we have the opportunity to be part of an old fashioned, soul winning, bus running, fundamental, King James Bible preaching and teaching church that does not use "strange fire." Psalm 37:16, "A little that a righteous man hath is better than the riches of many wicked." Take time today and praise the

Lord for a church, pastor and people that do not use "strange fire" in their worship. Do not let yourself get caught in the hype of "well, it is ok," when it is not. It is "strange fire." Something to think about.

We need to be very careful of the world's religious practices using "strange fire."

February 11

Leviticus 11-12   Psalm 37:23-40   Proverbs 11   Luke 3

Proper Care

Good morning! Life growing up for me was so different from many today. Being raised in a small farming community where everybody had a garden and many had chickens, maybe even space to raise a calf or even enough room to have a dairy cow, was what life was like for me. What we ate we grew or raised ourselves. During gardening season, we spent time daily making sure the weeds were pulled, the ground was hoed and the pests were not eating the new plants. Each year when it came time to prune the fruit trees, there was that task and the cow had to be milked twice a day every day. Saturdays was when we churned butter and went to town to sell milk and cream. There were no sugar-coated candies. Pop was only purchased once a week and that was $.05 a bottle. There was no candy jar, just cookies that mom baked and you had to get permission to get one.

Leviticus 11 this morning teaches us about dietary and cleanliness laws. The older I get the more importance I see in taking care of myself physically in what I eat, drink and the importance of rest. Leviticus 11:44, "For I am the LORD your God: ye shall therefore sanctify yourselves, and ye shall be holy; for I am holy." Proverbs 11:23, "The desire of the righteous is only good." We need to look at our lives and see if we are taking care of the house where the Holy Spirit lives and that is our bodies. Luke 3:4, "The voice of one crying in the wilderness" is speaking of John the Baptist and he ate locusts and wild honey, but he took care of himself to be the voice of

God and was the forerunner for Jesus. As I read in Psalm 37:23, "The steps of a good man are ordered by the LORD: and he delighteth in his way."

May I ask the question today, are you taking care of and learning how to take care of the house the Holy Spirit lives in? So many are fighting sicknesses and I often wonder if we think about proper rest, exercise and nutrition or do we just push on and look to a doctor and medicine to fix everything? God laid out some guidelines for His people and even though we live in a modern world, we need to be under conviction to take care of the house where the Holy Spirit lives. Just something to think about today.

God has given guidelines for us to take care of the house
where the Holy Spirit lives.

February 12

Leviticus 13   Psalm 38   Proverbs 12   Luke 4

Never Give Up

Good morning! As I read about leprosy in Genesis 13 this morning, my mind went back several years to when we were raising dairy cows for a large dairy to help produce some income for the camp and to be a training tool for young men that were attending our "Young Men's Leadership Academy." We would go to the dairy and get the newborn calves every couple of days and bring them back to the camp to raise them up to about 700 pounds. We would get them ready to eventually send back for milk production. We only received little heifer calves. It was quite a hard-working learning experience for all of us. One main thing I observed was if a calf got sick and even though we vaccinated it, it had to have a will to live. The veterinarian said on several occasions that when an animal loses its will to live, nothing can keep it alive.

When sin controls, it is like a leprosy that destroys. Jesus' return is only tarried because of His love for sinners. In Luke 4:32 we read, "his word was with power." And on down in verse 36, "And they were all amazed, and spake among themselves, saying, What a word is this! For with authority and power he commandeth the unclean spirits, and they come out." Jesus can help us overcome sin, but we have to desire to get victory over it. I am afraid too many are like the little calves that lost their desire to live. Sin deceives. Proverbs 12:20, "Deceit is in the heart of them that imagine evil: but to the counselors of peace is joy." We started playing relaxing music in the barn and we spent more time with the calves, and I know it sounds unbelievable, but the death rate went down. Spending time with Jesus, right friends, right music will help. We have to face our sins and the fact that all sinners are not just lost people. We need to quit feeling sorry for ourselves and giving excuses and realize there is victory in a walk with Christ. Proverbs 12:22, "Lying lips are abomination to the LORD: but they that deal truly are his delight." Psalm 38:18, "For I will declare mine iniquity; I will be sorry for my sin."

Quit letting sin eat like a cancer. Let God's Word, talking with Him in prayer, being around right folks, faithfulness to every church service you can, help you to get past and have victory over what is destroying you. Leprosy ate living flesh and destroyed lives, and so does sin. I used to talk to the calves and say, "Come on, little lady, you can make it. There is plenty of water and milk." Come on my friend, there is no need to quit and give up.

There is no need to give up, there is victory in a walk with Christ.

February 13

Leviticus 14   Psalm 39   Proverbs 13   Luke 5

Watch for Poison

Good morning! I cannot imagine the ill feeling of someone that was told they had leprosy. To stop and think how they got it and where they got it and wondering if they can be cleansed. Leviticus 14:57, "To teach when it is unclean and when it is clean." In Luke 5:12, "if thou wilt, thou canst make me clean." Luke 5:13, "I will: be thou clean."

I am so thankful that my grandsons enjoy the outdoors. Throughout the years, I have gotten poison on several occasions. Ivy, oak and sumac; I have had them all. One of my grandsons just recently got into a bad batch and he was very miserable until he got healed. The itching, oozing, trauma of the result of just rubbing up against something. That is why we as God's people have to be so alert to sin. Proverbs 13:13, "Whoso despiseth the word shall be destroyed: but he that feareth the commandment shall be rewarded." I felt so sorry for my grandson and I asked him, "Do you think you can identify the poison now?" He immediately said, yes sir. Life can be so blessed when we walk in the way of the Lord. Sin will draw us away, mark us and can destroy us. Psalm 39:4, "LORD, make me to know mine end, and the measure of my days." We need to walk in a careful direction of always pleasing the Lord in every area.

I have told many a young man, if you touch it, you will get it. Many a young man has said, I do not get that poison. That is just like sin, we think it will not affect us. Watch what you are around and watch what you touch. I do not think you want the poison.

We must be alert to sin so it will not affect us like poison.

February 14

Leviticus 15-16   Psalm 40   Proverbs 14   Luke 6

Are You Stubborn?

Good morning! Have you ever been called stubborn? I have had that said to me quite often and you know what? My wife is right. Sometimes I wonder if my stubbornness has been more of a negative than a positive.

In our reading this morning in Leviticus 15 and 16, we see Moses instructing Aaron the high priest what to do for the people's uncleanness. Leviticus 16:16, "And he shall make an atonement for the holy place, because of the uncleanness of the children of Israel, and because of their transgressions in all their sins." Stubbornness to do what is right in the eyes of the Lord is what will keep us from the full blessing of God upon our lives. We read in Luke 6:46, "And why call ye me, Lord, Lord, and do not the things which I say?" To fight God and what is right in His eyes is sin. To not do what is right is sin in the eyes of God. We are living in a world that talks God and goes on in life as if there is no God. Stubbornness will keep them from facing their sin and confessing that sin. There is a long list of things in my life that I have pushed to do because of my stubbornness and people have been hurt, projects ruined, money wasted, etc. Proverbs 14:16, "A wise man feareth, and departeth from evil: but the fool rageth, and is confident." May our stubbornness that is not all bad be used to do God's will in God's way in God's time. Psalm 40:8, "I delight to do thy will, O my God: yea, thy law is within my heart."

The last couple of days I have not felt very well at all, fever, coughing, headache, etc. A very wise wife said, you have abused your body and just kept pushing and the Lord must have said, I will stop you. May we be stubborn Christians against sin, and to stay right with God and in His will.

May our stubbornness be used to do God's will in God's way in God's time.

Leviticus 17-18   Psalm 41   Proverbs 15   Luke 7

Come Home to Roost

Good morning! Did you ever hear the statement, "the chickens will come home to roost"? Free range chickens, as they are called today, will wander around and pick and scratch to get something to eat but as the day draws to a close, they will head back to their nest. We had a chicken house and at night when all the chickens were in, I would go and close the door and we made the building so nothing could get in to bring harm to the chickens at night. They knew the chicken house was a safe place for them and we did not have to coax them in with anything. They just knew there was safety there.

God lays out safe boundaries for all of us in Leviticus 18:3, "After the doings of the land of Egypt (picture of the world), wherein ye dwelt, shall ye not do: and after the doings of the land of Canaan (world's picture of Christianity), whither I bring you, shall ye not do: neither shall ye walk in their ordinances." In simple language, God has a way for us to live and it is not the world or even Christians that set the standard; it is God that sets the standard. Proverbs 15:3, "The eyes of the LORD are in every place, beholding the evil and the good." Proverbs 15:14, "The heart of him that hath understanding seeketh knowledge: but the mouth of fools feedeth on foolishness." Why does a chicken that has a small brain understand there is safety in going to their roost at night instead of staying out and scratching? Luke 7 has many examples of people healed and in verse 47, "Wherefore I say unto thee, Her sins, which are many are forgiven; for she loved much: but to whom little is forgiven, the same loveth little."

Those chickens knew where safety was and where extra feed was and where a place out of the storm was, so every day they made their way to that place. The Psalmist wrote in Psalm 41:12, "And as for me, thou upholdest me in mine integrity, and settest me before thy face for ever." There is more than just safety in the place God has for us. God blesses beyond what we can imagine by being in God's place, God's way and in God's time. The next time you see a chicken out scratching around, just come back at sundown and see where the chicken went.

There is safety and blessing when we are in the place God has for us.

February 16

Leviticus 19-20   Psalm 42   Proverbs 16   Luke 8

Going All the Way

Good morning! As I was reading my Bible this morning and writing thoughts on a piece of paper concerning verses that were speaking to me, my mind went back many years ago to when I received a call from a church that was building a new building. The contractor did not reinforce the structure properly as they were doing the framing, the structure fell and the insurance company said they were going to count it all waste. We went and took several trucks and got the material that had fallen and helped the church clean up the mess. There was nothing that was wrong with any of the lumber. The problem was the contractor did not put up enough bracing to stabilize the framing as the building was going up.

Several times in Leviticus 19 and 20 we read, "be ye holy." We often want God to do things our way instead of God's way. We think we do things partially right and we expect God to do things the way we think. There was nothing wrong on the building except there was not proper bracing. In our lives we must do things God's way and wait on God's timing. Leviticus 19:37, "Therefore shall ye observe all my statutes, and all my judgments, and do them: I am the LORD." After the demons came out of Legion, Jesus told him to "Return to thine own house, and shew how great things God hath done unto thee." (Luke 8:39). Living in the will of God does not mean we do things part way the way God wants, and then the rest of the way how we want. Proverbs 16:9, "A man's heart deviseth his way: but the LORD directed his steps." We cannot receive the full blessing of God by only going half-way with God.

New building material came and we helped in framing the new building. We put a lot more bracing up and the building stands to this day. The Christian life is about doing things God's way. Psalm 42:11, "Why art thou cast down, O my soul? And why art thou disquieted within me? Hope thou in God: for I shall yet praise him, who is the health of my countenance, and my God." Doing things God's way brings God's blessing. Yes, there might still be trials and hard times, but God is teaching us to make us stronger in Him. Live God's way the whole way, which is the right way. Do right even when you do not feel like it. The right way is always the right way.

We cannot receive the full blessing of God by only going half-way with God.

February 17

Leviticus 21-22   Psalm 43   Proverbs 17   Luke 9

Focused on God

Good morning! As I finished praying this morning and began to read my Bible, I had to stop and almost start over with my prayer time because of being overwhelmed with the tasks of the day. Do you ever feel that way? You cannot get your mind to stop thinking about all that is on your "Things To Do List." I wish I could teach myself the lesson that God's will for my life is not the things on my "to do list." Let us stop, take a deep breath and focus on some Scriptures together.

Leviticus 21:6, "They shall be holy unto their God, and not profane the name of their God." Leviticus 21:8, "he shall be holy unto thee: for I the LORD, which sanctify you, am holy." Every day, each of us have responsibilities but it is so very important for us to stop and begin with a 100% focus on what God would have us to be, and that is to be separated unto Him. Our jobs and our responsibilities are the main focus of each day but before we head out to accomplish the tasks before us, we need to separate ourselves unto God so that we can be the testimony of His saving grace to a lost and dying world. Luke 9:56, "For the Son of man is not come to destroy men's lives, but to save them." My walk with God creates the spirit of Christlikeness within me. Proverbs 17:27, "a man of understanding is of an excellent spirit." This world that we all have to walk in needs to see us in fellowship with God and walking in the joy of the Lord. Psalm 43:5 "Why art thou cast down, O my soul? And why art thou disquieted within me? Hope in God: for I shall yet praise him, who is the health of my countenance, and my God."

Take time for God today and He will take time for you. Learn of Him today, walk with Him today, rejoice in Him today. May we be a walking testimony of the private time that we have had with Him. Let your light shine for Him today. Somebody is watching and going to be looking to you today. Be that spiritual encourager you need to be today. Our mates, our children, our grandchildren, our friends, our co-workers, etc., need us to be in a sweet, right fellowship with God today. Have a blessed day.

May we be a walking testimony of the private time
that we have had with Him.

Leviticus 23-24   Psalm 44:1-8   Proverbs 18   Luke 10

Harvest Time

Good morning! As I get up each morning and prepare myself for my personal time with the Lord and anticipate the time of reading the Bible, I am constantly in awe at the well that never runs dry. Leviticus 23:3, "Six days shall work be done: but the seventh day is the sabbath of rest, an holy convocation; ye shall do no work therein: it is the sabbath of the LORD in all your dwellings." Oh, the importance of setting aside the sabbath as a day of rest. Luke 10:2, "The harvest truly is great, but the labourers are few: pray ye therefore the Lord of the harvest, that he would send forth labourers into his harvest."

I can remember hearing a statement when I was a younger fellow, "make hay when it is time to make hay." I can remember pushing hard to get the hay cut, dried, raked and baled. Then out in the field we went to load the hay and take it to the barn to be stored. We would get done and our clothes would be soaking wet and our arms so tired, but the hay was up and it was time to rest. There must be more of an urgency in God's harvest. The time for sinners to be saved is running out. Proverbs 18:1 in our reading today, "Through desire a man, having separated himself, seeketh and intermeddleth with all wisdom." I wanted to be around those men that worked so hard. I was proud to be able to be around men that were men. They had a drive and a push that seemed to affect you in a way that you kept pushing when there was no push and when you hurt so badly, you kept working. As I read Proverbs 18:14, "The spirit of a man will sustain his infirmity; but a wounded spirit who can bear?" All the men focused on the harvest and not personal problems. Neighbors would come and help neighbors. Ladies would get together and bring enough food to feed several armies. It was harvest time and it did not matter what the harvest was about, it was harvest time and all worked to get the crops in.

May our hearts today and the rest of our lives be focused on the Lord's harvest and be in tune with the urgency of reaching souls and pushing on even when we do not feel like pushing. May there be praise in our hearts and lives so strong that it brings a lasting result in others. Psalm 44:8, "In God we boast all the day long, and praise thy name for ever." Push on, my brother and sister. It is time for God's harvest and when it is harvest time, it is time to win souls for God's glory. The soul of a man is far more important than any earthly harvest. May we be found faithful in the Lord's harvest.

May we be focused on the Lord's harvest
and have an urgency in reaching souls.

February 19

Leviticus 25   Psalm 44:9-26   Proverbs 19   Luke 11

Jubilee

Good morning! Our reading today is so full of our history here in America. Yes, Leviticus 25 has to do with the year of Jubilee for the Jewish nation, but as we read in Leviticus 25:10, "Proclaim liberty throughout all the land unto all the inhabitants thereof." That is also the inscription on the "Liberty Bell" that hangs in "Independence Hall." The year of "Jubilee" brings rest, forgiveness and freedom. "With malice toward none, with charity for all, with firmness in the right as God gives us to see the right, let us strive on to finish the work we are in... to do all which may achieve and cherish a just and lasting peace...." Abraham Lincoln's second inaugural address.

We also read this morning in Luke 11:4, "And forgive us our sins; for we also forgive every one that is indebted to us." May we search our hearts this morning to ask forgiveness of any malice or lack of forgiveness to another. God promises us a blessing for our forgiveness of others. Proverbs 19:17, "He that hath pity upon the poor lendeth unto the LORD; and that which he hath given will he pay him again." May we this day do as the Psalmist wrote in Psalm 44:25, "For our soul is bowed down to the dust: our belly cleaveth unto the earth." The Psalmist had arrived at a point of giving all to the LORD, and he had brought himself to lay prostrate on the ground to humble himself before God. Tear down hatred, anger or anything that is not Christlike. We must, as sinners, find our path of freedom back to Christ. Because of our acceptance of His forgiveness, we must have forgiveness toward others.

It is said that President Lincoln's body was laid to be viewed in "Liberty Hall" and miles upon miles of mourners passed by the body of the man that tried to lead healing to a nation full of hatred toward one another. May we follow the path of "Jubilee," or God's forgiveness, to others today.

Because of our acceptance of His forgiveness,
we must have forgiveness toward others.

February 20

Leviticus 26-27   Psalm 45   Proverbs 20   Luke 12

A Living Testimony

Good morning! Mrs. Smith and I took a brief drive yesterday to a little lake that is near where we have been preaching this week. We stopped the vehicle and just quietly looked across the lake. There was a lonely swan next to shore and we talked how they are a fowl that mates for life and we talked about where its mate was. Flocks of geese flew in and flew out. We counted each flock to see if there was an even or odd number of birds. There will come a day that one of us will be alone, but thank God for the comfort of the Scriptures.

Leviticus 26:12, "And I will walk among you, and will be your God, and ye shall be my people." Leviticus 26:13, "I am the LORD your God." I read in Luke 12:6 this morning how important we are to God, "Are not five sparrows sold for two farthings, and not one of them is forgotten before God?" "But even the very hairs of your head are all numbered. Fear not therefore: ye are of more value than many sparrows." (Luke 12:7). The swan quietly floated across the water as we watched and thought of God's love, grace and comfort. Proverbs 20:27, "The spirit of man is the candle of the LORD, searching all the inward parts of the belly." God so clearly can see every bit of HIS creation and yet we humans that were created in HIS very image seem to be so selfish and self-centered. May our life be as Psalm 45:17, "I will make thy name to be remembered in all generations: therefore shall the people praise thee for ever and ever:"

As the geese flew around and came back and landed upon the water, they would honk and somehow communicate with each other. May we be a living constant testimony of God's greatness, love, provision, and comfort. As we pulled away, that swan so beautiful, so pure white kept swimming with a contentment to go on, even if by itself. Live for the LORD today and every day.

May we be a living constant testimony of God's greatness,
love, provision, and comfort.

February 21

Numbers 1-2   Psalm 46   Proverbs 21   Luke 13

Our Standard

Good morning! As Mrs. Smith and I were driving down the highway yesterday, I said to her, look at the American flags flying. I love America, and I am thankful how she has stood so strong for so long. It is more than a flag; it is the principles behind the flag. There is an honor to God and the freedoms we enjoy, and those freedoms are paid for time and again by the blood of our patriots.

Numbers 1:52, "And the children of Israel shall pitch their tents, every man by his own camp, and every man by his own standard, throughout their hosts." Numbers 2:34, "so they pitched by their standards and so they set forward, every one after their families, according to the house of their fathers." May we and our houses be determined to stand by our standard, the Word of God. May we stand true and faithful to the heritage that has been passed down by men and woman who have given their lives for God and His Word. In Luke 13:34, Jesus cried out, "O Jerusalem, Jerusalem, which killed the prophets and stonest them that are sent unto thee." May we pray for revival and seek the face of our Lord to stand by our standard. The forces of Hell are fighting and they will not win, but we must be more determined to stand. Proverbs 21:30, "There is no wisdom nor understanding nor counsel against the LORD."

We must look to our God today and rededicate ourselves to HIM. Psalm 46:10, "Be still, and know that I am God: I will be exalted among the heathen, I will be exalted in the earth." I love patriotism and I am thankful for America, but more important than anything is to stand true and faithful to God who has blessed America. Let us be true and faithful to our God and His Word and His cause. Hold the standard high.

May we and our houses be determined to stand by our standard, the Word of God.

February 22

Numbers 3-4   Psalm 47   Proverbs 22   Luke 14

Serve with Humility

Good morning! I am so very thankful that the Lord wants to use all of us in His work and not just those with certain talents. As we began yesterday with our reading in Numbers for the Old Testament, we see how everybody is very important. Today we see the numbering of certain men's sons. Numbers 4:19, "appoint them every one to his service and to his burden." Numbers 4:24, "to serve, and for burdens." Life is filled with pride and to be blessed of the Lord and to be used of the Lord is to allow the Lord to humble us. God is looking for those that love Him, want to serve Him and to allow Him to get the glory. Luke 14:11, "For whosoever exalteth himself shall be abased; and he that humbleth himself shall be exalted."

I am so thankful God allows us to serve Him. I never want to get past the joy of being able to serve, even if most of what we do will never be known. God told us in Proverbs 22:29 to look upon hardworking men and learn from them, "Seest thou a man diligent in his business? he shall stand before kings; he shall not stand before mean men." Each one of us is different but very special to the Lord and He has a job or place of service for us. Psalm 47:4, "He shall choose our inheritance for us."

Make yourself available for service and not for position. Live to honor God and not be seen of men. Receive your reward in Heaven and not on earth. The earth's reward will pass away but the Heavenly reward will be given and honored by Jesus. Serve Him today.

Make yourself available for service and not for position.

February 23

Numbers 5-6   Psalm 48   Proverbs 23   Luke 15

Signature of Love

Good morning! I do not like saying goodbye. Those words have always brought sadness to me. Telling a loved one that has to travel back home after a visit or telling your children and grandchildren goodbye after getting to spend a wonderful few days with them. As I read in Numbers 6:24-26, my heart was convicted about saying goodbye and I thought about the words, "LORD Bless Thee." Let us read those verses together, "The LORD bless thee, and keep thee: The LORD make his face shine upon thee, and be gracious unto thee: The LORD lift up his countenance upon thee, and give thee peace." Those words are words of God's protection, God's blessing, God's comfort. They are words of God putting His arms around us and keeping us until we meet again.

Our grandchildren are growing older and it seems they are growing without us, but when I pray multiple times for them each day, it is as if I am with them even when I cannot see them. Those words that we just read are words that God's hand is with you and His blessings are upon you. Luke 15:10, "there is joy in the presence of the angels of God over one sinner that repenteth." Heaven is full of joy when that sinner trusts Christ and their eternity is changed from Hell to Heaven. How I need to rejoice as I know God's hand is on a loved one when we part. Proverbs 23:23, "Buy the truth, and sell it not; also wisdom, and instruction, and understanding." No greater words could I say to someone than, "The LORD make his face shine upon thee, and be gracious unto thee." Psalm 48:14, "For this God is our God for ever and ever: he will be our guide even unto death."

When that lump gets in your throat and the tears swell in your eyes, remember the words we read in Numbers 6:25, "The LORD make his face shine upon thee, and be gracious unto thee." I hunger for God's blessing on those I love. I hunger for them to grow in God's grace. I hunger for them to always have a love for God's Word and desire to serve the LORD with their lives. What better words to say when I have to say goodbye than, "The LORD bless thee, and keep thee." Always put that signature of "I love you."

We can rejoice, knowing God's hand is on a loved one when we part.

February 24

Numbers 7-8   Psalm 49   Proverbs 24   Luke 16

Stability in Maturity

Good morning! I love reading and hearing the stories of older men that never quit, never changed and just seemed to get wiser the older they got. I often picture in my mind the old Indian chief that had made it through many winters, many hard times, watching the people he loved struggle, and yet he stood strong. As I read about men like this, they seemed to get stronger and wiser when they failed physically.

I read this morning in Numbers 8:26, "to keep the charge." The men past fifty were not doing the physical labor in serving at the tabernacle but they were stable for keeping the guidelines, ordinances and commandments. I know that as I get older, I can feel my body changing but I hunger to keep my mind and spirit strong, stable and full of spirit for the Lord. Luke 16:10, "He that is faithful in that which is least is faithful also in much: and he that is unjust in the least is unjust also in much." Give us a generation that does not grow weak and inconsistent. Proverbs 24:5, "A wise man is strong; yea, a man of knowledge increaseth strength." Proverbs 24:10, "If thou faint in the day of adversity, thy strength is small." Give us men and ladies of wisdom, maturity, Godly in all ways. May our mouths be those filled with wisdom and guidance spiritually for the coming generation. Psalm 49:3, "My mouth shall speak of wisdom; and the meditation of my heart shall be of understanding."

I need to always be around a generation full of strength, energy and youthfulness, but let us give guidance and stability because of our walk with God and living a life of faithfulness. May the generation coming see a love and compassion in stability because of a relationship with the Lord. I can picture the young braves and the warriors ready to fight and yet listening to the wisdom of the chiefs that are stable. As we grow older, may we work "to keep the charge."

Let us give guidance and stability because of our walk with God and a life of faithfulness.

February 25

Numbers 9-11   Psalm 50   Proverbs 25   Luke 17

The Presence of God

Good morning! Can you picture in your mind a large cloud moving toward you and you know there is a storm coming? Have you ever stood and watched as the lightning shows itself through a large cloud before a good spring rain? I have no idea how large the cloud was that settled over the Tabernacle of God, but I know that all of Israel could see it and know that the presence of God was in that cloud. Numbers 9:15, "And on the day that the tabernacle was reared up the cloud covered the tabernacle, namely, the tent of the testimony: and at even there was upon the tabernacle as it were the appearance of fire, until the morning."

Do you hunger this morning for the presence of the Lord? The apostles said in Luke 17:5, "And the apostles said unto the Lord, Increase our faith." I fear that we go on too often in life without the presence of God, even though His presence can be ever with us. Proverbs 28:8, "Go not forth hastily to strive, lest thou know not what to do in the end thereof." Take time each day to pray and spend time in God's Word so that the presence of God will walk with you throughout the day. When in a time of frustration, confusion, and trial, stop and remember the words of Psalm 50:15, "And call upon me in the day of trouble: I will deliver thee, and thou shalt glorify me."

As long as the cloud was present with the children of Israel, He was there. When the cloud moved, they moved. May our God continue to lead us in every step throughout this day. Have a very blessed day and enjoy the presence of God.

Spend time in God's Word so that the presence of God
will walk with you throughout the day.

February 26

Numbers 12-14　　　Psalm 51:1-9　　　Proverbs 26　　　Luke 18

Empty the Hurt

Good morning! Words can cut so deeply. Picture this morning children playing together and seemingly getting along and then one says, are you my best friend? The other child says yes, and the third child says, I thought you were my best friend. And then the attacks begin. You did this to me, or you said this about me! I am not ever going to play with you again! We can all say we have seen this picture and we can probably all say that we have experienced this. You know what is even a sadder story? We as adults still act the same way, except the children will eventually get back together and we as adults seem to carry our disagreements farther and longer, and some adults will never get past the hurt, anger, jealousy, etc.

We read this morning about Miriam and Aaron talking against Moses and God bringing judgment on Miriam with leprous skin. They faced their sin and Aaron went to Moses and said in Numbers 12:11, "lay not the sin upon us, wherein we have done foolishly, and wherein we have sinned." What sin do we carry with us toward someone else that we need to deal with? Luke 18:14, "for every one that exalteth himself shall be abased; and he that humbleth himself shall be exalted." When someone does us wrong, we do not need to talk about it. Just give it to the Lord and pray for that one that has hurt us. If we are guilty about talking about someone, we need to realize how deeply that hurt can go and how destructive it can be. Proverbs 26:22, "The words of a tale bearer are as wounds, and they go down into the innermost parts of the belly."

It seems the world is full of hatred one toward another. This anger and hurt needs to be confessed and forsaken. Psalm 51:3, "For I acknowledge my transgressions: and my sin is ever before me." Do not hold a grudge. Empty the hurt and allow the Lord to bring the healing. Picture the children hugging and saying, "I am so sorry" and getting back to playing together. Think about it.

Do not hold a grudge. Empty the hurt and allow the Lord to bring the healing.

Numbers 13   Psalm 51:10-19   Proverbs 27   Luke 19

You Can Do It

Good morning! What does it take to stop you? What does it take to cause you to quit? What does it take to cause you to give up? I pray the answer is nothing and that you will determine by God's grace to keep on going for the Lord.

At camp we have some obstacles that we use as team events. Some of these obstacles are very difficult and you need a team member to help you. Some obstacles you can do by yourself but most all of them are made to create team effort. Moses sent spies into territory that God was giving to the children of Israel and as they came back, they brought a good report of the food and the land, but their focus was on the size of the people. Numbers 13:30, Caleb said, "Let us go up at once, and possess it." He had an attitude of "we can do it." Numbers 13:30, the other spies said, "We be not able to go up." Life is full of obstacles and God has never meant for us to go by ourselves. We have our part in a walk with God and that is to have faith in God. When Jesus entered Jerusalem, he told his disciples to "find a colt tied, wherein yet never man sat." I can imagine the look on their faces to get a colt that had never been ridden for Jesus to ride upon. They did and He did. When we do things in God's strength, we can accomplish great things. Proverbs 27:23, "Be thou diligent to know the state of thy flocks, and look well to thy herds." We must do our part and He will do His. It is our heart that needs to stay right with faith in God. Psalm 51:10, "Create in me a clean heart, O God; and renew a right spirit within me."

I have seen hundreds of boys throughout the years look at some of the obstacles that we have at camp and I have heard those words, "I can't," and yet I love the look on their faces when they say, "I did it." Let God be God and follow Him today and let Him be a team with you. Our God is the God of the impossible. "Let us go up at once, and possess it; for we are well able to overcome it." (Numbers 13:30). You can do it.

God never meant for us to go through life's obstacles by ourselves.

February 28

Numbers 14   Psalm 52   Proverbs 28   Luke 20

Watch for Signs

Good morning! The trees are starting to bud, the geese are starting to fly north, the weather is changing more rapidly, the signs of winter are ending, and signs of spring are all around. A neighbor the other day asked if he and his grandson could walk through the woods looking for deer sheds. One of the antlers of an eight-point buck was found and the neighbor and I talked about how that buck would come back bigger this next fall.

Numbers 14:11, "How long will this people provoke me? And how long will it be ere they believe me, for all the signs which I have shewed among them?" We as God's people fight doubt in God even when we know the signs to receive His blessings. In Luke, as Jesus continued His earthly ministry, there was a constant questioning of the signs that He was God. Luke 20:2, "Tell us, by what authority doest thou these things? Or who is he that gave thee this authority?" A good outdoorsman is always watching for the signs. The children of Israel only saw themselves and their situation and doubt came, and when doubt came, they turned from God. They would never see the Promised Land because they lost focus of the signs of God's leading and provision. Be careful not to lose the signs God puts in front of you. Proverbs 28:5, "Evil men understand not judgment: but they that seek the LORD understand all things." Proverbs 28:13, "He that covereth his sins shall not prosper: but whoso confesseth and forsaketh them shall have mercy."

God will always show us the right direction and will always bless our faithfulness in following Him. Pay attention to the signs of blessings and judgments. Learn to stay faithful in every area of life. Psalm 52:9, "I will praise thee for ever, because thou hast done it: and I will wait on thy name; for it is good before thy saints." Obey the spiritual signs before you.

Be careful not to lose the signs God puts in front of you.

| Numbers 15 | Psalm 53 | Proverbs 29 | Luke 21 |

Keep Your Eyes on God

Good morning! As a husband, father, grandfather, and I pray if the Lord tarries, someday a great grandfather, I desire to continue to learn and grow as a man and as a servant of the Lord. For years I have said that if a man ceases to learn, he ceases to lead. There is one area that I am a real slow learner. We can be driving down the road, and I will see something that I think is of interest and I will say, "look at that." For over fifty years of knowing my precious wife, she still has to say to me, what, where and what direction? Usually we have passed what I wanted her to see.

We as God's people must keep our eyes open to God, His leadership, His direction, His teaching, His protection, etc. Numbers 15:38, "that they put upon the fringe of the borders a ribband of blue:." Numbers 15:39, "And it shall be unto you for a fringe, that ye may look upon it, and remember all the commandments of the LORD, and do them; and that ye seek not after your own heart and your own eye." We must keep our eyes looking at and on what God wants, to be able to see sin and turn from it, to see what is right and what is wrong in God's eyes. That is what we need to learn to do, to see what God needs us to see. Luke 21:28, "look up, and lift up your heads; for your redemption draweth nigh." As we read the word of God daily, we must keep our eyes focused on God's teaching. Proverbs 30:5, "Every word of God is pure: he is a shield unto them that put their trust in him." God is looking at us. What does He see us looking at? Psalm 53:2, "God looked down from heaven upon the children of men, to see if there were any that did understand, that did seek God."

I have said it hundreds of times, "Honey, look at that." Each time I catch myself, realizing I did not say where to look. We can be right and safe by always keeping our eyes looking on God and what pleases God. Look the right way and that way always pleases God because our eyes are on HIM.

God is looking at us. What does He see us looking at?

Numbers 16   Psalm 54   Proverbs 1   Luke 22

Spiritual Authority

Good morning! Have you ever watched a mother cat deal with her kittens? Many times I have watched where a little kitten tries to get away from her mother and the mother will leave the comfort of where she has been laying and feeding her other kittens, and go grab that little stray kitten by the back of its neck and bring it back to the safety of where the mother was laying and feeding.

We are cautioned in Numbers 16 to give honor to the spiritual authorities over us in God's appointed position and to stay away from those spreading deceit. The Bible says in Numbers 16:30, "these men have provoked the LORD." God told the people in Numbers 16:26, "Depart, I pray you, from the tents of these wicked men, and touch nothing of theirs, lest ye be consumed in all their sins." The earth opened and swallowed all those that questioned and challenged what the Lord had set up and blessed. In Luke we read of how Judas was led away and used of the devil to betray our Lord. Luke 22:3, "Then entered Satan into Judas surnamed Iscariot." On down in verse 6 of Luke 22, "And he promised, and sought opportunity to betray him unto them in the absence of the multitude." Even Peter, who loved the Lord, was deceived and weakened. Luke 22:31, "And the Lord said, Simon, Simon, behold, Satan hath desired to have you, that he may sift you as wheat." I cannot imagine how Peter must have felt after he denied knowing the Lord three times and then heard the cock crow, and the eyes of Jesus looked upon him. Luke 22:61, "And the Lord turned, and looked upon Peter. And Peter remembered the word of the Lord." May we always see the importance of doing right. Proverbs 1:23, "Turn you at my reproof: behold, I will pour out my spirit unto you, I will make known my words unto you."

As a mother cat will drag her little kitten back to the safe place where it will be fed, cleaned, loved and protected until it is time to leave and have its own life, may we stay close in our walk with the Lord, realizing His love and desire to protect us. Psalm 54:7, "For he hath delivered me out of all trouble: and mine eye hath seen his desire upon mine enemies." Let us be faithful to God and His order of spiritual authorities in our lives.

God instructs us to give honor to the spiritual authorities
He has placed over us.

March 2

Numbers 17   Psalm 55   Proverbs 2   Luke 23

Doing it God's Way

Good morning! I have often said when I am trying to teach someone something, whether it be how to do a job as a summer staff member, or teach our children something when they were still in our home, or even a college student that is trying to learn; to stop and think. We get in a hurry, overreact, let our emotions lead us, do not think something through, etc., and we end up making a wrong decision.

God laid out the priesthood and who would serve in the Tabernacle, which was the tribe of Levi. God designated this to the tribe of Levi to be the priests and to do all the responsibilities of the priesthood. Others of other tribes challenged God and His plan. Each tribe brought a dead rod or branch. The rods were all put in the tabernacle of the congregation and when Moses went in, the rod of Aaron had budded and had blooms and almonds on it (Numbers 17:8). False religions have been and will always be a challenge to God's way. In Luke 23:14, "Ye have brought this man unto me, as one that perverteth the people: and, behold, I, having examined him before you, have found no fault in this man touching those things whereof ye accuse him." Christ did nothing wrong, but man was determined to do things their way and Christ was crucified. Faithfulness to church every time the doors are opened will help us grow. Reading daily the Word of God will help us grow, as well as tithing, giving to missions, and being obedient and holy as taught in the Word of God, and yet man tries his own way. Psalm 55:22, "Cast thy burden upon the LORD, and he shall sustain thee: he shall never suffer the righteous to be moved." God will sustain us but we are so stubborn and we want to do things our way. Proverbs 2:11, "Discretion shall preserve thee, understanding shall keep thee."

Let us live the Christian life God's way and quit making excuses why we can't read the Bible, why we can't get to church on time, why we can't, can't, can't. We can always do what we want. Let us rededicate today to do things God's way. Put God first. To learn a job the right way will bring a joy of accomplishment. The same is true in our walk with God. Let us live life God's way. Something to think about.

Let us rededicate today to do things God's way.

March 3

Numbers 18 Psalm 56 Proverbs 3 Luke 24

The Whole Picture

Good morning! Remember looking at a picture and trying to find other objects that are hidden within a picture? Once we see these hidden objects, they become so obvious to us. Numbers 19:2, "that they bring thee a red heifer without spot, wherein is no blemish, and upon which never came yoke." Numbers 19:2, "And Eleazar the priest shall take of her blood with his finger, and sprinkle of her blood directly before the tabernacle." This is a type of the sacrifice of Christ as the ground of the cleansing of the believer.

While Christ was on this earth, he continually taught from the Old Testament concerning His ministry and purpose for being on this earth. Luke 24:27, "And beginning at Moses and all the prophets, he expounded unto them in all the scriptures the things concerning himself." In this earthly life, we must realize that walking with God is seeing His leadership in each day. Reading His Word, spending time in prayer, and hearing His Word preached and taught is so very vital to strengthen our faith in Him.

Proverbs 3:1, "My son, forget not my law; but let thine heart keep my commandments." Psalm 56:4, "In God I will praise his word, in God I have put my trust."

The picture of life has many lessons if we just focus on what God is doing. There is a path where God is leading us and that is His will for us. He never allows us to compromise His principles, so if you cannot see where to turn or what picture you are to see, then it is a sign there might be sin that needs to be confessed and forsaken. God is not against us. Psalm 56:9, "for God is for me." Keep looking at the picture and see all that there is to see.

The picture of life has many lessons if we just focus on what God is doing.

March 4

Numbers 19   Psalm 57   Proverbs 4   John 1

A Hunger to Please Him

Good morning! How is it that an animal has more of an understanding of provision than a human? Each morning, I can walk out the back door and not say a word and the dogs will appear because they heard a door open. Often Mrs. Smith and I will be having devotions together by the glass doors by our deck and the dogs will come and stare at us, wanting me to come and feed them. I can go out in the morning and the horses are gathered in the corral over by the feed bins waiting.

Oh, that there would be a hunger in our hearts to be fed by God; food that will keep us stronger than any food we could eat! Numbers 20:6, "And Moses and Aaron went from the presence of the assembly unto the door of the tabernacle of the congregation, and they fell upon their faces: and the glory of the LORD appeared unto them." "They fell upon their faces." The dogs will obey and the horses will obey just to be fed or get a treat. John the Baptist said this about Jesus in John 1:27, "He it is, who coming after me is preferred before me, whose shoe's latchet I am not worthy to unloose." As I type, I am thinking maybe people are like my dogs and horses. They only come to God when they want from God. We only beg God when we are in great need. May we keep our eyes on Him because we love Him and hunger to please Him and serve Him. Proverbs 4:25-27, "Let thine eyes look right on, and let thine eyelids look straight before thee. Ponder the path of thy feet, and let all thy ways be established. Turn not to the right hand nor to the left: remove thy foot from evil."

I am glad to spend time with all the animals that I have, and I enjoy the response from them, but my relationship with God is far more important than any animal. May our hearts be full with a desire to please God, fellowship with God, serve God and be everything that we can be for Him. Psalm 57:7, "My heart is fixed, O God, my heart is fixed: I will sing and give praise." There is a joy unspeakable in living for and serving our God.

> *May we keep our eyes on Him because we love Him and hunger to please Him and serve Him.*

March 5

Numbers 20   Psalm 58   Proverbs 5   John 2

Think Before You Speak

Good morning! Do you remember your parents or grandparents teaching you, "Be careful, for what you say or do can turn around and bite you"? In Numbers 21:5, "And the people spake against God, and against Moses." Another lesson on not speaking against earthly authority, but let us read on to verse 6. "And the LORD sent fiery serpents among the people, and they bit the people; and much people of Israel died." "The people spake against God." Until we respect, honor and learn to follow authorities in our lives there will always be troubles. As we read on in verse 9, God instructed Moses to make a "serpent of brass, and put it on a pole." As the people looked at it, they lived in spite of the poisonous bite. This is a picture for us of how Christ became sin for us, a picture of divine judgment of God.

As we read on to John 2:5 we read the words of Jesus' earthly mother, "Whatsoever he saith unto you, do it." Godly authorities are given us to help us learn, grow, and serve. Proverbs 5:2, "That thou mayest regard discretion, and that thy lips may keep knowledge." Several things in life we must learn. I have often said, "if we cannot learn to follow earthly authorities that we can see, how will we ever be able to follow God whom we cannot see?" As we continue to walk on this earth, may we learn to think before we speak, control our emotions so our mouth is under control, and learn that leadership is not perfect but was given to us to guide us and prepare us for when it is time for us to lead.

May our words and actions be used of God to help people and strengthen people. May our words and actions not be used to turn and bite us. Psalm 58:1, "Do ye indeed speak righteousness, O congregation? Do ye judge uprightly, O ye sons of men?" May our lips, lives, and all our actions be used to glorify our God. What we say and do can be used for us or against us. Stop and think before you speak.

Godly authorities are given us to help us learn, grow, and serve.

March 6

Numbers 21   Psalm 59   Proverbs 6   John 3

Do Right the First Time

Good morning! Think back with me, and I will think back many years, to high school and college. That takes me back to the 60s. We have a test to prepare for and we study and study and study. The day of the test comes and that test lays on our desk. We have studied and yet as we begin to write down answers, we question our answers. Can you remember doing that? We actually over thought on some answers, and we should have left the first answer on our paper.

Numbers 22:18, "I cannot go beyond the word of the LORD my God, to do less or more." Balak is trying to lure Balaam away from what God has told him to do. Numbers 22:22, "And God's anger was kindled because he went: and the angel of the LORD stood in the way for an adversary against him." We know that in Balaam's stubbornness, he beat his ass three times and then his ass fell and spoke to him, and then Balaam saw the angel of the LORD. We need to learn to walk with God and never question His will and His way. We need to always do what is right the first time. John 3:36, "He that believeth on the Son hath everlasting life and he that believeth not the Son shall not see life; but the wrath of God abideth on him." Oh, that this world could accept the love of God and be saved! Oh, that we who are saved would follow the voice of God and do His will and stay in His will!

My parents taught me many Biblical principles of life and as I have grown older and spent more time in God's Word, I see even more of God's principles to live by. Proverbs 6:22, "When thou goest, it shall lead thee; when thou sleepest, it shall keep thee; and when thou awakest, it shall talk with thee." Do what God says and do not question it. Do God's will God's way the first time, not questioning that His way is always the right way. Psalm 59:17, "Unto thee, O my strength, will I sing: for God is my defense, and the God of my mercy." Do right the first time.

We need to always do what is right the first time.

March 7

| Numbers 22 | Psalm 60 | Proverbs 7 | John 4 |

A Strong Relationship

Good morning! Remember the phrase, "It hit me like a brick wall"? In all of our lives, we look at pleasing the Lord as doing the things that please Him, or we ask the question often, "what is God's will for my life?" It is good and right to do things that please the Lord, and He does have a will for our lives, but God is looking for something more and it is so simple.

This May I will have been married to Mrs. Smith for forty-nine years. We have seen the Lord do so very much in our lives and we have strived to be in the will of the Lord doing the will of the Lord. In our relationship I try to do things that will help and please Mrs. Smith, but I have learned it is not what I do but what I am to her. More than anything I do in action for her, what really pleases her is time with her that builds our relationship. Tasks can be done by anyone, but relationship building takes a lifetime. The more time together, the stronger the relationship. That is really what will please the Lord. Yes, He wants obedience, but He really wants a relationship and that will bring obedience. Numbers 23:26, "All that the LORD speaketh, that I must do." John 4:24, "God is a Spirit: and they that worship him must worship him in spirit and in truth." He is God and He wants to be all our God.

Jesus said in John 4:34, "My meat is to do the will of him that sent me, and to finish his work." Jesus said His very existence is to do what the Father wants. Proverbs 7:2-3, "Keep my commandments and live; and my law as the apple of thine eye. Bind them upon thy fingers, write them upon the table of thine heart." Our lives should show forth a relationship with God that brings about obedience. Psalm 60:4, "Thou hast given a banner to them that fear thee, that it may be displayed because of the truth. Selah." The greater the relationship, the greater the obedience. Think about it.

God wants obedience, but He really wants a relationship and that will bring obedience.

March 8

Numbers 23   Psalm 61   Proverbs 8   John 5

Surrendered to God

Good morning! The more years that pass, the more I hunger to know and love the Lord. At fifteen years of age I began working as an apprentice printer or, as I was called, a "printers devil." Printing then was a craft, a trade. I worked under a master printer, a journeyman, a man that had learned a trade. I loved what I did. I hungered to learn and I earned the right to be called a printer. It has been said that once printing gets in your blood it never leaves. My heart was under conviction to serve the Lord and

I thought I could use printing as the way to serve the Lord. I surrendered my life, but it was not enough; I was called to be a preacher and I knew it.

As I read this morning, many thoughts came to my mind of when I surrendered to the Lord. Numbers 24:13, "but what the LORD saith, that will I speak." John 5:30, "I seek not mine own will, but the will of the Father which hath sent me." Proverbs 8:11, "For wisdom is better than rubies; and all the things that may be desired are not to be compared to it." I hunger for my love for God and desire to serve Him to grow and grow greater than I can imagine. Proverbs 8:17, "I love them that love me; and those that seek me early shall find me." Have you told God lately that you love Him and give your life to Him for whatever He wants? Not everyone is called to preach, but we are all called to love and serve Him. Psalm 61:5, "thou hast given me the heritage of those that fear thy name." Have you given the Lord your whole heart and desires? He loves you and longs to use you. Do not limit what you think God can do in and through you.

Yes, printing is still in my blood. I love the smell of ink and I love to hear a press running, but there is a burning in my heart greater and that is to please God with my whole heart and to be in His perfect will. Let God have everything.

Do not limit what you think God can do in and through you.

March 9

Numbers 24   Psalm 62   Proverbs 9   John 6

Keep On Keeping On

Good morning! Today was one of those mornings that it was hard to get up. I wanted to, I needed to, I knew I should, and I did. Our flesh gets so weak. To want to do right and to do right are two different things. As I read in Numbers 25:11, "while he was zealous for my sake." In the beginning of Numbers 25 we read, "the people began to commit whoredom." How sad, and God said in Numbers 25:5, "Slay ye every one his men that were joined unto Baal-peor." The people began to bow down to other gods and commit ungodly immoral acts. God had enough and "Phinehas, the son of Eleazar, the son of Aaron the priest, saw it." He "took a javelin in his hand," and "thrust both of them through," and "the plague was stayed" (read verses 1-8). Someone needed to step forward, stay with it and do right.

As we read this morning in John 6:66, "From that time many of his disciples went back, and walked no more with him." Then picture with me in verse 67 as Jesus looks at his disciples and says, "will ye also go away?" Stay faithful. Don't quit. Don't fall away. Keep doing right. When we say we can't, we are not just giving up, we are turning our back on the Lord. Proverbs 9:6, "Forsake the foolish, and live; and go in the way of understanding." Every one of us gets tired, gets discouraged, feels like quitting, feels like we can't make it. Take another step, keep going, you will be glad you did. Psalm 62:6, "He only is my rock and my salvation: he is my defense; I shall not be moved." Psalm 62:8, "Trust in him at all times; ye people, pour out your heart before him: God is a refuge for us. Selah."

A bird will keep pecking away at the ground to find food. A hawk will keep flying and searching for prey. That big old oak tree will keep standing through every storm. The seasons will keep coming. The sun will shine again. Keep going, my friend. Refocus on God and not what you think is more important. My wife and I received a little note from a young person. We are unworthy for what was said, but we must keep going. My wife, my children, my grandchildren, my Lord must see me keep going. Don't turn back. Keep on keeping on. God is faithful to us, let us be faithful to Him.

Refocus on God and not what you think is more important.

March 10

Numbers 25   Psalm 63   Proverbs 10   John 7

Longing For God

Good morning! The importance of getting up each morning and spending time alone with the Lord can never be emphasized enough. As I read in Psalm 63 today, my heart was challenged with the words in verse 1, " . . .early will I seek the: my soul thirsteth for thee, my flesh longeth for thee . . "

When I was dating my wife during our years in college, I would walk her back to the girls' dorm and would say goodbye. I would long for and be so eager to see her again. When I was away from her and our new baby daughter when I was training in the army, I would long for or be eager to see them as soon as possible. Verse 6 in our text says, "When I remember thee upon my bed, and meditate on thee in the night . . " Each night I would lay on my bunk and think of being home with my wife and daughter. I would hear my wife's voice and I would see her face. I longed to be with her and to hold our new little baby girl.

Do you long to be with God that sent His Son to be our redeemer? Do you long to hear His voice? Do you long to see His face? That is why we must read His Word and spend time in prayer talking to Him. When I spent time with my wife and we had to part, I longed for more time to spend with her. After almost fifty years of being with her, I long to spend more time with her. I think of her when we are apart, and I call her to hear her voice. I love spending time with her. My heart loves my Lord. As the Psalmist wrote, "my soul thirsteth for thee, my flesh longeth for thee."

We should long for God, just as we long for our loved ones.

March 11

Numbers 26　　　Psalm 64　　　Proverbs 11　　　John 8

Spiritual Counsel

Good morning! Man and beast by nature are stubborn and independent. Dogs will run in packs and be dangerous if not tamed and controlled. Horses will never be ridden unless broke, bridled and saddled. Man, unless he humbles himself before God and submits himself to God, will not be led by God. Proverbs 11:14, "Where no counsel is, the people fall." John 8:47, "He that is of God heareth God's words:." Teenagers will go to teens their own age to get counsel they want to hear because of the friendship.

Disgruntled adults will usually not seek counsel from someone of honest love to tell them the truth, because they want sympathy and not truth, healing and growth. Moses is about to leave this earth and God tells him to "set a man over the congregation," Numbers 27:16. As we read on in verse 17, this man will "go out before them, and which may go in before them, and which may lead them out, and which may bring then in; that the congregation of the LORD be not as sheep which have no shepherd."

We all need leadership, counsel and guidance that will keep us straight and help us to stay right with God. Running and not seeking counsel on how to deal with a problem and overcome a problem will only cause us to postpone getting things right. We need solid spiritual leadership that will tell us the truth and have the heart of a shepherd that loves and cares. The world lives in darkness and has always rejected the truth of the gospel. John 8:12, "Then spake Jesus again unto them, saying, I am the light of the world: he that followeth me shall not walk in darkness, but shall have the light of life." When we are sick, we do not go to the doctor to hear him say, just stay away and you will learn to deal with it, or we do not need him to say it will pass. We need the doctor to find the problem and tell us how to fix it. John 8:32, "And ye shall know the truth, and the truth shall make you free." There is so much immaturity in this world and running away instead of seeking spiritual counsel from the Word of God and a pastor who has a love of a shepherd to help us find and apply biblical truth to have victory over a situation. Psalm 64:10, "The righteous shall be glad in the LORD, and shall trust in him." Trust God and His Word. Humble yourself, seek spiritual biblical counsel, not a man's opinion.

My heart breaks as I have seen so many run, run, run and not deal with a situation and keep working with it to get victory. I cannot fix anyone else and there will always be that someone else that will remind me of a situation of the past. So the real problem is myself that I look at each day in the mirror. Listen to Proverbs 11:14 again, "Where no counsel is, the people fall." I want to go to a doctor that will tell me the truth, and I want to go to my pastor that will lead me to the truth of the Word of God. We do not have to run. We have God and His Word and our pastor.

Humble yourself and seek spiritual counsel to have victory over a situation.

March 12

Numbers 27   Psalm 65   Proverbs 12   John 9

Giving Our All

Another day is before us. How will you live it for the Lord? A couple of days ago toward evening, I stood on a battlefield where over thirty thousand troops met during the war between the states. Men and woman gave the ultimate sacrifice because of what they believed. As we read in Numbers 28:2, "Command the children of Israel and say unto them, My offering." As I stood and thought of the offering those soldiers gave, my mind went to the offering of our KING as He freely gave His life and shed His blood for all mankind.

As I read on this morning in John 9:4, "I must work the works of him that sent me, while it is day, the night cometh, when no man can work." Man gets so tied up in personalities, fame of certain people, chasing the dream of our lives, running after the "almighty dollar," finding something that will bring satisfaction to our flesh. Those soldiers that gave their lives on the battlefield where I stood, gave all that day. As a Christian, I must give all I have to and for my Saviour. I ask myself, who and what am I living for? When is the last time you tried to reach out to someone that needed Christ and you knew it? When was the last time you passed out a gospel tract? When was the last time, or has there ever been a time, that you invited and brought someone to church with you? Proverbs 12:25, "Heaviness in the heart of man maketh it stoop: but a good word maketh it glad."

It might seem unusual to you, but as I stood on the battlefield, I hungered for a determination to live more for my Lord. I hunger to have the fight for the cause of Christ more. I hunger more to have the power of God upon my life. As I read on this morning in Psalm 65:5, "O God of our salvation; who art the confidence of all the ends of the earth." May we hunger for a breath of God's power to win the lost, be an encourager to others, reach out to the hurting, spread the Gospel of Jesus Christ. Live for His return and that beautiful meeting in the air. The battle is not over and yet I live on the side of victory. Fellow Christian, live for Christ today.

As a Christian, I must give all I have to and for my Saviour.

Numbers 28-29   Psalm 66   Proverbs 13   John 10

The Good Shepherd

Good morning! The older that we get the more we see the errors of our past. The past cannot be changed but to learn from the past and to not repeat the same mistakes is wisdom. As I began to read this morning, I noticed in Numbers 29 the words, "sweet savour," and I thought how our lives are to be a beautiful fragrance to our God. Words that I also read were, "continual burnt offering," and I thought how our lives are to be given continually for His use and for His glory.

How do we arrive at the point of putting God first place every day? The answer to that is to hear His voice and to follow His leading and to be obedient unto Him, just as the sheep are to a shepherd. John 10 gave us so very much to consider today. John 10:4, "And when he putteth forth his own sheep, he goeth before them, and the sheep follow him: for they know his voice." The sheep know the shepherd will lead them to fresh pasture and cool water. The good shepherd will protect the sheep from harm. He loves them and they love him. Jesus said in John 10:11, "I am the good shepherd: the good shepherd giveth his life for the sheep." John 10:27-28, "My sheep hear my voice, and I know them, and they follow me. And I give unto them eternal life; and they shall never perish, neither shall any man pluck them out of my hand." Oh, that we would understand our Shepherd is there always for us! Proverbs 13:15, "Good understanding giveth favour: but the way of transgressors is hard."

As we look back this morning at the Scriptures, we have a life to give to Christ since He gave His for us. He is our Shepherd and He knows best. We cannot be lost from Him, and He is there if we will just listen and follow. Psalm 66:8-9, "O bless our God, ye people, and make the voice of his praise to be heard: Which holdeth our soul in life, and suffereth not our feet to be moved." May we who have entered the gate of salvation heed to the Good Shepherd's call and follow Him.

Oh, that we would understand our Shepherd is there always for us!

March 14

Numbers 30   Psalm 67   Proverbs 14   John 11

Always the Same

Good morning! Have you ever had this statement said to you, "you have not changed a bit"? A friend, a relative, a past acquaintance looks at you and makes that remark. We physically change because of the aging process. I once had hair on the top of my head; now it is gone. Mrs. Smith has had to shorten some of my pant lengths because I seem to be getting shorter. I have sat and thought on the Scriptures this morning quite a long time. We live in a world that is constantly changing. Just this morning before I started typing I noticed I needed to do four updates on my phone. Yet in a changing world, God stays the same. His love is the same, His position is the same, His forgiveness is the same, His location for eternity is the same, His promises are the same. He is unchanging.

Are we growing more like Him in holiness and separation unto Him or are we now justifying things that we said we would never change? Numbers 30:2, "If a man vow a vow unto the LORD, or swear an oath to bind his soul with a bond; he shall not break his word, he shall do according to all that proceedeth out of his mouth." I am speaking of when you and I confessed a sin and said we would never do it again. We made a commitment to the LORD to faithfully read His Word. A man and a woman say, "for better, for worse, in sickness and in health, until death do us part." That is said before family, friends, and God. John 11:42, "And I knew that thou hearest me always:." God is always there to listen. Proverbs 14:26, "In the fear of the LORD is strong confidence." We know God will always be there, but will we always seek to please Him? Psalm 67:5-6, "Let the people praise thee, O God; let all the people praise thee. Then shall the earth yield her increase; and God, even our own God, shall bless us."

They say to keep my phone updated keeps it working better. Maybe we need to check out if we have kept our promises to God and stay with our vows to HIM. As I typed this morning, the world is full of fear over the new virus and yet to seek God's face seems to be the farthest from our minds. I think it is time for us to get on our faces before God and check out if we are keeping the commitments that we have promised HIM. May it be said, we stayed faithful to HIM. Some thoughts to consider.

We know God will always be there, but will we always seek to please Him?

March 15

Numbers 31-32   Psalm 68:1-18   Proverbs 15   John 12

The Power of the Tongue

Good morning! As I was reading this morning in Proverbs 15, I kept marking words and phrases that had to do with the tongue, the lips, and the mouth. I thought about the power of words that proceed from this area of our bodies. A person can be weak in physical strength but powerful in their tongue. The tongue can be an encourager, but it can also be used to destroy. The tongue can be used to express love, but the same tongue can be used to express hate. The tongue can say words of hate and anger, and this same tongue can ask forgiveness. Verse 23 says, "A man hath joy by the answer of his mouth: and a word spoken in due season, how good is it!"

I have stood beside a casket and heard people say to a deceased person that can no longer hear or say anything, "Please forgive me, I am so sorry." I have seen and heard weeping people say, "I love you and I will miss you." It is then too late. Let us be challenged today about what comes from our tongues and mouths. Verse 1 says, "A soft answer turneth away wrath: but grievous words stir up anger." Verse 4 says, "A wholesome tongue is a tree of life." Verse 7 says, "The lips of the wise disperse knowledge . . "

Proverbs 15 is full of guidance about controlling and using our tongue and mouth in a Godly way. Let us decide every day to give full control of our tongue and mouth to ways that please the Lord. When our children were young, I used to love and live to hear these words come from their mouths after I had prayed with them and tucked them in bed: "I love you, Dad and Mom! You are the greatest dad and mom in the whole world." Those days are now gone. Our children are grown and have their own families, but I still get to hear from their mouths, "I love you, Dad and

Mom." The words we say can never be taken back. May our words be a blessing to those to whom we speak.

Use your tongue to bless and encourage someone today.

March 16

Numbers 33-34   Psalm 68:19-35   Proverbs 16   John 13

Staying on God's Path

Good morning! For my Old Testament reading, the last two days have been about the journeys of the children of Israel to Jordan and them receiving their inheritance. As I read, I thought about our journey through life. It can be a journey of God's blessings. Even though there will be trials and testing, they are there to strengthen our faith and walk with God. Our journey through life can also be one of rebellion, sorrow, frustration, anger, hate, and emptiness toward others and toward God.

In Numbers 33:3, " . . the children of Israel went out with an high hand in the sight of all the Egyptians." They went out with God's blessing, guidance, and protection, and as they would soon see, His provision. They were led by God through a pillar of fire by night and a cloud by day. The Egyptians were destroyed even though there was doubt by many of the Israelites that God would save them. As they approached the Promised Land, God told them through Moses to "drive out," "destroy," and "pluck down" things that God wanted destroyed. We see this in Numbers 33:50-53.

Let us now think about where we are in our journey with the Lord. Have we been obedient to His guidance, or have we allowed our journey to drift far from Him? Those that doubted never received their inheritance. In these days of apostasy and turning away from God, we need to focus more on things that are Godly and pleasing to the Lord. Our faith in God and His Word must be strong. We are all on a journey, and at the end of this life there is an eternity that is perfect for those who know Christ as their Savior and a Hell that has eternal punishment for those who have rejected

Christ. As Titus 2:13 says, "Looking for that blessed hope, and the glorious appearing of the great God and our Savior Jesus Christ;" What will He find us doing in our journey when He returns?

Trials in life are there to strengthen our faith and walk with God.

March 17

Numbers 35-36   Psalm 69:1-15   Proverbs 17   John 14

God is in Control

Good morning! Always let God's Word be your guide, your strength and your comfort. Never let emotion and circumstances be the control of your life. John 14:1, "Let not your heart be troubled." As we read in Numbers 35 this morning, we saw the importance and reason God gave instruction for cities of refuge, or prisons and jails in our day. We also learned about trials, juries, and judgments, even capital punishment. We must teach the truth to every generation. As I turned to John 14 this morning, my heart received comfort. John 14:6, "I am the way, the truth, and the life: no man cometh unto the Father, but by me." Let us not stop there. John 14:13-14, "And whatsoever ye shall ask in my name, that will I do, that the Father may be glorified in the Son. If ye shall ask any thing in my name, I will do it." Just asking is not enough, we must live it.

In this world there is not peace nor comfort. I went to the store yesterday and saw the fear in people, the anger, the high emotions, the hurry. The leaders are trying to calm the masses, but God is the only one that can bring the peace and calm we need. In Numbers, the cities of refuge are a type of Christ that shelters the sinner from judgment that we all deserve. Then we read in John 14:27, "Peace I leave with you, my peace I give unto you: not as the world giveth; give I unto you. Let not your heart be troubled, neither let it be afraid." Sing, my brother and sister, rejoice in the Lord, He is in control. Proverbs 17:22, "A merry heart doeth good like a medicine." Proverbs 17:27, "a man of understanding is of an excellent spirit." Psalm 69:13, "But as for me, my prayer is unto thee, O LORD."

God is in control. Look to Him, spend time talking with Him, spend time meditating on His Word. Let those opening words in John 14:1 be on your lips and in your heart all day long and into the night, "Let not your heart be troubled." Have a blessed day in the Lord.

Rejoice in the Lord, He is in control.

March 18

Deuteronomy 1   Psalm 69:16-36   Proverbs 18   John 15

Claiming God's Promises

Good morning! My heart is daily refreshed that God has a plan for all of our lives, no matter our circumstances or abilities. I believe we so often miss the will of God and His blessings because we only see ourselves and our circumstances, instead of allowing God to be God in our lives. Today in my Old Testament reading, I am beginning the journey through the book of Deuteronomy. This book consists of the parting counsel of Moses to the children of Israel, a review of their wilderness wanderings, the judgment of God for the lack of following His direction, and God's punishment after that judgment. My heart was again stirred as I read in Deuteronomy 1:8, "I have set," "go in," and "possess." Then, in the last part of verse 8, God reminds us of His promise that He made to Abraham, Isaac and Jacob.

Just think! We have all the promises of God in our hands preserved for us in the Bible. Oh, that we would read God's Word, study God's Word, meditate on God's Word, memorize God's Word, and apply God's Word in our daily lives. It is given to us to strengthen us, comfort us, direct us, encourage us, challenge us, convict us, lead us, and assure us . . and I could keep going on. The Word of God needs to be our all in every area of our lives. I challenge you today to stop and make a fresh commitment to God to put His Word in the forefront of everything. II Timothy 3:16-17 says, "All scripture is given by inspiration of God, and is profitable for doctrine, for reproof, for correction, for instruction in righteousness: That the man of God may be perfect, throughly furnished unto all good works."

The Word of God is full of promises to help us in every area of life.

Deuteronomy 2-3   Psalm 70   Proverbs 19   John 16

Refocus on God

Good morning! What a day that will be when our focus is completely on the Lord, His leadership, His guidance, and we have placed full confidence in Him. Several phrases stuck out to me this morning in Deuteronomy 2 and 3. Chapter 2, "Meddle not with them," "Now rise up," "Rise ye up." Deuteronomy 3:22, "Ye shall not fear them." We listen, we watch, and we dwell on what the media tells us. I am so thankful for this day and age we live in, but our hope and confidence should never be in what man says or does.

Deuteronomy 3:24, "what God is there in heaven or in earth, that can do according to thy works, and according to thy might?" Daily we must take time and refocus on our God and His Word. John 16:30, "These things I have spoken unto you, that in me ye might have peace. In the world ye shall have tribulation: but be of good cheer; I have overcome the world." This world believes that it can control everything, but we as God's people know better. Proverbs 19:3, "The foolishness of man perverteth his way: and his heart fretteth against the LORD."

Seek the Lord and learn to rejoice in Him. Learn to walk in prayer, enjoy His presence. Psalm 70:4, "Let all those that seek thee rejoice and be glad in thee: and let such as love thy salvation say continually, Let God be magnified." God is still on the throne and Jesus is coming again.

Daily we must take time and refocus on our God and His Word.

Deuteronomy 4   Psalm 71:1-16   Proverbs 20   John 17

What Are You Known By?

Good morning! Our focus today comes from Proverbs 20:11, "Even a child is known by his doings, whether his work be pure, and whether it be right." I asked myself this question: What am I known by? The people that know me, how do they look at me? Is my work that I do done correctly and completely? Am I known as a person that is on time and dependable, or am I a person that is late and they never know for sure when I will be there? Am I a person that can be depended on to fulfill a responsibility? Am I an encourager, or when I have a conversation with someone, is it always about me? Am I a complainer, or do I see good in situations and circumstances?

As a parent, we want to focus on building a Godly character in our children because when they grow older, it will be with good habits or bad habits that have been formed. In order to grow in the Lord, we need to take a detailed look at our lives. We are known by who we are. My work shows who I am. My consistency, or lack thereof, shows who I am. I often wonder why people are too sick and tired to come to Sunday School and church on Sunday, but they can make it to work on Monday. We see the importance of keeping a job, but we do not see the importance of being faithful to God's house. We pay our bills, but we do not show our love to God by being faithful in our tithes and offerings. We hear a filthy joke and we do not walk away. Are we always complaining and never thankful? When there is a need or an opportunity to serve, do we volunteer, or do we always have an excuse? Proverbs 20:11 is very convicting.

Another example I found is in Proverbs 22:1, "A good name is rather to be chosen than great riches, and loving favour rather than silver and gold." Would the world know that I am a Christian by my name and my actions? "A child is known by his doings," and so is an adult. Let us take a long look at ourselves and answer the question: What am I known by?

Our consistency, or lack thereof, shows who we are.

March 21

Deuteronomy 5-6   Psalm 71:17-24   Proverbs 21   John 18

Emptied of Self

Good morning! It was very dark this morning when I went to the front porch to bring in wood for the fire, and I stopped for just a moment and felt the coolness of the morning and the humidity in the air. I asked the Lord to let me learn more of Him today. After I spent some time in prayer, I turned to Deuteronomy 5:1 and read the first verse, "that ye may learn of them, and keep, and do them." And then in Deuteronomy 6:23, "And he brought us out from thence, that he might bring us in."

Did you ever consider what we have to get cleaned out of our lives before we can have more of Him in our lives? This world builds a constant fear. Even as we read in John 18 how the soldiers and Judas are coming to get Jesus, He asked "Whom seek ye?" twice and answered them three times, "I am he." The world is so full of itself and what it seeks that we cannot even understand that we must constantly be emptying ourselves of ourselves so that we may get more of Him. The world and all of its pride does not even understand the words of Proverbs 21:30, "There is no wisdom nor understanding nor counsel against the LORD."

There is a hunger in my heart to finish right so that when that day comes for my journey to end on this earth, it may be said as it was written in Psalm 71:8, "Now also when I am old and gray headed, O God, forsake me not; until I have shewed thy strength unto this generation, and thy power to everyone that is to come." May we work more on getting the old man out that more of Him may come in. Everything is going to be alright.

We must constantly empty ourselves of ourselves
so that we may get more of Him.

March 22

Deuteronomy 7-8   Psalm 72   Proverbs 22   John 19

Every Word

Good morning! Have you ever begun to walk down a trail in the forest not knowing what you will find at the other end, only to come across one of the most beautiful sights that you have ever seen? As we walk through the pages of Scripture, we will always find the most beautiful, encouraging, strengthening truths. You must realize every word is so vitally important. We need to read every word and not just our favorite passages.

In 1750, the thirteen colonies had arrived at the point of expansion and the great Appalachian mountain ranges stood in the way of an easy passage, but in that year a pass was found, which was named the "Cumberland Gap." My wife and I have stood there and looked at the beauty and dreamed what the view must have been when first seen. It was a new land and much to be explored, much to be learned. Deuteronomy 8:3, "man doth not live by bread only, but by every word that proceedeth out of the mouth of the LORD doth man live." Every word needs to be read and studied. Can you only imagine the trails and the passes that must have been looked at before the "Cumberland Gap" was found? As Pilate looked and questioned Jesus in John 19, he said, "I find no fault in him." May we read every word to discover the heart of God. He sent His Son, who had no fault and yet gave everything for you and me, and finally said in John 19:6, "It is finished." God's Son completed His work. May we read every word of God so that we may learn and do the work of God. Proverbs 22:19, "That thy trust may be in the LORD." How can we only read a small portion? It is like we begin a trail and never come to the end and see the beautiful falls or valley. Psalm 72:17, "His name shall endure for ever." Read every word of God's Word. See the truth of God's love, God's leading and God's purpose for our lives. Search the Scriptures to find the promises of His Word.

Yes, they searched and searched and they found the clear way to a westward expansion for our country. Keep searching the Word of God and find the truth for every need and every trial and enjoy and live every promise. Men and women of the past did not quit. May we of this generation have the same drive to search the Word of God that we may find the strength to finish our course that is before us.

We will always find in Scripture the most beautiful, encouraging, strengthening truths.

March 23

Deuteronomy 9-10   Psalm 73:1-14   Proverbs 23   John 20-21

The Solid Rock

I just went to my wife's piano and got a hymnal and turned to the song, "In Times Like These." This is the first verse, "In times like these you need a Savior, In times like these you need an anchor; Be very sure, Be very sure, Your anchor holds and grips the Solid Rock!" My wife and I have been humming that song since yesterday.

What a joy to open the Scriptures and read in Deuteronomy 9:3, "Understand therefore this day, that the LORD thy God is he which goeth over before thee." Our Lord is never surprised and never overwhelmed. Read with me Deuteronomy 10:12, "what doth the LORD thy God require of thee, but to fear the LORD thy God, to walk in all his ways, and to love him, and to serve the LORD thy God with all thy heart and with all thy soul." The wisdom from Proverbs 23:19, "Hear thou, my son, and be wise, and guide thine heart in the way." Peter lost his focus and said in John 21:3, "I go a fishing." Others followed and said in the same verse, "They say unto him, We also go with thee." It is time for us to stay faithful, stay focused, stay fervent in prayer, stay following the LORD and His Word. We must eep ourselves right with God. Psalm 73:1, "Truly God is good to Israel, even to such as are of a clean heart." Those words, "even to such," is all of us.

Sing verse three with me of our hymn today, "In time like these I have a Savior, In times like these, I have an anchor; I'm very sure, I'm very sure, My anchor holds and grips the Solid Rock!! Hang on, our ROCK is secure.

Our Lord is never surprised and never overwhelmed.

March 24

Deuteronomy 11-12   Psalm 73:15-28   Proverbs 24   Acts 1

Are You Satisfied?

Good morning! How full, how comforting, and how strengthening the Word of God is! As I read in Psalm 73:26 this morning, I noticed this: "My flesh and my heart faileth: but God is the strength of my heart, and my portion for ever." This globe that we live on has more people on it than ever before, yet I see a world of loneliness, frustration, discouragement, depression, and emptiness. People are never happy and never fulfilled. It is because we are seeking what we think we need outside of a walk and relationship with God.

A couple of days ago, I stood beside a mountain stream that had water flowing into it from streams coming out of the side of the mountain. The place where I stood was peaceful, comforting, quiet, relaxing and satisfying. My wife and I just sat and watched God's beautiful creation. Nothing was said or done. We were just watching what God had created and feeling full, refreshed and at peace. We drove to town and watched as people in a rush honked their horns, got impatient, and ran around getting to where they thought they needed to be. This simple verse in Psalms tells us that our flesh faileth and that God is our strength.

I cannot stress enough the importance of spending time in God's Word and spending time in prayer with Him. I just read yesterday a shocking statistic that less than 20% of the people that go to church spend daily time in God's Word. How sad! May the challenge to us today be the words of the Psalmist as he wrote, "God is the strength of my heart, and my portion for ever." Psalm 73 ends with this phrase, "I have put my trust in the Lord God, that I may declare all thy works." Put God in first place today and let Him have the lead in your life. He has never, ever failed and He will never forsake us.

True satisfaction and fulfillment comes from a
walk and relationship with God.

March 25

Deuteronomy 13-14   Psalm 74:1-11   Proverbs 25   Acts 2

Controlling Our Speech

Good morning! I have often said that the last words you say may be the last words you say. As I was reading in Proverbs 25 this morning, I found in verse 11, "A word fitly spoken is like apples of gold in pictures of silver." I took out a 3 x 5 card and wrote this:

1. Communicating words

2. Comforting words

3. Correct words

The words we say should be words that will build and encourage. They should be words of comfort. They should be correct words. As we go through this day, let us be very careful to think before we speak. Let us be careful to choose words that will build and not destroy. Once a word has been said, it can never be taken back. You can be sure that today someone will pull in front of us without turning their car's signal on, someone will cut in line in front of us, or someone will be grumpy toward us. Their attitude is not our fault, but these things, and more, will happen. Let us prepare ourselves to respond in the right way and to say the right words. Proverbs 25:28 challenges us about our own spirit, "He that hath no rule over his own spirit is like a city that is broken down, and without walls." Stop, take a breath, ask God for strength, and choose words that will be right words.

The last words you say may be the last words you say.

March 26

Deuteronomy 15-16   Psalm 74:12-23   Proverbs 26   Acts 3

The Fire of the Tongue

Good morning! Our daily reading in Proverbs today is Chapter 26. There is so much that I would like to say, but I want our thoughts to focus on one word. Take a look at verse 20; "Where no wood is, there the fire goeth out: so where there is no talebearer, the strife ceaseth." This verse applies to my words and gossip. We are not to be spreading stories that create strife. Our tongue can be used to build, encourage, correct, and destroy. I would just like to look at the word "fire."

As I awoke this morning and walked by the woodstove that we use to heat our home, I wondered if I should start a fire in it. During the early days of spring, the house is a little chilly in the morning, so I start a fire. As I keep putting wood in the stove, my precious wife will say, "Honey, please do not get the house too warm." There have been days that I have built up the fire too much, and I have come home to find the windows and doors open to let a little cool air in. I enjoy a fire, but that same fire can destroy.

I want to share some thoughts about fire. It can create warmth. To feel a warm fire, see the beautiful blaze, and hear the crackling of the wood is so comforting and enjoyable; however, that same fire that was comforting can get out of control, cause a house fire, and bring total destruction to a home and lives. We can also cook food over that fire to give us nutrition, which will give us physical strength. Oh, how I enjoy camping and cooking over an open fire! I think food tastes better over a fire.

Our tongues can be used to provide comfort and encouragement to others, yet that same tongue can be used to hurt and possibly destroy relationships. I can choose to use my tongue to guide, instruct, help, and strengthen someone. Oh, I love a fire, but how I use that fire determines the outcome of the fire. May we focus today on proper use of our tongues.

We can choose to control our tongue and use it for good.

March 27

Deuteronomy 17-18   Psalm 75   Proverbs 27   Acts 4

A Sharpened Life

Good morning! Oh, that all of our leaders would see the importance of using the Word of God as their guidance. All the kings of Israel were instructed to have it, read it, learn it and follow it. In Deuteronomy 17, verses 14-20, and especially verse 19, we see the importance of not only having the Word of God, but reading it, learning it and following it. Deuteronomy 17:19, "And it shall be with him, and he shall read therein all the days of his life: that he may learn to fear the LORD his God, to keep all the words of this law and these statutes, to do them." Wow!!! In Acts 4:20, after being questioned about the lame man being healed, the disciples said, "For we cannot but speak the things which we have seen and heard;" speaking of what they were taught by Jesus which is the WORD.

I thought about how hard a file is when I sharpen mower blades. The file brings the dull mower blade back to a sharpened blade because it cuts away the steel that was worn dull or nicked. That is how the Bible reveals a dull, backslidden life with sin in it, or a hardened heart toward God; it brings conviction of sin. Thank God for His preserved Word that is sharper than any two-edged sword. We should praise Him as the Word of God is our guide, our strength, our sharpener. Psalm 75:1, "Unto thee, O God, do we give thanks, unto thee do we give thanks."

Remember the quote that is often said, "Sin will keep you from the Bible or the Bible will keep you from sin." Read the Bible, memorize the Bible, quote the Bible, think on the Bible, let the Bible be your guide. Let the Bible be the file that sharpens your life to fight the sin of this world. Love your Bible and spend time in the Bible. Cherish the Word of God in your life.

Let the Bible be the file that sharpens your life.

March 28

Deuteronomy 19-20   Psalm 76   Proverbs 28   Acts 5

Weeds of Sin

Good morning! Two days ago I had finished picking up limbs, cutting brush and raking so that I could begin mowing. I mowed and my wife said, the area you mowed sure does look beautiful. I thanked her and went on mowing in other areas and called it a day. As the sun came up yesterday and I went about the day's events, I went back to where I had mowed and all over the area I had mowed were these bright yellow weeds blooming as brightly as you can believe, called dandelions. I looked and thought they were not there when I mowed. Oh yes, they were, but they had not bloomed yet.

Just like the Christian life, the more we try to do right, the more sin sticks its ugly head up. I loved Deuteronomy 20:4 this morning, "For the LORD your God is he that goeth with you, to fight for you against your enemies, to save you." A walk with God in His Word and in prayer is what we must do to fight sin as it pops its head up. Acts 5:42, "And daily in the temple, and in every house, they ceased not to teach and preach Jesus

Christ." Fighting sin in our lives is a daily battle that must be fought. The weeds must be destroyed in a yard or the weeds will destroy a yard. Proverbs 28:13, "He that covered his sins shall not prosper: but whoso confesseth and forsaketh them shall have mercy." Sin must be removed from our lives, for we cannot enjoy the blessings of God and live in sin. It is time to attack that sin, pull it out, destroy it and fill that spot with God and His Word. Psalm 76:11, "Vow, and pay unto the LORD your God." How can we do less than give Him our best?

People will spend hours upon hours in their yards and hundreds of dollars to have a beautiful lawn. We must spend that daily time with God so that we can live for God and serve Him with all that we have. Do you value a beautiful lawn more than a blessed life in Christ? Something to think about today.

Fighting sin in our lives is a daily battle that must be fought.

March 29

Deuteronomy 21-22   Psalm 77   Proverbs 29   Acts 6

Spiritual Fences

Good morning! As I was mowing again yesterday and mowing along a fence row, I stopped and thought about fences. I thought about their purpose, the good, the bad, the sharp looking and the bad looking. As I read this morning in Deuteronomy 21 and 22, I noticed over and again the "Thou shalt not," "Thou shalt," and "They shall." Guidelines to live by to please the Lord, bring judgment, bring life, bring death - do's and don'ts. These two chapters provide guidelines, just like a fence around properties. Some of the fences at the ranch have been removed, but I know where the boundaries are so that I do not cross over onto a neighbor's property, but what about when I am gone? Some fences provide a closed in area for animals so that the animals do not wander off and get on the road, go to a neighbor, get lost and get stolen. Boundaries and fences are not bad, they are a great help. Fences have to be repaired and kept in good shape or they are of no value.

Spiritual fences help us live a life unto the Lord, a holy life, a fruitful life for Christ. In Acts 6, the disciples were looking for men to help them with the ministry. Look what kind of men they were looking for. Acts 6:3, "look ye out among you seven men of honest report, full of the Holy Ghost, and wisdom, whom we may appoint over this business." These men must have controls and boundaries in their lives to qualify for these spiritual positions. When we fight spiritual boundaries, we will fall away from a right relationship with the Lord and miss His blessings. Proverbs 29:1, "He, that being often reproved hardeneth his neck, shall suddenly be destroyed, and that without remedy." The Psalmist wrote in Psalm 77:2, "In the day of my trouble I sought the Lord." There are times I and the summer staff get tired of weeding the fences and keeping them in repair, but they are a need to keep the animals in. Even if we did not have the animals, we need to know where the boundaries of the property are. What "Thou shalt nots," do we need to deal with in our lives? What "Thou shalt," do we need to be doing in our lives?

The Christian life has to be lived by boundaries. God gave each man a free will but take a look at the world and look at almost 60 million babies that have been killed. Look at the homes that are destroyed and the deaths from alcohol. How many lives and homes are destroyed from drugs? What about the attitude of many Christians that say, I will dress how I want to and I will go and do what I want? I think today we need to saddle our horses and ride the fence row to check if we need to do some repair on our fences. A fence used properly and kept in good repair is a great blessing and help.

Spiritual fences help us live a holy, fruitful life unto the Lord.

March 30

Deuteronomy 23-24   Psalm 78:1-20   Proverbs 30   Acts 7

Life's Vultures

Good morning! Have you ever noticed animals in God's creation that are not the most attractive to look at and seem of no importance, but they have a very important purpose in God's plan? Animals that we would not want for a pet, you would not want to hold them, etc. As I read this morning in Proverbs 30:18 and the first phrase in 19, "There be three things which are too wonderful for me, yea, four which I know not: The way of an eagle in the air." It is not the time of year to be seeing eagles where we live and it is a bad comparison, but I saw several turkey vultures flying around and I wondered what they saw. God's perfect plan is not what we always see. A turkey vulture to me is very ugly, but God created and uses the vulture to keep dead, decaying animals cleaned up so there is not the smell of a dead animal. Deuteronomy 23:14, "For the LORD thy God walketh in the midst of thy camp, to deliver thee, and to give up thine enemies before thee; therefore shall thy camp be holy: that he see no unclean thing in thee, and turn away from thee." God wants to bless us and use us, but He cannot unless the sin stays cleaned up in our lives.

I had you look at verse 14 before verse 5 because there are things that maybe we do not like or people we do not want to be around, but God has allowed things in our life to teach us, help us, turn us, lead us. Listen to verse 5, "The LORD thy God turned the curse into a blessing unto thee, because the LORD thy God loved thee." Stephen was giving a testimony before he was stoned and we read in Acts 7:51, "Ye stiffnecked and uncircumcised in heart and ears, ye do always resist the Holy Ghost: as your fathers did, so do ye." God has a purpose far greater than we can see. The vulture is ugly. It is not something you would want for a pet and it searches out dead animals and garbage, but in God's eyes it has a very important purpose. We need to set our eyes on God and allow His purpose to be fulfilled in our lives. Psalm 78:7, "That they might set their hope in God, and not forget the works of God, but keep his commandments."

When you see a turkey vulture, think about something in your life that you do not like, but God used it for a purpose to bring you to a closer walk with Him. In God's plan there are things that happen to us that we cannot see the value of, but God does. Do you have any vultures in your life today? Be thankful God allowed them to be.

God allows things in our life to teach us, help us, turn us, lead us.

Deuteronomy 25-26   Psalm 78:21-33   Proverbs 31   Acts 8

A Call for Consistency

Good morning! The Christian life is to be lived the same all the time. Not just Sundays but every day. Our language, the places we go, the words we say, the clothes we wear, etc. Too many Christians live a life one way at church and another way at work, have a friend at church and different kinds of friends that they do things with. Ask yourself this question this morning, am I the same in all areas of my life all the time? In Deuteronomy 25:13, "Thou shalt not have in thy bag divers weights, a great and small." Deuteronomy 25:14, "Thou shalt not have in thine house divers measures, a great and small." Deuteronomy 25:15, "But thou shalt have a perfect and just weight, a perfect and just measure shalt thou have." The measures and weights were to be correct and consistent.

In our mind this morning, let us take a trip to the grocery store and go over to the meat section. Let us just look at hamburger. Look at the different prices. Three different prices for ground hamburger. All three packages are hamburger, but the cut of the meat, or the filler (fat) in the meat makes the difference. When we were saved, God saved all of us and forgave us of every sin. But I am afraid there are times that we are not honest with ourselves and do not use a just measure because we want to do things that we would not do in front of our pastor or other Christians. What kind of Christian are you? All the packages say they are ground beef, but they are not the same. In Acts 8 the church was under great persecution but in verse six, "And the people with one accord gave heed unto those things which Philip spake." They were the same in action and spirit all the time. In Proverbs 31:9 I saw two words that spoke to me, "judge righteously." There will be great turmoil in a Christian's life when they live inconsistently. Psalm 78:22, "Because they believed not in God, and trusted not in his salvation." Oh, that we would follow God and His Word all the time and stay the same in our life's standards.

Have you ever watched a hamburger shrink in size under the heat of the grill and watched another hamburger that did not shrink? The one that shrank in size was not the quality of meat. How is your life holding up under the teachings of the Word of God? Are you the same or are you different because you are not the same? Our God is the same all the time. Should we not be as the God we follow?

There will be great turmoil in a Christian's life when they live inconsistently.

Deuteronomy 27-28   Psalm 78:34-55   Proverbs 1   Acts 9

Blessing or Curse?

Good morning! I am so very thankful that I was raised by a generation that did not fear or even talk of being offended or of being afraid of disciplining their children. My parents just said and did what needed to be said and did what needed to be done. This day that we now live in, there is such a fear of saying something or doing something where somebody might get offended. It is like we have raised a generation that has chips on their shoulders just waiting for somebody to knock them off.

I love how God just says it like it is. I think that is one of the reasons man has constantly tried to change the wording of the Bible. I had a fearful respect for my parents so much that I wanted to please them, and a fearful respect knowing that when I did wrong and they found out (and they always did), judgment was not far behind. In Deuteronomy 27 and 28 we read the words, "Cursed be" over twenty times, along with the words "Blessed shall be" many times, and many references to God blessing for obedience. Deuteronomy 28:58, "If thou wilt not observe to do all the words of this law that are written in this book, that thou mayest fear this glorious and fearful name, THE LORD THY GOD."

The attitude of Paul when he was struck with blindness before he was saved is recorded in Acts 9:6, "Lord, what wilt thou have me to do?" As we read on in Proverbs 1:33, "But whoso hearkeneth unto me shall dwell safely, and shall be quiet from fear of evil." Psalm 78:35, "And they remembered that God was their rock, and the high God their redeemer." I thought of the little chorus this morning, "Obedience Is the Very Best Thing." Let that little song be on our lips and hearts throughout this and every day. Decide, are you looking for God's blessing or God's curse?

Obedience is always blessed by God.

April 2

Deuteronomy 29-30   Psalm 78:56-72   Proverbs 2   Acts 10

Following the Path

Good morning! As I was reading today in Proverbs 2, the little word "path" stood out to me. I would like us to consider today, for a moment, a path. I enjoy the outdoors very much. I love watching nature, listening to water flowing down a stream, the chattering of squirrels and seeing them jump from tree to tree or birds picking through the grass to find a seed or a worm to eat. If we take the time, we can often see a path that animals have made as they journey through the outdoors. I have followed some of these paths in the past. You can see where a deer followed a path and bedded down in safety. The path will take you by a place where they fed on some new growth of some type of plant, and if you follow long enough, you can follow this path to where they found water to drink.

In verse 9 of our reading today, we see the three words "every good path." If we look before this phrase, we see three parts of a good path to take. The first part is "understand righteousness." In our lives, we should follow a path of doing things that are right in the eyes of God. The second part of our path leads us to understand "judgment," meaning God will bless us for making right decisions. The third part of our path today is "equity," or the quality of looking at things fairly or in a right way.

Sin will always bring destruction and a ruined life. Each of us are on a path, and that path can take us to a closer relationship with Jesus Christ or our path can take us far from God, His will, and His blessing. In verse 8 of chapter 2, we see if we keep on the right path, He "preserveth the way of his saints." The devil is a wicked hunter and he is trying to ruin our lives. Stay on the "good path" toward a wonderful, blessed relationship with God.

Staying on the right path will always bring God's blessing.

Deuteronomy 31-32   Psalm 79   Proverbs 3   Acts 11-12

He's Always There

Good morning! I tried to picture myself standing there and listening to Moses say his last words before the Lord was to take him. Deuteronomy 31:6, "Be strong and of good courage, fear not, nor be afraid of them: for the LORD thy God, he it is that doth go with thee; he will not fail thee nor forsake thee." Then as we read in Acts 12 how Peter was in the depths of jail, chained to two guards, and yet prayer was going to God for him. Acts 12:5, "Peter therefore was kept in prison: but prayer was made without ceasing of the church unto God for him." The angel awoke Peter, the chains fell off, he walked through open gates that were chained, past guards that were asleep and said in Acts 12:11, "Now I know of a surety, that the Lord hath sent his angel, and hath delivered me."

I stood yesterday in the woods a little after daybreak and observed high up in a tree a large hawk. I stood as still as I could, and I watched the head of the hawk turn from side to side. The sun shown on the hawk and it was a large red-tailed hawk. I observed how it was as if the hawk was commanding and observing all that was going on, sitting so very high on the tallest tree. Proverbs 3:21, "My son, let not them depart from thine eyes: keep sound wisdom and discretion." That hawk was not going to let anything move that did not catch his eyes. God challenges us that "wisdom and discretion" must never depart from us. Proverbs 3:22-23, "So shall they be life unto thy soul, and grace to thy neck. Then shalt thou walk in thy way safely, and thy foot shall not stumble." That big red-tailed hawk was in full observance of everything that moved in that valley. God pleads with us to not let sin cause us to stumble but to live to show forth His praises. Psalm 79:13, "So we thy people and sheep of thy pasture will give thanks for ever: we will shew forth thy praise to all generations." Our God is sitting high in Heaven and observing everything that is going on. He is there to lead us, protect us, lift us up, encourage us.

As I had to leave and get to work, that hawk just sat there and kept constantly scanning the hills and valleys. My heart rejoiced as I thought how our God is constantly there watching us and is there for us every moment of every day. Oh, how our God is High above all of His creation. Praise Him today!

God is there for us every moment of every day.

April 4

Deuteronomy 33-34　Psalm 80　　Proverbs 4　　Acts 13

Keeping a Clean Life

Good morning! Good morning! Good morning! God is still on His throne. He is still answering our prayers and He is still coming again. Springtime brings a fresh time. Cleaning, raking, clearing, planting flowers, getting the garden ready, taking an early morning walk, a walk in the evening before calling it a day. There just always seems to be a special happiness in the air. You might ask, Bro Smith, are you living in the same world that I am? The answer is yes. Listen to these phrases out of Deuteronomy 33, "The LORD came" (verse 2), "he loved the people" (verse 3), "The eternal God is thy refuge, and underneath are the everlasting arms" (verse 27).

Yesterday some fellows from the college came out to help me with work at the camp. Dirty work, grubby work, back breaking work, but when we were finished the area looked so very much better. It was the same place, but it looked different. Take a tree that has some fallen and broken branches on the ground. Some people will mow around them, and the grass grows up and the small limbs begin to look like brush. The weeds grow in the flower bed, but when the weeds get pulled out, the flower bed looks fresh and clean. Acts 13:47, "For so hath the Lord commanded us, saying, I have set thee to be a light of the Gentiles, that thou shouldest be for salvation unto the ends of the earth." We cannot be the light that God wants us to be until we get the sin out and have that daily fresh walk with the Lord. The weeds will continue to grow, and the limbs will continue to fall, but if we keep things cleaned up, there is a joy of looking at the freshness and cleanliness. Proverbs 4:23, "Keep thy heart will all diligence; for out of it are the issues of life." Keep your heart clean from sin or out of your heart will come forth the filth of the sin within. Psalm 80:3, 7, 19, "Turn us again, O God, and cause thy face to shine."

Ask God to let you see the dead branches in your life. Ask Him to let you see the weeds that are growing and pull them out and rake them up. It takes work to keep a yard clean, a flower bed free of weeds, a garden hoed and the soil broken up so the plants can grow, but the results are beautiful. May our lives be a beautiful sight for the honor and glory of our God that saved our soul. A little work brings a whole lot of satisfaction. Confession of sin brings the sweetness of a clean heart and a brighter relationship with the Lord.

We cannot be the light that God wants us to be until we get the sin out.

April 5

Joshua 1-2   Psalm 81   Proverbs 5   Acts 14

God Believes in You

Good morning! To believe in somebody is to be an encourager to somebody. Our reading in Joshua chapter one this morning brings us to the time when Moses is gone and it is time for Joshua to lead. What a responsibility! Joshua 1:5, "as I was with Moses, so I will be with thee: I will not fail thee, nor forsake thee." I went to the boys staff cabin several times this past week and thought and prayed about many of the young men that have worked on camp staff. Each summer as the young men and young ladies arrive to give a summer serving the Lord, it is easy for Mrs. Smith and me to detect the nervousness of each staff member. They do not want to do wrong; they do not want to be a disappointment. I have learned in working with people that the greatest thing I can do is believe in them and let them know that I believe in them.

Moses believed in Joshua and, by all means, God let Joshua know in Joshua 1:9, "Have not I commanded thee? Be strong and of good courage;

be not afraid, neither be thou dismayed: for the LORD thy God is with thee whithersoever thou goest." In Acts 14 we read of Paul being stoned, and yet he stood later and in verse 22, "Confirming the souls of the disciples, and exhorting them to continue in the faith." The word "confirming" means he stood and encouraged them to keep going and he believed in them. God saved our souls, not because of our talents, abilities, finances, etc., but because He loves us and wants to use us. That is God believing in what He can make us for Him, and He desires us to love Him and believe in Him. Proverbs 5:7, "Hear me now, therefore, O ye children, and depart not from the words of my mouth." As I watch our grandchildren grow and develop, they need me to believe in them. My children, as grown adults, need me to believe in them. My wife needs me to believe in her. But more than anything, I need to believe that God can and God will. Listen to the Psalmist in 81:7, "Thou calledst in trouble, and I delivered thee, I answered thee in the secret place of thunder: I proved thee at the waters of Meribah. Selah."

God is saying to us today, you believed in me enough to get saved, believe in me now with the rest of your life. All that know us must see that we believe in God and His Word, that is why we live it. Wherever you are in your spiritual life, know that God has not forsaken you and ask yourself if you have forsaken Him. "As I was with Moses, so I will be with thee." Think about it.

God saved our souls because He loves us and wants to use us.

April 6

Joshua 3-4   Psalm 82   Proverbs 6   Acts 15

Stand Firm

Good morning! Reading the Word of God daily is a must in a walk with God. God has told us that He preserved every word. Often, we look at the miracles and miss the characters and their actions in looking at what God did in the lives of different people.

Joshua 3:17, "And the priests that bare the ark of the covenant of the LORD stood firm on dry ground in the midst of Jordan." The children of Israel have arrived at the bank of the mighty Jordan river and need to cross. The priests were instructed to pick up the ark of the covenant and walk into the water. As they stepped in the water, the waters separated and they walked forward. Now, I want our minds to focus on what the priests did. Joshua 4:10, "For the priests which bare the ark stood in the midst of Jordan, until every thing was finished that the LORD commanded Joshua to speak unto the people." The priests stood still and firm until all the people had passed over and until stones had been picked up to build an altar for the people, for generations to come to remember what God did. Our focus today is on the fact that the priests "stood firm on dry ground." You and I that are saved need to "stand firm" for God and on His Word. Psalm 82:1, "God standeth in the congregation of the mighty."

In Acts 15 there was an argument about Jewish law and fully following Christ for the Jews and Gentiles. Acts 15:11, "But we believe that through the grace of the Lord Jesus Christ we shall be saved, even as they." God's Word and God's ways are unchanging. They are the same in the good times as in the bad times. We have looked in the past at the firm strength of that generation, and this generation needs to stand firm on God's Word for this generation and for the coming generation. Proverbs 6:21, "Bind them continually upon thine heart, and tie them about thy neck." Stand firm today, tomorrow, in good times and in bad. Stand firm on God's Word. As the priests "stood firm," all of God's people passed by and saw those men standing firm. Decide today that you are going to "stand firm" on God's Word for God's glory.

Stand firm today, tomorrow, in good times and in bad.

April 7

Joshua 5-7   Psalm 83   Proverbs 7   Acts 16

The Accursed Thing

Good morning! Our readings this morning are overflowing with truth, conviction and guidance. We must stay on our Bible reading schedule to not miss one word or one truth that God desires for us to know and apply to our lives. The children of Israel have crossed over on dry ground as we read yesterday, and today they have a seven-day march around the city of Jericho. The first day they went one time around and on the seventh day they marched seven times. Joshua 6:15, "And it came to pass on the seventh day, that they rose early about the dawning of the day." That one phrase is an admonition for us to rise at the beginning of the day and have our personal time with the Lord. Joshua 6:18, "keep yourselves from the accursed thing, lest ye make yourselves accursed, when ye take of the accursed thing, and make the camp of Israel a curse, and trouble it." I wish we had time to spend on just studying the word "accursed." It is anything in our possession, or as we will soon see, our "household," that God says we are not to have because it is not pleasing to the Lord.

My heart is convicted today to check my life, my marriage, my home, my dress, my music, my books, etc., what I have in possession, which is not pleasing to God. Achan "coveted," "took," and "hid," that which was "accursed." Why was it accursed? Because God said so!!!!! There is one word that was in our Old Testament, New Testament, Proverbs and Psalms reading this morning, and that word is "house." They had in their possession what God said should not be, and thirty-six men lost their lives because of what one man thought he could hide from God. Acts 16:31, "Believe on the Lord Jesus Christ, and thou shalt be saved, and thy house." The word "house" is mentioned five times in Acts 16, and four times in Proverbs 7. Psalm 83:12, "Who said, Let us take to ourselves the houses of God in possession."

From our personal lives to our homes to our churches, it is important to God that we do not possess the "accursed" thing, and when I speak of the "accursed" thing, I am speaking of anything that is not pleasing to God. We must quit seeing only through our eyes and our wants and look through the eyes of what is pleasing to God. Let us stop today and do a thorough examination of the stuff in our lives, our homes and our churches. Are there things hidden that need to be cleaned out? Something to work on.

It is important to God that we do not possess anything
that is not pleasing to God.

Joshua 8-9   Psalm 84   Proverbs 8   Acts 17

Stability in Unstable Times

Good morning! There is strength in stability. When something is stable, there will be strength. When there is stability in a relationship, there will be strength in that relationship. Couples that have been married over many years have learned to be stable in their strength. Strength without stability will not last very long.

Psalm 84:5, "Blessed is the man whose strength is in thee; in whose heart are the ways of them." Joshua's leadership was so strong when it was stable. Joshua 8:18, "And the LORD said unto Joshua, Stretch out the spear that is in thy hand toward Ai." Joshua 8:26, "For Joshua drew not his hand back, wherewith he stretched out the spear, until he had utterly destroyed all the inhabitants of Ai." We read in chapter nine how the Gibeonites were afraid and "They did work wilily," Joshua 9:4. Joshua 9:14, "And the men took of their victuals and asked not counsel at the mouth of the LORD." They weakened and sought not the Lord's guidance and leadership. Now we read in Joshua 9:18, "And all the congregation murmured against the princes." The people had lost confidence because of a lack of stability in leadership. The apostle Paul was constantly moving forward to win people to Christ by spreading the gospel. Acts 17:16, "Now while Paul waited for them at Athens, his spirit was stirred in him, when he saw the city wholly given to idolatry." Paul never lost his focus, his calling, his burden; he stayed stable in his direction and service for the Lord. Proverbs 8:32-33, "Now therefore hearken unto me, O ye children: for blessed are they that keep my ways. Hear instruction, and be wise, and refuse it not."

We are living in a very unstable time. It is time for God's people to remain stable in our walk with God, focused on God's will and have a determination to do God's work. Stability brings strength. Be stable in your walk with God, marriage, family, church, and service for our KING. Remember, our God is the same yesterday, today and forever.

God's people must remain stable, focused, and determined to do God's work.

April 9

Joshua 10-11   Psalm 85   Proverbs 9   Acts 18

God Can

Good morning! God's daily strength and guidance from His Word is so amazing to me. The storm that came through last night awakened me with the hail hitting the ranch house so strongly. I got up and asked the Lord to please put a hedge of protection around the camp. The wind, rain, and hail was so strong. As Joshua and the people of Israel prepare to take the land that God has promised, we read in Joshua 10:8, "And the LORD said unto Joshua, Fear them not: for I have delivered them into thine hand." The enemy was large in number, tall in stature, strong in military strength and we read in Joshua 10:11, "The LORD cast down great stones from heaven upon them unto Azekah, and they died: they were more which died with hailstones than they whom the children of Israel slew with the sword." Then we read in Joshua 10:12-13, "Then spake Joshua to the LORD, "Sun, stand thou still, And the sun stood still, and the moon stayed, So the sun stood still in the midst of heaven, and hasted not to go down about a whole day." PRAISE BE THE LORD!!!

God always blesses obedience and righteousness, in His time and in His way. Do not say that God cannot or God will not. The problem is with us, not God. I sat here this morning, got back down on my knees and asked God to bring sin to my mind so that I can confess it. I hunger to stay away from anything that is not pleasing to God. God can and God will, the problem is not God. Joshua 11:15, "As the LORD commanded Moses his servant, so did Moses command Joshua, and so did Joshua; he left nothing undone of all that the LORD commanded Moses." Have we done all that we need to do? Acts 18:9-10, "Be not afraid, but speak, and hold not thy peace: For I am with thee, and no man shall set on thee to hurt thee." God used hail again to destroy and teach that He is God. Proverbs 9:10, "The fear of the LORD is the beginning of wisdom: and the knowledge of the holy is understanding."

God is looking for us to live what we say HE is. Psalm 85:6, "Wilt thou not revive us again: that thy people may rejoice in thee?" Wow!!! God's Word sure hit home in my heart today. May we take some time and meditate on God's Word and let His Word strengthen, convict and motivate us for His glory. Have a blessed day.

God always blesses obedience and righteousness, in His time and in His way.

April 10

Joshua 12-13　　　Psalm 86　　　Proverbs 10　　　Acts 19

Headed Toward Heaven

Good morning! I would like for you to ride with me in your mind this morning in my truck and imagine that we are going on a vacation. You pick where you would like to go. All expenses are paid, and we are going to stay in the most beautiful place that you can imagine. We have never been there before. The longer we travel the more excited we get because of getting to our beautiful vacation and destination.

As I read Joshua 13:1 this morning, my heart got excited, and I thought about a destination that is a perfect place to go. "Now Joshua was old and stricken in years; and the LORD said unto him, Thou art old and stricken in years, and there remaineth yet very much land to be possessed." Do you ever feel tired, worn out, exhausted? The answer to that question is we all feel that way at some time. Let us reread the last part of the verse, "there remaineth yet very much land to be possessed." God was not done with Joshua. He is older and has fought many battles and yet the Lord says there is more that I need you to do. My brother and sister, there is more that the Lord has for us to do. You may not see what it is, and you may not feel like you can do any more, but the Lord sees what we cannot see and knows what our next step is. Acts 19:20, "So mightily grew the word of God and prevailed." Proverbs 10:25, "As the whirlwind passeth, so is the wicked no more: but the righteous is an everlasting foundation." There is still work to be done. God wants to use us all. Psalm 86:7, "In the day of my trouble I will call upon thee: for thou wilt answer me."

There is an excitement as we travel and know that we are getting close to our destination. We think about the time of rest and what we will see and what we will be doing. As a Christian, our place of rest is Heaven, and our hearts should be full of excitement as we draw closer to our place of rest. Let the excitement build as we continue to serve God and get closer to that place for eternity with our KING. Don't quit and don't give up. Fire up, keep your eyes looking forward and up, keep seeking to serve Him. Psalm 86:12, "I will praise thee, O Lord my God, with all my heart: and I will glorify thy name for evermore." "There remaineth yet very much land to be possessed." Keep going. Life only gets better as we think on the place of rest and peace.

Our hearts should be full of excitement as we draw closer to our place of rest.

April 11

Joshua 14-15   Psalm 87   Proverbs 11   Acts 20

Our Daily Strength

Good morning! The Word of God and prayer must be our daily strength. As I read this morning in Joshua 14, two words drew my attention. In verses 8, 9, and 14, we see these two words: "wholly followed." The land is divided, and now we read of Caleb stating that he is as strong now at 85 years old as he was when he was 45. Oh, that my strength would maintain and stay stable until the end!

How did this happen? Where did this enthusiasm come from? Where did he get this drive? How can we keep a determined heart like this? I suggest three observations:

1. He kept faith in God and His promise.
2. He followed the leadership of Moses, the man of God.
3. He stayed committed to God and the goal of reaching the Promised Land.

I can hear him say to Joshua in verse 12, "Give me this mountain." Let your faith be strengthened in God's Word and His promises today.

Keep your focus on goals that please the Lord and stay committed to live for Him, no matter what is ahead. There is a mountain at the end of the trail. Keep on!

Let God's Word and His promises be your strength today.

April 12

Joshua 16-17   Psalm 88   Proverbs 12   Acts 21

A Praying People

Good morning! He Is Risen!!!! As I read my Bible this morning and thought of the history of America and the history of the followers of Christ, as well as the faith of the saints in the Old Testament, there is a common factor in all. We constantly read that there were times that all sought the face of God in prayer. Joshua 16:17, "Thou art a great people, and hast great power." As we read in Acts 21:5, "And when we had accomplished those days, we departed and went our way; and they all brought us on our way, with wives and children, till we were out of the city: and we kneeled down on the shore, and prayed."

We must be a praying people to see the hand of God move. We must be a people that seek the hand of God and His power. We must be a people that plead for the will of God to be accomplished. Selfishness has no place in the heart of a yielded saint. Proverbs 12:7, "The wicked are over thrown, and are not: but the house of the righteous shall stand." We serve a risen Saviour who hungers for a relationship with those that He shed His blood for. That relationship grows its strength through the time we spend in prayer and His Word. May it be said of us today as the Psalmist wrote in Psalm 88:1, "O LORD God of my salvation, I have cried day and night before thee:." Psalm 88:9, "LORD, I have called daily upon thee, I have stretched out my hands unto thee." Psalm 88:13, "But unto thee have I cried, O LORD; and in the morning shall my prayer prevent thee."

As Jesus spent the time in prayer before His betrayal, may we hear those words that He said to His disciples that night. Luke 22:40, "Pray that ye enter not into temptation." May we first of all always seek the face and will of the Father. May we continue and grow in our time of prayer with the Father. The strength of every believer is the strength that they attain through the time they spend in prayer. May our Lord bless you greatly.

We must be a praying people to see the hand of God move.

April 13

Joshua 18-19   Psalm 89:1-18   Proverbs 13   Acts 22

Don't Miss the Joyful Sound

Good morning! In Psalm 89:15 we read the phrase, "Blessed is the people that know the joyful sound." The two words "joyful sound" drew my attention this morning. As I meditated on these two words, I reread the phrase and I focused on the word "know." Last night was the opening of our first camp activity for this year. I caught myself laughing at myself, because I saw young people that I thought were not old enough to be at this activity. Then it hit me like a storm- these young people are growing up and getting older.

As an adult, the older I get, I keep shocking myself by thinking young people will always stay young. There were those here that were new, and I watched to make sure that they would be included and make new friends. As all of us have seen before, if someone does not feel a part of things, they will not have fun. That brings me to our verse. We that are saved have benefits and joys of the Christian life that we will miss if we do not get involved and truly live the Christian life. The "joyful sound" brought hope, peace, and confidence in God. Many that are saved have not learned to enjoy the Christian life and its many pleasures. Just like young people that do not get involved, they will miss things they do not know they are missing. The verse tells us there were those that "know the joyful sound." Can I throw out a challenge to us all to enjoy the "joyful sound"? It was a trumpet that was blown that caused the people to focus on benefits that they had. It developed confidence in God's favor, and the sound of that trumpet gave a peace to their hearts. Hey, brother and sister in Christ, let us:

1. Enjoy the benefits of being saved.
2. Have a greater confidence in God and His Word.
3. Enjoy peace that He is in control and He is preparing an eternal place for us to be with Him.

"Blessed is the people that know the joyful sound." As I watched new young people make new friends and enjoy time together, and as the preacher preached, I saw their spirit become tender. When the invitation was given, they left their seat and came to the altar. Let us enjoy the blessings of being saved and serving our Lord. LISTEN!!! Can you hear the "joyful sound"?

We will miss the benefits of the Christian life if we
do not get involved in the Christian life.

April 14

Joshua 20-21   Psalm 89:19-37   Proverbs 14   Acts 23

A Cause Worth Standing For

Good morning! Can I begin this morning by asking a question? What drives you? Maybe I should ask, what motivates you? Or maybe the question could be asked, what is your purpose in life? As I was reading in Acts 23, I saw the story of Paul being held and appearing before the Sanhedrin, the religious leaders. Part of them had banded together (verse 12), made a promise to each other, made a commitment, and promised themselves that, whatever it took, they were going to kill Paul. There was a great hatred that had built up in them toward this man of God and the truth that he spoke.

The sadness of this true story is that they were "bound" by wrong principles to accomplish this goal of killing Paul. They were so driven that they also said in verse 14, "that we will eat nothing until we have slain Paul." I asked myself and I ask you this morning, "Do I have a love for Christ and a drive to stand for Him, live for Him, be faithful to Him, and

125

be in His perfect will as strong as these men that "bound themselves with an oath" (verse 21)?

This world that we live in is showing how much they hate life by all the abortions we have. Daily in the news there are reports of robberies and killings. Christians around the world are living in fear for their lives, just because of their belief in and love for Christ. This passage convicts my heart to have a stronger conviction in my principle to stand, live for, and serve Christ. I must be faithful to the Lord's house when the doors are open. Hebrews 10:25 says, "Not forsaking the assembling of ourselves together, as the manner of some is; but exhorting one another: and so much the more, as ye see the day approaching."

We should be convicted to not only tithe (10%) out of our finances, but out of our time as well. There are 24 hours in a day and 168 hours in a week. Have we thought about serving the Lord, not only by being a testimony, but by serving Him in some way 16.8 hours each week? These forty men were strong in their desire to kill Paul and "bound themselves with an oath." You know what they really did? They said, "We will stand together for this purpose of the deep hatred in our hearts." Let us bind our hearts together for the love of Christ to reach lost souls with the most wonderful truth man will ever hear. We must bind ourselves to encourage brothers and sisters to be faithful to God's house, to encourage and serve together in unity, and to reach the fields of lost souls. These forty men had a cause. May we, like David In I Samuel 17:29, say, "Is there not a cause?"

May we be fervently committed in our cause to stand for and live for Christ.

April 15

Joshua 22-24   Psalm 89:38-52   Proverbs 15   Acts 24

Popcorn or Sweet Corn?

Good morning! This morning at the top of the page where I write notes from my Bible reading, I wrote, "Is it popcorn or sweet corn?." Many years ago, when I started working in the garden, my father saw my love for planting and working in the garden and asked if I would like to plant the garden that year. I was thrilled but almost made a great mistake. My dad just asked a simple question. He asked, "You are not planting popcorn next to sweet corn, are you?" I had not thought about the cross pollination that would happen. You see, if I had planted these two different crops next to each other, they would have developed ears of corn with both sweet corn and popcorn on the same cob.

We read in Joshua 22:10, "the children of Reuben and the children of Gad and the half tribe of Manasseh built there an altar by Jordan, a great altar to see to." The rest of Israel were in an uproar when they heard about the altar, and they thought these tribes on the other side of Jordan were going to begin to worship other gods and bring God's wrath on all Israel, just like Achan did when he hid the gold and silver and the Babylonish garment. The children of Reuben and Gad said, no, it is not an altar of a strange god, "But that it may be a witness between us, and you, and our generations after us," Joshua 22:27. They wanted to keep things separated from the false gods and build unity with the other tribes on the other side of Jordan. Paul was accused of heresy, but we read in Acts 24:14, "But this I confess unto thee, that after the way which they call heresy, so worship I the God of my fathers, believing all things which are written in the law and in the prophets." To keep the separation from wrong doctrine, there must be a daily searching and learning from the Scriptures. Proverbs 15:14, "The heart of him that hath understanding seeketh knowledge: but the mouth of fools feedeth on foolishness." The world and Christ do not mix and cannot be brought together. In our reading in Psalm 89 this morning, we read ten times the words, "thou hast" and three separate times the word "hast." God has done His part and we must do our part by separating from the world and its ways.

I am thankful that my father taught me the importance of separating crops that can cross pollinate and to keep them separate or I will have fruit from the garden that I cannot eat. That is why the Christian that keeps the ways of the world in their lives cannot fully live a life full of the joy and blessings of the LORD. Keep in mind, is it popcorn or sweet corn?

The world and Christ do not mix and cannot be brought together.

April 16

Judges 1-2   Psalm 90   Proverbs 16   Acts 25

Prepared with God

Good morning! Do you ever feel like you are not ready for the day? You did not sleep soundly. You tossed and turned all night. The house was too hot or too cold. You laid there, heard things, and wondered what that noise was. When morning arrived, you said, "I am not ready for the day." As I read in Proverbs 16 this morning, words and phrases just kept drawing my attention about how important it is to prepare for the day. I love a quote that I have often heard my pastor say, "By failing to prepare, you are preparing to fail." (Benjamin Franklin). Many days I carry that quote in my pocket on a three-by-five card, and I take it out and read it often. Proverbs 1:16 states, "The preparations of the heart in man." I began to think about that phrase. I finished reading the chapter, and as I read, phrase after phrase kept jumping at me, letting me know that it is so important every day to seek the Lord, His wisdom, His understanding, His ways, His leadership, and His guidance.

It is no wonder we as God's people lose our direction in serving Him, our zeal in serving Him, and our heart in serving Him. We are not prepared for the day because we did not allow Him to prepare us. An athlete prepares himself continually physically, a teacher has to be prepared to teach, a business has to be prepared to meet the needs of the clients. To be a success in anything, we have to prepare. Please read this statement slowly: The word "preparations" means I am not sufficient by myself. I must be prepared by God to live a life pleasing to Him. How many have tried to live the Christian life and failed? We get fired up for God, and then we think we can make it without Him. We miss church and say, "I can make it without," and we fail. We headed on into the day and had no personal time with the Lord to prepare ourselves, and the day fell apart. Many have failed and will fail because we are not sufficient enough in ourselves to make it without being strengthened by God. He does not want us to do it alone. Take a little time this morning, read slowly, and mark some phrases and verses in Proverbs 16. Verse 16 says, "How much better is it to get wisdom than gold! and to get understanding rather to be chosen than silver!" Have a blessed, prepared day.

*Often, we are not prepared for the day because
we did not allow Him to prepare us.*

April 17

Judges 3-4   Psalm 91   Proverbs 17   Acts 26

A Refuge in the Storm

Good morning! It is that time of year when the temperatures keep fluctuating so much. One day, it is so warm a coat is too much, and the next day, I feel as if I need two coats. The beautiful spring blossoms are filling the countryside. The gobble of turkeys can be heard so often, and the singing of birds is all around us. With the weather changing so often, the hot and cold winds clashing together bring those dangerous storms. I am constantly amazed at how all of creation, such as animals, flowers, and trees, continue through the storms, yet we as humans have a fear, distrust, and lack of faith as the storms of life approach us.

As I read Psalm 91 this morning, my heart was filled with such a calmness, comfort, and fresh confidence in the protection, provision, and peace that a right relationship with God can bring. Look at verse two. "He is my refuge (a place of shelter and safety), my fortress (a place of defense, safety, security), and my God (my Lord, my Savior, my Redeemer). Psalm 91 is a psalm of protection for all believers. There is no need for me to walk alone today, for He is with me. There is no need for me to feel discouraged today; He wants to be my encourager. There is no need for me to be confused today; He is my Guide. "He is my refuge and my fortress: my God; in him will I trust." Head into this day knowing He is there. Allow the Lord to guide you, wait on Him for direction, and cling to Him for patience. Have a wonderful day in the arms of our God, for He is there.

There is no need for us to walk alone today, for He is with us.

April 18

Judges 5-6   Psalm 92   Proverbs 18   Acts 27

Flourishing

Good morning! I love trees. As a young boy, I loved to climb trees. The bigger they were, the more I enjoyed climbing them. I have said many times that the Lord made trees for boys to climb and explore what they cannot see from the ground. Oh, I heard my mom say many times, "Be careful and don't fall." I fell many times because I slipped, a branch broke, or I thought I could reach the next limb and I would miss and fall. One day I fell, caught my chin on a branch, split my chin, and had to have stitches. I have the scar to this day. By the way, it never stopped me from climbing.

As I read in Psalm 92 this morning, verse 12 states, "The righteous shall flourish like a palm tree: he shall grow like a cedar in Lebanon." We never had palm trees when I was a boy, and I only saw pictures of them for many years. They are tall, and the fruit of the tree is at the very top. I have seen men climb right up the trunk and get to the top even though there are no limbs. Verse twelve also speaks of a cedar tree. The cedar has so many limbs and is much easier to climb. Both of these trees have something to teach us. They both have roots that make them stable, have wood that will make them useful, and have wood that is beautiful. Verse 13 tells us that if we are planted in the house of the Lord we shall "flourish" (grow). We read on to verse 14, and we see by being faithful (planted), as we grow, we will "bring forth fruit" (our life will produce). It does not stop there. We shall also "flourish" (grow stronger). It takes many years of growing to grow a strong, tall tree. It is the same in growing a stable, strong, fruit-producing life for the Lord.

I love a big, old, shade tree, and I also love a fruit-bearing tree. I love to watch the wind blow through a willow tree, and I love to hear the song a pine tree can sing as the breeze blows through its limbs. There is so much to say about trees, their beauty, their fruit, and the precious wood that only comes from years of being planted, letting the roots grow deep, withstanding all kinds of weather, and growing through the years. We are like these beautiful trees of all kinds. Get planted in church, grow, and produce. It is God's plan and God's way. Have a growing day.

By being faithful to the Lord, we will bring forth fruit.

Judges 7-8   Psalm 93   Proverbs 19   Acts 28

What Do You Need Deliverance From?

Good morning! I love the story of Gideon in Judges 6-8. He was quite a fellow. As I was reading this morning in chapters 7-8, a word caught and kept my attention. That word is "deliver." Before we go further, let us look at the character of the man that became the next judge of Israel, Gideon. His name means: feller, hewer, destroyer, hacker, and one who hewed down. His first task that the Lord asked of him was to "throw down the altar of Baal" (6:25). We jump ahead to chapters 7 and 8, and we see God using Gideon and his men to get things back in order.

Now let us look at the word deliver. Deliver means to set free, to assist, to aid. So many are bound by financial stress, physical stress, family stress, addictions, employment stress, marriage problems, and vehicle problems. Today, let us look to the Lord to be delivered. Gideon had to have the Lord's help. He looked to the Lord, and that is what brought the victory. I John 5:4 says, "For whatsoever is born of God overcometh the world: and this is the victory that overcometh the world, even our faith." Jeremiah 33:3 says, "Call unto me, and I will answer thee, and shew thee great and mighty things, which thou knowest not."

Matthew 11:28 says, "Come unto me, all ye that labor and are heavy laden, and I will give you rest." We need to quit feeling sorry for ourselves, look up to God, seek His face, humble ourselves, and seek His guidance. Quit saying, "I can't." Get strength from Him and say, "I can." Let God be God, our deliverer. As Gideon needed God, so do we. To enjoy the vegetables from the garden, we must plow the ground, plant the seed, let the rain nourish the ground, let the sun help the seed to germinate and grow, hoe the ground to keep it broken up so that the tender plant can grow, and keep the weeds pulled out so they do not overtake the garden. All of this takes work, but the wonderful delicious taste of fresh garden vegetables is worth it. It takes work, but so does the Christian life. God is desiring to be our Lord and deliver us that we may be fruit-bearing, joyful, Christians. Have a day of deliverance.

Quit saying, "I can't." Get strength from Him and say, "I can."

April 20

Judges 9-10   Psalm 94:1-11   Proverbs 20   Romans 1-2

On the Right Course

Good morning! As I was reading this morning for my devotions, I noticed as I read in the Old Testament, New Testament, Proverbs, and Psalms that there was a theme in all of my readings. Opposites always are going different directions. They never go the same direction but are always in conflict. The truths and principles of the Old Testament are still truths and principles in the New Testament. Righteousness is right in the eyes of God, and unrighteousness is wrong in the eyes of God.

In Romans 1:16 we read, "For I am not ashamed of the gospel of Christ: for it is the power of God unto salvation to everyone that believeth; to the Jew first, and also to the Greek." The first part of the next verse says, "For therein is the righteousness of God revealed…" God warns us in just a few verses about changing the truth of God. Verse 25 states, "Who changed the truth of God into a lie, and worshipped and served the creature more than the Creator, who is blessed forever. Amen."

God's way is truth; our flesh and the devil's way is a lie. Verse 26 through the end of the chapter gives us a sad truth about man in total rebellion against God. When I was a Boy Scout, I learned how to use a compass and read a map to do land navigation. I love hiking and the outdoors. I love to observe nature and all its beauty. But I will not let nature keep me from being in the Lord's house when the doors are open. When I was in the Army, I also had land navigation courses and had to learn orienteering. An orienteering course is using a map and compass to go through a designated course. You are given your starting point that will give you information to make it to the next location and, finally, to the end of the course. Most of the time the course takes you places that are not clear and you have to stay right on course, or you will not make it to the next location, and you could get lost. It is vital that I know how to use a compass, read a map, and go through different types of terrain. I might have to go through thick brush, cross a river, or go over a mountain. I must correctly use everything that I have been taught. I cannot question the accuracy of the compass or the fact that my map might show a building that is no longer there. The distance between points must be followed accurately.

The Christian life can be compared to this. I must not question the truth of the Word of God. I must listen to the Holy Spirit that dwells inside of me to convict me when something is not right and to guide me in God's perfect will. I must apply the principles of holiness and obedience that I learn from the Word of God. Both in the Boy Scouts and in the Army, there were those who did not listen and got lost because they did not follow the right directions. Sometimes on the trail, I felt alone, but I kept going in the direction that I knew was right. There were times on the trail that were rough, difficult, and it seemed impossible to go on, but I kept going. There were times on the trail that I could not trust myself, and I knew I had to focus on what I had been taught. I followed the reading of the compass and applied the right principles that had been taught. I am still on my course in life, and as Paul wrote how he had finished his course, I hunger to finish my course in a way that pleases the Lord. Stay faithful and stay on course.

God's Word is our compass to keep us on the right course.

April 21

Judges 11-12   Psalm 94:12-23   Proverbs 21   Romans 3-4

Keep Your Vows

Good morning! I have seen many a young person and adult kneel at an altar during a week of camp and shed tears. I have seen those tears become a puddle on the floor or in the sawdust. There was a sincerity of heart and a full heart to keep the commitment made. When those buses, cars and vans pull out and go under the camp entrance sign, there is an urgency in my heart to keep praying that those campers and counselors will keep their promises to God. A time away from the world and all its sin and distraction is what brought them to their point of brokenness before the Lord. Bible preaching, right standards, the world shut out and so much more.

We read in Judges 11:30, "Jephtah vowed a vow unto the LORD." He was a "mighty man of valour" (Judges 11:1). He had a sad beginning and was rejected and yet he was brought back to lead the people of Israel to victories in battle. He vowed to the Lord that if the Lord would give them victory, "that whatsoever cometh forth of the doors of my house to meet me, I will offer it up for a burnt offering" (Judges 11:31). It was his daughter. Judges 11:35, "I have opened my mouth unto the LORD, and I cannot go back." Greater than this is what God did for all mankind. In Romans 3:23, "For all have sinned, and come short of the glory of God." We are all sinners and in our sin, we have no hope, and yet look what God promised and did. Romans 3:24, "Being justified freely by his grace through the redemption that is in Christ Jesus." God did so much greater than Jephthah and yet men cannot keep their vow of faithfulness, service, yielded life to God. We read in Proverbs 21:3, "To do justice and judgment is more acceptable to the LORD than sacrifice."

Are you keeping your vows to the Lord? He is always there for us and is always willing to welcome us back to Him in our walk with Him. Psalm 94:22, "But the LORD is my defense; and my God is the rock of my refuge." Oh, that we would be faithful to the Lord to live for Him and to serve Him daily and with everything we have. Can you see the tears on the floor or in the sawdust? Can you remember how your heart was brought under great conviction? Remember the words of Jephtah, "I have opened my mouth unto the LORD, and I cannot go back." (Judges 11:35). He kept his vow unto the Lord.

Are you keeping your vows to the Lord?

Judges 13-14   Psalm 95   Proverbs 22   Romans 5-6

A Good Day, or a Bad Day?

Good morning! Another day is about to begin for each of us. Have you ever asked yourself the difference between a good day and a bad day? Do I allow things, situations, circumstances, people, or frustrations to determine what kind of day I am going to have? Have you ever gotten up in the morning and thought about how refreshed you feel and how beautiful the sunrise is and enjoyed the fresh smell of spring air? Then the day falls apart, and everything seems to fall apart. Have you had those nights that you could not sleep, and you laid there and thought of all the things you needed to do?

Let us stop, before we let ourselves get discouraged, and look at a couple of words in Romans 5 and 6. I must face the fact that I, and no one else, determine what kind of day I am going to have. Romans 5:21 states, "That as sin hath reigned unto death, even so might grace reign through righteousness unto eternal life by Jesus Christ our Lord." The first word we need to focus on is the word "reign." Reign means to possess, to rule, to have supreme power, to prevail. Before I was saved, sin was what "reigned" my life. Sin is a controller, a destroyer. When I faced the fact that I was a sinner, I faced what controlled my life and kept me from God. Even though I have been saved and have new life in Christ, I must still be aware that sin can control me.

That brings us to the second word in Romans 6:13. The word is "yield," which means to permit, to grant, to allow, to give in return. I must "yield" my heart, my body, my thoughts, my circumstances, my everything to God. I cannot let this world and the negatives of life and sin "reign." It is important every day, and every moment of every day, that I "yield" everything to Christ. Romans 6:4 challenges us to "walk in newness of life." So, what determines if I am going to have a good day or a bad day? I do, by what I allow to "reign" my life and how I "yield" my life to the Lord and His will. What a blessing Romans 5:17 should be to us! "For if by one man's offense death reigned by one; much more they which receive abundance of grace and of the gift of righteousness shall reign in life by one, Jesus Christ." Only walking with Jesus can give me a great day. Have a blessed walk today.

Yielding to God and allowing Him to reign determines if we have a good day.

April 23

Judges 15-16   Psalm 96   Proverbs 23   Romans 7

Don't Take the Bait

Good morning! I love fishing. I enjoy sitting beside a country pond and relaxing or being in a boat out on a lake. A few years ago, I enjoyed going fishing for trout with all five of my grandsons and my son. As we prepared to go fishing, we talked about the different types of bait. I have gone to the garden and dug many worms or gone to the bait shop and purchased many minnows. Throughout the years I have used different kinds of lures and special, colored flies. I can remember many different kinds of stink bait, garlic, marshmallows, etc. I have caught a lot of fish on sweet corn and just plain, old chicken livers. There are probably as many different baits as there are fishermen.

This morning as I was reading in Judges 16, I read the story of the Philistines trying to catch Samson. As you might already know, or I encourage you to take time to read it, that three different times they tried to catch him, but they failed. Oh, that Delilah who he should never have been around! Did you get that? He should never have been around her! She baited him with the words, "thine heart is not with me," in verse 15; and in verse 16, we see that she "pressed him daily." That is just like the old devil baiting you and me to try to get us to turn from God. He throws things in our path that will lead us away from living for God and being faithful to God. The stories have been told many times of a big, old fish in a lake or a pond that keeps getting away, and many hours are spent, along with many different baits, to try to catch him. The devil tries everything he can, and he never tires of trying to lure us away from the Lord. When Sampson, in verse 18, "told her all his heart," he was caught. Each day we live, the devil is working hard, and the lusts of our flesh are so tempted by the things of this world to lure us away. He baits us to get us away from what the Lord has for us. Be aware of the temptations of your flesh, and do not let the bait of this world catch you and pull you away from a victorious life in Christ. Pray a hedge around yourself today and keep your eyes on the Lord.

The devil never tires of trying to lure us away from the Lord.

April 24

Judges 17-18   Psalm 97   Proverbs 24   Romans 8

Led by the Light

Good morning! Have you ever awakened during the night and been in confusion of what day it is or what time it is? I have woken up and got right up and walked into a wall in the dark. Go ahead and laugh, Mrs. Smith did. When our lives are not in order spiritually, we will live in confusion and the devil will mount an attack on us. We must keep our lives in spiritual order even in trials and times of discouragement.

Judges 17:6, "In those days there was no king in Israel, but every man did that which was right in his own eyes." How can anyone try to live for God without God? We cannot make a decision that is right spiritually without the mind of Christ. Judges 17:5, "And the man Micah had an house of gods, and made an ephod, and teraphim, and consecrated one of his sons, who became his priest." Basically, Micah did what he thought and wanted. Romans 8:5-6, "For they that are after the flesh do mind the things of the flesh; but they that are after the Spirit the things of the Spirit. For to be carnally minded is death; but to be spiritually minded is life and peace." We must always do what God wants and in God's way and in God's timing. Confusion spiritually will always come along with sin when we do things our way and just what we want. Consistency in our walk with Christ is a must if we are going to stay in God's will and do God's will. Proverbs 24:21, "My son, fear thou the LORD and the king: and meddle not with them that are given to change." We need to settle down in our walk with God and live one step at a time.

When I have been startled in the night or wake up and jump right out of bed, I almost always stub my toe or walk into something. That is just what we do in our walk with God when we do not wait on Him and get His guidance in our lives. Living for God is not living in darkness and confusion. Jesus is the light, so why not be led by the Light? Jesus is the way, so why not be patient and let Him guide us in the way? Psalm 97:11, "Light is sown for the righteous, and gladness for the upright in heart." It was funny when I have walked into a wall or stubbed my toe, but there was also pain. Let us end with the thought that we read in Judges 18:18, "What do ye?" Live in the light and not in the darkness of confusion.

Jesus is the light, so why not be led by the Light?

April 25

Judges 19-21   Psalm 98   Proverbs 25   Romans 9

Henpecked

Good morning! I would like to invite you to go out to the chicken house with me this morning. We are going to observe something about chickens that I have never understood but it is a reality. I remember as a boy asking my mom why a certain chicken had an area on them where all the feathers were gone. Mom just simply said, the other chickens are picking at it, and they will eventually pick all the feathers or maybe even kill that chicken. If a chicken will see what it thinks is a bug on another chicken, it will begin to peck and pick at that spot. That is right, they will peck away at their own kind.

How sad the story that we read in Judges 19-21 this morning. Basically, I can say they killed their own. Judges 19:30, "There was no such deed done nor seen from the day that the children of Israel came up out of the land of Egypt unto this day." How did this happen? Judges 21:25, "In those days there was no king in Israel: every man did that which was right in his own eyes." A chicken will pick at and possibly kill their own because of what they think they see. We must look at all situations of life through the eyes of God and not what we think we see. Romans 9:32, "Because they sought it not by faith but as it were by the works of the law. For they stumbled at that stumblingstone." They could not and would not see the love of Christ and it caused them to miss by faith God's gift to man. Proverbs 25:8, "Go not forth hastily to strive, lest thou know what to do in the end thereof, when thy neighbor hath put thee to shame." We must not live in the flesh but the spirit. Sin and our emotions will cause us to often react in a way that we will soon regret, and even cause us to attack the ones we love the most. Psalm 98:2, "The LORD hath made known his salvation: his righteousness hath he openly shewed in the sight of the heathen."

I used to feel so sorry for the chickens that had been picked by the others, but it is much worse for us to attack and almost destroy others with our mouths and with our actions. Pray for others, see this world through the eyes of Christ and be the soul winners we need to be. Be patient with a younger brother in Christ or a brother that might not see things exactly the way that you see them. I remember seeing one chicken get another one down and pick at it, and how it disturbed me. Let us encourage, pray, and lift others up for the glory of Christ.

We must look at all situations of life through the eyes of God
and not what we think we see.

April 26

Ruth 1-2   Psalm 99   Proverbs 26   Romans 10

No Excuses

Good morning! The Word of God is so full. I feel so sorry for those who do not daily take time to read and search the Scriptures. As I read today in Proverbs 26, I noticed that the word "fool" is mentioned eleven times. There are many definitions for the word "fool." Here are some of them: destitute of reason, one who acts contrary to sound wisdom, wicked or depraved, one who prefers trifling and temporary pleasure to the service of God. Quite convicting, isn't it? My focus today was on one verse, and that is verse 7. "The legs of the lame are not equal: so is a parable in the mouth of fools."

My father was born with polio. One leg was deformed and shorter than the other. That imperfection never stopped my father, nor did it slow him down at all. The word "parable" is defined as this: a way to teach a spiritual or moral lesson. I hear excuses all the time about why people miss church or cannot help in an area of service. It has always amazed me how people can't make it to church, but they can make it to work. They will work because they need the money, but they will miss church because they do not see the need of learning God's Word, Christian fellowship, or just being faithful to God's house. I have heard the statement many times, "I do not have to go to church to worship God."

One of the dogs at the camp was attacked by two other dogs, and our dog was hurt so badly that she walked "lame." We cared for her, but nothing kept her down. She was always with me, hopping around on her three good legs. She came to eat her food and drink the water that was given to her. Wherever I went, she wanted to be with me. Nothing stopped her. This verse in Proverbs 26:7 teaches us that a lame person is impaired, but it does not say they stop. It does not say they can't; it does not say they quit; it does not say they give excuses. I watched my dad work and do everything, and I never heard him say, "I can't." A fool looks for excuses, refuses wisdom, does not seek counsel, has little or no reason, and seeks pleasure more than service for God. My father has now gone to Heaven, but so often, I remember my dad and his determination to press on, even when I knew it was hard for him. The word "fool" is mentioned eleven times in Proverbs 26. May our character be challenged today to walk as wise men and not as fools. We must not walk as a lame one, but we must be determined to serve our Lord.

A wise man will not quit, even if impaired or slowed down.

Ruth 3-4   Psalm 100   Proverbs 27   Romans 11

Separate, But Together

Good morning! Yesterday, before I left the church office, I straightened a picture that I have on my desk. It was taken several years ago of our family at Thanksgiving. It is a picture of my wife, myself, our children, their mates, and our grandchildren. I stopped, sat down, and took time to think about each one in the picture. Three generations were before me in the picture. The picture is several years old, and all have grown older. Each has his own personality and his own likes and dislikes, but there is a similarity in us all.

As I read this morning in Romans 11:36, I read, "For of him, and through him, and to him, are all things: to whom be glory for ever. Amen." I love my wife and our family more than I know how to express. My wife and I have been alone for many years now, and our children have their own families. Their children are growing and will soon be gone from their homes. Even though we are apart, we are together. Our hearts and our prayers keep us together. We all have seen potential in each other, believe in each other, and try to encourage each other. We are different, but we are similar. Likewise, when we received Christ, we became part of an eternal family, and Romans 11:36 tells us some very important truths about our heritage.

1. "of him:" His will should be the most important priority of our lives.

2. "through him:" He promises to sustain us and provide for us in His will.

3. "to him:" Everything we do should be to bring glory to Him and His name.

God loves us and made us in His very image and has a perfect will for our lives. We love our children and grandchildren, and we want them to be happy and enjoy life. God gave His Son for us and loves us. He will provide for us. How can we do less than live for Him and serve Him with our lives? Our family has a bond just as our Heavenly family has a bond. A parent experiences joy when a child grows, matures, and finds purpose in life. In Christ we should grow, mature, and let His purpose be fulfilled in our lives. We must remember that we are "of him, and through him." Let us live our lives "to him." Do not miss the joy of living in God's perfect will.

We have a Heavenly bond with Christ, just as we do with our family.

April 28

1 Samuel 1-2   Psalm 101   Proverbs 28   Romans 12-13

"I Will" To "I Did"

Good morning! As I read Psalm 101 this morning for part of my daily reading, I took notice of two words used in conjunction eleven times. Those words are "I will." An old quote immediately popped into my mind that says, "Good intentions never accomplished anything." Throughout life, many people have said, "I will," and they never did. It seems as though honesty, commitment, loyalty, and faithfulness are not character traits with much meaning these days. I have been excited many times by statements such as, "I will be in church Sunday," "I will make sure I am there," or, "I will be in my place." We have all heard these "I wills" and even possibly said them.

This Psalm was written around the time David was made king. He is writing about his commitments to the Lord. I'd like to point out three uses in this Psalm that can apply to us.

1. "I will behave" (verse 2): We see David's desire to be an obedient servant of the Lord.

I believe he means obedience in every area of his life. Obedience should be the first step in the new life of every new believer and in the daily life of all Christians.

2. "I will walk within my house with a perfect heart" (verse 2).

This phrase points out the importance of a clean heart where sin is confessed and forsaken. We would not eat a freshly cooked meal on a dirty plate, so why do we try to live the Christian life with a dirty heart?

3. "I will set no wicked thing before mine eyes (verse 3)." "I will not know a wicked person" (verse 4).

These verses challenge us to walk a pure life. We cannot have the Lord's blessing and constantly be filling ourselves with this world's ways.

We need to pay attention to ourselves and stay away from the world's music, dress, associations, and fads. We are not to use the language or slang of this world, nor dress the dress of this world. We should walk, talk, and act like a Christian. II Corinthians 6:17 says, "Wherefore come out from among them, and be ye separate, saith the Lord..." Ephesians 5:11 says, "And have no fellowship with the unfruitful works of darkness, but rather reprove them." Let us become a people, not of intentions who just say, "I will;" but let us say today, "I did."

Good intentions never accomplished anything.

April 29

1 Samuel 3-4   Psalm 102:1-17   Proverbs 29   Romans 14

My Way and God's Way

Good morning! My Old Testament reading this morning took me to I Samuel 4. As I was reading chapters 3-4, my mind went to children playing, getting into an argument, and saying, "I want it, it is mine!" Or when they are fighting and saying, "I had it first." I often wonder if, when God sees us sin, He thinks in His heart how childish and immature we are. God looks at our actions as nothing less than sin. In chapter 4 of I Samuel, we see where the ark of God is taken by the Philistines. This came about because the children of Israel sinned and took the ark of God to the battlefield, instead of leaving it in its place. Any time we do things our way instead of the Lord's, we will get into trouble.

Too often, I have heard Christians say, "I do not care. I will do it my way," or, "I am going to do what I want." Israel sinned by taking the ark into the camp. They should have repented of their sin and reformed for battle, but they did things their way, and the ark was taken by the Philistines. The chapter ends in verses 21 and 22 as we read the sad statement, "the glory is departed from Israel." Why? Because the presence of God was gone. As we head into this day, may we walk close to the Lord, listen to His voice, and follow Him in every way. Proverbs 19:3 states, "The foolishness of man perverteth his way: and his heart fretteth against the Lord." As children would argue and say, "I want it my way," let us be mature Christians who are right with the Lord. Let us walk and serve in His way. We must have God's presence and blessing to lead a victorious life in Christ. Let us repent and reform for battle today. The devil is alive and ready to rob us of our joy in service for the Lord. May we enjoy the presence of the Lord in our lives.

Anytime we do things our way instead of the Lord's, we will get into trouble.

April 30

1 Samuel 5-6   Psalm 102:18-28   Proverbs 30-31   Romans 15

A Helping Hand

Good morning! For most of my life, single and married, I have lived in a rural area; a small town that is peaceful, where everybody knows almost everybody (that can be bad). Most folks wave when you pass by them, and the paper is filled with community news. As I read this morning in Romans 15:1-3, I thought about neighbors through the years that have reached out a helping hand. When someone was sick, the neighbors brought in food. When a new baby was born, all the neighbors came and brought gifts. When it was planting or harvest time, the neighbors came to help, or when there was an extra hand that was needed for something, a neighbor came and helped.

The opening three verses of Romans 15 tells us that the "strong ought to bear the infirmities of the weak." The verse finishes with a strong statement against selfishness: "not to please ourselves." Selfishness never sees the needs of others, never encourages others, never builds others, never builds a team spirit, and never helps others. Selfish people only see themselves. The word "bear" drew my attention today. It means to carry, to support, to sustain, to maintain. The question will be asked, "How can I be strong to "bear" another's burden and to help them?" Our answer is in Romans 15:14. When I am walking with God, given to His will, faithful in my prayer life, and focused on serving the Lord, I will possess three things that can be used of the Lord to help a brother in Christ. Verse 14 challenges me to be (1) "full of goodness," (2)"filled with all knowledge," and (3)"able to admonish" (encourage).

There is no greater way to be the Christian that Christ desires us to be than to see the needs of others, reach out to meet that need, and do it with a heart full of joy. Christ set the example for us and challenged us to see the "fields white unto harvest." Helping someone today could open a door to share Christ and see a sinner saved. Helping a brother or sister in Christ today could encourage them and help them to not quit. Look at verse 3 in Romans 15, "For even Christ pleased not himself; but, as it is written, The reproaches of them that reproached thee fell on me." Reach out and help today.

*There is no greater way to be what Christ wants us to be
than to help someone today.*

May 1

1 Samuel 7-8   Psalm 103   Proverbs 1   Romans 16

Wise Decisions

Good morning! For many years I have enjoyed the quietness of the early morning hours. There is a stillness, as if nature is still asleep. The birds are not singing, there is little movement of any kind, and there is a calmness that is just right to be able to hear the Lord speak as I read His Word. I love those words in II Thessalonians 5:17, "Pray without ceasing." I also love the quiet time that I spend with Him after I read the Scriptures each morning.

Today as I read in Romans 16, my thoughts pondered two words in verse 19. The words are "wise" and "simple." Paul is ending his writings to the Christians in Rome before his arrival. He is letting these Christians know how their obedience has been known abroad, but he is also challenging them to be "wise unto that which is good, and simple concerning evil." Good and evil never have and never will get along. Proverbs 1:10 says, "My son, if sinners entice thee, consent thou not." Proverbs 1:3 tells us "To receive the instruction of wisdom," and verse four says, "To give subtilty to the simple." We must pay very careful attention to that which will help us. We must think before we act. A child does not always think things through, and their actions get them in trouble.

Here are three simple thoughts:

1. If in doubt, don't.

2. If it is contrary to Scripture, don't.

3. If it goes against Godly counsel, don't.

God always blesses right, and He never blesses wrong. Right never goes against Biblical principles. More decisions are made out of emotion than from seeking wise counsel. Proverbs 1:5 says, "A wise man will hear, and will increase learning; and a man of understanding shall attain unto wise counsels:" Proverbs 1:33 says, "But whoso hearkeneth unto me shall dwell safely, and shall be quiet from fear of evil." Only the Lord knows how many times I have stopped before making a decision and heeded the simple counsel I was given. What might be a difficult decision can become a simple answer if we stop and listen to simple wisdom. Have a blessed day.

Heeding wise counsel will result in making wise decisions.

May 2

1 Samuel 9-10   Psalm 104:1-17   Proverbs 2   1 Corinthians 1-2

Hidden Among the Stuff

Good morning! Has anyone ever told you to quit hiding among the stuff? Turn to I Samuel 9:21. Saul had been sent to find some lost mules, and when they could not be found, his father's servant that was with him said, "Behold now, there is in this city a man of God, and he is an honorable man; all that he saith cometh surely to pass:" (verse 6). Little did Saul know or understand that the people of Israel wanted a king, and God in His providence had selected a man. That man was Saul. To make a long story short, Saul and the servant traveled on and found the man of God, Samuel. When "Samuel saw Saul, the Lord said unto him, Behold the man whom I spake to thee of!" (verse 17).

Today, I thought about how we never see in the beginning of our walk with God how God wants to use us, but we must know and understand that, when He saved us and gave us a life to live, He had, and still has, a purpose for us. In verse 21, Saul lets us see his heart, and this is the same spirit that we must keep for the Lord to use us in His way.

1. "Am not I a Benjamite" (He knew who he was).

2. "Of the smallest of the tribes of Israel" (He knew where he came from).

3. "And my family the least of all the families of the tribe of Benjamin" (He knew he was unworthy).

In the next chapter, after he had been anointed with oil, "the Spirit of God came upon him," in verse 10. We see him now in verse 22 that "he hath hid himself among the stuff." God has a plan for us, and He is looking for us to keep ourselves humble before God, unworthy, in total dependence on Him for every decision, and looking continually to Him for guidance. Israel and Saul were blessed and used by God until Saul thought he would do things his way. In I Samuel 15:17, "Samuel said, When thou was little in thine own sight." This challenges my heart in whatever I am doing in my Christian life to stay humble, submissive, and surrendered to my Lord and His will for me. God wants to use us all. We must never arrive at a point of doing things our way. We must stay true to the Lord and His Word. Do not "hide in the stuff," because God knows where you are. God is looking for complete obedience in every area of our lives. May we begin this day on our knees with a humble, submissive, surrendered heart toward our Lord that saved our souls. Have a blessed day and stay away from the "stuff"-anything that will keep us from being in the Lord's perfect will.

God is looking for complete obedience in every area of our lives.

May 3

1 Samuel 11-12 Psalm 104:18-35 Proverbs 3 1 Corinthians 3-4

Stop and Meditate

Good morning! Are you ready to charge into the day? Have you had the coffee you need to get you awake? Do you have your list of tasks that need to be done today? Are your plans well made to accomplish all the goals that you have before you? Do you have your laptop, tablet, iPhone, and iPad? Is your presentation completely ready for that big meeting today? Is your project completed, and are you prepared for that big conference call? We must get everything done so that we can hurry to the activity tonight. We have to go here, get this, do that, run over here, be there, finish this, and answer that. I can't forget this! I must remember that! Will they be ready? We must get there on time. Do the above statements sound familiar, or can you relate with any of the hurry?

As I was reading my Bible this morning, I read in Psalm 104:23, "Man goeth forth unto his work and to his labor until the evening." That sounds like a man that has character to work, is a provider, is not a slacker, and has an accountability for his responsibilities. But then as I kept reading, I came to verse 27, "These wait all upon thee; that thou mayest give them their meat in due season." Who waits? I reread the above verses, and it is talking about the animal kingdom, the seasons of the earth, the rivers, the mountains, the trees, and all of creation.

I am for scheduling and making lists. We must have goals and plans to accomplish these goals. But I ask the question, "Is not stopping and meditating on God's Word more vital than anything that we do?" Do we get up, get our Bible and our Bible reading schedule, read what we should read for the day, have a short prayer time, and charge into the day? As this earth and all of God's creation in the air, land, and sea waits on God, should not we as humans, created in His image and after His likeness, do the same? I challenge you to spend more time waiting on God in meditation over what you have read instead of getting up at the last minute and charging down through your list of things to do for the day. Isaiah 40:31 says, "But they that wait upon the Lord shall renew their strength; they shall mount up with wings as eagles; they shall run, and not be weary; and they shall walk, and not faint." Take time with God today, tomorrow and the rest of your life. Learn to stop and meditate on His word. Spend more time in silence and meditating on Him and His greatness. Psalm 104:27 says, "These wait all upon thee." I am not against goal setting, being on time, or being disciplined. Could we not have a more blessed walk with Christ if we took the time to stop and wait on Him to speak and teach us? Take time for Christ today, for He has time for us. Jeremiah 33:3 says, "Call unto me, and I will answer thee, and shew thee great and mighty things, which thou knowest not." Have a blessed day.

Spend time in silence, meditating on God and His greatness.

May 4

1 Samuel 13-14   Psalm 105:1-15   Proverbs 4   1 Corinthians 5-6

Individually Special

Good morning! Do you have something in your possession that is very special to you? Something that was given to you and has a story behind it? Each time you look at it, it brings back memories of something very special, or someone very special. Some time back, one of my grandsons asked me if I could show him my coin collections. My wife and this grandson had been talking about some coins he found, and Mrs. Smith told him to ask me to see my coin collection. We went to where I have them, and we sat together on the floor. I got the coin books, and we began to go through them together. His eyes, his attention was focused on everything I said and showed him. There were two other grandsons there also. One saw some knives I have collected, and another saw some old guns that I no longer shoot. Each one held and looked at what they have an interest in. They asked me questions about what they had an interest in.

As I read this morning in I Corinthians 6:11, these three words caught my attention: "washed, sanctified, and justified." As I watched each grandson look at what they had a special interest in that day, I thought this morning how special each of us that are saved are to our Lord. We are all different, but we are very special to our Lord. Mrs. Smith and I have six grandchildren, and they are all different, but each is very special to us as an individual. We love them each in their own way. If we have trusted Christ as our personal Saviour, then we are (1) "washed"- we have been cleansed or saved. (2) We have now been "sanctified" - set apart for a special use by our Lord. (3) We have also been "justified"- secured, made innocent. Our sins would condemn us to hell, but, through Christ, I have been redeemed and forgiven. Romans 6:23 says, "For the wages of sin is death; but the gift of God is eternal life through Jesus Christ our Lord."

Each of our grandchildren is special to us, and they are each different. As I sat on the floor and looked at the coins, knives, and guns, my heart rejoiced that even though they were different, we all had a common bond.

Christ is the bond by which we should love and serve. If you are not saved today, please let Christ save your soul. If you are saved, then rejoice that you have been "washed, sanctified, and justified" and live for God. Know that you are special, and He loves you in a very special way. Have a special, blessed day.

You are special to God and He loves you in a very special way.

May 5

1 Samuel 15-16   Psalm 105:16-45   Proverbs 5   1 Corinthians 7

How is Your Spirit?

Good morning! My Old Testament reading today was from I Samuel 15-16. They are powerful chapters in the Word of God. In chapter 15, we read of Saul's incomplete obedience. Instead of doing things the way he was instructed, he decided to do things his own way. We read the statement of God in verse 11, "for he is turned back from following me." In verse 17 we read that Saul's pride brought about disobedience. As we read on to verse 22, we read those true words, "to obey is better than sacrifice." Saul's life is on a downhill run, and we read of him pleading with Samuel and repenting, but Saul has lost the power, presence, and peace of God. The page turns to chapter 16, and Samuel is sent to anoint a new man that will be king. Seven men, sons of Jesse, pass before Samuel, but we must return to verse 7 to see that powerful, convicting statement, "man looketh on the outward appearance, but the Lord looketh on the heart."

I ask myself, what does God see in me that He wants to use me for? What plans does my Lord still have for me? I must stay in His will and not look at what I think I can do. I must keep a willing heart and be prepared for whatever is before me. Saul was qualified until his pride, disobedience, and rebellion caused the Lord to depart from him. Then we see David, the most unlikely son, to be obedient and humble, with the presence of God about him; and he is anointed with oil to be the new king. The blessing of watching David after he was anointed is that others, as well as the Lord, saw his abilities, humility, strength, and leadership; and yet he stayed as

Saul's servant until the time that was appointed by God for him to become king. My heart is challenged to stay faithful to what I am doing, keep walking with God, serving in any way I can, and keep growing, because God has a special plan for the next chapter of my life. Is our spirit today a spirit of Saul or a spirit of David? One will be rejected, and one will be used greatly. Have a blessed day.

God will greatly use a person with a spirit of humility and obedience.

May 6

1 Samuel 17-18   Psalm 106:1-15   Proverbs 6   1 Corinthians 8-9

Running to Serve

Good morning! As I read the Word of God each day, I remind myself that there are principles that God wants me to learn, live, and leave for another generation. I am afraid that many of us, as we get older, get a critical spirit toward those coming behind us, instead of having a patient, teaching spirit. The Bible is a well of spiritual nourishment that is to be taken in, lived, and taught to the next generation. I say all of this because of my reading in I Samuel 17-18 this morning. We see David, a young man, comes to the battlefield to deliver food, check how the war is going, check on his brothers, and bring the report back to his father. What a turn of events!

May our attention be brought to two, 3-letter words. I want to focus on David's actions as he comes to where the army is, observes what is going on, and moves into action.

1. In verse 17, we see David was told to *run,* in obedience to his father, by taking the food to the camp.

2. In verse 22, David "ran into the army, and came and saluted his brethren," out of honor for those fighting in the battle.

3. In verse 48, we see that David "ran toward the army to meet the Philistine." This was the enemy's army, but David ran because he saw the need and the opportunity to serve.

4. In verse 51, we see that the giant Goliath is down from being hit with the stone from David's sling. "David *ran*, and stood upon the Philistine, and took his sword, and drew it out of the sheath thereof, and slew him, and cut off his head therewith." David *ran* to have absolute victory.

May there be an urgency to be obedient to God, to bring honor to those serving God, to stand to serve God, and to take nothing less than victory with God. What an example is set before us! May this convict us as we see David, a young man who has a faith in God and a desire to serve God, take an opportunity to do the impossible with strength from God. God is not looking for another David, but He is looking to us today to have faith in Him, be ready to serve Him, and live in victory through Him. Those two little words, "run" and "ran," surely have a lot in them. Live for Christ today.

May we have an urgency to be obedient to God and to serve Him.

May 7

1 Samuel 19-20   Psalm 106:16-33   Proverbs 7   1 Corinthians 10

Who Knows Best?

Good morning! Do you remember the words from your parents, "Be careful, you are going to fall!"? Or, "Be careful, you are going to get hurt!" It is a hard lesson to learn, but I have learned (or I am trying to learn) that you can't live somebody else's life. Watching our children and grandchildren grow is difficult. Do not get me wrong, I love watching them grow, mature, and develop in the areas that they love or the talents that they have. I will put it another way: The statement my mother said to me many times was, "Dave Smith, you are going to be the death of your mother." Every boy, and I am sure some girls, jump ramps with their bicycles. If you are like Dave Smith, getting your knees skinned up, getting a cut, twisting an ankle, and getting bruised are just part of life.

I Corinthians 10:12 says, "Wherefore let him that thinketh he standeth take heed lest he fall." Too often, I have seen Christians make wrong decisions, quit doing what they know they should do, or start something they know they should not start. Before you know it, they are out of church. God delivers them from a habit, but if they get back around the old crowd, they become weak, and as the Bible says in Proverbs 26:11, "As a dog returneth to his vomit, so a fool returneth to his folly." Many new Christians have had a new joy after salvation, followed the Lord in baptism out of obedience, were faithful to every service, but then they started missing. In the beginning, salvation was the greatest decision they made, and then it happened. They got out of church for whatever reason, quit reading their Bible, lost the excitement, and just barely hung on. Look at I Corinthians 10:13, which says, "There hath no temptation taken you but such as is common to man: but God is faithful, who will not suffer you to be tempted above that ye are able; but will with the temptation also make a way to escape, that ye may be able to bear it."

We must do right. We must stay faithful. We must not say, "It won't hurt," or, "I will be alright." May we learn to do what is right in God's eyes. May we do things that cause us to grow. I Corinthians 10:23 says, "All things are lawful for me, but all things are not expedient: all things are lawful for me, but all things edify not." Let us do those things that bring us closer to the Lord and give us strength for our daily life. We must walk the right path in the right direction and in the right way that helps us to grow in the Lord and be the servants He desires us to be. Some of the scares I have had from life came because I knew better, but I did it anyway. I did not listen and heed to what was told to me, and I got hurt. James 4:17 says, "Therefore to him that knoweth to do good, and doeth it not, to him it is sin." Get in church and stay in church. Get up every morning, and get alone with God. Stay away from the sin that keeps you from God, and serve God in any way you can. Do not say, "It won't happen to me," because it will. Have a blessed day.

Be committed to staying on the right path and faithful to God.

1 Samuel 21-22   Psalm 106:34-48   Proverbs 8   1 Corinthians 11

Examine Yourself

Good morning! This morning, my New Testament reading took me to I Corinthians 11. This chapter teaches us the order of the Lord's supper and emphasizes the importance of the meaning behind what we are doing. I Corinthians 11:24 says, "This do in remembrance of me." Go back to the first verse of this chapter. We are challenged by Paul, "Be ye followers of me, even as I also am of Christ." Now look at verse 28, which says, "But let a man examine himself."

When I was in the military and attending a leadership academy, there was a mirror at the door where we had to stop and look at ourselves. There was a sign beside the mirror that stated, "What you see is what your men are about to see." That has stuck with me in many areas of my life. As I read those two words this morning, "examine himself," I thought as a Christian, we should not just "examine" ourselves when we observe the Lord's supper, but we should be under constant self-evaluation in every area of our lives continually. The devil would love nothing more than for us to weaken in some area of our life and let something enter that would not please the Lord.

We have been mowing a lot of grass at the camp and I made a statement yesterday as I was teaching someone working with me. I said, "we do not mow to cut grass, we mow to paint a picture." Everything we do or say says something about who we are and the relationship that we have with the Lord. In Proverbs 8:32, I read these words this morning, "blessed are they that keep my ways." As born again Christians, we not only bear the name of Christ, but everything we do or say is an example of either Christ likeness or this world. The way we dress, the words that we speak, the work ethics we display, the attitude we have - all are a reflection of our walk with the Lord. Do we display the world and all that it tempts us with, or do we dress, talk, and do our work as a testimony of what Christ is to us? Is my attitude toward all that I do and say to honor Christ or to fit in to this world's culture? I am challenged today to "examine" myself and all that I do or say. Will my actions today display a walk with Christ or am I focused on being accepted by this world? May our lives be a reflection of Jesus Christ today. Have a blessed day.

Everything we say and do is a reflection of our walk with the Lord.

May 9

1 Samuel 23-24   Psalm 107:1-22   Proverbs 9   1 Corinthians 12-13

Praising the Lord

Good morning! Psalm 107 starts out by stating, "O give thanks unto the Lord, for he is good: for his mercy endureth for ever." Verses 8, 15, 21 and 31 begin, "O that men would praise the Lord for his goodness, and for his wonderful works to the children of men!" Do you see the exclamation point at the end of these verses? Are we thankful and do we praise Him like we should?

This time of the year is a very busy time. Graduations, weddings, getting ready for another full summer, details upon details preparing for staff to arrive, planning and preparing, and special church activities. I'm not complaining, but just enjoying being busy for the Lord. Yesterday morning I was working on a piece of equipment. Did you ever notice nothing breaks until you use it? A neighbor stopped by and when he got out of his truck, the first words he said to me were, "How are you doing today?." I had dirt on me mixed with grease, mud, and yes, a little frustration. I answered him and said, "I am doing great, especially after I get this repaired." He then responded with, "I told my grandchildren that when I wake up each morning, it is a good day." I told him how thankful I was to have another day that the Lord has given me to serve Him. The truth of the matter is, I meant it from the depths of my heart, but do I really praise the Lord for His goodness, and for his wonderful works? There was a leak in the hydraulics on this piece of equipment that I was working on and I could not find it. Before I started working on the equipment, I asked the Lord to please set my eyes on where the leak was. When I brought the equipment out of the barn, washed it and starting taking things apart, I stopped and prayed again, and then I started the equipment. The first spot my eyes went to I saw the leak. There are so many things in our life every day for which we could continually praise the Lord. The leak was repaired, and I began to think how many areas daily I take the Lord's goodness for granted.

It came time for dinner and Mrs. Smith and I sat on the front porch and ate, but as I looked at the birds searching for food, my mind went to the Scripture and how He provides for the birds of the field. Oh, that we would praise Him more! I have a brain to think, hands to use, eyes to see, feet to walk, ears to hear, nose to smell, tongue to taste, and blessings far beyond enough words for which to praise Him. Stop, look around, and observe the goodness of the Lord. His wonderful works are everywhere; let us praise Him. He knows our needs before we ask, so praise Him that He knows our needs. Let me encourage you to start your prayer time with PRAISE TO OUR LORD!

Yes, the neighbor is right, it is a good day when we wake up, so let us use this day and every day to praise Him. Psalm 107 is full of praises to our Lord. May this day and every day be full of PRAISE TO THE KING OF KINGS AND LORD OF LORDS. Have a praiseful day.

Let us notice the wonderful works of God and praise Him for them.

May 10

1 Samuel 25-26   Psalm 107:23-43   Proverbs 10b   1 Corinthians 14

Known by Our Name

Good morning! I received a phone call yesterday afternoon and the conversation started out like this, "Is your name?." The first thing that was asked was about my name. This individual that I was speaking to had been told to call me, but we had never met. As I was at the hospital visiting, there was an individual sitting in the parking lot on a bench, and the Lord gave me an opportunity to pass out a gospel tract and try to win a soul to Christ. Through the conversation, this individual made this statement, "Is the name of your pastor . . . ?." Two different conversations within one hour brought up the question, "Is the name . . ?."

We are known by our name. We were given a name to identify us. Our name is who we are or what we are known by. Reading this morning in I Samuel 25, we read the story about David and his men being hungry and coming to the farm of Nabal and Abigail. The farm was beautiful and had provided a bounty of crops. David's men were hungry. They approached Nabal for food and water. In verse 9 we read, "they spake to Nabal according to all those words in the name of David." Nabal refused and was very curt and unkind. The servants of Nabal were treated kindly by David's men and they took word to Abigail about how Nabal treated David's men so unkindly and refused to help them. Abigail then "made haste, and took two hundred loaves," and much other food and drink to David and his men. My thoughts today take us to verse 25. "Let not my lord, I pray thee, regard this man of Belial, even Nabal: for as his name is, so is he; Nabal is his name and folly is with him:." Abigail was trying to cover for the wickedness and unkindness of her husband because his name tells all about him. Go down to verse 28 and see what she says about David; "evil hath not been found in thee all thy days."

What is thought about us when our name is mentioned? When our name is spoken, are there good thoughts or negative thoughts? Do people remember kindness or selfishness? Do people think of a friendly person or an unkind person? Proverbs 22:1 says, "A good name is rather to be chosen than great riches, and loving favour rather than silver and gold." When our name is spoken, what impression is left in the mind of others? May our name be a lasting testimony that brings honor to Christ. May our name be a name that leaves a picture of steadfastness, Godliness, humility, unselfishness, meekness, kindness, and many attributes of Christ. Our name tells everyone who we are and what we are. Our name will go before us and it will remain after we are gone. My father taught me that your name will always outlive who you are. Have a blessed day.

What do people think of when they hear your name mentioned?

1 Samuel 27-28   Psalm 108   Proverbs 11   1 Corinthians 15

Assuming the Worst

Good morning! Have you ever been told, "you think too much"? I am speaking about when we sit around and stew over something that we are not sure is going to happen and we overthink what could happen. The word "assume" is an action word and it can bring discouragement and final destruction.

In our Old Testament reading today in I Samuel 27 and 28, there is a change of events that brought sin and final destruction because of overthinking, or making an assumption, about a possible circumstance. We find David in a time of weak faith, which brought self- discouragement. It all starts out in verse 1 of chapter 27, "And David said in his heart, I shall now perish one day by the hand of Saul:." Had David forgotten so soon how the Lord had protected him time after time? David now goes to the enemy, takes up residence with the enemy, lies to the enemy, prepares for battle with the enemy, and we read in chapter 28:1; "And Achish said unto David, Know thou assuredly, that thou shalt go out with me to battle, thou and thy men." What is going on? Now we read of Saul. He cannot hear God (verse 6), so he goes to a witch to seek Samuel who has died; and Saul says in verse 15, "God is departed from me, and answereth me no more." God did not leave David nor Saul; they departed from God.

Many have been saved and excited about living for God and serving Him, and then there is a departing from God. We allow the voice of the devil, our flesh, our past, our old friends and relationships that we had left, to tempt us and distract us from what the Lord was doing in our life. Psalm 108:1, the Psalmist writes, "O God, my heart is fixed;." In the same chapter, verse 13, "Through God we shall do valiantly: for he it is that shall tread down our enemies." Paul wrote in I Corinthians 15:31, "I die daily." What he was writing was to quit thinking and start listening to God. We assume too much bad about a possible situation and if we are not careful, this assumption will cause us to believe an untruth, and this unknown could be what the devil uses to get us away from God and His will for our lives. Look at verses 57-58 in I Corinthians 15, "But thanks be to God, which giveth us the victory through our Lord Jesus Christ. Therefore, my beloved brethren, be ye steadfast, unmovable, always abounding in the work of the Lord, forasmuch as ye know that your labour is not in vain in the Lord." STAND FIRM!!!! We must keep strong faith in the Lord. Let the flesh, the world, and wrong influences go. STAND FIRM IN THE LORD! David did not need to run to the enemy. Saul could have confessed his sin. You and I can keep growing, serving, and living for the Lord. STAND FIRM! Have a blessed day.

Assuming a negative outcome will bring discouragement
– stand firm in Christ!

May 12

1 Samuel 29-31   Psalm 109:1-13   Proverbs 12   1 Cor. 16 & 2 Cor. 1

Staying Right with God

Good morning! Yesterday I was out soul winning and making some visits on folks that have been missing Sunday School and church. As I was speaking to one person that had been saved recently and promised to come to church and be baptized, but had never attended yet, I noticed they began to have tears well up in their eyes. I listened to the story of their past and I heard how they felt they did not deserve to have Heaven as their home, and they felt that their life had been such a mess that things could never be fully turned around. I listened to every word, and then I said, "Don't you know God knows you better than you know yourself and He is the one who, through His grace, saved your soul?" They looked at me and said yes. I told them to take the first step and be obedient to Christ to let others know they had been saved.

In our reading again today in I Samuel, we see David preparing to go to war with the enemy to fight against Israel. When we get away from God, we are in bad shape and things will just continually get worse. What a sad statement as some of the enemy recognized who David was and said he must go back because he might turn against them in battle. What a sad statement in verse 9 of chapter 29, "I know that thou art good in my sight." What a sad place for David and any Christian to be, to have the world look at us and think we are okay when we are not right with God. David returned with his men to where they had made their homes and in chapter 30, we see his wives and children were taken and their homes burned. The men with David spoke of stoning him and David was in the depths of discouragement. There are three things that David did in verses 6-8 that we should all keep in our hearts and minds when we are tempted to sin or when we are away from God.

1. He sought spiritual counsel. "David said to Abiathar the priest."

2. He went to the Lord in prayer. ." . . bring me hither the ephod."

3. He sought God's guidance. "David enquired at the Lord."

It is not time for you and me to run from God. If you have fallen, it is time to be in fellowship and a right relationship with God. Look to Him and confess your sin and get back to Him. I Corinthians 16:13 says, "Watch ye, stand fast in the faith, quit you like men, be strong." Fight the flesh and the devil with everything you have. "Sin will take you farther than you want to go; it will keep you longer than you want to stay." Proverbs 12:7, "The wicked are overthrown, and are not: but the house of the righteous shall stand." Stay with the Lord, Stand for the Lord, Serve the Lord. The blessing will be there. David got right with God, got in the place God had for him, and God said that David was "a man after his own heart." Have a blessed day.

Stay right with the Lord and the blessing will be there.

May 13

2 Samuel 1-2   Psalm 109:14-31   Proverbs 13   2 Corinthians 2-3

Dealing With The Curve

Good morning! Remember the statement we all heard when we were younger, "Life just threw me a curve"? I did not understand how life could throw a curve. Now after many years, I have received many curves in life, as we all have. There are times when we do not understand why these circumstances of life have to happen the way they do. In II Samuel 1-2, David received word of the death of Saul and Jonathan. In II Samuel 1: 19, 25 and 27, we read the statement from David, "how are the mighty fallen." Verse 17 in chapter one tells us, "David lamented;" he was in mourning. His heart was broken. He tells us in verse 23 how they loved each other and how they were an example of unity and strength. "Saul and Jonathan were lovely and pleasant in their lives, and in their death they were not divided: they were swifter than eagles, they were stronger than lions." In David's grief he sets an example for us, as in verse 1 of chapter 2 he seeks the guidance of the Lord.

I do not know what this day will bring forth, but I do know that there is strength in the Lord. II Corinthians 3:5, "Not that we are sufficient of ourselves to think any thing as of ourselves; but our sufficiency is of God;" David is now focused on the future. In Psalm 109:26-27, David penned these words; "Help me, O Lord my God: O save me according to thy mercy: That they may know that this is thy hand; that thou, Lord, hast done it." May we live today for Christ, no matter what is thrown at us. Seek the Lord, His strength, His power, His guidance. Psalm 109:30, "I will greatly praise the Lord with my mouth; yea, I will praise him among the multitude. This day is not determined by what I go through, but it will be determined by how I respond to what comes my way. I do not need to walk alone because He is there and ready to guide me all the way as we walk together. Enjoy your day with the Lord and see His hand in all this day brings. In the battle as well as the victory, our Lord is there. Why walk alone and feel lonely and sorry for ourselves? "He is a friend that sticketh closer than a brother." In God's strength we can deal with the curve. Have a blessed day.

God is always with us, regardless of the curves life may throw at us.

2 Samuel 3-4   Psalm 110   Proverbs 14   2 Corinthians 4-5

Vengeance or Forgiveness?

Good morning! Have you ever said the words, "I am going to get you," or "I will never forgive you"? Sounds like words we said when we were kids and we got in trouble for something we did to our brother or sister or something that happened in school and we got caught. After reading in II Samuel 3-4, I looked up the word "vengeance:" the infliction of pain on another, in return for an injury or offense. I am sorry to say, but vengeance is never satisfied. In II Samuel 3:8, we see the phrase, "Am I a dog's head," and in II Samuel 3:24 we see the phrase, "What hast thou done?" I turned back to I Samuel 24:13 where David could have taken the life of Saul but he said, "Wickedness proceedeth from the wicked: but mine hand shall not be upon thee," and in the next verse he says, "whom dost thou pursue? after a dead dog, after a flea." There was so much killing and vengeance going on between those following David and those that had followed Saul. David had fasted because of the death of Abner and the people saw the heart of David, but the very next chapter brings the death of Ishbosheth and in verse 11 of chapter four, we read the words of David, "How much more, when wicked men have slain a righteous person in his own house upon his bed?"

We cannot go forward until we die to ourselves and focus on the love of Christ for a dying world. Proverbs 14:14 says, "The backslider in heart shall be filled with his own ways:." Lack of forgiveness will destroy. All of us get hurt or offended and we make statements like, I will never forget what they did to me. When we cannot forgive and go on, even when forgiveness has not been asked, it will cause us to not have full focus on the love of God for a world that really does not deserve the forgiveness of God. Truly, we are at the head of the list. II Corinthians 5:14 says, "For the love of Christ constraineth us:." Verse 17, "Therefore if any man be in Christ, he is a new creature: old things are passed away; behold, all things are become new."

How can I accept God's forgiveness of my sins and not forgive others for what they have done to me?

I got into fights when I was a boy, and there were times my folks stopped the fights and said, get up and shake hands and forgive each other. Throughout the years of being a camp director, there are sometimes that there are staff that just do not get along with each other. On a few occasions I have told them, you guys are going to work side by side until you can get along. You know, it is amazing how they become friends when they start seeing the good instead of only seeing the bad and how they were offended. I cannot be the soul winner or the brother in Christ that I need to be until I let the love and forgiveness of Christ be my driving force. King David wanted to see unity in Israel and the blessings of God on all. If someone is not going the same direction that I am, it does not mean that they have to be my enemy. I do not want my unforgiveness to so consume me that I cannot show the forgiveness of God to a lost sinner. Walk today in a spirit of God's forgiveness and not the vengeance of Satan. We will look at others in a different light. Have a blessed day.

Let the love and forgiveness of Christ be your driving force.

May 15

2 Samuel 5-6   Psalm 111   Proverbs 15   2 Corinthians 6-7

Doing It God's Way

Good morning! It is that time of the year when tests are being given at school, final exams are being studied for and graduation plans are being made. There are long hours at night preparing and studying for the final that must be taken to complete the course of study. The answers must be correct, and the work must be done correctly to meet the requirements for the course. Things must be done the way the instruction has been given.

Not doing things God's way caused the death of a man In II Samuel 6. David is now king of Israel and the ark of God is being brought to Jerusalem. Can you imagine the excitement and the joy? But sorrow is soon to come because God explained the rules that the ark should only be carried and, in this chapter, it was placed on a cart. Uzzah reached out and touched it to stabilize it and in verse 7, "God smote him there for his error;." It was on a new cart, they were careful, and Uzzah was not a bad man. What is the problem? The ark was not moved God's way. Proverbs 15:5 states, "A fool despiseth his father's instruction: but he that regardeth reproof is prudent"(wise). Remember our teacher telling us to do the math problem this way, do not count on your fingers, put the decimal in the right place, that is not a complete sentence, and so on? God is expecting us to live the Christian life the way that He has instructed us. A wrong answer is not the right answer and close is not correct. They were moving the ark to the right place, but in the wrong way. Proverbs 15:7, "The lips of the wise disperse knowledge: but the heart of the foolish doeth not so." Doing things right gets the job done right and brings a right satisfaction. Doing things wrong will never bring a right ending. A Christian that desires to please the Lord will desire to live the Christian life in every way he can, the way God says. Proverbs 15:14, "The heart of him that hath understanding seeketh knowledge:." There is a joy in taking the test when the time has been spent to study and when we know the correct answers.

Many Christians say, I am going to live the way I want, and nobody is going to tell me differently. The end result will be a life lived the way you want and missing the blessings that the Lord had. Psalm 111:10, "a good understanding have all they that do his commandments:." Tests will be given but only the correct answers will bring a passing grade. The end of an obedient life will bring eternal blessings from the Lord. Let us decide today to do it right by doing it God's way. Have a blessed day.

Living the Christian life God's way brings eternal blessings.

May 16

2 Samuel 7-8   Psalm 112   Proverbs 16   2 Corinthians 8-9

No Place Like Home

Good morning! For almost forty years my wife and I prepare for young people to come and serve a summer with us in the camping ministry.

These young people leave their homes, families, friends, local churches and much more to come and serve the Lord with us. As I was reading in II Samuel 7-8 this morning, I wrote on a piece of paper beside me, "no place like home." David is king, the wanderings are over, and there is a desire in David's heart to build a house for the Lord. In II Samuel 7:2, he said, "See now, I dwell in an house of cedar, but the ark of God dwelleth within curtains." Through the following verses, David is told his seed will build an house and "thine house and thy kingdom shall be established for ever before thee:." What a promise!

What is a home? I took a piece of paper and I began to write - home is not a building; it is a place of peace, love, security, counsel, memories, maturing, learning, chastening, companionship. As a young boy I went to a place where at one time was home for my father, but there was nothing there. Dad and I walked down a path that once was a drive to a farm. Dad stopped and I saw parts of several old foundations. I watched and listened as memories of lessons, times of sadness, times of laughter, times of learning, times of labor, sickness, birth, death, reunions, harvest, planting, and much more, came into reality for me. With my eyes I saw little, but with my heart and mind I saw much.

David had a love for God and a desire in his heart. In II Corinthians 8:3, I read these words that challenge my heart for missions giving and service; "to their power, beyond their power, were willing of themselves." I read Proverbs 16 this morning and came to verse 7, "When a man's ways please the Lord, he maketh even his enemies to be at peace with him." I then read Psalm 112 and came to verse 2, "His seed shall be mighty upon earth: the generation of the upright shall be blessed." I read on to verse 7, "his heart is fixed, trusting in the Lord." As David sat in his house and dreamed for God, may our hearts this day be stirred to dream for God, but also to live for God so that generation after generation may be saved, grow and win another generation. There are many lessons of life that we learn in different places and in different ways. Home is not a building. Home is where the will of God has led me to serve Him. Home is the place where God and I meet together, where I grow in a relationship with Him, where I serve Him. As the song writer wrote, "this world is not my home, I am just passing through." Home is not a building; it is building a life that pleases the Lord, it is serving the Lord where and how it pleases Him. As was recorded in II Samuel 7:29, "let the house of thy servant be blessed for ever." I am looking for the day that I am welcomed home by the Lord, but while I am on this earth, may my life that He dwells in be a Heavenly Home on earth. Let us serve Him all that we can in every way we can. Have a blessed day.

Home is not a building; it is building a life that is pleasing to the Lord.

May 17

2 Samuel 9-10   Psalm 113   Proverbs 17   2 Corinthians 10

Choose Your Battles

Good morning! The life of a Christian is a life of victory, but victory never comes without a battle. An athlete must train and through the training comes pain, scratches, bruises, aches, but the focus is victory. A soldier must face the enemy to win a battle and in that battle there will be the wounded and those that give the ultimate sacrifice. But there is never the victory of battle without the facing of sacrifice. There are battles of life that do not have to be fought. I trust the above statement draws your attention. In II Samuel 9-10, we see David desiring to show kindness to the house of Saul and he seeks to find if there are any of his household and Mephibosheth is found. Land is set aside for Mephibosheth's income and provision and in II Samuel 9:10, David said that Mephibosheth "shall eat bread alway at my table." David's love for Saul and honor given to his family is seen by these actions. In chapter 10, David desires to honor a family because of the loss of a king. David's intentions were questioned and war broke out.

I wrote this morning the word "contention" on a piece of paper and looked up the definition. The word contention means strife, quarrel, controversy, given to angry debate. I read this morning in Proverbs 17:14, "leave off contention, before it be meddled with." Life has its bumps and hard times, disagreements and discouragements, unfairness and wrong judgments. What is important is how we handle these battles, because they are life's battles. Proverbs 17:22, "A merry heart doeth good like a medicine: but a broken spirit drieth the bones." Our trials do not have to be our battles. There are times to battle, times to stand and fight; but be wise and bathe the possible battle in prayer. Stand for truth, do not compromise, but use wisdom. " . . be ye therefore wise as serpents, and harmless as doves." (Matthew 10:16). Do not misjudge a statement or action and let contention develop. Do not let bitterness set in and end up with a "broken spirit." My wife and I love to go to the Smokey Mountains and observe the bears when we can. We have seen many and I have seen many unwise people trying to get too close. You never want to get between a momma bear (sow) and her cubs. Proverbs 17:12, "Let a bear robbed of her whelps meet a man, rather than a fool in his folly." Our foolishness of judging others is worse than a mother bear that will fight for her cubs. We constantly hear arguments between political parties and it has caused us to doubt truth and true intentions. The same happens to us in battles of life. Be careful today, know truth, be kind even when kindness is not shown, be a blessing even when it does not come your way, be patient even when patience is not shown. The hard feelings, bitterness, anger toward someone else will only destroy you. It is like a cancer that will eat away and destroy. Proverbs 17:28 is a great verse for us to meditate on today; "Even a fool, when he holdeth his peace, is counted wise: and he that shutteth his lips is esteemed a man of understanding." Choose wisely your battles today. Have a blessed day.

Our trials do not have to be our battles.

May 18

2 Samuel 11-12   Psalm 114   Proverbs 18   2 Corinthians 11

Staying Faithful

Good morning! I read a statement many years ago that helped me understand why God has put some stories that are real stories about real people in the Bible. The Bible is about real people in real life situations and how God deals with these real people. God does not condone sin. He brings judgment on sin. Galatians 6:7 says, "Be not deceived; God is not mocked: for whatsoever a man soweth, that shall he also reap." God blesses righteousness and God brings judgment on sin! As we read and study the Bible, there are lessons for us to learn.

Each time I read II Samuel 11, my heart is grieved at the sin of David; but I must focus on the lessons to be learned. First, we must learn that David was not in the right place doing what he was supposed to be doing. It was the time for kings to go forth to battle. The troops are in the battlefield and their leader is not with them. Any time we are not in the place we are supposed to be and not doing what we are supposed to be doing, there will always be a price to pay. David saw Uriah's wife, lusted after her and committed sin. Now David tries to cover his sin. David brings Uriah in from the battlefield, feeds him and sends him home to be with his wife. Word the next morning gets to David that Uriah slept at the door of the king's house. The lessons are so many in this chapter, but I want to turn our focus on why Uriah did what he did. Why did he not go down to his house? Why did he not go see his wife? Why did he sleep with the servants? Verse 11 gives us the answers.

1. "ark," he must be where the presence of the Lord is (he must be in God's will).

2. "Israel," the family of God is depending on him to be a soldier in the battle field.

3. "Judah, abide in tents and my lord Joab." He must be faithful in the fight for those that are before, that had taught him and had been an influence in his life are fighting in the battle.

4. "servants of my lord." Other men like him are still fighting in the battle.

One word describes Uriah, and that is the word FAITHFUL. What an example for us today when we think about quitting, giving up, saying we have had enough, looking at others instead of keeping our position! We need to be faithfully doing our work until the Lord calls us Home. Paul wrote to Timothy in II Timothy 4:7, "I have fought a good fight, I have finished my course, I have kept the faith." He stayed FAITHFUL! Don't quit. STAY FAITHFUL! "Quitters never win and winners never quit." Life is not about you and me. Life for a Christian is about being in God's will, doing God's will, as God wills, where God wills, and staying faithful. You are needed, you are important. Be the Christian God wants you to be. Have a blessed day.

Quitters never win and winners never quit.

May 19

2 Samuel 13-14   Psalm 115   Proverbs 19   2 Corinthians 12-13

His Grace is Sufficient

Good morning! Do you ever get overwhelmed? Have you ever arrived at a point that you said, I do not know what I am going to do? You look at your life and the circumstances that surround you, and you do not know what to do. STOP! God is never surprised, He is never confused, He is never at the end of His grace, He is never so far away that He cannot be reached. PRAISE THE LORD!

As I read in II Samuel 13-14 this morning, king David's house is in turmoil. I read in II Corinthians 12:10, "for when I am weak, then am I strong." How could Paul pen these words? Then in verse 15 he wrote, "I will very gladly spend and be spent for you." Sometimes we become overwhelmed with situations of life and we do not look to the Lord for guidance. Is something in your life discouraging you? Is it breaking your heart? Is it draining life right out of you? When we are weak, He is strong. When we do not see what to do, He does. Ammon had done wrong. Tamar had been violated, humiliated, and now was rejected. Absalom was now filled with anger and impatience. David was broken and had lost leadership as a father and as a king. Things are in a mess.

We might be saying, what are we going to do? II Corinthians 12:9, "And he said unto me, My grace is sufficient for thee: for my strength is made perfect in weakness. Most gladly therefore will I rather glory in my infirmities, that the POWER OF CHRIST may rest upon me." Proverbs 19:3,"The foolishness of man perverteth his way: and his heart fretteth against the Lord." Proverbs 19:20-21, "Hear counsel, and receive instruction, that thou mayest be wise in thy latter end. There are many devices in a man's heart; nevertheless the counsel of the Lord, that shall stand." Take the situation to the Lord in prayer, leave it there, do right, be faithful in every area of life, and learn to wait on God. Psalm 115:11, "Ye that fear the Lord, trust in the Lord: he is their help and their shield." Let the Lord be your strength. He is there for us. Have a blessed day.

God's strength is made perfect in our weakness.

May 20

2 Samuel 15-16   Psalm 116   Proverbs 20   Galatians 1-2

The Security of God's Will

Good morning! Have you ever had to move and leave your friends behind? The area you move to is unfamiliar, you know no one, and you do not know how to get around. It is like you have to start all over. In 1963, the day after Christmas, our family moved from Missouri where I was born and raised, and where all my friends and family lived. Dad moved us to the state of Iowa. I wanted to be happy, but I knew no one. The first day of school was terrible. My very first day I got into a fight. It was wrong and I hated being in this unfamiliar place.

Our reading today in II Samuel has king David on the run because of the conspiracy of his son Absalom. Absalom had reached out to the people against his father. He showed personal interest in them and had showed compassion toward them in II Samuel 15:5-6. That does not sound bad, but it was a conspiracy set up to overthrow God's appointed king. II Samuel 15:12, "the conspiracy was strong; for the people increased continually with Absalom." There are times we feel all is going wrong, especially right after we try to get things right with God. The devil makes his attack. David was running, but in II Samuel 15:26 he said something that I want to focus on; "let him do to me as seemeth good unto him." In 1963, when my parents moved our family from all of the security I had to a new place where I had no security; that was the best move of my life. At

171

the time it seemed terrible, but today as I look back, that move brought me into a relationship with God that would change my life and put me on the path to serving the Lord.

When we go through times that our world seems to be caving in, look to God and His Word for guidance, comfort and assurance. Galatians 1:4, "Who gave himself for our sins, that he might deliver us from this present evil world, according to the will of God and our Father." David asked the Lord to turn the counsel of Ahithophel into foolishness. God was in control when man thought he was in control. Absalom thought everything was going his way but soon he would see differently. David sought God and Absalom sought man. Whatever we are going through, however hard it seems, when there is no light to see at the end of the tunnel, stay strong with the Lord. Stay faithful. The devil loves when he can distract us from God. I love what we read today in Psalm 116:1-2, "I love the Lord, because he hath heard my voice and my supplications. Because he hath inclined his ear unto me, therefore will I call upon him as long as I live." There is victory in serving the Lord and being in His will. Psalm 116:16, "O Lord, truly I am thy servant; I am thy servant." Have a blessed day in victory.

There is always victory and security in God's will.

May 21

2 Samuel 17-18   Psalm 117   Proverbs 21   Galatians 3-4

What Is Driving You?

Good morning! I asked myself this morning a question that is a question of evaluation. What drives me? My heart is grieved when I see hatred in a child toward their parents. Or hatred of any kind from one adult to another. Why can we not forgive? Proverbs 21:2, "Every way of a man is right in his own eyes: but the Lord pondereth the hearts." It is time for a self-evaluation. We need to be careful when pointing a finger at someone else, because there are three fingers of our own pointing back at us. In II Samuel 17 we find Absalom driven to destroy his father and to be king, and in II Samuel 18:5 we see David telling Joab and the soldiers to "Deal gently for my sake with the young man." Absalom is found, killed, buried and according to verse 17, they laid "a very great heap of stones upon him." David receives word and grief sets in.

What is the driving force in our lives today? A lost world that needs to hear of Christ's love for them? Money, position, fame, a new car, a new house, envy, retirement, hatred? In Galatians 3:11 we read, "the just shall live by faith." What is driving us today? What is in our hearts? May we step out today with a right heart toward others and a right heart toward what God has for us today. Life is too short to be lived with anger or any other sin in our hearts. We, in ourselves, are self-centered. Let us look beyond us today and see others. In II Samuel 18:13 we read, "there was no matter hid from the king." They were speaking of David, but the Bible teaches us that God is all knowing. He sees our hearts and knows our thoughts. Let us live today as a child of the King. Galatians 4:7, "Wherefore thou art no more a servant, but a son; and if a son, then an heir of God through Christ." We should live today as a family member of Christ. Have a blessed day.

Faith in God and a heart right toward others should be our driving force.

May 22

2 Samuel 19-20   Psalm 118:1-14   Proverbs 22   Galatians 5-6

A Tender Heart and Thick Skin

Good morning! The very second verse of our Old Testament reading in II Samuel 19:2 is something that we should strongly consider; "And the victory that day was turned into mourning." Soldiers had put their lives on the line to secure a victory and yet David turned to mourning. We give time to people, try to help people, sometimes sacrifice finances and they turn around and shun us or do not even give a simple thanks. It was so sad that Absalom was killed and division came but David has now locked himself away from those that loved him, have served him and fought for him.

I do not know what David felt, but God has spoken to my heart in several ways this morning. Don't stop doing for others. Don't stop caring for others. Just because we get hurt by someone who often does not even know they have hurt us; do not stop seeing the needs in others. There are those that only see themselves and they want our pity, our time, our attention and yet they say they want counsel, but they do not heed anything we say. I have seen many a preacher become bitter, discouraged, and quit over the frustration of those that said they wanted counsel and they truly only wanted a listening ear. Psalm 118:14, "The Lord is my strength and song, and is become my salvation." Galatians 6:10, "let us do good unto all men." Do not do for someone because of what you will get in return. Do for others because it is what the Lord would have us do. Galatians 5:25, "If we live in the Spirit, let us also walk in the Spirit." Serve today for a Heavenly blessing, not looking for an earthly blessing. David regained his focus and said to the people, "ye are my brethren, ye are my bones and my flesh." Live and serve God, keep a heart for God, be a blessing to others and look for Him to bless. Do not get discouraged for what someone is not; be the someone that is. As the old preacher said, keep your heart tender and your skin thick. There is a blessing just around the corner. Do not miss the blessing because of someone else. Have a blessed day.

Serve for a Heavenly blessing, not looking for an earthly blessing.

May 23

2 Samuel 21-22   Psalm 118:15-29   Proverbs 23   Ephesians 1-2

Here He Comes Again

Good morning! I've entitled this morning's devotional, "Here He Comes Again." We see David as an older man, with his mighty men, in II Samuel 21 and the Philistines are attacking again. This time it is four that "were born to the giant" (verse 22). Praise God, the mighty men that fought with David faced them and defeated them. We must face the fact that we deal with the weakness of our flesh and the temptations of the devil daily. The enemy keeps coming, but I love David's song of victory and deliverance in chapter 22. He praises our Lord for who He is and for what He does. Verses 31-33, "As for God, his way is perfect; the word of the Lord is tried: he is a buckler to all them that trust in him. For who is God, save the Lord? And who is a rock, save our God? God is my strength and power: and he maketh my way perfect."

God is on our side and is our strength. Ephesians 1:9 lets us know He has a purpose for us, "Having made known unto us the mystery of his will, according to his good pleasure which he hath purposed in himself." God knew David would have the victory if David just kept his faith in God, and David did. The battles are going to keep coming but God has a purpose to glorify His name if we will stand strong and stand faithful. Generations before have proven this. Proverbs 23:10, "Remove not the old landmark; and enter not into the fields of the fatherless:." God tells us to see the principles of living and serving God that helped previous generations stay faithful to the Lord. Psalm 118:28 gives us a boost in the fight, "Thou art my God, and I will praise thee: thou art my God, I will exalt thee." Hold your head high, stand for holiness and truth. God will bring the victory. There is a generation coming that is right behind us. Hold the ground in your battle; reinforcements are on the way. Have a blessed day.

God is on our side and He is our strength.

May 24

2 Samuel 23-24   Psalm 119:1-16   Proverbs 24   Ephesians 3-4

Again and Again

Good morning! Did you ever think of the things in your life that you keep doing over and over? You get up and go to work or get up and go to school. Every day we get up and bathe, shave, brush our teeth, comb our hair (when I had hair), dress and begin the day. The washing has to be done over and over. The yard has to be mowed again and again. There are things that each of us do over and over almost on a daily basis. Each day in my Bible reading, I read some in the Old Testament, New Testament, Proverbs and Psalms. I have no idea how many times I have read the same passage and yet I find the Word of God fresh every morning. I am afraid that there are things we do over and over and keep doing them, but when it comes to reading our Bible, having family devotions and having a personal prayer life, we may find ourselves putting off private time with the Lord.

Proverbs 24:16, "For a just man falleth seven times, and riseth up again: but the wicked shall fall into mischief." When the dishes are washed after eating the meal and they are put back into the cabinet, does the use of them end? When the grass is mowed, do we put the mower away for the year? When we finish a work week, do we say, I am ready for my annual pay or do we realize if we are going to get a weekly paycheck, we have to keep going back to work and doing our job? Proverbs 24:30-34 teaches us that the slothful allowed his vineyard to grow over with thorns and nettles and the stone wall was broken down. He had arrived at a point of poverty. Such is the Christian life if we do not feed ourselves daily with the Word of God, attend all the church services and activities that we can, and spend as much time in prayer as we can. As a matter of fact, I Thessalonians 5:17 says, "Pray without ceasing." We need to spend as much time in prayer with God as we can. Psalm 119:11, "Thy word have I hid in mine heart, that I might not sin against thee." We know what happens if we do not show up for work or school, but what about showing up and spending time with the Lord and being in His house? Let me encourage you today to stay with your walk with God and if you have missed some, get back to it. Proverbs 24:16, "For a just man falleth seven times, and riseth up again: but the wicked shall fall into mischief." The grass needs cutting again and we need the Bible again and again. We need the preaching and teaching again and again. We need Christian fellowship again and again. We need to keep serving God again and again. We do not quit washing the dishes when we have finished a meal. We prepare another meal and fill the plates over and over. Keep going, do not quit. The joy of the Christian life gets better and better. The blessings keep coming when we do not quit. Have a blessed day.

Keep serving God faithfully again and again.

1 Kings 1-2   Psalm 119:17-32   Proverbs 25   Ephesians 5

The Charge of the Lord

Good morning! It is graduation time. Has your mailbox been full, like ours, with graduation announcements? It is that time of year when the caps and gowns our worn, family arrives, pictures are taken, there are tears of joy, practice for the graduation ceremony and the evening arrives. There is excitement, the nervousness, the accomplishments, and all eyes and ears are open to hear about the accomplishments and plans of the graduates. I love to listen to the charges and challenges given to the graduates. It is like a new charge for me as well.

In I Kings 2, David is about to die and he is giving a charge to the new king, his son Solomon. Look with me at I Kings 2:2-3, "Be thou strong therefore, and shew thyself a man; and keep the charge of the Lord thy God, to walk in his ways, to keep his statutes, and his commandments, and his judgments, and his testimonies, as it is written in the law of Moses . . ." I can see the old king tired, worn, feeble and yet strong in his charge. His words pierce the heart of the new king Solomon. Can you picture Solomon facing his father, his king, his example? There is a big lump in his throat and yet there is a strength and challenge that is growing in his heart. Then those powerful words of promise at the end of verse 3, "that thou mayest prosper in all that thou doest, and whithersoever thou turnest thyself."

That same challenge to Solomon is for us as well. We need to step up, just as the graduates are challenged to go forth. Ephesians 5:8, "For ye were sometimes darkness, but now are ye light in the Lord: walk as children of light." As new graduates are looking ahead to what is before them, so should we look forward to finishing and proving what God has for us. Ephesians 5:10, "Proving what is acceptable unto the Lord." As Christ said, we need to "walk as children of light." May we be challenged as Solomon to walk with God, seek His wisdom, walk in His path, and live holy unto Him. A new day is before us; yesterday, last week, last month, and last year is behind. Let us go forth and serve the Lord with a new freshness and a renewed vision. Have a blessed day.

Serve God with a new freshness and renewed vision today.

May 26

1 Kings 3-4   Psalm 119:33-48   Proverbs 26   Eph. 6 - Philippians 1

A Godly Heritage

Good morning! Yesterday my son called and was asking me questions about our heritage. I have a grandson that is fascinated with family trees. I used to love listening to my grandparents tell the stories that they were told. I have heard the stories of Jesse James eating at my great aunt's house and leaving a $20 gold piece. I have heard the stories that my great grandmother on my father's side was a daughter of Kit Carson from Kentucky. As I talked, my grandson was saying, "yes, that is the name" or "yes, that is the location."

Today I read of the beginning of King Solomon's life and how God asked him the question in I Kings 3:5, "ask what I shall give thee." His answer was "an understanding heart," and in verse 9 we read, "and the speech pleased the Lord." Only if king David could have seen what God did to and for his son. I thought this morning about what God has in store for us and the heritage that will come after us, or what we have done with the heritage before us. In Ephesians 6: 2-14, we are challenged to obey, honor, be strong in the Lord, wear the armour of God, withstand and stand. I do not know which stories that I was told are true and which stories are not true; but I do know God wants to bless all of our lives and our heritage after us if we do as those words in Philippians 1:27, "that ye stand fast in one spirit." May our cry not be of those things in the past, but may we live life daily as the Psalmist wrote in Psalm 119:33-38, "teach me, give me understanding, make me to go in the path of thy commandments, incline my heart unto thy testimonies, turn away mine eyes from beholding vanity, stablish thy words unto thy servant." Those things will leave a heritage that God will use, bless and reproduce for another generation. I cannot change the past, but I can sure lay a solid foundation for the future. Build a heritage to honor God.

God will bless our heritage as we stay faithful to Him.

May 27

1 Kings 5-6   Psalm 119:49-64   Proverbs 27   Philippians 2-3

What is Your Goal?

Good morning! Do you ever find yourself tired, weary, heavy hearted but you cannot put your finger on what is really bothering you? Working and serving people is tiring, but it is a good tired. The problem that we often face is not having "purpose" and we just do activities with little or no goals to reach. This morning I read in I Kings 5:5, "I purpose to build." Solomon had direction, he had a goal to reach, direction for his life. As I read on in chapter 6, the dimensions and materials are coming together to begin construction for the house of God. In verses 11-13, Solomon hears the voice of God say, "if thou wilt, then will I." What could we do for God if we kept in our minds and in our hearts those very words, "if thou wilt, then will I"? Those two phrases will spark a vision, give direction and cause us to focus. Do you have a goal for God? Solomon did, because his father David did and passed it on and it burned in both of their hearts. I read this morning in Philippians 2:2 these phrases, "same love, one accord, one mind." Is our heart on fire to do something for God? Has God given us clear direction on building a Sunday School class, a bus route, a Godly family, a marriage that has Christ in the center? We need to let God do with us, in us and through us what He desires. In Philippians 3:14, Paul writes, "I press toward the mark for the prize of the high calling of God in Christ Jesus." Do you have a mark in front of you that you are pressing toward?

Reading the stories of fallen soldiers during these days around Memorial Day stirs my heart, and that is good; but how about my heart staying stirred for God and what He has for my life? Summer camp is getting close and the excitement is building, but I stay stirred about camp all the time because it is what God has given me to do with my life. I daily ask God to keep my heart stirred for the task before us. My challenge to you today is to take a look at your purpose, your mark, your vision, your goals for God. Psalm 119:59, "I thought on my ways, and turned my feet unto thy testimonies." Maybe we need to take a new look at our marriage, our faithfulness to God, our service for God, our families, every area of our lives and regain or take ground that is before us for the Lord. Could our tiredness, weariness and heavy heartedness be because we have lost the "purpose to build"? Focus today on God's words, "if thou wilt, then will I." The joy of the Christian life is growing in Christ, coming closer to Him, learning to serve Him, reaching the lost for Him, having His Word come alive in our daily lives. He has a plan for us and He wants to use us. Focus today on these two phrases, "if thou wilt, then will I." Have a blessed day.

Setting a goal for God will give direction and purpose in life.

May 28

1 Kings 7-8   Psalm 119:65-80   Proverbs 28   Phil. 4-Colossians 1

God in First Place

Good morning! Oftentimes our pastor has made a statement about our church, "church the way it used to be." In I Kings 8-9, we see the temple finished, the ark moved in and the presence of God so great in I Kings 8:11, "So that the priests could not stand to minister because of the cloud: for the glory of the Lord had filled the house of the Lord." How powerful is the presence of God! In verse 23, as Solomon is having a prayer of dedication, there is a challenge for the people to "walk before thee with all their heart." The people are challenged in verse 53 to remember, "For thou didst separate them from among all the people of the earth."

When we get saved, there should be a turning away from sin and a drawing close to the Lord. Our lives should be lives of prayer and walking in the ways of the Lord, not in ways of the world. Philippians 4:1, "stand fast in the Lord," and the challenge is before us in verse 6, "Be careful for nothing; but in every thing by prayer and supplication with thanksgiving let your requests be made known unto God." At the end of verse 8 in Philippians 4 we read, "think on these things." Solomon challenged the children of Israel to face sin, confess to God and keep his commandments. Paul wrote to the church at Philippi and it is for us today in verse 9, "Those things, which ye have both learned, and received, and heard, and seen in me, do." That word "do" lets us know to stop giving excuses and just do what we have been taught. Our lives are to be lived for God, to bring glory to God, and to be a living testimony of God. Colossians 1:18, "that in all things he might have the preeminence." God needs to always be FIRST PLACE. Can you imagine the presence of God being so powerful, filling the house of God, that the priests had to step outside? Should not that be the testimony in our lives to others today? A life lived so filled with God that it overflows in what we say, how we work, in our appearance, in our attitude. Let us "do" today what pleases God in everything we "do." Have a blessed day.

We ought to be a living testimony of the preeminence of God.

May 29

1 Kings 9-10   Psalm 119:81-96   Proverbs 29   Colossians 2-3

Grounded and Growing

Good morning! I love the mornings, when the sun is just starting to rise and the new day is breaking. The birds are beginning to come to the feeders, their songs are being sung, the morning breeze is moving the branches of the trees. I noticed the growth of one of my wife's rose bushes and I saw how it had grown and the roses are so beautiful. I looked at the large maple trees. I saw the willows that we had planted over ten years ago, but then I thought about a giant ash tree and a pine tree that was over thirty feet tall and two beautiful blue spruce trees that died and I had to cut up and dig out the roots. The trees had been killed by bores that were so small and yet so powerful.

In I Kings 9 and 10, the blessings of God are seen, experienced and heard of around the world. Solomon's wisdom and riches "exceeded all the kings of the earth," I Kings 10:24. I thought for a moment of some of the greatest trees that have been killed by something so small as a little bore. In Colossians 2:6-7, Paul is cautioning the Christians to "walk in him," speaking of Christ. He gives us four words that are our focus today; walk, rooted, built, and stablished. The strength, riches, wisdom and power of Solomon can be lost. What makes a tree grow so large? It is rooted, has time for growth, and it becomes established. I then looked at the beautiful rose bush and I thought about each fall as it gets pruned back. Proverbs 29:17, "Correct thy son, and he shall give thee rest; yea, he shall give delight unto thy soul." He has to be pruned back or disciplined to develop properly. God desires to bless us, just like Solomon. We are challenged to go after wisdom and knowledge, but the blessings of God only come when we are grounded, growing and letting God prune us. Our faith must be stablished firmly so that we can hold on to the Godly strength that we need. The beauty of a tree or a bush only comes from being rooted and stablished. May we be more beautiful in the eyes of the Lord because of our faith in Him. Let us grow in Christ, and when we need pruning, let us grow forth much stronger. The Psalmist said in Psalm 119:88, "Quicken (to become alive) me after thy lovingkindness; so shall I keep the testimony of thy mouth." Grow for God today.

Being rooted and grounded in Christ makes us strong Christians.

May 30

1 Kings 11-12   Psalm 119:97-112   Proverbs 30   Col. 4-1 Thessalonians 1

Green Apples

Good morning! How many times have I heard a statement from my folks when growing up, and I did not heed what they were saying? The statement is, "you better listen and do what I am telling you." That statement could have been said for my safety, or to do something correctly, to keep myself out of trouble, or even to learn a lesson of wisdom so that I would mature as I grew older. As I was reading this morning, I thought about green apples. In all the wisdom Solomon had, he allowed his heart to get turned away from God. We read this sad but true story in I Kings 11. What was it that caused him to not heed the words of the Lord? Verse one of chapter 11 says, "Solomon loved many strange women." He was told of God not to have anything to do with certain nations because, "surely they will turn away your heart after their gods:."

At the back of our little farm in Missouri where I was raised, were some very big apple trees. I was cautioned every year, do not eat the green apples. If you would ask my wife today, she would tell you that I love anything that has apples in it. The truth is, I love apples. Apples are good for you and can be prepared many ways. My parents knew I loved apples, but they always cautioned me to not eat the apples until they were ripe. Do you know my love for those apples got me very sick several times? I ate them before they were ripened enough to be eaten. In chapter 12 of our reading today, we see a nation splintered because of rejection of wisdom of the old men, in verses 6-13. What a mess we get into when we do not heed the words of wisdom! We know we need to read God's Word daily, spend time in prayer, give our tithes, be faithful to church, live separate from the world; but do we? Proverbs 30:15, "The horseleach hath two daughters, crying, Give, give." The horseleach is one of the largest blood sucking leeches. Never satisfied, always wanting more. Solomon wanted more, Rehoboam wanted more, our sinful nature wants more. Oh, I wanted those apples so badly I ate them before I should have and I did not just eat one, I ate several and I got very sick. Psalm 119:97, "O how love I thy law! it is my meditation all the day." Get into God's word, meditate on it, memorize it. Psalm 119:103, "How sweet are thy words unto my taste! yea, sweeter than honey to my mouth! Our daily walk with God will keep us next to him, strengthen us, guide us, encourage us, prepare us. Yes, it takes time and it takes patience, but it is what we need. It was not that my parents did not want me to eat apples, it was that they wanted me to wait until they were ready to eat. God knows what is best, when it is best and when he is ready for us to move on to the next learning place in our life. Solomon was so blessed of God, but he let his flesh overpower what he knew was right and wrong. Stay on the right path with God today. Enjoy a good apple.

God knows what is best and when it is best.

May 31

1 Kings 13-14   Psalm 119:113-128   Proverbs 31   1 Thessalonians 2-3

Learn to Serve

Good morning! We live in such a demanding society. Graciousness seems to be depleting. I heard a statement yesterday that bothered me. I have to be tough to get things done. What happened to the joy of serving? In I Kings 14:8, "thou hast not been as my servant David." God is looking for servants and those that are willing to serve and not be served. My wife and I are so blessed each year as the summer staff begins to arrive here at the camp. They are all different and yet when we all work together and learn to serve, we work like a fine-tuned machine. Each one of us have things that we like to do and there are things that we do not like to do, but they have to be done. We have often heard that it is hard to live the Christian life. I say it is a matter of decision to do what is right.

Yesterday at the dinner table, I overheard a discussion about how we should do a job. I jumped in and said we always do the job the best that we can do. None of us are perfect but we should strive for perfection. When I was in the Army, I heard a statement, "it is close enough for government work." How sad, and how wrong. Our walk with the Lord should be to be everything that He would want us to be. Verse 8 goes on to say, "who kept my commandments, and who followed me with all his heart, to do that only which was right in mine eyes;." Those words, "to do that only," pricked my heart this morning. Before we begin our day, let us decide "to do that only" that pleases the Lord. When we do our tasks, whatever they may be, let us "do that only" which is right. I Thessalonians 2:12, "That we would walk worthy of God, who hath called you unto his kingdom and glory." Psalm 119:125, "I am thy servant; give me understanding, that I may know thy testimonies." Today, let us begin to walk with a servant's attitude, to please the Lord in everything we do or say, and to walk worthy of being called a child of the King. I will tell the staff every day that we are here to serve all, there are no big shots, none of us are perfect; but let us be the best we can be for the honor of Christ that saved our souls, gave us eternal life, and is preparing a place for us in Heaven. So many young people have come and gone here at the camp and they have often said, it has blessed my life to learn to serve. We are called to be servants of the Lord. Let us serve the King of Kings by learning to serve. Husband, wife, children, and home can be happier if we do for others instead of waiting for them to serve us. Ask the Lord to help you see what you can do for others instead of complaining that no one cares for you. Jesus did. That is why He died for us all and shed His blood. Have a blessed day serving.

We serve the King of Kings by serving others.

June 1

1 Kings 15-16   Psalm 119:129-144   Proverbs 1   1 Thessalonians 4-5

Strong Senior Saints

Good morning! As I grow older, I do not know what age you have to be to be older, but I do know the older I get, the more I pray to not be old in my actions, my attitude and in my spirit. I hunger to be a blessing to the next generation. As I was reading in I Kings 15:4, "for David's sake did the Lord his God give him a lamp." A new king is coming into power over Judah and he is walking in his sins. You would think that God would immediately deal with the sin but look in verse 5, "Because David did that which was right in the eyes of the Lord, and turned not aside from any thing that he commanded him all the days of his life, save only in the matter of Uriah the Hittite." I am not justifying any sins, but I think we that are older should realize we can be a blessing to the next generation by us doing right. God will have his day, God will judge sin, God will take care of what does not please Him. I cannot quit doing right because I might see this generation going in the wrong direction. In I Thessalonians 4:1, "ye ought to walk and to please God, so ye would abound more and more." Look on down to verse 7, "For God hath not called us unto uncleanness, but unto holiness."

Please do not look at this generation and give up and say it does not matter. Young people of today, young adults of today, need to see strong senior Christians. They need to see senior adults serving, soul winning, maintaining standards, loving lost people, having blessed marriages, living clean lives, being faithful in church. God is blessing Israel because of the faithfulness of past generations, because God has kept His promises. This generation needs to see older Christians living Psalm 119:131, "I longed for thy commandments;" Psalm 119:140, "thy word is very pure: therefore thy servant loveth it." Yes, I know it gets frustrating when we see foolishness,

186

immaturity, and lack of spiritual desire; but so did we at a time in our lives. May I encourage all of us old, mature, hurting with arthritis, has been adults to realize Proverbs 1:33, "But whoso hearkeneth unto me shall dwell safely, and shall be quiet from fear of evil." The first part of Proverbs 1 gives wise counsel and then God talks about foolishness.

Let us as senior adults live for God to the end of our life. If you are a young person reading this, realize that we as senior adults have scars that we regret and we often wish we could live life over. We want to finish right, so please know we do want to set a Godly, blessed example before you and when we get impatient, give us some space because we really do need you in our lives. Have a blessed day.

Young adults of today need to see strong senior Christians.

June 2

1 Kings 17-18   Psalm 119:145-160   Proverbs 22   Thessalonians 1-2

The Impossible Is Possible

Good morning! When I was in junior high school, we would go to the gym for breaks if it was raining outside. At one end of the gym were ropes tied to a bracket hanging from the ceiling. Those ropes were for climbing. Now a days there would have to have pads and safety equipment all around and there would have to be helmets, gloves, instructors, harnesses and the such. There was nothing but a rope hanging and we could climb it if we wanted. Sometimes during gym class, the teacher would have the students try to climb the rope. I loved climbing the rope, some students never tried and some that tried never made it to the top.

As I read in I Kings 17, Elijah has come on the scene and God is preparing to show Himself great. I wrote, "the impossible is possible" and "if the Lord be God then follow Him." In I Kings 18:37, fire is about to come down and Elijah prays, "Hear me, O Lord, Hear me, that this people may know that thou art the Lord God." I climbed that rope to the top of the gym every time because I wanted to do it, I was determined to do it, and I would stay at it until I did it. There were students that did not even try. God has great things for us, and I believe He is waiting to see how badly we want Him. Psalms 119:145, "I cried with my whole heart." Verses 145-159 have some words of plea that I want you to see; "hear me, save me, I hoped, deliver me, quicken me." The Psalmist cried (Psalms 119:145) with his whole heart in an earnest plea to see God work. II Thessalonians 1:12, "That the name of our Lord Jesus Christ may be glorified in you, and ye in him." God is ready and waiting for us to show Him how badly we hunger for Him to do a work through us.

I had no special talent to be able to climb that rope. I climbed to the top because I was determined to. Do you hunger for God today? Do you hunger to sense His presence? Do you hunger to see His power? Do you hunger to see Him save souls? The Psalmist said, "I cried with my whole heart." Elijah kept telling the servant to go look for the clouds of rain. Proverbs 2:3, "Yea, if thou criest." Life is not about us; it is about God and His will. God promises to take care of us, provide for us; but stop and think about how God is ready and waiting for us to climb to a higher height in our relationship with Him. Quit looking at what you think you cannot do and grab a hold and start climbing. The impossible is possible with God. As was written in I Kings 18:37, "that this people may know that thou art the Lord God." When I was climbing that rope, I was always looking up. Look up to God today. Have a great climb.

God has great things for us and is waiting to see how badly we want Him.

June 3

1 Kings 19-20   Psalm 119:161-176   Proverbs 3   2 Thes. 3-1 Timothy 1

How Is Your Spiritual Vision?

Good morning! Have you ever heard the statement, "What you see is not really what you are seeing"? Yesterday, three different times, it was said to me that the summer staff at camp seem to be getting younger. I agreed and then I said, they are not any younger than others have been, we are just looking through older eyes. Much of my life I have had to wear glasses. When I was much younger, I had to wear glasses for a short time because my eyes improved, and then I had to go back to glasses. As I grew older and was having trouble reading, I got bifocal lenses and the last several years I have had to have trifocals. Why? Because what I was seeing was not in focus so I could not see what I was seeing.

The prophet Elijah said in I Kings 19:10, 14, "I, even I only, am left." That was not true, but that was all Elijah could see. God pointed out to Elijah in verse 18, "I have left me seven thousand in Israel, all the knees which have not bowed unto Baal." Sometimes we get so tired we do not think we can keep going, and we do not see what we need to see. II Thessalonians 3:13, " . . be not weary in well doing." In I Kings 20, King Ahab of Israel is afraid he cannot win the battle and God says in verse 13, "I will deliver it into thine hand this day; and thou shalt know that I am the Lord." In verses 14, 15, 17 and 19, God tells him, "Even by the young men." We need to quit looking at what we cannot see and start seeing what we really see. A generation needs us to stay faithful, stay in the battle, "hold fast" (I Thessalonians 5:21). Elijah, look ahead; Elisha is plowing with twelve yoke of oxen; it is time to start training him for service. Proverbs 3:1, "My son." I was convicted this morning with the words in I Timothy 1:18, "This charge I commit unto thee." Look and see a generation coming that wants to learn, wants to lead, wants to serve; and they are fresh. In war there are fresh troops coming into the ranks to strengthen those fighting and to replace those that are tired, but the old troops never leave their position until the fresh troops are in position. Old soldier, stay in the battle and learn to train, encourage, believe in the Elisha's that are ready and already serving. I love the closing words of I Kings 19:20, "Then he (Elisha) arose, and went after Elijah, and ministered unto him." I wish we could sing together this morning, "Hold The Fort, For I Am Coming." Take a good look and really see what is there. Have a blessed day.

Learn to train, encourage and believe in the next generation
that is ready to serve.

June 4

1 Kings 21-22   Psalm 120   Proverbs 4   1 Timothy 2-3

Too Special to Exchange

Good morning! What have you been given that you never want to lose? Think of something so special that you would do anything to never misplace it or lose it. Is there something or someone in your life that you would never exchange for anything else?

In I Kings 21, we read the story of Naboth's vineyard. He told the king it was his "inheritance of my fathers." He was offered money, exchange of property, and even offered a better vineyard; but Naboth said no. In chapter 22 we read of the prophet Micaiah that spoke true words from God and the king hated him for it so very much that he was put in prison (verse 27). Naboth was killed, Micaiah was put in prison for living and willing to die for principle.

In I Timothy 2 and 3 we read today of orders and principles for men, women, pastors, deacons and their wives. God's Word gives us examples of people that were willing to die for what they were given and for what they believe. How did someone grow to this point of never giving up or compromising what they have been given or what they have learned to do? In reading Proverbs 4 this morning, I wrote down four words that I pray will help us. In verse one we must "hear" what is being told us and taught to us. Secondly, we must "attend" to what we hear and give total focus and attention. Thirdly we must "know" or be prepared to use, live and apply what we have been told and learned. Fourthly, we must "retain" from verse 4 those things so that as we continue in life, we may live a victorious Christian life. We must live to do right in God's eyes, in God's ways, for God's will to be done. I will never forget two days in my life as I stood on the edge of the street and watched as my daughter and son-in-law pulled away from the church after their wedding. Before they pulled away, my daughter saw me just staring and she said, dad I am leaving. One year later I stood in almost the exact same spot and saw my son and daughter-in-law get in their truck and pull away. As a dad, in my heart I let go and prayed and I am still praying that those children will continue to live and grow by principles that they heard, learned, lived and will always retain in life. What I have been given I am not willing to give up or change. Have a blessed day.

May we never give up or compromise the Bible
principles we have been taught.

June 5

2 Kings 1-2   Psalm 121   Proverbs 5   1 Timothy 4-5

A God Who Is Never Overwhelmed

Good morning! I am so thankful, and I love it when Pastor Fugate steps behind the pulpit and makes the statement, God is never surprised and never overwhelmed. Getting prepared for summer brings times of being overwhelmed and I have to continually stop myself, take a breath, look beyond where I am and regroup. Each year there are new staff members. They come with a desire to serve, they want to do right, they do not want to make mistakes. Getting ready for our summer schedule is not only mowing grass, cleaning buildings, making repairs, practicing songs, learning skits, getting a schedule ready, etc. It is spending time with each staff member and training them how to work, learning what their abilities are, watching them interact with other staff, encouraging them since they will spend a summer away from home, helping them to learn how to walk with God or being the spiritual influence to keep them growing in their walk with God, and much more. I always say, we are going to make it and camp will begin whether we are ready or not.

In II Kings 2, Elisha has now come on the scene and his desire is easily seen as in verses 2, 4 and 6 we read the statement, "As the Lord liveth, and as thy soul liveth, I will not leave thee." This is a perfect example of God in the life of a Christian. God will not leave us or forsake us. He is there with us no matter the circumstances or the situation. He is there. Elisha hungered for the power Elijah had and the relationship Elijah had with God. In verse 9 Elisha said, "I pray thee, let a double portion of thy spirit be upon me." Oh, that we would desire the presence and power of God in everything that we do and in our walk with God. We are cautioned in I Timothy 4:1, "in the latter times some shall depart from the faith;" in verses 7-8, "exercise thyself rather unto godliness;" and "godliness is profitable unto all things." Mrs. Smith and I are not looking for what a summer staff member knows, but we are looking for a humble heart to serve, learn and have a desire to grow. Many Christians begin a backsliding process when they do not build a strong daily walk with the Lord. In I Timothy 4:16, "Take heed unto thyself, and unto the doctrine; continue . . .." That word "continue" means to keep doing the same thing over and over again. If it was right yesterday to read your Bible, pray and walk with God, it is right today, tomorrow and the rest of our lives. Proverbs 5:21, "For the ways of man are before the eyes of the Lord." God sees all that we are and all that we are not. The Psalmist wrote in Psalms 121:1, "I will lift up mine eyes," verse 2, "My help cometh from the Lord." What a blessing that God is there. He is my help, my strength, He knows everything about me and He is never overwhelmed. May we "continue" to have a desire to be with God, know God, and grow in God. Elisha took the mantle of Elijah, walked to the waters edge that he had crossed before and cried out, "where is the Lord God of Elijah?." The water parted and a great man of God began his service with and for the great God. It is not what you know that matters, it is what you hunger for that keeps you growing in the Lord. Have a blessed day.

God knows everything about us and is never overwhelmed.

June 6

2 Kings 3-4   Psalm 122   Proverbs 6   1 Tim. 6 - 2 Tim. 1

What's in Your Pot of Stew?

Good morning! Do you ever get your mind on a food, soup, stew, casserole, special dish, special pie, and you think so much about it that you can smell it and even taste it? Maybe it is just me but as I was reading my Bible this morning, I began to smell a good beef stew. Big chunks of beef, potatoes, carrots, onions, maybe throw in some green pepper. I found myself beside a campfire this morning, cooking a stew in a Dutch oven over an open fire. Let it cook slowly and simmer a long time.

In II Kings 4:38-41, "there was dearth in the land;" and "the sons of the prophets were sitting before him (Elisha). "And he said unto his servant, Set on the great pot, and seethe pottage." He told his servant to make a stew. The servant gathered "a wild vine and wild gourds." When the stew was done and they began to eat, one of the men cried out, "there is death in the pot." I thought on that this morning. Let us look at the pot as our life and what we put in the pot, or our life, as the things we do, say, see, listen to, the places we go, the books we read, the type of friends we have, the type of habits we have, etc. There was bad food and in verse 41 Elisha said, "bring meal," and he stirred the meal and the stew was safe to eat. In I Timothy 6:6-12 we are challenged by this statement, "godliness with contentment is great gain," and to follow after righteousness, godliness, faith, love patience, meekness." I do not want to live a life that is poisoned by sin. I want to enjoy a life lived by Godly traits. What are you putting in your life? Is there poison that is causing you to drift from God and not grow in your spiritual life, or are you putting in good ingredients that will bring the Lord's blessing? Timothy was charged in verse 20 of chapter 6, "keep that which is committed to thy trust." In Proverbs 6:6-8 we are challenged to "go to the ant." Does an ant have more wisdom than we as humans? The ant has purpose, it has a plan and it knows what it must do to provide. If you have "death in your pot," or life, it will destroy you. Let us be challenged today from our reading to only put those things and activities in our lives that produce a safe, sold out life for Christ that will be a blessing and testimony of praise to our Lord. Enjoy your stew today.

We need good ingredients in our spiritual life to bring the Lord's blessing.

June 7

2 Kings 5-6   Psalm 123,124   Proverbs 7   2 Timothy 2-3

Look to the Master

Good morning! As I prepared myself to read my Bible this morning, I asked the Lord as I do each time, to please speak to me, strengthen me, teach me and so on. I find that the longer I walk with God, the more I want to trust Him, depend on Him, yield to Him. Last evening as the staff was working on the opening program for camp, I walked out to the porch of the dining hall and my two dogs were laying there. They both looked up before I said a word, and their tails began to wag. Why were they so happy to see me, why did they look up, and why did I draw their attention? I am their master.

Psalm 123:2, "Behold, as the eyes of servants look unto the hand of their masters," and then look down to the end of the verse, "so our eyes wait upon the Lord our God, until that he have mercy upon us." Does a dog understand a Biblical truth more than a human? In II Kings 5 we read the story of captain Naaman that had leprosy. A little slave maid living in his home made the statement in verse 3, "Would God my lord were with the prophet that is in Samaria! for he would recover him of his leprosy." A little maid, not in her own home, away from her family and friends, tells of the power of God that could heal her master. We know how the story ends, but my heart was touched this morning how even in her condition as a maid, her faith in God's power was so strong. In II Kings 5:13 we begin the story of Elisha's servant awakening to a city surrounded by soldiers, horses and chariots. The servant asks, "how shall we do?" I love the words of Elisha that had learned so well to look to God for strength and guidance, "open his eyes, that he may see." When we look to God for strength, we are able to see differently than what we see in our weak flesh. II Timothy 2 gives us a good path for a soldier of the cross. I thought about my dogs that watch and wait for me because I provide food for them to eat, water to drink, companionship, affection. They walk with me when I am walking, they run beside the truck when I go from one end of the camp to the other. Wherever I am, they are close by. Is a dog more faithful to his master than we are to our KING? Let us look unto the Lord today, enjoy a walk with Him, stay close to Him, wait on Him, enjoy His love for us. Look to the eyes of the Master. He is a loving Saviour, He cares for us, He wants to be our all. As the servant could only see all the soldiers and chariots, Elisha knew God was greater that all the armies of the world.

I bent down and reached out to my dogs and they looked up at me. Their tails began to wag and it was like they were saying, thank you. My challenge for us today is to look up to the Master in every moment of this day, thank Him, praise Him. Have a blessed day.

When we look to God for strength, we see differently
than we do in our weak flesh.

June 8

2 Kings 7-8   Psalm 125,126   Proverbs 8   2 Tim. 4 – Titus 1

Soldiers in God's Army

Good morning! The last several days there have been a lot of pictures and videos posted in memory of those that fought and gave their lives for freedom. I enjoy reading and studying history, but my focus is studying the character of those warriors of days gone by. What was their motivation, their drive, their desire to never quit? I have found that it was always a cause, even if they did not completely understand. There have been many victories won by soldiers around the world, but they never saw the final victory because they gave the ultimate sacrifice.

In our daily lives as Christians, I have a fear that because we do not always see the end result, we quit before the victory. These words in II Kings 7:2 and 19 spoke to me this morning, "Behold, thou shalt see with thine eyes." We will not always see what God is doing through us when we serve Him. In II Timothy 4:1, "I charge thee," are words that convict me to pay attention because in the battle we sometimes get weak, discouraged, feel like we are not having any effect for the cause of Christ, and yet in verse 7 we see three words that give us a plan. "*Fight*," stay faithful doing the work that God has called for us to do. " *Finish*," do the work, whatever it is, the best that we can. "*Faith*," the work that we are doing must be in God's strength. We are not alone. II Timothy 4:17, "the Lord stood with me, and strengthened me." We are alive today because God has a purpose for us. Just think about those wonderful words in Proverbs 8:17, "I love them that love me." Something all of us can do and should do is to love God. In Proverbs 8:32, "blessed are they that keep my ways." Every generation that stands for God will not always see how God used them, but thank

195

the Lord for every generation that keeps standing. Soldiers have fought and died because they believed in what they were doing. Our motivation as God's army should be to reach a lost world. As the oppression of an enemy drove our soldiers to fight for freedom of the oppressed; so should the doom of a lost world even be a great motivation for us. Psalm 126:5-6, "They that sow in tears shall reap in joy. He that goeth forth and weepeth, bearing precious seed, shall doubtless come again with rejoicing, bringing his sheaves with him." Victory is on the side of a surrendered Christian. Stand today, Christian soldier, stand for souls. There is a place for all of us in the battle for Christ. May the Lord bless you as you serve.

Our motivation as God's army should be to reach a lost world.

June 9

2 Kings 9-10   Psalm 127   Proverbs 9   Titus 2-3

Grow Up

Good morning! When is the time to grow up and accept responsibility and be accountable for your actions? Did you ever think about how we try to live in a shadow? A shadow is not the true image, it is a reflection of what is real. The Christian life is not a difficult life to live, it must just be lived in truth.

In II Kings 9:1 we read "Gird up thy loins." In this passage Elisha "called one of the children of the prophets." This child of one of the prophets is given a job. He was to take a box of oil, run to Ramoth-gilead, find Captain Jehu, pour the oil on his head and tell him, "I have anointed thee king over the people of the Lord, even over Israel. And thou shalt smite the house of Ahab thy master." What a responsibility! This is a son of one of the prophets. He did what he was told to do, how he was told to do it, immediately when he was told to do it.

Our children were 7 years and 11 years old when we started in the camping ministry. I remember how it was just us as a family. We worked together, cried together, prayed together and had faith in what God was going to do together. It is a hard task to consistently teach and train our children. Life is a building project. In Proverbs 9:1, "Wisdom hath builded her house, she hath hewn out her seven pillars. I thought about "*Wisdom*" (applied knowledge), "*builded*" (under construction) and "*seven pillars*," balance of completion and strength. All of us have seen adults that have not grown up yet. In Proverbs 9:6, 8-10, there is a hunger to grow, mature and develop a life. In Titus 2:1 we see "speak" words of "sound doctrine ," and in verse 7 "In all things shewing thyself a pattern of good works:" Life is difficult, but if there has ever been a time for a generation to be taught and held accountable for their actions, attitude and accountability, it is now. We are allowing a generation to do what is right in their own eyes and if they get under any pressure, they fold. Our world needs to be challenged to live by principle from the Word of God and live by faith in God. We will all be held accountable for our lives and we will not be able to blame somebody else. We have more people saying, well, I was mistreated, life was not fair. Now I hear and read adults blaming preachers for how their life is so rough because they were made to feel guilty. My dad would have told me to grow up. That prophet's son was told to "Gird up thy loins." Get up, face up, be up, Christian. We need to quit sucking our thumb and grow up. I do not mean to be attacking, and my spirit is right. We must quit living in the shadows and face our responsibility and be accountable for our own lives. Hold your head high and walk like a victorious Christian should walk. We need to let God build us the way He wants to. Psalm 127:1, "Except the Lord build the house, they labour in vain that build it:." We are all under construction. May we let the Lord keep building our lives. Have a blessed day.

It's time to face our responsibilities and be responsible for our own life.

June 10

2 Kings 11-12   Psalm 128   Proverbs 10   Philemon 1- Hebrew 1

Godly Unity

Good morning! As I read the Bible this morning in the Old Testament, New Testament, Proverbs and then the Psalms, there kept coming a thought to my mind and heart. Unity with God brings unity in a marriage, unity in a family, unity in right friendships. When I was an eight year-old boy, I joined Cub Scouts and I was part of what was called a "den." We met weekly and learned many things. That den was part of a "pack." We used to have regular pack meetings where all of the dens came together for competitions, awards, etc. When I turned eleven, I became a Boy Scout and became part of a "troop." The troop consisted of several "patrols," and each patrol had a patrol leader.

As I read my Bible this morning, I saw that unity in doing right and opposing wrong brought about a seven year-old Jehoash becoming king and God blessing (II Kings 11:19). In Philemon, Paul is in prison and writes to Philemon, asking him to forgive Onesimus for being unprofitable, because Paul knows he will be a "brother beloved." I am not encouraging being a compromiser or dropping any standards, but I am challenging us to walk a path together that brings God's blessing. We need to pray for each other, see the needs of others, focus on others' hurts instead of ours and be an encourager instead of a complainer. Proverbs 10:16, "The labour of the righteous tendeth to life; the fruit of the wicked to sin." Proverbs 10:20, "The tongue of the just is as choice sliver: the heart of the wicked is little worth." You know, when I was part of a den, pack, troop, or patrol, I was working to better myself and advance in rank. I do not remember ever focusing on the weaknesses of other scouts. I just wanted to be the best scout I could be to have the best den, pack, patrol or troop. Psalm 128:1 and verse 6, "Blessed is every one that feareth the Lord; that walketh in his ways. Yea, thou shalt see thy children's children, and peace upon Israel." I cannot fix anyone else, but I can be a brother serving and going in the right direction and be a testimony that brings glory to Christ. The game of tug of war is about the team pulling together. When we run a race as a team, it is not about the fastest or the slowest runner, it is about which team runs the fastest. Our summer staff for camp comes from different homes, churches, states, backgrounds, likes and dislikes; but when we start working together, we become a unit that will be everything the Lord needs for Him to work in the hearts of the campers. Selfishness only sees self, cares about self and focuses on self. There were twelve disciples and they were all different, but Christ pulled them together to spread the Gospel of salvation to all mankind. Have a blessed day, my "beloved" brother or sister. I am blessed to serve on the team. Let us win souls, disciple new converts, build lives for Christ.

Unity with God brings unity in marriage, family and friendships.

2 Kings 13-14   Psalm 129   Proverbs 11   Hebrews 2-3

I Should Have

Good morning! Have you ever said to yourself, "I should have"? I parked the truck the other day and I left the keys in the truck because I thought I was going to drive it again, and when I got ready to go to bed, I remembered leaving the keys in the truck. I said to myself, "I should have" pulled the keys. So many times in our daily lives, we say, "I should have." Studying for a quiz or test; we think we know the material and then we sit down to take the test, and we realize "I should have" studied better. Have you ever gone to the store to get some needed items and you get to the store, and said, "I should have" brought my list with me?

There will come a day that we all stand before God and I am afraid that we might say, "I should have" listened to the preaching and the counsel that was given to me. Sin will always take us farther than we want to go, and it will keep us longer than we want to stay. Sometimes the Holy Spirit speaks to us and we realize we "should have" turned away and run from sin. In II Kings 13:14, Elisha has fallen sick. The king comes to him and pleads to him for guidance. Elisha says, take my bow and arrows, put your hands on mine and shoot. Then he said to take the arrows and "Smite upon the ground." The king smote three times and stopped. Elisha said, "Thou shouldest have smitten five or six times;" (II Kings 13:19). If his faith and obedience had been greater, the enemy would have been destroyed, but they were not because of the lack of faith of the king.

What is it in our lives that we have not done or held back in a spiritual decision that the Lord has been speaking to us about? Hebrews 2:1, "Therefore we ought to give the more earnest heed to the things which we have heard, lest at any time we should let them slip." Verse 3, "How shall we escape, if we neglect so great salvation;." How often have we heard the voice of God and not heeded and repented? How often have we heard the voice of God calling us and we have not yielded? How often has God showed us a way we can serve in our church and we have not stepped forward? I do not want to miss one blessing, opportunity, or reward and end up saying at the end of my life, "I should have." Is the Lord speaking to you this morning about something He has talked with you about before? Be obedient or there will be a day that you will say, "I should have." "Thou shouldest have smitten five or six times; then hadst thou smitten Syria till thou hadst consumed it:." God has our best in His plan. Obey and yield. Have a blessed day.

Better to yield now than to say "I should have" at the end of life.

June 12

2 Kings 15-16   Psalm 130-131   Proverbs 12   Hebrews 4-5

Partial Obedience

Good morning! I asked myself a question this morning as I read in II Kings 15 and 16. Why do we think a partial right can be right and a partial wrong is not really wrong? You may say, Bro Smith, a partial right is not right and a partial wrong is wrong. So if that is true, we could then say that partial obedience is not obedience.

In II Kings 15:1-5, Azariah began to reign at 16 years of age, and he reigned 52 years. In verse 3 the Bible says, "he did that which was right in the sight of the Lord." If we would stop reading there, we would be able to say, he was a good king and God blessed him greatly for his obedience. But read on to verse 4 and you will see one word and that is the word "save." He did not tear down the temples to false gods and he did not stop the sacrifices and burning of incense to those false gods. So how did God look at his partial obedience? In verse 5 we read, "And the Lord smote the king, so that he was a leper unto the day of his death, and dwelt in a several house." He was separated, he was cast out, he was shunned, he was not clean because his wrong was not right. Hebrews 4:1, "Let us therefore fear, lest a promise being left us of entering into his rest, any of you should seem to come short of it." I cannot lose my salvation; it is secure. But God cannot bless me fully because of partial obedience which is nothing more than disobedience. Verse 14 says, "let us hold fast our profession." As I read that, I remembered my dad saying often, "make hay while you can." There can be beautiful hay growing in the field and it comes time to cut it down, rake it in windrows and bale it. If you cut it down and it gets rained on and you bale it, it will mold and that mold can make livestock sick and even die. That is why a farmer watches the weather and "makes hay while he can." Thank the Lord for His grace, but why not live the Christian life, as what is right in God's eyes is right. Proverbs 12:3, "the root of the righteous shall not be moved." Verse 5, "The thoughts of the righteous are right." Verse 7, "the house of the righteous shall stand." God cannot bless my life and use me the way He wants to when there is only partial obedience. How can my prayers be answered when I am asking a Holy God to bless me when I am living an unholy life in His eyes? God let king Azariah reign 52 years, but he did not reign from the king's house. Thank our Lord for Psalm 130:7, "for with the Lord there is mercy." Let us live our lives in truth and not in a lie. A partial truth is a lie. Wrong is not right. Do right while there is time to get right. Make hay while you can. Have a blessed day.

Partial obedience is nothing more than disobedience.

June 13

2 Kings 17-18   Psalm 132   Proverbs 13   Hebrews 6-7

Secret Sins

Good morning! In Hebrews 6:1 we read, "let us go on unto perfection." As I looked at the word "perfection," I thought nothing is perfect except God, but then I thought how God is the perfect example for us to do the best we can and to reach the potential that He has for us. In verse 19 we read, "Which hope (assurance) we have as an anchor (stability) of the soul, both sure and steadfast." God has a perfect plan for us if we will face the reality of ourselves.

In II Kings 17:9, "Israel did secretly those things that were not right against the Lord their God." These secret things are sins that caused them to turn away from God and turn to ways of the world. In II Kings 18 we begin the chapter reading about Hezekiah that "clave to the Lord, and departed not from following him." Why do we not stay right with God? My heart breaks any time I hear or see of someone that is turning from the Lord. How does this happen? Proverbs 13:1 says, "A wise son heareth his father's instruction" and in verse 20 we read, "He that walketh with wise men shall be wise:." Who are you walking with, listening to, reading about, wanting to be like? Look closely at your friends because that is what you are like or will soon be like. Hebrews 6 is a challenge for us to be what God wants us to be. Hebrews 6:12, "That ye be not slothful, but followers of them who through faith and patience inherit the promises." Who is leading you today? Who are you following?

I love horses. Do you know that in every herd, large or small, there is what is called the dominant horse? The leader, the one they all follow. We as humans are the same. We are following someone, some fad, some thing. We need to make sure we do not have those secret things that will cause us to be led away from a victorious life in Christ. The children of Israel "hardened their necks, followed vanity, went after heathen nations and made gods of their own." They arrived at a point of not listening to God. Psalm 132:4-5, "I will not give sleep to mine eyes, or slumber to mine eyelids, until I find out a place for the Lord." Keep the Lord in the right place in your life and you will stay in the right place. Get rid of those secret sins that are destroying you like a cancer. Walk with God today and obey His voice. Be everything that He would have you to be. Look up to Him, listen to Him and follow Him. It is a wonderful path.

Secret sins will destroy you like a cancer.

2 Kings 19-20   Psalm 133-134   Proverbs 14   Hebrews 8-9

Spending Time with God

Good morning! There is so much in our reading today that has spoken to my heart, that it is hard to know where to begin. As a camp director, I pray a lot about the weather because it affects so very much in a day's schedule. I love to walk across the grass in the evening and look down at my boots and see the moisture on the toes of my boots; then I know that it will be clear the next morning. I love to look at the sunset in the evening when it is clear as the last rays of light settle so slowly in the west. I then know we will have a clear day tomorrow.

Before I began to type, I went to the door and looked out and I thought about the words in II Kings 19:4, "lift up thy prayer for the remnant that are left." Hezekiah is afraid because of the "words which thou hast heard" (verse 6). I am learning that God always has a plan that is greater than my plan. There is often a concern in our lives that turns into a worry and we all know that worry is sin. God tells Hezekiah in verse 20, after he prays for deliverance from the enemy, "That which thou hast prayed to me, I have heard." I believe a priority in all of our lives should be a greater awareness of spending time in prayer and seeing the power of God. In verse 34 we read, "For I will defend this city, to save it, for mine own sake." My challenge to us today is that God is looking for us to spend more time with Him in prayer, fellowship and faith in His promises. Hebrews 8:10, "I will put my laws into their mind, and write them in their hearts:." God told Hezekiah in chapter 20:1, "Set thine house in order." We need to spend more time rejoicing in the goodness of God's grace to us, as is written in Hebrews 8:12, "their iniquities will I remember no more." Our Lord wants us to believe in Him, trust in Him, yield to Him, surrender all to Him. Proverbs 14:6, "knowledge is easy unto him that understandeth," v. 16, "A wise man feareth and departed from evil," v. 26, "In the fear of the Lord is strong confidence." Too much time is spent listening to the news, hearing the bad reports, worrying about things that we cannot change instead of just enjoying the presence of the Lord. After every storm is a rainbow somewhere in the sky. We need to look forward to the rainbow instead of fearing the storm. God heard the prayers of Hezekiah and turned time backwards and mankind with his computers found the gap in time. We need to quit standing in the shadows of darkness and get out in the light of our Saviour. God is always going to do what He needs to do, so why don't we do what we should do, and that is praise Him, rejoice in Him, serve Him and be faithful to Him? Yesterday the chilly winds blew and there was a concern in my heart whether we should have a bonfire for the children. We prayed all day for the moving of the Spirit of God, and by faith the trail was set, the fire was prepared, and at the end of the service there was an altar full of those yielding and surrendering their lives for whatever the Lord wanted, along with eight being saved for this week. We stepped out the door to go to the bonfire and no wind, plus a beautiful full moon shining down on us all. God is waiting to hear our prayers today. He is waiting to fellowship with us. Take time today for God. He will spend time with us. Have a blessed day.

Look forward to the rainbow instead of fearing the storm.

June 15

2 Kings 21-22   Psalm 135   Proverbs 15   Hebrews 10

A Thorough Cleansing

Good morning! Have you ever gone to a restaurant and picked up a fork, spoon or knife and saw dried food on it, and knew it was not washed properly? Have you gone to a smorgasbord where you go up to the line of food and pick up a plate and when you look at the plate, you find dried food on it because it did not get washed thoroughly? How about putting a cup to your mouth and before you drink the water you see something floating in the water? Many, many years ago when I was in school, I used to wash the dishes for the school lunch program so I could get free meals. Not only did I get free meals, but I became friends with the cooks and they gave me extra desserts. I consumed a lot of brownies and pieces of apple, peach and pineapple desserts.

In II Kings 21, God had had enough of the abominations and wickedness of the king and in verse 21 he said, "I am bringing such evil upon Jerusalem and Judah, that whosoever heareth of it, both his ears shall tingle." God is mad and has had enough. In verse 13, "I will wipe Jerusalem as a man wipeth a dish, wiping it, and turning it upside down." God is wanting a thorough cleansing. I thought for a moment about us bathing, brushing our teeth, cleansing ourselves, making sure we are clean before putting on a set of clean clothes. We would not put on clean clothes over a dirty body, neither would we put clean food on a dirty plate or use a dirty fork that had not been washed thoroughly. Why do we try to live the Christian life without being thoroughly clean and right with the Lord? A new king is now on the throne and there is a cleaning being done and in chapter 22 of our reading, in verse 8, they "found the book of the law in the house of the Lord." They "read it, heard it," and in verses 11-20 we see their hearts became tender, they humbled themselves, rent their clothes, and wept. This is a perfect example of why we must read the Word of God, be in Sunday School to hear teaching and be in church to hear preaching. In Hebrews 10 this morning we read of the importance of doing the will of God, drawing near to God to keep the assurance of our faith that will keep us from wavering and will cause us to encourage each other. In Proverbs 15:13, "A merry heart maketh a cheerful countenance," and that comes when we let the Word of God lead us and instruct us. When I did not wash the dishes thoroughly, the cooks would say, wash it again and then I can hear those convicting words, "would you eat off of a dirty plate?." Do you need a good washing today? Spend time alone in God's Word, make sure you are in church under good preaching and teaching, encourage each other in the Lord. The cooks would give me extra desserts and smile when the dishes were clean but there was no dessert if the dishes were dirty, and I had to keep washing them again and again until they were thoroughly clean. Do we need a thorough cleansing today?

We need to be thoroughly clean in our Christian life.

June 16

2 Kings 23-25   Psalm 136   Proverbs 16   Hebrews 11

The School of Hard Knocks

Good morning! To learn a lesson the hard way is most of the time the best way to learn a lesson. I often heard the generation before me say, "I was raised by the school of hard knocks." We read in II Kings how the temple is destroyed, the walls of Jerusalem are broken down, the people are taken captive. All of this happens right after king Josiah has had the Word of God read (II Kings 23:2) and "the king stood by a pillar and made a covenant before the Lord, to walk after the Lord, and to keep his commandments and his testimonies and his statutes with all their heart and all their soul," (verse 3). Then we read that wonderful word, "perform."

As a young fellow, I often heard a phrase said, "put up or shut up." Many decisions are made spiritually but never carried through. Josiah kept his word and sin of the people was dealt with, ungodly places were destroyed. There was a thorough house cleaning. As I read on and finished the book of II Kings, we see God allowing, and I mean God allowed, this to happen. The people were taken into captivity. I remember my parents would often say to me, "it is for your own good." Whatever it was that I had to be disciplined for, if I did something wrong and had to correct it or if going through a trial that I did not understand, many times I would say, "but it is not fair." See, being the oldest in the family, I got accused and punished for things that I did not do. I might have been the provoker, but I did not always do the act that was wrong.

God always knows what He is doing and as people were taken into captivity and Jerusalem was in a mess, God knew what He was doing. In our reading in Hebrews 11:25, we find the statement, "pleasures of sin for a season." God had had enough, and the faith, focus, and future of His people had to be put back on the right track. Proverbs 16:7 teaches us, "When a man's ways please the Lord, he maketh even his enemies to be at peace with him." God does not forget about us. God loves us and His compassions are forever. We need to realize from Hebrews 11:6 that "he is a rewarder of them that diligently seek him." The entire 136th Psalm, in every verse we read, "for his mercy endureth for ever." God will have His day to even teach us through the "school of hard knocks." I stand proud to have known my father-in-law and to have been raised by my father who were both out of broken homes, had hard times and many setbacks. They stayed faithful to their families and set many examples that a person can make it and grow strong through "the school of hard knocks." Stay faithful, Christian brother or sister. I know there are times that life does not seem fair, but God has a plan, He has a purpose. Stay faithful to what is right in the eyes of the Lord. Keep on keeping on. Have a blessed day.

God does not forget about us; He always knows what He is doing.

June 17

1 Chronicles 1-2   Psalm 137   Proverbs 17   Hebrews 12-13

A Heavenly Heritage

Good morning! Did you ever lose something that was very special to you? As parents, we have all said to our children, especially when they were young, you better hold on tight to it or you will lose it. The "it" may have been a toy, a book, a blanket, or something that was of value to them. When our children grow up, graduate, go to college or get a career we seem to lose something that was of great value to us and we can never gain it back. It is a part of life that we cannot stop but we can hang on to memories and we can enjoy the ride of watching them grow, mature and have their own families.

As I read I Chronicles 1-2 this morning, I thought of the heritage that I was reading. Where people came from, how they turned out and what purpose God had for their lives. Each evening at the camp, all the campers gather at the flagpole and before we take the flag down and properly fold it, I have some type of reading about our American heritage. I love America. We are so blessed to live in this great land. Throughout the history of our country, there have been many struggles from without and from within, but it is our heritage that makes us a great nation and the battles of each generation to maintain the principles of our founding fathers is what keeps us a nation blessed of God. As I read in I Chronicles, I kept reading a phrase, "the sons of." Hebrews 12:1, "Wherefore seeing we also are compassed about with so great a cloud of witnesses." As God's people, we have a great heritage that has gone on before us, and it should motivate us to know God as they did, serve God as they did, live and teach our generation as they did. The record is there of the bad, but the record of the good and faithful should be our focus. Hebrews 12:1 tells us to "lay aside every weight, and the sin which doth so easily beset us, and let us run with patience the race that is set before us." Jesus is our inheritance, our heritage, our example, our life. Hebrews 12:3, "for consider him that endured such contradiction of sinners against himself." We must not lose the example that Jesus set for us. Psalm 137:1, "By the rivers of Babylon, there we sat down, yea, we wept, when we remembered Zion." The people were broken because they had lost what they thought they would never lose. This past week at camp, young campers would come up to me and say, I have lost my Bible, I lost my flashlight, I cannot find my coat. I looked into those eyes and I saw hurt and my heart was touched to help. We need to look into the eyes of Jesus and remember the heritage that has been given us. Proverbs 17:24-25, "Wisdom is before him that hath understanding; but the eyes of a fool are in the ends of the earth. A foolish son is a grief to his father, and bitterness to her that bare him." I have read many a statement of men that led other men in battle and they would challenge the men by saying, "we are here today for our wives, our children, and our country." May we stand for the heritage that has been given to us through Christ and teach this and other generations. Hebrews 12:28, "Wherefore we receiving a kingdom which cannot be moved, let us have grace, whereby we may serve God acceptably with reverence and godly fear:'. We need to hang on to what we have or we will lose it. Freedom has always come with a high price, and Christianity came with the blood of Jesus being shed for all mankind. We have a Heavenly heritage.

Jesus is our inheritance, our heritage, our example, our life.

1 Chronicles 3-4   Psalm 138   Proverbs 18   James 1-2

Just Keep Going

Good morning! Do you ever have those days that are full of trouble? By trouble, I mean everything seems to be going wrong or there is just so much happening you do not think you can take any more. We all have those days, but what we do with them or how we handle them is what really matters. I have a picture in my office right above my desk at the house, that is a picture of horses pulling a heavy load in the blizzard. You can feel the wind blowing the snow, you can feel the struggle the horses have in pulling the heavy load. Below this picture and inside the frame is a little brass plate that has this engraved in it; "When the going gets tough, the tough get going."

In our reading this morning, we read the story of a man called "Jabez." He is only mentioned three times in the Scriptures, and it is like the listings of the genealogies stop and we read, "Jabez was more honourable than his brethren" (I Chronicles 4:9). This verse continues, letting us know "his mother called his name Jabez, saying, Because I bare him with sorrow." We can assume that something very exceptional, more painful or of great trauma happened at his birth. His name "Jabez" would define God's plan, God's purpose, and God's promise for his life because of his prayer in verse 10. Jabez "called on God" and said, "bless me," "enlarge my coast, be with me," and "keep me from evil." Isaiah 44:3 says, "I will pour water upon him that is thirsty." We read this morning in Proverbs 18:14, "the spirit of a man will sustain his infirmity," and in Psalm 138:7, "Though I walk in the midst of trouble, thou wilt revive me." Trouble is going to come to all of us, but how we handle trouble when it comes is what really matters to God. James 1:4 says, "let patience have her perfect work." Just the meaning of the name "Jabez" means "he causes pain." This mother loved her son and God wrote in His eternal Word that "Jabez was more honourable than his brethren." He was an overcomer, you could not keep him down, you could not stop him. As I meditated on this passage this morning, I was challenged by Jabez's desire to be blessed by God. We need to quit looking at the trouble, quit being defeated by the trouble, quit complaining about the trouble and just keep going. In our reading in James we read, "faith without works is dead." It takes work to keep walking with God, serving God, staying faithful to God, but that is where the blessings are. Let me challenge you that "when the going gets tough, the tough get going." There is a blessing on the other side of the hill. There are two beautiful mountains on each side of the valley. Keep going, my brother and sister. Keep going!

Trouble is going to come, but how we handle trouble
is what really matters to God.

June 19

1 Chronicles 5-6   Psalm 139   Proverbs 19   James 3-4

The Tie That Binds

Good morning! Mrs. Smith and I have six grandchildren, five boys and one girl. Two of my grandsons live over six hundred miles away and we only get to see them usually once a year. Three grandsons live two hours away and our granddaughter serves with us here at the camp, and she is presently a student at Commonwealth Baptist College. This week we were surprised to have all of the boys come to see us. It has thrilled our hearts to see them all together; we are family. We are all different, but the binding is that we are family.

As I read today in the genealogies of I Chronicles 5-6, I noticed the appointed jobs that were given in the listings. Notice chapter 6, verse 10, "executed the priest's office in the temple," verse 32, "they waited on their office according to their order," verse 33, "a singer," verse 48, "appointed," verse 49, "were appointed." Each was a member of a family that had a specific job or position. Our grandchildren are all different, but they are all special to us. We do not like one over the other. We live in a time of such hatred, and that hatred is so expressed with the tongue if you do not agree with someone else. We that are saved are family. We need to be careful how we talk and criticize others. We are not all the same and that is God's plan. James 3 speaks to us about the tongue. Verse 6 lets us know how the tongue "setteth on fire the course of nature, and it is set on fire of hell." Verse 8 tells us "the tongue can no man tame," and 4:1 says, it causes "war in your members." Then as we read down through chapter 4 of James, we see we are to "submit, resist, draw nigh to God, cleanse your hands, purify your hearts, humble yourselves, speak not evil one of another, brethren." And then chapter 4 ends in verse 17, "Therefore to him that knoweth to do good, and doeth it not, to him it is sin." May I ask, is your tongue a builder or destroyer? Does it praise the Lord or does it destroy others? Is it used to gossip or to speak truth? Proverbs 19:1, "he that is perverse in his lips, and is a fool." I am afraid that if we do not like someone, they hurt us, or they just bug us that we spend time trying to destroy them. Our tongue is given to us to praise the Lord.

I have spent a little time this week enjoying our grandchildren, watching them spend time together. They love each other and will all be sad when they head to their different homes at the end of this week. Their binding is not their likes, their talents, their age; their binding is they are family. Quit being critical of others that are in the family of God. If we do not agree, we need to keep our mouths shut. The devil would like nothing more than to divide a team that serves together in a local church or ministry. We need to look deeply today at Psalm 139:23-24, "Search me, O God, and know my heart: try me, and know my thoughts: And see if there be any wicked way in me, and lead me in the way everlasting." Let us use our tongue to praise God and strengthen the brethren. We be brethren. Have a blessed day.

Is your tongue a builder or destroyer?

June 20

1 Chronicles 7-8   Psalm 140   Proverbs 20   James 5 - 1 Pet. 1

Perfect Stock

Good morning! As I was reading this morning, several phrases caught my attention. In I Chronicles we are reading a lot of different lists of names and if we are not careful, we can get bogged down or just pass through them and miss the reason God has them in the Scriptures. In I Chronicles 7, verses 11 and 40, there are two phrases I want to bring to our attention; "fit to go out for war and battle" and "choice and mighty men of valour, chief of the princes." In I Chronicles 8: 13, 28, and 40, we see these phrases, "who were heads of the fathers; by their generations, chief men," and "mighty men of valour, archers." These lists of men tell us a different story.

Have you ever heard the statement, "they are out of good stock"? I had never been around race horses until we moved to Kentucky. I have always loved horses as long as I can remember, but there is a major difference in the horses that I have owned and the horses that are on many farms here in Kentucky. The difference is the "stock" or "blood line" or "breed" that they are and come from. A horse is not just a horse and these men listed were not just a list of men. Some of these men were very special because of what they were. We read that they were, "choice, mighty, chief, men of valour." They were from a different stock than the average man. I read in Proverbs 20:27, "the spirit of man is the candle of the Lord." When God saves us, He has a very special plan and He desires to work His plan through us. In James 5 this morning, we read several places where we are to "be patient, stablish, endure, be fervent in prayer, word of the Lord endureth." We are special to God; we are not just a human being. If you will allow me to say it in comparison to horses; we have a perfect blood line that should produce a victorious life. It was the blood of Jesus that was shed that washed our sins away and we became new in Christ. I love those wonderful words in I Peter 1:18-19, "Forasmuch as ye know that ye were not redeemed with corruptible things, as silver and gold, from your vain conversation received by tradition from your fathers; But with the precious blood of Christ, as of a lamb without blemish and without spot:." We are special in the eyes of God. We are a special breed. We have been born again and we are made from perfect stock. There is no reason for us not to live the victorious life in Christ. We are a special breed, we are Christians. My sins are washed away, I was forgiven, I have eternal life in and through Christ. I can hold, read and grow through God's Word. I am now redeemed and a special "stock." The world should see a difference in me from what they see in the average man. I am a special "breed" of a man. We are not just an old plow horse. We have a race before us and we need to run the race and finish as a victor. David wrote in Psalm 140:1, "Deliver me, preserve me." God has given us the victory, so run with a spirit to please Him and honor Him. I have gone to many horse and livestock sales and heard the statement many times, "they (meaning horses or cattle) have a good blood line." Think today about the blood line that you and I have.

We have a perfect blood line that should produce a victorious life.

June 21

1 Chronicles 9-10   Psalm 141   Proverbs 21   1 Peter 2-3

Basic Training

Good morning! As I was reading this morning, my mind kept going to II Timothy 2:3-4, "Thou therefore endure hardness, as a good soldier of Jesus Christ. No man that warreth entangleth himself with the affairs of this life; that he may please him who hath chosen him to be a soldier." We have been chosen to be soldiers of Christ and we have been given the most important mission that any soldier could ever have been given. It does not matter what branch of service a soldier is in because every soldier, whether Army, Navy, Air Force, Marines, or Coast Guard, must be trained to be combat soldiers. The first training all soldiers receive is basic combat training. They learn the basics of being a soldier, such as discipline, physical training, use of weapons and so much more.

Today in I Peter we are given the guidelines of basic training for the Christian soldier and then we see the guidelines for the advanced training for a Christian soldier. We see that every Christian soldier must "know" that he was saved by the "precious blood of Christ" (I Peter 1:18-19). Secondly, we see that every Christian soldier must "grow," (I Peter 2:2); "As newborn babes, desire the sincere milk of the word, that ye may grow thereby:." Thirdly, we see that every Christian soldier must "shew," (I Peter 2:9); "But ye are a chosen generation, a royal priesthood, an holy nation, a peculiar people; that ye should shew forth the praises of him who hath called you out of darkness into his marvelous light." Fourthly, every Christian soldier must "follow," (I Peter 2:21); "For even hereunto were ye called: because Christ also suffered for us, leaving us an example, that ye should follow his steps." After basic training, a soldier goes to a school to develop a skill with which he may serve in his given position as a soldier. We see in I Peter 2:17 our advanced training; "Honour all men. Love the brotherhood. Fear God. Honour the king." In I Peter 3:15 we receive our orders; "But sanctify the Lord God in your hearts: and be ready always to give an answer to every man that asketh you a reason of the hope that is in you with meekness and fear." Our orders are very clear in Psalm 141:8, "But mine eyes are unto thee, O God the Lord: in thee is my trust:." We must stay faithful to the mission to win a lost and dying world and to be a disciple of Jesus Christ, an encourager to the brethren and above all, to be faithful Christian soldiers. Some today are in basic training and some have moved on to advanced training, but all of us who are saved have a mission, or a will of God for our lives. May we be found as faithful soldiers in the Army of the King of Kings.

Our orders are to be faithful Christian soldiers in God's army.

June 22

1 Chronicles 11-12   Psalm 142   Proverbs 22   1 Peter 4-5

No Excuses

Good morning! I was watching a young child eat the other day and I noticed that they were using their left hand. I asked the parents if their little boy was right-handed or left-handed. They said, he uses both hands and it depends on what he is doing. In I Chronicles 12:2, we read the statement, "They were armed with bows, and could use both the right hand and the left in hurling stones and shooting arrows." I am left-handed, but I have had to learn to use both hands. In America we drive on the right side of the road, but we drive from the left side of the vehicle. When we go into a building that has double doors, we use the right door. When we walk up steps, we walk on the right side to be out of the road of possible people walking down the steps on their right side. When we enter a vehicle on the driver side, we use our left hand to open both the front and rear doors, and when opening the passenger side doors, we use our right hand. In many things we use our dominant hand, but we do use both hands. I have to wear glasses and I have one dominant eye, but I use both eyes.

I read in I Chronicles 12:8, "men of war fit for the battle, that could handle shield and buckler." It did not matter if they were left or right-handed, they just needed to be fit and ready for war. As we read in verse 38, these men of war needed to "keep rank," which means they needed to stay in order and stay in their proper position. It did not matter whether they were left or right- handed. What did matter about these fighting men was also told to us in verse 38, that they "were of one heart." There was a camper at camp this week that only had one arm. I watched this young man with amazement. He has come to camp before and he participates in every activity with the fellows that have two arms. He is at a disadvantage in most games but as I watch him, he has a great advantage. He has chosen to not let anything stop him. Excuses hold no weight when serving the Lord. God sees our abilities and He sees no limits. I am so thankful that I had to learn to use both hands even though I use my left hand most of the time. Life is full of lefts and rights, and we learn to keep on going. A teen boy with one arm ran, sang, jumped, pulled, set, stood, read his Bible, wrote in a devotional book; nothing stopped him. He made a choice and that choice has caused him to try just about anything. Sure, he is at a disadvantage with only one arm, but he kept participating in every activity and service. In I Peter 4:1 we read two words, "same mind." We need to have the mind of Christ and be the Christian that God wants us to be. In Proverbs 22:29, we read about a man "diligent in his business;" I wonder if he was left-handed or right-handed or if he only had one hand. It did not matter; he was a very hard worker. We read in Psalm 142 as David was in a cave, he cried, "I looked on my right hand, and beheld, but there was no man that would know me: refuge failed me; no man cared for my soul. I cried unto thee, O Lord: I said, Thou art my refuge and my portion in the land of the living." We need to quit looking at why we can't do something and get involved and do something. We do not have any excuse in not serving the Lord. It does not matter what we do not have or what we cannot do. Jump in and serve the Lord with what you do have. We are not all made the same, but we still should serve the Lord as best we can with what we have. Yes, I am left-handed, but I have learned to use both hands

In the Saddle with Dr. Dave Smith

because that is what I have and that is what I have to do. Get in the race and use what you have.

Excuses hold no weight when serving the Lord.

June 23

1 Chronicles 13-14   Psalm 143   Proverbs 23   2 Peter 1-2

Do It God's Way

Good morning! The older I get, the more I am reminded of the wisdom of the past generation or those that have gone before me. I and II Chronicles are often referred to as a newspaper that is reporting things that have already happened. As we read this morning in I Chronicles 13, we read the story of David doing the right thing the wrong way. Uzza touches the ark and dies. The ark of God was to be carried by men and not carried on a cart.

When new staff comes each year to serve a summer on camp staff, they are very nervous and do not want to make a mistake and do things the wrong way. All I desire for them to be is to have a heart to serve, ears to listen, eyes to watch and obedience to do what is told. When something does go wrong, I always try to turn things around, and I ask the question, explain to me why you did whatever you did. Just yesterday we had a couple of lady staff working hard to clean some buildings and they had the air conditioner going with the windows opened and the door opened all at the same time. I noticed this as I came by and stopped and asked why the windows and doors were open with the air conditioning going? Yesterday was a very hot and humid day, and I knew the humidity would fill the building and it would be hard to get the temperature and humidity back down in the building. The answer I received is an answer that I have often received. The ladies looked at me and they said, I do not know. That is not what they were taught to do. They thought they had a better idea. Teaching young men to run a string trimmer is quite an interesting series of lessons, from teaching them how to start it to teaching them how to not scalp the ground or not cut the bark from a tree. We often have toilets plugged in the buildings and I was told several times this week they had tried to plunge them and they could not get the toilet unplugged. I would go to the buildings and use the plunger and free the toilet of whatever it was and I would hear the statement, how did you do that?

In Proverbs 22:28 we are told, "Remove not the ancient landmark, which thy fathers have set." Generations before us walked with God, did things God's way and they did not change. In Proverbs 23:10 we read, "Remove not the old landmark; and enter not into the fields of the fatherless." A new generation comes on and does what they think is the right thing, the wrong way. I love those words in Psalm 143:5, "I remember the days of old." God has His way of living and serving Him and we are seeing a generation try to do things their way instead of God's way. There is so much for us to learn in life and the best way to learn is God's way. Psalm 143:6, "my soul thirsteth after thee," verse 8, "Cause me to hear," verse 9, "Deliver me," verse 10, "Teach me," verse 11, "Quicken me," verse 12, "I am thy servant." I tell the staff often, my way is not the only way, but there is a reason why I do things the way we do them. In the Christian life there is joy when we do things God's way. Since the beginning of time man has tried to do things his way and we always see how man messes things up, so let us humble ourselves before God and learn to do things God's way. There are limitless blessings for being obedient to God's way. Enjoy your walk with the Lord today; please do it God's way.

The best way to learn is God's way.

June 24

1 Chronicles 15-16   Psalm 144   Proverbs 24   2 Pet. 3 – 1 John 1

Pulling Weeds

Good morning! When I was living at home many years ago, I had a daily responsibility to keep the garden weeded and to keep the yard trimmed, mowed and weeded. There were chores with the animals, but my main responsibility was to keep the weeds out of the garden and to keep the garden hoed and the ground broken up around whatever we had planted. Our garden grew most all the food that we ate and canned for winter. I hated weeding. Every time it rained and then the sun came out, I knew the new weeds would be coming up. I had a job to do and I was expected to do it.

In I Chronicles 16:4, we see that David "appointed certain" to "minister," "to record," "to thank and praise." According to verse 11, these selected individuals were to "Seek the Lord and his strength, seek his face continually." The selected needed to be faithful at their position and faithful in their position. Dad would say to me, "if you do not keep the weeds pulled, the weeds will take over the garden." I hate weeds. To this day weeds consume me. I pulled into the drive yesterday and I said to my wife, look at those weeds. We can have a beautiful gravel parking lot at the camp and all the gravel smoothed and a weed pops up and it drives me crazy. In our daily walk with God we must keep the weeds (sin) out. It is a constant battle. If we let weeds (sin) creep in, it will start by keeping us from reading the Bible, and then weeds (sin) will keep us from praying, and then weeds (sin) will keep us from church; and before you know it, weeds (sin) have taken over our lives, and we find ourselves far from God. Daily I had to weed the garden. I can hear him say now, keep those weeds out of the fence row or we soon will not see the fence. In II Peter 3:14 we are challenged to "be diligent that ye may be found of him in peace, without spot, and blameless." We must keep the weeds (sin) out of our lives daily and continually. Proverbs 24:30-34 tells us about a slothful (lazy) man, that his vineyard was overtaken with "thorns, and nettles," "the stone wall thereof was broken down." A beautiful vineyard was ruined by not keeping the weeds out and the walls repaired. I remember in the fall of the year as the fruit from the garden was slowing down, the weeds began to overtake the garden. It looked awful and dad would say, those weeds will go to seed and they will come up next year, so keep them pulled out. We would fall plow the garden and let the stubble of the plants die and in the spring we would plow, disk and prepare the ground for the new seed to be planted, and guess what always came back and had to be pulled? The weeds. Our lives are to be fruit bearing for the Lord and weeds (sin) will keep our lives from producing the fruit that we could produce. Psalm 144:15 says, "happy is that people, whose God is the Lord." We can apply that verse to say, happy is that people who keep the weeds (sin) out of their garden. No matter how hard I worked in the garden, the weeds kept coming back and they had to be pulled. Christian, keep the weeds (sin) pulled or the weeds (sin) will keep you from enjoying a victorious life. I love fresh garden vegetables, so it was important to keep the weeds pulled. I love the blessings of the Lord because we work to keep the sin out. Why don't we step back and look to see if there are any weeds (sin) in our lives and pull them out?

Sin will keep our lives from producing the fruit that we could produce.

June 25

1 Chronicles 17-18   Psalm 145   Proverbs 25   1 John 2-3

Our Advocate

Good morning! This week of camp is Spanish week. I am so thankful for Spanish pastors that are reaching Spanish speaking people. I have a language barrier because I do not speak Spanish, but a smile is a universal language. There are Spanish campers that I have known for several years and have gone to their church and I have spoken through an interpreter. Just because I cannot speak their language did not stop my heart from being blessed as they drove on to the camp property yesterday and we waved at each other and smiled. There was common ground even though we do not always understand each other; there is a binding that brings joy.

We read in I John 2:1 this morning those powerful words that "we have an advocate." We have a communicator in Heaven that sits at the right hand of God and pleads for God's mercy on us. Jesus is our attorney pleading the case for us. There are a multitude of different languages around the world and Jesus speaks them all. There is no language that He does not understand. Jesus is the "propitiation for our sins" (I John 2:2). He shed His blood that I might be saved and receive the forgiveness of God. It does not matter how bad of a sinner or how many sins I have committed, God is satisfied through the blood of Jesus. I do not understand the love of God, but I am so thankful for it. I do not understand how God can love me so much, but I enjoy it. I do not understand why God would want to talk with me, but I enjoy every moment of prayer that I have with Him. I do not understand why He would want to use me, but I enjoy serving Him. I love Spanish family camp; not because I understand all that is being said, but I love watching the Lord work in their hearts through the preaching of the Word of God and the yielding to His Spirit. Proverbs 25:11, "A word fitly spoken is like apples of gold in pictures of silver." The universal word of God says, "I write unto you, little children, because your sins are forgiven you for his name's sake." At the name of Jesus, we are forgiven. When we fall, He is there to pick us up. I cannot understand it, but in Psalm 145:14 we read, "The Lord upholdeth all that fall, and raiseth up all those that be bowed down." Even though I do not understand the Spanish language, there is a binding in our hearts through the love of God that joins us as brothers and sisters in Christ. Just as I do not understand Spanish, I do not let it keep me from enjoying the fellowship through Christ. Even though you do not understand the love and forgiveness of Christ, please do not let it keep you from getting right with Christ and living for Him. The love of Christ and His forgiveness of our sins is the language that all languages can and should understand.

There are a multitude of different languages and Jesus speaks them all.

June 26

1 Chronicles 19-20   Psalm 146   Proverbs 26   1 John 4-5

Do You Know for Sure?

Good morning! There are so many things in life that are unsure. Summertime is a time for family outings, but it can be said, we are unsure of the weather. We order so many things on the internet and we are unsure of the quality because we cannot hold it or check it out. An item can be on sale in a catalog, but we are unsure if the item is still in stock. We can go to a place on vacation and say, it would be fun to come back next year and we make plans to return, but when we come back things changed and we did not like it as much because we do not like the changes. We could say life is constantly changing and nothing stays the same. The climate changes, our health changes, vehicles change, clothing styles change. It seems everything around us is in a constant change. Even nature has its different seasons, spring, fall, winter and summer.

There is something that is sure and unchanging and that is God's promise to us of eternal life. We read today in Psalm 146:6, "which keepeth truth for ever." I counted three words in I John 4-5 this morning. The words are "knoweth, known, know." I looked up the meanings and I also took my concordance and dictionary and spent time reading definitions. The words mean, "to allow, to be sure, to understand clearly, to know a thing precludes all doubt." The words "know, known and knoweth" are mentioned in the two chapters of John, fifteen times. We have heard the statement that no one can know for sure they are going to heaven. That statement is untrue and is a lie of the devil. I am not married because Mrs. Smith and I live together, have had children and we wear rings. We are married because on May 22, 1971 in front of God, family and friends we both said, "I take thee." You might not remember the exact day or time but if there has been a time in your life that you told God you were a sinner, you were sorry for your sin, and you asked Him to forgive you, and by faith you asked Him to come into your heart, you are saved. When I was born, they gave my parents a birth certificate. When Mrs. Smith and I got married, we received a marriage license. When I got saved, I received the promises of God and a record. I John 5:11, "And this is the record, that God hath given to us eternal life, and this life is in his Son." As I have a birth certificate, a marriage license, I also have God's Word that says in I John 5:13, "These things have I written unto you that believe on the name of the Son of God; that ye may know that ye have eternal life." My birth record is recorded, my marriage license is recorded, and my salvation is recorded. Revelation 20:15, "And whosoever was not found written in the book of life was cast into the lake of fire." My salvation is sure; is yours? If not, please bow your head today and by faith make it sure. Life will keep changing but my eternal destiny is for sure and unchanging. We live in a world of doubt and confusion. I am sure of my eternal home because of God's record for me. Tomorrow might be too late. No one knows when life will end so we must be ready for eternity. I know my God is a "know so" God. Please trust Him today. As of this writing, I have been married for over 48 years and life with Mrs. Smith gets sweeter as each year passes. My life in Christ gets sweeter, stronger and more blessed the more time I spend in His Word, and the more time I spend in prayer. If you know Him, please spend time growing in Him and if you do not know Him, meet Him today and accept His salvation today.

God's promise of eternal life is sure and unchanging.

June 27

1 Chronicles 21-22   Psalm 147   Proverbs 27   2-3 John

Focused on God

Good morning! As I read in Psalm 147:10-11 this morning, I looked at the notes I had written as I read this morning in I Chronicles, II & III John, in Proverbs and now in Psalm 147. I picked up the paper that I had written on and sat and thought on the Scriptures. I find myself enjoying more time meditating on what I am reading than ever before in my life. I read a note I had written in my Bible by Psalm 147, "It is not in what we can do; but in awe of Him and what He is doing." Let us look for a moment at what God is doing in our lives and not what we are doing. We focus too much on what we do, and do not always see what He is doing.

David made a major mistake in having Joab number the people instead of David focusing on all that God had done and could do. David allowed Satan to "provoke" Him, as we read in verse one. Joab tried to help David in verse 3 by saying, "why then doth my Lord require this thing," and we read in verse 6 how Joab knew this was wrong; "the king's word was abominable to Joab." Judgment then fell because David lost focus on God and looked at a situation through his own eyes. We need today to set our hearts on what God is doing and not on what we think should be done or what we can do in ourselves. Many times I have said to the Lord in preparing for a week of camp, I will do all that is before me, but it is not in what I do; it is always in what God does in the hearts that really matters. I often hear a testimony about plans that someone is making and then they say they have given up on their plans and are listening to the Holy Spirit of God. Mrs. Smith and I talked much yesterday about how we can work and serve in our flesh instead of working and serving in the Spirit. II John 4 says, "walking in truth," and III John 4 says, "I have no greater joy than to hear that my children walk in truth." Let us ask ourselves this morning, are we walking, serving and living in the Spirit of the Lord or in our own flesh? I see those leaving the Lord's service, quitting on God, dropping of standards, living in sin, and I ask myself, what happened? Could it be that we focus on our strength and not on the strength of the Lord? Do we want to see our results and not the results of the Lord, or are we so busy looking for results that we miss what God is really doing? Are our eyes only seeing the "strength of the horse" and the "legs of a man," and not the working of God? III John 11, "Beloved, follow not that which is evil, but that which is good. He that doeth good is of God: but he that doeth evil hath not seen God." Work being done in our strength and time and not God's time could be wrong. Give some thought to, "It is not in what we can do; but in awe of Him and what He is doing." Have a blessed day.

We need to focus on what God is doing and not on ourselves.

June 28

1 Chronicles 23-24   Psalm 148   Proverbs 28   Jude-Rev. 1

Stay on Guard

Good morning! Each summer we take one day with the summer staff and leave the camp and go someplace to relax, have some fun activities and just stop. I think using the word stop is probably not the right word because we do not stop with a group of 45. Yesterday we went to the Levi Jackson State Park here in Kentucky. We hiked, played miniature golf, ate and hiked again and played some games. There is an area that has some old buildings and a very interesting collection of items from the 1800's. Along the road is a small graveyard and I stopped to read the sign and looked at the old head stones. As a group of settlers were moving into the area and establishing their farms, they gathered at this spot to have an evening meal together, but they did not post a guard for their safety. As they were eating and enjoying time together, they were attacked by some Indians and many died. Some lived to tell the story of what happened.

As I thought about this incident, even this morning as I was in I Chronicles 23:30, there were those appointed to "stand every morning to thank and praise the Lord," and in verse 32 we read, "keep the charge of the holy place." There were those appointed with responsibility. In Jude we read in verse 3, "contend for the faith." James warned that we should, "keep yourselves in the love of God." There was apostasy rising and false teachers deceiving in their teachings. Recorded for us in Revelation 1:3, "Blessed is he that readeth, and they that hear the words of this prophecy, and keep those things which are written therein: for the time is at hand." The settlers were warned and I am sure had faced Indians before. The sign read, "they failed to post guards." We must be aware of the attacks of the devil and not let our hearts become insensitive toward sin. There is not a safe place where a Christian can let down his or her guard. Proverbs 28:14, "Happy is the man that feareth alway: but he that hardeneth his heart shall fall into mischief." After the massacre, there were those that came back and buried the dead, and I am sure as they dug the graves they remembered how there were no guards posted for safety. We must live in the Word of God and spend time in prayer, asking the Holy Spirit who dwells inside of us to stay on guard for us. The guards that night would have cried out and warned others, but there were no guards. We must stand guard against the devil, his workers and our flesh. Proverbs 28:18, "Whoso walketh uprightly shall be saved: but he that is perverse in his ways shall fall at once." Stay on guard.

There is not a safe place where a Christian can let his guard down.

June 29

1 Chronicles 25-26   Psalm 149   Proverbs 29   Revelation 2-3

Teaching and Learning

G ood morning! The change of one generation to another is more of a struggle than I ever realized it could be. The older generation spent time, or should have spent time, in teaching and training a generation that was coming behind. Raising our children to be the men and women they should be is difficult, but very rewarding. We must be patient in our training of this generation. I am often asked, how did you learn to do that? Life is so different now than when I was a young man. I am sitting at a keyboard that is connected to a phone to write this devotional. I will send it in just a moment and it will be posted on a Facebook page. It sure is different than sitting in a class and learning how to put a piece of paper in a typewriter. I remember trying to learn to type and getting the keys stuck together or just learning how to place my hand on the typewriter. As a young man, I was led to see the importance of learning a trade, or now we would call it a vocation. My father was a printer and so I thought this is what I should be. So at twelve years of age I began working in a print shop as an apprentice, learning the printing trade from printing craftsmen. A young man like me was called a printer's devil. A master printer would have to take time to teach an apprentice and it would be frustrating sometimes, so the term "printer's devil" was given to the young man learning the printing trade.

As I read this morning in I Chronicles 25:1, the phrase "separated to the service," and also the phrase, "the number of the workmen according to their service." Then in verse 6, "All these were under the hands of their fathers," and in verse 7, "even all that were cunning." I have thought on these phrases this morning of the importance of teaching and learning. I asked some of the boys on staff yesterday if they knew the difference between latex paint and oil-based paint. The fellows that I asked are good boys with a desire to work and a heart to serve. Not one of them knew the difference. My heart broke as I thought, why do they not know the difference? Every generation must have those that teach and those that learn. I have told myself that I must keep learning for the simple fact that life is constantly changing. But then I read in Revelation 2 and 3 this morning these convicting words, "because thou hast left thy first love" (verse 4). My love for God should keep me motivated, no matter what my age, to be everything that I can be for any service that I would do for the Lord. We read several times in both chapters of Revelation the phrase, "I know thy works." As an older man, I sometimes feel I have nothing to teach because life is changing so fast and then my heart breaks as I see a young man or lady just simply struggling because no one has taken the time to teach them simple facts, such as the difference in latex and oil paint. I am convicted this morning because as an older Christian, have I taken the time to teach a younger generation how to serve, work, win souls, walk with God, pray, and how to stay encouraged in a walk with God? Then I stopped and thought, we have learned how to walk the Christian life without walking with God. Do we have a tenderness toward the things of God? Proverbs 29:1, "He that being often reproved hardeneth his neck, shall suddenly be destroyed, and that without remedy." I came up on hard preaching, sin naming preaching, hot preaching.

Now we get offended over everything. Psalm 149:4, "For the Lord taketh pleasure in his people:." Do we take pleasure in the Lord? Do we take pleasure in our walk with Him? Do we take pleasure in our study of His Word? My heart is convicted today of setting a Spirit filled example and training a generation to walk with God. Brother or sister, we cannot train what we are not. Please think and pray about it.

Every generation needs those that teach and those that learn.

June 30

1 Chronicles 27-29   Psalm 150   Proverbs 30-31   Revelation 4-5

Be in Your Place

Good morning! I am so thankful that we have had some days without rain. We have not been able to get work done that needed to get done. As the summer staff has been working the last couple of days, I have been so blessed as they faced their responsibilities, dug in and did whatever it took to prepare for the next week of camp. To most people, getting ready for camp is cleaning buildings, mowing the grass, purchasing the food and preparing some games, songs and skits. Every year, new staff say, I had no idea it took so much work and time to just prepare for a week of camp. Then I smile and say, unless they serve with us no one has any idea.

As I was reading this morning in I Chronicles 27, I kept seeing the two words, "his course." I got my Strong's Concordance and looked up the word "course." The word "course" means company, division or army.

David had assigned certain men to lead other men. Then as I read on, verses 25-31, David assigned men to be in charge of treasures, storehouses, work of the field, over vineyards, olive trees, over herds, over camels, etc. Every area had a leader in charge who led other men. We read in verse 31 that these men were "rulers of the substance." In verses 33-34, we read that David had a counselor, companion, and then he named Joab as "general of the kings's army. We then read on that he brought the men together and counseled them all in chapter 28, along with his son Solomon, to "be constant" and "to know God with a perfect heart and a willing mind." My heart was challenged afresh this morning to be in my place, faithfully fulfilling my responsibility. Too many of us look at church as a place to go to receive, but want no responsibility. The work behind the scenes in preparing anything is so much more that what is ever seen. God does not just bless what is seen; He blesses the preparation. There is no delicious meal without planning a menu, purchasing the food, preparation of the food and making the table look beautiful. All of that needs to be done before we enjoy the delicious meal.

In Proverbs 30:11-14, we read the words, "There is a generation" and all that follows is negative. We that are in position today, men and woman, must take time to train and work alongside the next generation. Obedience will not come just from command. Obedience comes from working together, explaining, teaching, producing together. Each summer I challenge the summer staff with a new project for which they will be able to say we, the staff of this year, did this. In the last couple of days there have been some past staff members come and asked if they could help us get ready for this coming week of "Family Camp." What a joy to see them jump in and ask what they could do. I stand amazed each year as the Lord brings together young people that are all different and makes a team out of them. The unity is because they are serving in their position and doing the work to bring praise to the Lord. It does not matter the task; it is for the Lord. Sure, some will be seen and some will not, but we have seen what needs to be done and we do it together. You are important to your local church. You might be used of the Lord to encourage someone by just spending time talking with them. You might be used of the Lord to be a nursery worker and hold a baby, change a diaper, play with a toddler, empty a trash can, greet at the door. Christian brother or sister, you do not have to know how God is using you, just be in your place and I promise you He will use you. We think, I am not important or nobody even knows when I am not there. That is a lie from the devil. We all have a "course" and we need to be in our place. God sees and that is what matters. Is church about us or is it about Him? Whatever the activity of your church, be in your place. Psalm 150:6, "Let every thing that hath breath praise the Lord." Church is about a family getting together and being strengthened in our walk with God through preaching, teaching, fellowshipping and serving. It does not matter who we are or where we are from; God sent His Son to die for us and His blood washed our sins away. Life is not just about us, but about reaching a lost world with the gospel and being in our place to bring praise to our Lord. Someone needs you today, and the Lord wants to use you.

God does not just bless what is seen; He blesses the preparation.

2 Chronicles 1-2   Psalm 1   Proverbs 1   Revelation 6-7

Pass On A Godly Heritage

Good morning! It is coming to the time of the year that we will see flags waving everywhere we look. Red, white and blue decorations will show the patriotism of the people of our country. I do fear the ignorance of generations to come, that they will not be taught the heritage of our country, the sacrifice of those from the past, the preservation that we enjoy. It must stay in our hearts and be taught to every generation. A tear in my eye, a lump in my throat comes from a heritage that must not be lost.

In II Chronicles 1:11, we read "And God said to Solomon, Because this was in thine heart." It was in his heart because his father David shared the vision and talked about building the temple. I believe it was due to David's love for God, thankfulness to God and desire to please God, that his son Solomon asked God, "let thy promise unto David my father be established:." Solomon asked for "wisdom and knowledge" because of the love of his father for God and Solomon had a strong desire to build a place for God. This love of David for God passed on to his son and his son said those words of humility in verse 6, "who am I then, that I should build him an house?"

Is the rejection of God by this generation because we, as an older generation, have not shown our love and dedication to our God? David's priority was to please God and that priority passed on to his son and his son's priority became to please God. As I read in Proverbs 1 this morning, I looked at the little word "to." "To know, to perceive, to receive, to give, to understand. I believe this is teaching us we need to have purpose; it is of importance; it will help us. I love America, but I want my children to know I love God more. I love apple pie, but I love God more. I love hiking, but I love God more. I love trucks, but I love God more. Proverbs 1:33,

"But whoso hearkeneth unto me shall dwell safely, and shall be quiet from fear of evil. What I love the most will shine through in every area of my life. Psalm 1:2, "But his delight is in the law of the Lord; and in his law doth he meditate day and night." In Revelation 6:9 I read and my mind went to those that have been slain for their love for Christ; "souls of them that were slain for the word of God." What is it that you love the most? It will be shown in everything that you do. We will hear songs of the heroes that paid the ultimate sacrifice for our freedom we enjoy today and we must not forget it. We will hear stories of those that volunteered and left their families to fight for freedom and we must not forget it. We will see the wounded that have returned from the battlefield who fought so that we may enjoy freedom, and we must not forget to be thankful for their sacrifice. We must talk, live, and remember the salvation that we enjoy. Remember the sins of the world that our Saviour bore for all mankind. We must serve because of our love for God. We must live for God because of our love for Him. May this and many generations to come have a love for God, service to God and lives lived for God because of what they saw, heard and received from our love for God. We must pass on our love for God. Live for Him today, serve Him, be faithful to Him, show your love for God in everything you do today and every day.

What we love the most will shine through in every area of our life.

July 2

2 Chronicles 3-4   Psalm 2   Proverbs 2   Revelation 8-9

A Continual Work

Good morning! Did you ever think about how life is a continual project? We are always building something at the camp. From building cabins for housing to cutting trails for campers to hike and enjoy the outdoors. As I drove to an area that we are greatly improving, I saw the fellows in the heat of the day pushing to complete another phase of a project. We are pushing so that campers can enjoy this activity.

As we read in II Chronicles 4:2 this morning, work is being done on the beautiful new temple and I noticed the two phrases, "brim to brim" and "round in compass." The project of building the temple is coming close to being finished and then in verse 11 of chapter 4, "Hiram finished the work." The construction part of the temple was complete; it is not yet ready for service, but it is getting closer. Our lives as individuals and our marriages are a continual work in progress. The situation that arises in us as individuals and in our marriages is that there are things that we need to change as we grow. In Revelation 9:20 we see that God's judgment is falling because the people "yet repented not of the works of their hands, that they should not worship devils, and idols." God will deal with mankind in His time. Just as I saw the boys on staff working so hard in the heat to further develop a project here at the camp, each day God is trying to help us grow in Him. In Proverbs 2:2-6 we read, "incline thine ear." God is telling us to listen, then "apply thine heart," God is telling us to focus on what He is saying. In verse 3 we read, "criest after knowledge." God sees our needs and He is telling us that help is there if we just ask. He goes on in verse 4 and we see the word "seekest," meaning we must have a desire to grow in our walk and relationships, and then in verse 6 we see, "the Lord giveth wisdom." God grows us and matures us. Then in verse 7 we read, "he is a buckler" and that means His truth becomes part of our lives and marriages.

As different staff come each year to serve with us at the camp, they need to arrive at a point of having a willingness to learn and grow. As they learn and grow, the projects that they are given begin to develop and there is a satisfaction and joy when they step back and say, I had a part in that. As we grow in the Lord individually and in our marriages, we see places that we need to grow and when we allow the Lord to help us, we can enjoy our walk with Him and enjoy the fruits of our marriages. Psalm 2:2 says, "Blessed are all they that put their trust in him." I love it when the staff ask, "may we finish what we started?." When a project is completed, they see the campers begin to enjoy that which was very hard work, but there is a satisfaction that they had part in bringing joy to the campers. Let God work in you and in your marriage. You might be going through difficult times, but listen, focus, ask, desire to find, and let God change you and bless you. Life is a continual work in progress. Let God finish His work.

Allowing God to help us grow results in joy and
satisfaction in our walk with Him.

July 3

2 Chronicles 5-6   Psalm 3   Proverbs 3   Revelation 10-11

Stand Tall

Good morning! I love to hear and say the Pledge to our flag. All over the camp are decorations of red, white and blue. Those colors are the colors of our flag, the flag that unites us, causes us to hold our head higher, stand taller each time it passes in a parade. When we hear or say the Pledge, there is something that happens inside of us. As the new temple of God had been built under Solomon's direction, it was now time to bring in the ark in II Chronicles 5. In verse 13 we read that the people "were as one," and in verse 14 "the glory of the Lord had filled the house of God."

I often think what it will be like when all the family of God is together in Heaven and we are one voice singing praise to God. Revelation 10:6 says there will be "time no longer." There will be an end to all this sin on this earth and sorrow will be gone. It is time we as God's army, the people His Son died and shed His blood for, to lift our heads high. Psalm 3:3 says that He is "the lifter up of mine head." The Psalmist wrote in verse 4, "I cried," "he heard me." Proverbs 3:5-6 is still in the Book and should be read often, "Trust in the Lord with all thine heart; and lean not unto thine own understanding. In all thy ways acknowledge him, and he shall direct thy paths." I thank God for America and the patriotism that we have, but much more than that, let us shine forth for the glory of our God so that we fill this earth with His story of redemption for all. Our theme verse this summer at Circle C Baptist Ranch is Romans 1:16, "For I am not ashamed of the gospel of Christ: for it is the power of God unto salvation to every one that believeth;." Stand tall, Christian, hold your head high, lift up your voice, and give praise to the King of Kings.

It is time for we as God's army to lift our heads high!

2 Chronicles 7-8   Psalm 4   Proverbs 4   Revelation 12-13

Standing in Awe

Good morning! Today is July 4th, "Independence Day." Across America there will be parades of all kinds, family get togethers, celebrations, fireworks and much more. I read my Bible this morning and then I went outside and stood awhile. It was dark, no noise except the sound of a few frogs chirping in the nearby pond, but as I looked up to the sky I saw the beauty of the heavens; the storm had passed and the stars seemed to bring a special quietness to the morning.

I read this morning in II Chronicles 7:1 how "the glory of the Lord filled the house." This is the temple that had been finished and the glory of the Lord had so filled the building that in verse 2 we read the "priests could not enter" because the presence of God was so powerful. In verse 1 and 3 we read that "fire came down from heaven" and consumed the sacrifices so powerfully that the house was filled with God's presence. The people heard then and we need to continually hear those words of verse 14, "If my people, which are called by my name, shall humble themselves, and pray, and seek my face, and turn from their wicked ways; then will I hear from heaven, and will forgive their sin, and will heal their land." Revelation 12 reminds us how there will be the day that "the accuser of our brethren" will soon be "cast down."

I stood in the dark and quietness of the morning and meditated on the words I had read in Proverbs 4:4, "Let thine heart retain my words." Today celebrations will come and go, children will run and play, adults will sit and visit, families will be together, quotations and songs will be said and sung about those who gave the ultimate sacrifice for our freedoms. Let us take the time and heed the words of Psalm 4:4, "Stand in awe and sin not." All the freedom we enjoy today and in the days ahead is because of the grace of our Lord. May we "stand in awe" and "humble" ourselves before Him, and "pray" and "seek His "face" and "turn" from our wicked ways.

Listen to these words recorded in Proverbs 4:18, "But the path of the just is as the shining light, that shineth more and more unto the perfect day.

As we enjoy this day of celebration and independence, let us not forget it is because of our God and Him alone. May we "stand in awe" at His greatness, power and glory. Have a blessed day.

All the freedom we enjoy today is because of the grace of God.

July 5

2 Chronicles 9-10   Psalm 5   Proverbs 5   Revelation 14-15

A Servant's Heart

Good morning! It is without doubt that the happiest people have always been, and will always be, serving people. I read in II Chronicles 9:7 this morning and thought about how beautiful were the things that the queen of Sheba saw when king Solomon showed her his riches and all that he had, but when all the beauty had been seen she said in verse 5, "it was a true report;" but then in verse 6 "one half of the greatness of thy wisdom was not told me:." In verse 7 she noticed that above all the beauty; "Happy are thy men, and happy are these thy servants."

This world and all of its riches will soon pass but the joy of learning to serve will shine above all that we can ever attain. In the very next chapter we see that "Rehoboam took counsel with the old men." In verse 6, he was challenged to "be kind, please them, and speak good words." But the last phrase of verse 7 is so very important, "they will be thy servants for ever." Leadership and followship will always be strengthened when there is present the heart to serve. We are living in a time that there is a demand to be served instead of to be the servant. True joy comes from seeing the need, responding to the need, and meeting the need more than being the need.

As I watched and listened to the staff recite words of history yesterday and I watched pictures of soldiers that put their lives on the line, I thought how America has been blessed in victory after victory because America has seen the need to fight, protect and preserve freedom around the world.

Christians that are servants are the happiest people around the world. We read this morning in Revelation 14:13, "their works do follow them." What lasts forever is what we do, not what we receive; what we give, not what we want or demand. Proverbs 5:21, "For the ways of man are before the eyes of the Lord, and he pondereth all his goings." God knows all we do. Selfishness is destructive and serving is satisfying. There is always a place to serve. Step up and be a servant instead of desiring to be served. What the queen saw was beautiful but what was the best was the joy and happiness in the people that served. Be a servant today.

True joy comes from seeing a need, responding to the need, and meeting the need.

July 6

2 Chronicles 11-12   Psalm 6   Proverbs 6   Revelation 16-17

Who is Influencing You?

Good morning! Fellowship with Christian brothers and sisters of like faith and practice is so important. The people that I let influence me can either strengthen me or weaken me and my walk with the Lord. We should be around those that strengthen us in our walk with the Lord. It should be the deep desire of our heart as a Christian to grow more like Christ for all that He has done for us. In II Chronicles 10 we saw the division of the kingdom. In chapter 11 there is preparation to fight each other and in verse 4 we read, "Ye shall not go up, nor fight against your brethren:." I will not always agree with my brethren, so I need to humble myself and walk away. In verse 16 we read the statement, "set their hearts to seek the Lord God." I will not have fellowship with someone that departs from sound doctrine, but I do not have to have battle with them. The most important thing I must continually do is seek the Lord. My strength is a personal walk with God and doing things that strengthen me.

Several times this past week at family camp, I heard testimonies of the friendships that have been made through the years by coming and being with other Christians that are desiring to bring their families to a place where the music is right, the dress is right, and the preaching and teaching of the Word of God helps them to grow. We read in II Chronicles 12:5, "Ye have forsaken me." I am afraid some Christians have so looked at the world that they have lost any desire to maintain a strong growing relationship with Christ. May we take time to stop today, look around us and see what is influencing us. In Proverbs 6 we read of six things the Lord hates, and in verse 19, "A false witness that speaketh lies, and he that soweth discord among brethren." Let us decide today to be a strength to our brethren and not a division or discouragement. That is why it is so important to be at church when the doors are open. We all need it and our lack of discipline, character or wrong influence will keep us from growing in the Lord. The Lord hears our pleas. Psalm 6:8, "the Lord hath heard." Be an encourager today and let someone know that you care with a note, text or call. Invite them to be with you in Sunday School and church. I can hear the choir sing, and what a joy to join in and sing hymns together and grow as we hear the Word of God taught and preached. Make plans on purpose to be in church. See ya soon.

Be a strength to the brethren, not a division or discouragement.

July 7

2 Chronicles 13-14   Psalm 7   Proverbs 7   Revelation 18-19

The Wedding Day

Good morning! I would like to take a look at one simple phrase this morning found in Revelation 19:7, "the marriage of the Lamb is come, and his wife hath made herself ready." This reminds me of a young bride anticipating her wedding day. I remember over 48 years ago as I asked my wife's parents for permission to marry their daughter. How nervous I was and the joy in my heart when they said yes! I purchased an engagement ring and wedding band and asked my soon to be wife to marry me and she said yes. Oh, the joy, the thrill, and excitement of being married to the one I love! My soon to be wife and I began to make plans. We looked at invitations and made a list of those that we wanted to send invitations to;

there was a picture and article placed in the newspaper. So many people were excited for us. The day was fast approaching and so many things had to be done. The few days before the wedding arrived and we worked on the details of making sure of flowers, food, clothing, arrival of the wedding party, etc. I remember the conversation of the hair appointment for my wife to be, the dress, the details.

We that know Christ as our personal Saviour are the bride of Christ. I asked myself this morning and I would like to ask you, what preparations are we making to meet our Saviour, our groom? My wife and I wanted the wedding day to be perfect, just as every couple does. Every detail is checked and rechecked. All couples and families want everything perfect. The day of the wedding is what we have been waiting for.

How about us and the details of our relationship with Christ? Are we checking every detail and making sure that our lives are being lived to please Him? II Chronicles 13:10, "we have not forsaken him." No groom or bride would ever think of forsaking the one they love. In premarital counseling the couple is challenged to do certain things to have a blessed marriage. In II Chronicles 13:11, I read the words, "we keep the charge of the Lord our God." I ask, is our love and detail of wanting everything perfect for our wedding day on earth more important than our preparations to meet our Lord and Saviour who died for us and shed His blood that our sins may be washed away? Let us stop and look at our preparations to meet our Heavenly groom, our Lord, our Saviour. The wedding day is fast approaching.

We need to anticipate and prepare to meet our Heavenly groom.

July 8

2 Chronicles 15-16   Psalm 8   Proverbs 8   Revelation 20-21

God is Right There

Good morning! I do not very often sleep a night through. When I awake, I will listen or sometimes I get up and walk through the house and check to see if everything is ok. Often the dogs are barking at the coyotes or chasing something. I have learned through the years that when

I lay back down, I will begin to pray. I heard a preacher long ago say that when he awakes at night, one of the first things he does is ask the Lord if He wants to talk with him. Some of my greatest waking hours have been spending time with the Lord in the middle of the night.

The summer staff ladies that work in our "Granny's Sweet Shop" in our cowboy town have to meet a dairy truck early in the morning once a week to get the ice cream mix. I knew we had an extra day this week and I often call the ladies as they make their trip to town just to make sure they met the dairy truck and that they are okay. This morning when I woke, I noticed my wife was not in bed, so I quickly got up to check where she was. I could not find her anyplace in the house. I quickly went outside and our car was gone. My heart sank and I got scared. Where is she? I took my phone and tried to call her, but she had left her phone in our kitchen. Fear came all over me and I called the girls that were getting the ice cream and they answered and told me Mrs. Smith was driving them. Mrs. Smith could not sleep, so she got up and took the girls to meet the dairy truck. She did not wake me, as it was 3:15 a.m. I was thankful she was okay. When she got home, I asked her what she was doing and she told me she could not sleep and she wanted to take the girls to meet the dairy truck.

The fear that came across me when I could not find the one I love convicted me as I read this morning in II Chronicles 15:1, "The Lord is with you, while ye be with him; if ye seek him, he will be found of you; but if ye forsake him, he will forsake you." I thought, how many Christians have no idea that they have lost communication and companionship with the Lord? Fear came across me as I could not find my wife. I needed to hear her voice and see her with my eyes. Proverbs 8:6 says, "Hear, for I will speak." When is the last time you had a conversation with God and walked with Him? Proverbs 8:17 says, "I love them that love me; and those that seek me early shall find me." May we stay in constant communication with God. Proverbs 8:35 states, "For whoso findeth me findeth life, and shall obtain favour of the Lord." When my wife walked in the house, there was comfort, peace and assurance that everything was okay. Do not walk in this world without the Lord by your side. He is there but He will not force Himself on us. He wants to be wanted. Take time and tell the Lord that you love Him and want Him and want to walk with Him every day, everywhere. He is there. Do not walk this day without Him by your side.

Have you told God lately that you love Him and want Him by your side?

July 9

2 Chronicles 17-18   Psalm 9   Proverbs 9   Revelation 22

Maturing in Christ

Good morning! This week at camp is a Combo week. There are young people that are in fourth grade all the way up to twelfth grade. That is quite a broad spread of age and maturity. The foolishness of the young campers sometimes frustrates the maturity of the older campers but yesterday at the afternoon activities, I noticed the energy of the youth was a driving force for the mature. Each age looks at life a little differently, but the older were younger one day and the younger will be older soon. I talked with the counselors yesterday about the older campers being the right type of mentors for the younger campers. Proverbs 9:6 says, "Forsake the foolish, and live; and go in the way of understanding. Sometimes the immaturity of the younger camper causes the older camper to not want to be around them. I understand this situation but God does not separate an age or grade level when it comes to a walk and relationship with Him. We are all in a growing process. We do not destroy the young plants because they have not fully developed; we nurture and patiently wait until they mature. Then we can enjoy the fruit or vegetable.

Revelation 22:11 states, "he that is holy, let him be holy." No matter our age, all that have trusted Christ and have been saved are set apart or should be growing in Christ. Each day life is changing as we grow in age and maturity, and this also happens as we read God's Word and spend more time growing in our daily walk. I then thought that if Christ returned today it would not matter our age, we that are saved would be taken out of this world and would be in the presence of our Lord. All of us, no matter our age, are to be holy or set apart and growing in our walk with Christ.

Where are you today? Keep growing. Keep learning. Keep your heart tender to the things of God. As we mature in our walk with Christ, look back over your shoulder and be an encourager to a new Christian. Set the right example of a life given to Christ. Someone took the time to show you the love of Christ and explained to you God's plan of salvation. Also, the younger should be looking at those who have paved the way to live a holy life in Christ. No matter where you are in your walk with Christ, keep walking. Jesus is coming soon.

As you mature in Christ, look back over your shoulder and encourage another.

July 10

2 Chronicles 19-20   Psalm 10   Proverbs 10   Matthew 1-2

Stay Fixed in the Right Direction

Good morning! I often say, stay on the trail and you will get there. Have you ever been on a trip taking a vacation and it seems like you will never get there? You are following your map or now days, following a GPS, and you doubt what you are seeing, reading or hearing. When giving directions to come to camp, I hear people say it seemed so far they thought they had missed their turn, and they make a turn too soon and get lost. Even though you put the correct address in your GPS, you had that feeling that you were not going the right direction.

I am afraid that is what too often happens to us spiritually. We are heading the right direction in our walk with the Lord but we do not stay fixed on the Lord, and the devil gets us to turn down a wrong road in life. There are three phrases I want us to look at in II Chronicles 20 and verse 17 this morning. First, we read to "set yourselves;" stay fixed on the direction you need to be going in your walk with God. As you know, all roads are not straight. There are curves, crossroads and sometimes intersections where we need to make a turn. It is important that we keep our eyes spiritually set on where we should be going.

The next phrase that I want you to look at is, "stand ye still." A camp staff member was sent on an errand one day and I said if you get turned around, stop, give me a call and I will help you. He got lost and called but instead of staying where he told me he was, he kept driving and we looked for him for a long time. He did not stay where I told him to wait. We found him and he made it back to the camp, but it took me longer to find him than needed because he did not stay where I knew he was. Spiritually speaking, stay and stand for what you know is truth and right. When we are following our GPS, we do not see our destination until we arrive, but we must keep going until we do see where we were headed. That brings me to the third statement in verse 17, "see the salvation of the Lord with you." When we "set" ourselves on the right path to walk with God and "stand" without wavering or moving away from God, we will soon "see" His blessings come true in our lives. As you and I head into this day before us, let us "set" ourselves, "stand" firm on what we know is right, and we will soon "see" the Lord bless our lives and labors for Him. Keep your eyes on the destination of pleasing the Lord and you will have a blessed day.

Set yourself, stand firm, and see the Lord bless your life!

July 11

2 Chronicles 21-22   Psalm 11   Proverbs 11   Matthew 3-4

Faithful, Focused and Fervent

Good morning! Several years ago, the Lord led us to a place down in the woods that is very secluded to be able to clear a spot and construct an amphitheater here at the camp. Each morning during the summer time this is where we have a men's split session, and during our week of *Take the Challenge*, this is where our preaching services are held. I have listened to many different preachers preach and teach in this amphitheater. This week as I sat on the bench and listened to one of our preachers, I thought how this particular pastor came as a camper, then a summer staff worker, and now he is a guest preacher and bringing his young people to camp.

I read this morning in Psalm 11:3, "If the foundations be destroyed what can the righteous do?" As I looked at this preacher and listened to him preach with power from God, conviction from his heart and an urgency in his message, my heart was thrilled. In Matthew 4 we read today of the calling of the first disciples in verses 18-25. I wrote in my notes how they left the place they were, stopped doing the work that they were doing, and left the security they had to follow the Lord Jesus. I sat there during the split session and asked the Lord to keep calling young men and women into His service.

I turned this morning to Proverbs 11 and began reading and stopped as I read verses 2-4 and wrote in the margin of my Bible, "Give us a generation that is humble, honest, and hardworking." Jesus was tempted as we are with our flesh, fame and our future and He gained the victory. We read in Matthew 4:11, "Then the devil leaveth him, and, behold, angels came and ministered unto him. The foundations must stand firm for generations to come. We must see the need to keep going for our Lord. Stay faithful, focused and fervent in your life in Christ for the past, present and future generations. The foundations must not be destroyed but built upon. Stand firm for Christ and build on the foundation that has been there for us. Have a blessed day.

The foundations must stand strong and be built upon for future generations.

July 12

2 Chronicles 23-24   Psalm 12   Proverbs 12   Matthew 5

Dealing with Opposites

Good morning! Life is full of choices and most of the time the choices are not hard to make. Think about opposites for a minute. Right versus wrong, good versus evil, up versus down, in versus out, left versus right, heat versus cold and day versus night. They are all connected but different. We read this morning in Psalm 12:1, "Help, Lord." Daily life is full of decisions and most of the time the decisions are far apart but they must be made.

In Matthew 5:11, God says, "Blessed are ye, when men shall revile you, and persecute you, and shall say all manner of evil against you falsely, for my sake." If we can get this Biblical truth in perspective, we will be able to have a closer walk with the Lord. I love a sunrise and I also love a sunset. They are different but they are connected. A new day cannot begin until a day ends. When we find ourselves going through a trial, it will be connected to a victory. A battle can bring a victory. Good can conquer evil. Right can overcome wrong. Look down to verse 44 in Matthew chapter 5, "Love your enemies, bless them that curse you, do good to them that hate you, and pray for them which despitefully use you, and persecute you." Look at the first phrase of verse 45, "That ye may be the children of your Father which is in heaven." The Christian life is a life of constant decisions, and facing these decisions will help us to grow and become closer to the Lord. There is no joy in living in sin. There is no peace in not doing right. We need to face the opposites today and have victory in our lives. We will never have the victory until we face the battle. We will not see the break of day until the night is past. Get past what is keeping you from the joy of living for Christ. Get past what is defeating you and walk in victory. Sorrow helps us to understand joy. Walking in the light of the Lord helps us to see the darkness of sin. A trial helps us to look for the victory. Deal with the opposites of this day. The sun will not bring forth the beauty of a flower unless the storm brings the rain. There will never be the birth of the beautiful baby without the travail of delivery. The song writer was right when he wrote, "joy cometh in the morning." Deal with the opposites today. Do what is right. Turn from sin and walk in victory today.

We will never have the victory until we face the battle.

July 13

2 Chronicles 25-26   Psalm 13   Proverbs 13   Matthew 6-7

A Hunger for God

Good morning! For many years I have watched as young people have pulled out of camp with a smile on their face and joy in their hearts.

My heart is always blessed when a young person yields their heart and life to the Lord and His will for their life. I often ask myself, what could we have done more to help this person prepare for the return to their home? In II Chronicles 26:5 we read, "as long as he sought the Lord, God made him to prosper." In verse 7, "God helped him;" verse 8, "he strengthened himself exceedingly." Oh, that we would learn to walk with God, stay right with God and seek Him in everything that we do! In Matthew 6-7, we read through the Sermon on the Mount where Jesus taught how God provides for the animals, and then teaches how to pray, the importance of prayer, and the results of prayer.

Have we become like a dog that is obedient to its master when that dog knows it will get a treat? Do we hunger for God only when we are wanting something from Him? A dog will wag their tail when they see their master because they know they will be fed, watered, petted and talked kindly to. I have noticed how my dogs will follow me wherever I go just to be with me. Every morning when I go out to the front porch, the dogs are there. Does a dog understand loyalty more than a human that has received salvation from God? A dog is loyal, faithful, and when rewarded, obedient.

Matthew 7:20 says, "by their fruits ye shall know them." As the campers pull out of the gate, our prayer is that they have been strengthened in their walk with the Lord so that they will have a love in their heart to live, serve and be faithful to the Lord in a greater way than when they came. The more time I spend with my dogs, the more obedient they are to me. They do not understand the language that I speak but they do understand the provision I provide, the attention I give and the affection I show. Has not God done so much more for us? Psalm 13:6, "he hath dealt bountifully with me." A camper goes home having been away from the world and its influences and we try to give them a refreshing time to strengthen them in the Lord. Spend time with the Lord and enjoy Him. Let God love you today and listen to His voice.

Spending time with God will strengthen us in Him.

2 Chronicles 27-28   Psalm 14   Proverbs 14   Matthew 8-9

Every Need Met

Good morning! My wife and I have been observing a robin's nest. Each summer a new nest is built in this same place. As spring arrived and then the weeks of summer rolled by, we saw the nest being built and then the female robin spending time laying the eggs. How did I know the eggs were there? I looked but did not touch. Two days ago, I noticed a male robin sitting with a worm in his beak. He sat on the power line for the longest time and then he flew to the nest and brought the worm. He not only brought one worm but he made several trips with a worm each time.

All of us have needs and our God wants to and will meet those needs. I am afraid it is almost always our faith that is lacking. In Matthew 8 we read about many miracles that the Lord did for the needy. Look at the requests of the people. Verses 2-3, "If thou wilt," and the Lord said, "I will." In verse 7 a servant is home sick, and the Lord said, "I will come." In verse 13 we read, "as thou hast believed," so be it done unto thee." Matthew 9:2, "seeing their faith," and in verse 22, "thy faith hath made thee whole." In Matthew 9:35, Jesus was "healing every sickness and every disease among the people."

If two robins can build a nest, have babies, and be fed by God without any problem, what can God do for those that He loves and died for? Proverbs 14:30 says, "A sound (content) heart is the life of the flesh." It is time for us to take a fresh look at God's love and provision for us. We need to have a revival in our faith in God. Psalm 14:1, "The fool hath said in his heart, There is no God." More robins will be flying soon because God took care of them, provided for them and they will soon be singing praises to God. Brother and sister in Christ, look up! Our Redeemer has not left us or forsaken us. Have faith in God today.

Take a fresh look at God's love and provision and revive your faith in Him.

July 15

2 Chronicles 29-30   Psalm 15   Proverbs 15   Matthew 10

A Clean Heart

Good morning! Each week before a camp activity I go into all the camper cabins and spend time praying, asking the Lord for His presence and to work in the hearts of each camper. Last night I spent time going through and praying in each cabin because we have two churches that drove through the night so they can get to camp early. As I was going through each cabin, I was so thankful for the ladies staff that works so hard to clean the cabins. As I looked at the mowed and trimmed grass yesterday morning, I thanked the Lord for the men's staff and their hard work in keeping the property looking good. If we never cleaned the buildings or never mowed and trimmed the lawn, the camp would not look the same even though it is the same. I remember my dad saying when we washed the family car that it would run better, last longer, look better and we would appreciate it longer.

That is the same with our lives as the Lord's people. When we keep our hearts clean from sin, we have joy in our heart and a better spirit and a desire to serve the Lord. In II Chronicles 29:15, orders were given to "cleanse the house of the Lord." In verse 16 we read, "to cleanse it, brought out all the uncleanness," and to "carry it out abroad." The campers' cabins can be used dirty or clean but the campers have a better attitude and spirit when they are clean. We teach the staff the importance of keeping the tables in the Dining Hall in alignment and clean, as well as the good spirit it sets when the chairs are all straight and in order. When things are in order in our lives, we have a better attitude and we have a better spirit about things. Sin in our lives discourages us, causes us to have a bad attitude and we do not see any need to serve the Lord. When our lives are free from sin, we can enjoy our walk with God, carry a burden for others and have a greater desire and willingness to serve the Lord.

In Matthew 10:8, Jesus told the disciples to "Heal the sick, cleanse the lepers, raise the dead, cast out devils." It is all about God cleansing a life and making it free from sin. When we wash the car, it looks better, seems to run better and we enjoy it more. The buildings are the same buildings when they are clean or when they are dirty, but the campers have a better time, the buildings look better and they last longer when we spend the time cleaning and repairing them. Psalm 15:2, "He that walketh uprightly, and worketh righteousness, and speaketh the truth in his heart" does make a difference. Jump down to verse 5, "He that doeth these things shall never be moved." Being clean does make a difference, inwardly and outwardly. Let us keep a clean heart and watch the difference on the outside. What I fill myself with on the inside does make a difference on the outside. Dad was right, when I take care of something, it does cause it to last longer and I enjoy using it more.

Cleanliness does make a difference, inwardly and outwardly.

July 16

2 Chronicles 31-32   Psalm 16   Proverbs 16   Matthew 11

Do You Understand?

Good morning! In this morning's reading in Proverbs 16, some simple and yet powerful statements and words caught my eye. How many times have we heard or said to someone or a group, "Do you understand?" This question has been asked in teaching instruction by teachers, parents, pastors, by leaders of all kinds. Do you understand? I have some information that I want you to get and not only get it, but I want you to use it or be aware of what I am telling you.

In verse 16 of Proverbs 16 we read, "How much better is it to get wisdom than gold! and to get understanding rather to be chosen than silver!" I looked up the word wisdom and it is defined as *the right use or exercise of knowledge.* The definition of understanding is *to know the meaning of what is being said.* God said to have wisdom and understanding is better than the precious metals of gold and silver. We read God's Word, we hear the Bible taught and preached and we do not comprehend what God is saying, and we do not apply it to our daily lives. I believe that all of us who are saved want the Lord's blessing on our lives, marriages and service for Him. I asked myself this morning, do I listen to God when He speaks and do I understand and apply it to my daily life? How often have we said to children, "Do you understand what I am saying?" and "How come you did not do what I said to do?" This truth challenges me today to be more aware of what God is saying when I read my Bible and listen more closely to preaching and teaching. This truth today that we have read not only challenges me to be a better listener, but to also spend more timing applying and living the truths that I am hearing and learning. "Get wisdom, Get understanding;" it is better than some of the finest metals in the world and worth a whole lot more. Do you understand?

Listen closely, apply and live the truths that are preached and taught.

July 17

2 Chronicles 33-34   Psalm 17   Proverbs 17   Matthew 12

Stand to It

Good morning! There are things that I wish I had learned when I was younger. I did not pay attention, I saw little or no importance, I did not think I would ever use the information; I just wanted to get past this time and go on to what I enjoyed doing or what I thought was important.

Proverbs 17:24 says, "Wisdom is before him that hath understanding." As I read this morning in II Chronicles 34, my heart was once again convicted that I have let so much spiritually pass me by which I should have learned as a younger man. We read in verse 1 that Josiah was only eight years old when he began to reign. So young, and yet so wise. How did this happen? Verse 3 says, "he began to seek after the God of David." That is a good place for all of us to start no matter our age. When we put the Lord first and seek His will, we will be convicted of sin. We will want to be clean and right with God, His Word will come alive to us, and in our response, there will be a desire to serve the Lord. As I read on down through the chapter, in verse 24 we read, "thine heart was tender" and this tenderness of heart brought humility. Oh, we might be a lot older than eight years of age but we can still keep a "tender" heart to "seek" the Lord.

You have heard the phrase, "get to it," which means get busy, quit standing around, you know what to do. Well, we read this morning in verse 32 to "stand to it." It is time each day that we live to "seek" after God, "purge" our hearts from sin that tempts us or already controls us and "humble" ourselves before God. In Psalm 17:15 there is a wake up call; "I shall be satisfied, when I awake, with thy likeness." No matter our age today, there is peace, joy, satisfaction and fullness of life when we walk after the Lord, keep His commandments, and "perform" (serve Him). Look at verse 31 of II Chronicles 34 and "stand to it" today. Live victoriously in Christ today. Thank the Lord it does not matter our age or stage of life, God is ready and waiting to use us if we seek His face and humble ourselves before Him. Have a blessed day.

Always keep a tender heart to be used of the Lord.

July 18

2 Chronicles 35-36   Psalm 18:1-15   Proverbs 18   Matthew 13

May We Never Forget

Good morning! I have heard many stories and read many books about great revivals and how the power of God came down in a service like never before. To describe a service where the presence of God was and the Spirit of God was working is an impossible task.

I read in Matthew 13:17 this morning, "men have desired to see those things which ye see." Last night's chapel service was a service like that. God moved in an indescribable way. I read this morning also in II Chronicles 35:1, "Moreover Josiah kept a Passover." You see, this was a time for the people to remember when they were held captive in Egypt. The death angel of the Lord passed over and the angel saw the blood of the lambs and the people of God were able to be set free from the bondage of Egypt. In verse 6 of this chapter, we see the people were told to "sanctify yourselves," set yourselves apart unto the Lord; and then they were to "prepare your brethren." It is time we encourage others that are saved to live for God and His Glory.

As I continued to read in verse 6 there was the little phrase, "that they may do." Do what? Serve the Lord! Oh, that we would never forget what God has done for us. He saved us and set us apart for Him. The Psalmist in Psalm 18:1 said, "I will love thee, O Lord, my strength, my rock, my fortress, my deliverer, my God, my buckler, the horn of my salvation, my high tower." We must stop daily and evaluate our love for God and our love for what He did for us and all mankind. Praise Him today for who He is, serve Him today for what He did, and be faithful to Him for what He is preparing for us. Shout it today, HE IS MY GOD!!!!!! Have a blessed day in the Lord.

We must daily evaluate our love for God and never forget His love for us!

July 19

Ezra 1-2   Psalm 18:16-36   Proverbs 19   Matthew 14

Living by Principle

Good morning! I am so thankful every day that God loves me even though I am so unlovely. I am not speaking of outward appearance, but of my sinful heart. As "the Lord stirred up the spirit of Cyrus" (Ezra 1:1) to restore the temple of God, I hunger for God to keep me stirred for His cause in my life. We must live by principle with purpose - principles to know right from wrong by reading and applying the Scriptures, principles for our lives personally, principles for our marriages and for training our children, principles to stand for in an ever-changing world that is denying Christ and going in every direction except toward Him.

As we read this morning in Psalm 18:16-21, we see in verse 16 how "He took me" as I was a sinner with no hope, "He drew me" unto Him with His love, "He delivered me" from the depths of my sin, and the "Lord rewarded me" with a new life to serve Him. May it be said of us today as we read verse 21, "For I have kept the ways of the Lord, and have not wickedly departed from my God." Do not forget all that He has done for us. When campers walk up and thank me for a week of camp, I feel so unworthy because all that made their week special is what God did, not me or our staff. We just gave Him our life and asked our Lord to use us.

Have you allowed the Lord who saved you the permission to use you? As you and I have accepted His gift of salvation, have we in turn given our lives to serve Him? It is stated very well in Psalm 18:30 and 32, "As for God, his way is perfect: the word of the Lord is tried: he is a buckler to all those that trust in him. It is God that girdeth me with strength, and maketh my way perfect." He is my Lord; I must serve Him.

Give your life to serve God and never forget what He's done for you.

July 20

Ezra 3-4   Psalm 18:37-50   Proverbs 20   Matthew 15

What is Your Motivation?

Good morning! I would like to ask a series of questions this morning. Why should we serve God? Why do some quit after they have been serving? Why do some Christians decide to serve God their entire life? What is our motive in serving God? Let me take time and say that serving God is not a position and it is not a task. Serving God is having a heart for the work of God and doing whatever we have to do to reach the multitudes.

In Ezra 3, the people were daily, morning and evening, offering the "burnt offerings." Verse 8 says, they "set forward" the work of God, and in verse 12 the older men were so blessed to see the work of God going forward and the people working together that the "shout of joy" (verses 12-13) "was heard afar off." Then in chapter 4 we see the work was stopped by those outside. It was a worldly distraction from outside the people of God.

As I read this morning in Matthew 15, I saw the word "multitude" mentioned six times. I thought about how there have always been a remnant of God's people that have been moved by God to keep going forward. The word motive means "that which determines the choice or moves the will." Motivation is putting into action the motive. As Christians, we need to look at the multitudes without Christ that will go to Hell for eternity if they are not reached with the gospel. That is exactly why there are those that keep serving for a lifetime. It is because they took their eyes off themselves and were motivated by the multitudes.

It is our spirit that is moved by God for God. Proverbs 20:27, "The spirit of man is the candle of the Lord." May our motive be for Christ because we see the lost multitudes. It takes all of us doing whatever we can to reach a lost world for Christ. All of us can do something and whatever that something is, we must keep doing it and train another generation to see the multitudes. Our motive and motivation to live a life for Christ must be reaching the multitudes in our neighborhoods, cities, states and around the world. Matthew 15:32, "Then Jesus called his disciples unto him, and said, I have compassion on the multitude." What is your motivation today?

Having a vision for lost multitudes should be
our motivation for serving Christ.

July 21

Ezra 5-6   Psalm 19   Proverbs 21   Matthew 16-17

God Knows Best

Good morning! As I was reading my Bible this morning and seeing the miracles of God printed for us to read and remember in the Scriptures, I stopped and wrote on a piece of paper: "Nothing will stop what God wants done." In our reading today, God moved the heart of several kings and the temple was rebuilt.

We should learn that God is always in control of all of life's situations. The important thing for us to always do is to learn what God wants, do what God wants, and always be faithful living in God's will. Matthew 16:24 teaches, "If any man will come after me (doing God's will), "let him deny himself" (put what God wants first), "take up his cross" (face every situation in life with God's strength and grace), "follow me" (stay true and faithful to God no matter what circumstances or situations arise).

In our flesh, we often question God and become hardened to Him and His voice. Proverbs 21:1, "A wicked man hardeneth his face: but as for the upright, he directeth his way." We must not think that we know better than God. Proverbs 21:30, "There is no wisdom nor understanding nor counsel against the Lord." There is peace, joy and strength in walking with God. Psalm 19:14 "Let the words of my mouth, and the meditation of my heart, be acceptable in thy sight, O Lord, my strength, and my redeemer." We need to decide every day that God knows best and He will get His way. There is joy and peace in serving Him. When we have our hearts broken, His grace is always there for us. I wish we could sing together this morning, "'Tis So Sweet to Trust in Jesus." The last verse says, "I'm so glad I learned to trust Him, Precious Jesus, Savior, Friend; And I know that Thou art with me, Wilt be with me to the end." Sing the chorus, "Jesus, Jesus, how I trust Him! How I've proved Him o'er and o'er! Jesus, Jesus, precious Jesus! O for grace to trust Him more! Have a blessed day.

Decide every day God knows best and He will get His way.

July 22

Ezra 7-8   Psalm 20   Proverbs 22   Matthew 18

Which Way to Turn?

Good morning! Have you ever felt like you have come to a "T" in the road and you do not know which way to turn? Yesterday my wife and I were driving to try and find a new hiking area that I might want to take some boys hiking during our *Take the Challenge* camp. The signs were not clear for directions and we came to a "T" in the road. I had two decisions to make; turn left or turn right. Which is the right way? The decision was made when we looked at the map on our phone. There was a source that was there in our hand that would help us know which way to turn.

Ezra 7:5 tells us Ezra was a "ready scribe in the law of Moses." He knew the Word of God. The Word of God was his source of authority, his source of guidance, and he had confidence in it to follow it. In verse 10 we see he "prepared his heart to seek the law of the Lord, and to do it." We come to so many "T's" in life and we turn the wrong direction because we think we know what is best and we do not stick with our source of direction, the Word of God. Matthew 18:4, "Whosoever therefore shall humble himself as this little child, the same is greatest in the kingdom of heaven." We all have watched a child hang on to their parent because of the protection of the parent. Psalm 20 gives us a perfect map for walking with the Lord. When we do not know what to do or which way to turn, "The Lord hear thee in the day of trouble" (verse 1), He will then (verse 2) "Send thee help." When we seek his face instead of trying to figure out which way to go and we ask, He will "Grant thee" (verse 4). As we read on in Psalm 20, we see in verse 5 how the Lord will "fulfil all thy petitions," when we "remember the name of the Lord our God" (verse 6). Christian, do not give up, do not quit. Verse 8 challenges us to "stand upright." Yes, there will always be "T's" in the road of life and there will be blessings of the Lord when we turn in the direction of the authority of the Word of God. We are living in a time when people are doing what they want, how they want and when they want. God's Word has always been there to guide us and lead us. Each of us will come to the end of the trail someday. I personally want to be blessed by the Lord and not face a lot of regrets for not turning in the right direction and serving the King of Kings who has given me life eternal. Which way have you been turning at the "T's" in your life?

The Word of God is our source of true guidance and direction in life.

July 23

Ezra 9-10   Psalm 21   Proverbs 23   Matthew 19

What Principles Guide You?

Good morning! When we were all young there were principles that we were taught that were guidelines to live by. I looked up the word *principle* this morning. The definition goes as follows: "the cause, source or origin of any thing." It is why a person believes what they believe and lives what they believe. We read in Ezra 9 how the remnant had lost their separation. Verse 2 says, "holy seed have mingled themselves with the people of those lands." Sin does not and will never mix with righteousness. God's Word teaches us principles of God, given by God, for us to live by. In verse 6 of Ezra 9, Ezra says, "I am ashamed and blush to lift up my face to thee." We need to constantly be growing in God's principles to live by. Proverbs 23:5, "Wilt thou set thine eyes upon that which is not?" We keep looking at the world and desire to be like them. When we received Christ, we were to step away from sin and that which was destroying us. Ezra told the people in Ezra 10:11, "separate yourselves" and in the very next verse, "As thou hast said, so must we do."

It is so important for those in an operating room in the hospital to keep things sterile and sanitary. Can you imagine going in for surgery and the doctors and nurses not being washed and clothed in clean garments? Can you imagine the doctors using instruments that had not been cleaned and sterilized? Sin of this world does not mix with holiness of God. The problem is we have not sought the principles of God and we have done what is right in the eyes of the world. As Christians, we are to be living to honor Christ. Ezra stated the problem this way in Ezra 9:2, "holy seed have mingled themselves with the people of those lands." Can you hear the words of the old man of God, "separate yourselves"? Proverbs 23:23 states, "Buy the truth." There is no peace in not being right with God. Ezra fell on his face before God and said, "I am ashamed." May God shame us today, for He is holy and we should desire to be like Him. I love to use the quote of the old preacher, "I do not know much, but what I do know I know real good." Live by God's principles. Walk in the guidance of God's Word. Learn how a Christian is to live and let us bring honor to God through all areas of our lives. Live by principle.

Sin of this world does not mix with the holiness of God.

July 24

Nehemiah 1-2   Psalm 22:1-21   Proverbs 24   Matthew 20

A Team Effort

Good morning! Do you remember hearing the statement, "We have too many chiefs and not enough Indians"? As I was reading today in Matthew 20, I read down to verses 26-28 and I kept rereading part of verse 26, "whosoever will be chief among you, let him be your servant."

Yesterday during *Take the Challenge* camp, it was time to get our camp sites set up. Since the fellows are only here for a week and our time in the woods is so short, we have wood cut up of dead trees and have it stacked someplace so they can go get it and have firewood for their fires. I suggested to the leaders to have the fellows go two by two and when those two get back, send two more and keep going until all the fellows in the group share in bringing back firewood. I noticed right away two groups had more wood than the third group. I watched and noticed that not all the boys were taking turns going down a hill to the stack of wood and bringing their share back up. They were expecting someone else to carry the wood.

As we read in Nehemiah chapters 1-2 this morning, we see that Nehemiah is so moved to get the wall rebuilt, but notice how he shared his burden with others, "some few men" in verse 12 of chapter 2. Look down to verses 17-20 and look how often the words "we" and "us" are used. In just about everything in life, it takes a team effort. A good marriage must have both partners working together. A good home will have all family members working together. A good Sunday School class has all the members inviting others to come and when needs are seen, all will pray and see what they can do to help the one in need. Just about everything we do in life takes a team effort. The baseball team is not only about the pitcher; it takes the whole team. Do we only see our needs or are we focusing on the needs that are around us? Nehemiah carried a burden but he knew he needed a team. Yes, some have a greater ability in leading, but it still takes all of us working together to complete the task, reach the goal, build the class. There is no choir without members singing together. There is no church without people coming together. I love the words in Nehemiah 2:20, "The God of heaven, he will prosper us; therefore we his servants will arise and build:." Whatever team, group, class, that you are part of, participate and focus on being a servant instead of letting everybody else carry the burden. We can lift a heavier load if we all lift together. Let us do our part so we all serve together.

Focus on being a servant instead of letting others carry the burden.

July 25

Nehemiah 3-4   Psalm 22:22-31   Proverbs 25   Matthew 21

Training Another Generation

Good morning! Each time I read the passage in Nehemiah 3, I love the words,"they builded" or the words, "next unto him." As I sat by a fire last evening camping with the young men from *Take the Challenge* Camp, I thought of another generation learning and working together. As the wall began to be built, the enemies came. Enemies will always come to question, create doubt, discourage and, if possible, stop the work of God. The devil and his workers will try to stop every generation that tries to live and serve God.

I am challenged to keep teaching and working and striving to keep on as I read in Nehemiah 4:14 the challenge to stand your ground and stay in your place. Listen to those words that have been said to generation after generation who have taken a stand and decided to fight, preserve and train another generation. "Fight for your brethren, your sons, your daughters, your wives, and your houses." Our faith in God, His Word and His gift of salvation must be spread to every generation. Psalm 22:31 speaks of "a people that shall be born." Matthew 21:21, "have faith and doubt not," and verse 22, "whatsoever ye shall ask in prayer, believing, ye shall receive."

I sat by the fire last night and I looked to my left and there sat a husband, father; a man that I have watched grow in the Lord from his teen years, and to my right I saw a young boy, one of my grandsons. Before my very eyes was a fire burning and a reflection on three men of different ages, generations going forth for the same purpose - to live, serve, stand for the King of Kings. Let us in our generation live for God and train another generation that will do the same. As those men in the days of Nehemiah stood building and repairing the wall, there were boys watching and ready to come forth and do their part. May we set an example for another generation. Someone is watching today to see if we will stand in our place, do the work that is before us and live for God to the end. May our hearts be challenged afresh and anew for God to stand, train and preserve for our God and His Glory. "They builded" and "they repaired."

Someone is watching today to see if we will live for God to the end.

July 26

Nehemiah 5-6   Psalm 23   Proverbs 26   Matthew 22

The Comfort of God's Word

Good morning! Every morning as I read the Bible, my heart becomes so full. I wish that I could glean the wisdom that is there for us in every word that I read. I read this morning in Nehemiah 6:3 the words, "I am doing a great work." In Matthew 22:32, "God is not the God of the dead, but of the living," and in Proverbs 26 we read about a "fool" and about being "slothful." The Bible is so full of wisdom, guidance, challenge and so much more for our daily life.

When I began to read Psalm 23 there was a rest in my heart, a peace, a comfort. So often we get so caught up in the things that we do and we miss the simple things that can help us in our daily struggles. Look at just four things in Psalm 23. Verse one, "I shall not want" (God can keep me satisfied), verse 4, "for thou art with me" (God is always present), verse 5, "thou preparest a table" and "my cup runneth over" (my needs are always met), verse 6, "surely goodness and mercy shall follow me all the days of my life" (God will be with me all of my days).

What a comfort and encouragement God can be through His Word! The more time I spend reading, meditating, memorizing God's Word, the more I love my walk with Him. Stop before the day starts and enjoy some time just sitting with God. Let His presence be there with you and enjoy His comfort. Have a blessed day.

The Bible has everything we need for guidance, comfort, and encouragement.

July 27

Nehemiah 7-8   Psalm 24   Proverbs 27   Matthew 23

Never Locked Out

Good morning! Have you ever locked yourself out of the house? This week I walked out of the house and accidentally locked the door. I have no idea how I did it, but the door was locked. I went to the front door and the deck door and the windows, and all of them were locked. My wife did not have her keys and even our car and truck keys were safely locked in the house. We were completely locked out from everything that we needed. Our clothes were inside, our identification was inside, everything we use to function with was inside. We looked at each other and said, what are we going to do? I did apologize and we both said we need to have another key placed somewhere in case this happens again. We were locked out and our lives were affected in many areas.

I read this morning in Nehemiah chapters 7-8, how the people were gathered together and listened as the Word of God was read. In chapter 8:17, "And there was very great gladness;" the Word of God had been lost and when it was found it was read, the people stood, they said "Amen, Amen." They understood and their lives were strengthened. The Bible is there for us to read, study, apply to our daily lives. The church doors are open for us to learn the Word of God and help us in our daily lives, to learn how to live, serve and be the Christians that the Lord wants us to be. Are we living like we are locked out?

We could do nothing until the door got opened. Praise the Lord we got the door open with the help of others. We are not locked out of the Word of God. We need to open it and walk right in every day and enjoy the fullness of its richness. There was a thrill in our hearts when we walked in and the door was open. Walk through today into the wide-open door of the Word of God and make sure you walk through the door of the house of God every time it is opened. You and I are never locked out from being with God.

The Word of God is wide open for us to enjoy the fullness of its riches.

July 28

Nehemiah 9-10   Psalm 25   Proverbs 28   Matthew 24

Are You Watching?

Good morning! Our Scriptures today are full of references to watching for the return of our Lord and the rapture of the church. In Nehemiah 9 we read of the new commitment of God's people because of all He allowed them to do. The remembering of His covenant caused them to "make a sure covenant" in verse 38. I like the promise that the leaders signed, and the Scriptures say they made a "seal unto it." Their signature was a "sure" promise to God. Chapter 10 shows us in verses 35-39 how they brought their "firstfruits" and "tithes" unto the Lord. We need to be committed like these people by also saying, "we will not forsake the house of our God."

I read in Matthew 24 down through the chapter of the caution to watch the signs that are now being shown for the coming of the Lord. Matthew 24:42, "Watch therefore: for ye know not what hour your Lord doth come." I ask the question this morning, is a dog more faithful to its master even though the dog has no soul, than a Christian who has a soul and an eternal home being prepared for them? I can leave the camp and run an errand into town and when I return the dogs run to meet me because they are watching for my return. The campers are gone, the cabins are empty, most of the summer staff has returned home; and the dogs still lay on the front porch of the Dining Hall where they daily met the campers. How can a dog be more faithful than us?

Psalm 25:15, "Mine eyes are ever toward the Lord." Be looking up and be living for Him. He is returning. What will He find you doing?

What will you be doing when the Lord returns?

Nehemiah 11-13   Psalm 26   Proverbs 29   Matthew 25

Daily Evaluation

Good morning! Summer has ended, the cabins are empty, no one is buying ice cream at "Granny's Sweet Shop," the chatter of young people talking is not heard, the tether ball just hangs still from the pole, the activity field is empty, the swimming pool and water slide are cleaned and put away. Each summer I walk and drive through the camp and try to remember each week and the blessings of God. Lives were changed, souls were saved, hearts were stirred, young people surrendered to God's will for their lives. It was a tremendous summer. It is time to reflect and plan again, go forward to the fall and winter retreats.

As I read Psalm 26 this morning, I noticed a series of words in verses 1-2, "Judge me, examine me, prove me, try my reins and my heart." As I pondered the meaning of each word, I thought of the importance of daily evaluation of our lives personally, looking deep in our hearts and seeing if there is anything that keeps us from having a fulfilling relationship with the Lord.

Every week a camper sits through eight messages, three split sessions, four flagpole devotions and four evening devotions in the cabins, as well as four daily devotional sheets and memorizing new verses from their devotional sheets. I believe it would help our relationship and walk with the Lord if we daily asked the Lord to look deep inside of us and asked Him to judge, examine, prove and try our hearts. As a camper goes home stronger and closer to God in their walk, what could the Lord do in and through us if we would allow Him to daily do a thorough examination?

Jesus is coming again. In Matthew 25:15, we are challenged to "Watch therefore, for ye know neither the day nor the hour wherein the Son of man cometh." We need to be ready every day for the Lord to come. How will the Lord find you when He returns? Let us daily take time to evaluate where we are in our relationship to Christ and in serving Him. The Lord bless you.

What could God do with us if we allowed Him
to do a daily, thorough examination?

July 30

Esther 1-2   Psalm 27   Proverbs 30   Matthew 26

Intentions or Actions?

Good morning! This morning my mind went back to November in 1963. I was in the 7th grade and sitting in English class, when over the loudspeaker our principal made an announcement and said we need to pray. I remembered that day as I read this morning the words that Judas said to the chief priests when he was willing to betray the Lord Jesus. In Matthew 26:15, we read, "What will ye give me . . ?." Just ten verses down in verse 25, Jesus has been talking about the one that will betray Him, and Judas says, "Master, is it I?."

President Kennedy said, "Ask not what your country can do for you, but ask what you can do for your county." That day as I sat in English class the principal said President Kennedy had been shot. A hush went not only across the classroom but the school, our town and our whole country was in shock. Just a few verses later Jesus had asked the disciples to "sit, tarry, watch," and yet they slept. He was betrayed and in verse 56 we read, "Then all the disciples forsook him, and fled."

We live in such a selfish time when we hear so often the words, "What do I get out of it?" or "What is in it for me?" or "I get nothing out of it." I am afraid the Christian life to many is not what we can do for Christ, but what we think Christ should do for us. When we think about how Christ gave all for us, how can we do nothing for Him? We might have good intentions, but intentions mean nothing if they do not become actions. I think we need to begin today a reverse action and say, "What can I do for Christ today?." How about starting with action instead of just intention? Have a blessed day serving the Lord.

Intentions mean nothing if they do not become actions.

July 31

Esther 3-4   Psalm 28   Proverbs 31   Matthew 27

Observing or Serving?

Good morning! I never know who is reading these morning thoughts, but I pray daily that they are used of the Lord to help us in our daily walk with Christ. There is so much in God's Word to help us daily, if we just spend the time and read His Word.

This morning in Matthew 27, we read about the path to the cross and the crucifixion of Christ. Each time I read these similar passages in the four Gospels, my heart is so convicted that Christ died for me. In verses 26-39 we see the chain of events. They "scourged Jesus, stripped him, platted a crown of thorns, mocked him, spit upon him, took the reed and smote him on the head, reviled him, wagging their heads." As I finished reading about all they did to Him, I went back to a phrase in verse 36, "they watched him there." My heart broke as I asked myself this morning, am I just watching? He went through all He did for me. As they watched, the sky blackened, the veil was rent, "the earth did quake, rocks rent, graves were opened." They that were watching said, "Truly this was the Son of God."

Oh, that we would right now get on our faces and thank Him for so great a salvation and get up off our knees and not be found merely watching, but get busy daily serving Him. We become so independent of Him and we need to say as the Psalmist wrote in Psalm 28:7-8, "The Lord is my strength and my shield; my heart trusted in him, and I am helped: The Lord is their strength, and he is the saving strength of his anointed." Let us not just be watching but living for Him and serving Him. Let us not just observe but serve.

Are we just watching or are we busy serving Him?

Esther 5-6   Psalm 29   Proverbs   1 Matthew 28

Access to the King

Good morning! I watched the other night as a person who was recently saved stood at the edge of the baptistry. Fear came over them as they watched a person get baptized before them. Throughout the years I have seen this scene often. A person gets saved and then they know they need to be baptized and a fear comes over them. My wife had a lady and man sitting next to her one evening. They were our guests and both had been saved and they were going to follow the Lord in obedience and be baptized. At the end of the message the lady jumped up and walked out. What fear today controls you and could be keeping you from doing exactly what you know the Lord wants you to do?

In Esther chapter 5, Esther faced a great fear and possible death when she knew she had to go before the king and she had not been called by the king. In the first eight verses we see two words that I want to take a look at, the words "petition" and "request." By approaching the king without his request could be death. If we go back to verse two, we see that "she obtained favour in his sight;" she had his approval to come forward. Then she made her "request" (act of asking politely) and then her "petition" (formal request with respect to a cause and position). How wonderful it is to read how God brought a great miracle that day and the king listened.

God is waiting for us to come to Him today. He is there waiting. He is not dead or deaf. We can approach Him. In Matthew 28:5-6, we have these wonderful words from the angel, "Fear not ye, for I know that ye seek Jesus, which was crucified. He is not here: for he is risen." Glory be to the KING! Do not live in fear or sorrow today. Do not live in discouragement. We read today in Psalm 29:11, "The Lord will give strength unto his people; the Lord will bless his people with peace." Even more so than for Esther, we can freely approach our KING any time and from anywhere. He has made a way for us to approach HIM and that is because of the gift of salvation to all who believe. Quit living in fear and take your fear, burden, frustration, discouragement or whatever it is to our KING. He will listen and He will answer. Go to Him now. Through His Son's blood we have obtained favour. He is waiting to hear your petition and your request.

We can freely approach our King any time and from anywhere.

August 2

Esther 7-8   Psalm 30   Proverbs 2   Mark 1

A Child of the King

Good morning! In Esther 7, the banquet was prepared and the king came right along with Haman the accuser. My reading stopped in Esther this morning and I thought about Revelation 12 where we read that the devil accuses us before God. The devil will never be happy, so his wickedness drives him on, and yet one day the sin and sorrow of this world will be stopped in an even greater way than Esther, Mordecai and all the Jews experienced that day. Haman was hanged, just as the devil will soon be cast into Hell. Esther 8:3 records for us how Esther "spake yet again before the king, and fell down at his feet, and besought him with tears."

We must never forget that Jesus is continually pleading for us and reminding our Heavenly Father that His blood was shed for our sins. The king had the scribes write into law letters letting all know that the Jews were free. My heart was thrilled as I looked at my Bible and thought how God's Word has been given and it is sealed in Heaven, so that all those who are saved are free from the destruction of sin. My heart was convicted afresh today for missions as I read in Esther 8:9 that the letter was sent "unto every people after their language." Mordecai went before the king and in 8:15 he was given "royal apparel" by the king.

Rejoice today, Christian brother and sister! We are children of the KING and we have been washed clean and we are a "royal priesthood." (I Peter2:9) We read in Mark 1:17 the call to "Come ye after me" and in verse 18 the word "straightway," meaning they were not begged but came and followed Jesus right after the first call. Rejoice today that your sins are forgiven as far as the east is from the west and we are a "royal priesthood." The Word of God is in print and is being taken to all people and languages. We need to quit looking at the gallows and start rejoicing that we are free and we have the seal of the King of Kings. Psalm 30:11, "Thou hast turned for me my mourning into dancing." Get busy today! We are free, the fate of Satan is sealed and a home is being prepared in Heaven. Rejoice and spread the Word to every nation and to every language that Jesus loves them and has paid the price in full. Quit looking at the gallows and get your eyes on the KING. Keep serving.

Get your eyes off the gallows and on the King of Kings!

August 3

Esther 9-10   Psalm 31   Proverbs 3   Mark 2

What Are You Saving?

Good morning! In the last several years, as it seems the number 70 is fast approaching, my wife and I have asked ourselves so many times, why are we saving this? Do you have things that you have saved and you ask yourself, why am I keeping this? As we have closed out our reading in the last two chapters of Esther, there has been a great victory of freedom for Esther, Mordecai and their people. There is now a day of remembering the day of victory. These days shall be called the "days of Purim." These days are to be "kept throughout every generation," according to verse 28 of chapter 9. God had saved His people and the world should hear about it.

Yesterday a veteran missionary and his family came to visit us at the Ranch. We talked and talked about memories; memories of what God has done, memories of prayers of faith and the provision of God. Some of the things that we save have no value, but the things that should be saved are

267

the prayers that God has answered, the miracles that we have seen the Lord do, etc. In Mark chapter 2 this morning, we read of the faith of the men that carried the palsied man to Jesus and there was no room, so they took him to the roof and removed the roof and let him down. Jesus "saw their faith" (verse 5), and Jesus said to the man in verse 11, "Arise, and take up thy bed, and go thy way into thine house." Keep the things that bring back the working hand of God, keep the things that strengthened your faith, keep the joy of the day of salvation, keep the memories of the day that you and I said there was no way and the Lord showed us the way. Keep the memories of God and His mighty power and tell "every generation."

It is not a sin to keep things but put a priority of saving and telling the stories of the great working of God. These memories will strengthen you, motivate you, and keep the fire of God burning in your soul so that you will stay faithful serving the Lord. Psalm 31:23, "O love the Lord, all ye his saints: for the Lord preserveth the faithful." Mrs. Smith and I sat with the missionaries last night who over 30 years ago had served on our summer staff and we talked of God's mighty hand then, and how His hand is still working today. They now have seen God work on their field of calling for over 20 years and now their children sat and listened of stories of the past, present and prayers of the future and continue to see the power of God working in lives. Keep the memories that must live as a testimony of our God. Make memories of the Lord today.

Keep the memories of God working in your life and tell the next generation.

August 4

Job 1-2   Psalm 32   Proverbs 4   Mark 3

Trusting Through Trials

Good morning! Today we begin our journey through the book of Job for our Old Testament reading. All of us have those times when life does not seem fair. We may ask ourselves, why am I having to go through this trial? Lord, what have I done wrong that you have allowed me to go through this valley? All of us have and will question the tough times. Job is a human example for us to look at and to learn from his Heavenly trust. We can and should learn from the example that is set before us in the Scriptures. In Job 1:5, we see Job "rose up early in the morning, and offered burnt offerings," and later in the verse we read, "Thus did Job continually."

We must be consistent in our worship of the Lord, every day reading the Bible and spending time in prayer. Be at church when the church doors are open. Be in your place and be ready to serve in any way that is needed. Give your tithes and offerings with a joyful heart and do not get behind in giving. In Job 1:8 we see the principles in Job's life that I believe caused God to allow the devil to test him. Look at these words: "perfect" (always did the best he could), "upright" (he was an honest person), "feared God" (respect and honor for God), "escheweth evil" (avoided wrong). Verses 20-22 tells us how he humbled himself before God. Trials and heartaches are going to come. We need to be walking with Him so that we do not turn from Him. Proverbs 4:26, "Ponder the path of thy feet, and let all thy ways be established." When going through a trial, stop and always seek the Lord for His grace, His love and His direction. Psalm 32:8, "I will instruct thee and teach thee in the way which thou shalt go: I will guide thee with mine eye." When Job's wife saw the one that she loved going through so much, she still knew what Job would do and we read in verse 10 of chapter 2, "In all this did not Job sin with his lips." God found Job prepared for the testing of Satan. The strength will not come until the time it is needed, and that is why it is so important for us to daily be walking and spending time with the Lord and be in our place of service. God's grace is there when His grace is needed. Job 1:21, "the Lord gave, and the Lord hath taken away; blessed be the name of the Lord."

We must be walking with God so that we do not turn from Him.

August 5

Job 3-4   Psalm 33   Proverbs 5   Mark 4

Keep Growing

Good morning! "Shall mortal man be more just than God?" That was the question posed in Job 4:17. I went back and reread verse 8, "they that plow iniquity, and sow wickedness, reap the same." Then after reading in Job, I turned in my Bible to the book of Mark and read in chapter 4:28, "For the earth bringeth forth fruit of herself; first the blade, then the ear, after that the full corn in the ear."

I love gardening and growing things. I love the fruit of the garden. We plant things that we enjoy eating. I trust we plant things in our lives that we want to reap. I love sweet corn right from the garden. The neighbors stopped by the other day and asked if we would like to go to their garden and get some fresh vegetables. They did not have to ask twice. I was on my way! As I walked through the rows of corn, I saw the large blades that were growing around the ears of corn, but I did not just grab any ear. I looked for those that were fully developed. I would stop at some stalks and pull the silk back to see what the kernels looked like. First comes the blade, then the ear develops, but it is not ready to be picked until the corn is fully developed on the ear.

I am afraid some Christians quit and give up, become critical, say the Christian life is too hard before there has been a chance to fully understand how to grow in the Lord. We were saved to produce beautiful fruit, to praise the Lord and show forth His praises. It takes time and patience to allow a full ear of corn to develop. I love to watch a tomato ripen, a cucumber grow out of the blossom, a green bean grow in length and a pea pod fully develop. There is nothing like standing in a garden and breaking open a fresh, fully developed pea pod and tasting the sweetness of new peas. As I walked through the garden there were some beautiful tomatoes but when I reached down, they were rotten on the bottom. I saw some ears of corn had developed a fungus. Those vegetables could not be enjoyed and prepared for a delicious meal. They had not been used when it was time and they were rotting.

That is just like a Christian that comes to church, hears teaching and preaching but never gets involved with serving. Keep growing, Christian, and keep developing for the Lord. It is the Lord's desire for us to be beautiful fruit for Him. Stay in the Word of God and let it grow in you to develop you. Psalm 33:4, "For the word of the Lord is right; and all his works are done in truth." Think about it. Have a blessed day.

God saved us to produce fruit – keep growing spiritually.

Job 5-6   Psalm 34   Proverbs 6   Mark 5

Lesson from a Bear

Good morning! Yesterday as my wife and I were driving slowly up a mountain road, a bear came running out of the woods and came right in front of us and just kept running. We were startled, excited, thrilled and all kinds of emotion ran through us. I looked to see if there were any more bears coming or going. I said to Mrs. Smith, why was that bear running? Had something frightened it, was it chasing something? The questions just kept coming to my mind. The road was not a back road. The traffic was moving between 40 and 50 miles per hour. Most of the black bear that my wife and I have seen move slowly, searching for food. There was an urgency for some reason.

As I read my Bible this morning, my mind went back to the urgency of the bear. Proverbs 6:20, "My son, keep thy father's commandment, and forsake not the law of thy mother." There are Biblical principles that have come down through the ages from our forefathers that we need to never forget. I get so tired of people saying, I was not raised that way or I was not taught that. If we just stop and look around us, God's principles are all around us - do not lie, pay your bills on time, no work-no pay, laziness will destroy a life, do not gossip, honor authorities. These and a multitude more of Biblical principles have been around for generations and yet the times are showing a turning from principles that have guided us for many decades. Proverbs 6:21, "Bind them continually upon thine heart, and tie them about thy neck." Principles are to be a constant reminder of how we are to live. Proverbs 6:22 says they will "lead thee, keep thee, and talk with thee."

That bear had an urgency that it had been taught, learned, or it was using a sense that God had given it. Sin is and has bound us to the path of destruction. Psalm 34:4 says, "I sought the Lord, and he heard me, and delivered me." We need to be quicker than a bear running through the forest to stay away from that which will destroy us, and running to God who will guide us, bless us, and reward us eternally. We hear good sound preaching and teaching and it should bring an urgency to stay right with God, do His will for our lives, serve Him in any way that we can. May that urgency come to us today. Look out for the bear, they just might teach us a lesson that we need to learn.

We need to have an urgency to stay right with God.

August 7

Job 7-8   Psalm 35:1-16   Proverbs 7   Mark 6

How Will You Finish?

Good morning! The older I get, the more I am reminded of the shortness of our time on this earth. I read this morning in Job 7:1, "Is there not an appointed time to man upon earth?" Life goes so fast, our children come and leave, the grandchildren grow so fast. We age and the transitions of life seem to come faster and faster. Job 7:9, "As the cloud is consumed and vanished away: so he that goeth down to the grave shall come up no more." We must finish right. The race is not done yet. The finish line is approaching and we must cross it in the right way.

For almost forty years I have read over and over Mark 6:30-31. The apostles had gathered themselves unto Jesus and He told them, "Come ye yourselves apart unto a desert place and rest a while:.." I have used these verses as the importance of camp being a place away from the influences of the world and getting ourselves alone with God and being refreshed in our walk with God. Camp cannot be every day but our personal time with the Lord can give us strength to keep going. Just after Jesus telling the apostles to get away, came the feeding of the five thousand and then seeing Jesus walk on the water. What great working of the Lord is ahead of us that we will miss, or not be ready for, if we have not been faithful in having that time of strengthening with the Lord? Each day we live is so important for us to spend time in God's Word, spend time in prayer and meditation of what we read. It is God's will for us to finish right. The Psalmist wrote in

Psalm 35:9, "And my soul shall be joyful in the Lord: it shall rejoice in his salvation."

Christian, how are you keeping your daily spiritual strength up? The work we do for the Lord is wonderful, but it cannot be done correctly and pleasing to the Lord if we do not do it in His strength. Many Christians start right, but it has often been said, "it is important how we finish." Know how to rebuild and keep going so that you will be faithful to the end. The finish line is approaching; finish strong in the Lord.

Finishing well is just as important as starting well.

August 8

Job 9-10   Psalm 35:17-38   Proverbs 8   Mark 7

Back Up Your Words

Good morning! I want to encourage you today to spend time thinking or meditating on what you are reading. I am afraid that we just read the Bible to check off a schedule and do not spend the time thinking about what we just read. Right now, I am reading a book the second time and I am going back through and marking things that will help me beyond just reading the book. Job 10:2 says, ." . shew me wherefore thou contendest with me." I believe Job wanted to see what God was doing in his life and understand what God was doing. In Job 9:32 we read, "For he is not a man, as I am, that I should answer him, and we should come together in judgment."

To see things as the Lord sees them is so very important. We often hear someone say they are a Christian, but their actions are far from those of a Christian. Mark 7:6, "This people honoureth me with their lips, but their heart is far from me." As the boys said on the playground before the fight of the day; "put up or shut up." In Proverbs 8:17, we read, "I love them that love me; and those that seek me early shall find me." Job was looking to learn and understand from God and so should we. It is God's will that we grow in Him, make decisions that please Him, live a life that is glorifying to Him. Proverbs 8:32, "blessed are they that keep my ways." My mother used to tell me all the time; eat your vegetables. I was ready for the fresh apple pie that had just come out of the oven. I looked down at my plate the other day and started laughing. My wife said, what is wrong? We were sitting at Cracker Barrel and I had ordered green beans, turnip greens and baby carrots along with grilled chicken. I want to take care of myself physically, so I have finally learned what I eat does matter. Spiritually speaking, we should do what Proverbs 8:33 teaches us; "Hear instruction, and be wise, and refuse it not." Let us today be Christians that live the life, walk the life, have the actions that show we are Christians and not just say it with our lips. I remember standing face to face with another boy on the playground as a little guy and saying those words, "put up or shut up." Don't just tell me, show me. Let us show the world, Christian brother and sister, with a life that backs up what we say. Have a blessed day.

Our actions ought to back up our words.

August 9

Job 11-12   Psalm 36   Proverbs 9   Mark 8

Even Nature Knows Him

Good morning! Mark 8:12 says, "Why doth this generation seek after a sign?' I walked by a mountain brook yesterday and listened to the water sing a song as it flowed over the rocks. The trees seemed to be saying something as their limbs swayed in the breeze with the leaves moving together. The rocks stood proud as they pierced the earth and withstood the storms day after day, along with the heat and cold of the different seasons. The trees stood so proudly with their strength. It was like they had a race to see who could stand the tallest before God. The animals of the forest moved freely with nothing to stop them and no fear of provision, comfort or protection.

Mark 8:16 states, "they reasoned among themselves;" verse 17 Jesus asked, "why reason ye," and in verse 18 He stated, "Having eyes, see ye not? and having ears, hear ye not? and do ye not remember?" In verse 21 we read, "How is it that ye do not understand?" Take time today and every day to see the greatness of God, remember His answers to your prayers, thank Him for always being there when you need Him. Never lose the desire to see His mighty hand at work. Praise Him in the good days and when He allows us to walk through the valley, still praise Him. Mark 8:34 challenges us to stand up and go forward today, "Whosoever will come after me, let him deny himself, and take up his cross, and follow me." Walk in the light with God today, for He is the light of the world. Psalm 36:9, "in thy light shall we see light."

We ended our day yesterday by a campfire. No words were said, just the joy of being together and being with the Lord. All the earthly possessions that we have and will have will never bring true happiness, but daily seeing and experiencing the hand of God will bring a joy unspeakable. The morning light will soon come, and the business of this day will begin. Please take time and begin your day with the Lord, walk with Him through this day, enjoy His fellowship, listen to His voice and allow Him to guide you today. All nature knows Him but He died for you and me. Have a blessed day.

Never lose the desire to see God's mighty hand at work.

August 10

Job 13-14   Psalm 37:1-22   Proverbs 10   Mark 9

What is Eating You?

Good morning! The attitude and spirit of Job is a strengthening reminder to me that God sees all, knows all, controls all and has a plan in everything. Oh, that our faith in God would grow to the point that we could say as Job did in Job 13:13, "let come on me what will." Job's expression of his faith in God and his love for God should convict us each time we try to figure things out. Job 13:15, "Though he slay me, yet will I trust him: but I will maintain mine own ways before him." Job was teaching us that he will maintain his walk with God no matter what he

275

goes through. Job 13:23 shows us there should be a constant cleansing of sin, "make me to know my transgression and my sin."

In Mark 9, we read of the father that had the son with the evil spirit. This father brought his son to the disciples believing he could be healed, and nothing happened until Jesus confronted the father and said, "If thou canst believe, all things are possible to him that believeth." The father responded in Mark 9:24, "Lord, I believe; help thou mine unbelief." What is it that is eating you alive, discouraging you, consuming you, slowly destroying you, and you cannot get past it? We read in Psalm 37:1, "Fret not." Verses 3-7 have key phrases for us today that we need to meditate on and give our burdens to the Lord today. "Trust in the Lord; Delight thyself also in the Lord; Commit thy way unto the Lord; Rest in the Lord, and wait patiently for him:." Life is short. Why let our lives be consumed by things that most of the time we cannot change? Let God strengthen you today and get past what you are letting destroy you. Proverbs 10:29, "The way of the Lord is strength to the upright:." Walk with Him today and watch Him take care of all of your situations. The Lord bless you today.

Commit your burdens to the Lord and let Him take care of them.

August 11

Job 15-16   Psalm 37:23-40   Proverbs 11   Mark 10

No Distractions

Good morning! My wife and I watched as a large male black bear meandered through the woods. We were driving along a back road slowly in the mountains, something caught my eye and it was this black bear. I stopped the car and got out and watched. There seemed to not be a path that this bear was following and yet he kept moving, sniffing, knocking logs with his paws and nose. I stood still and yet I knew he knew we were there. He stopped ever so often and took a glance at me, and yet he kept going. He was focused on finding food. Psalm 37:23, "The steps of a good man are ordered by the Lord: and he delighteth in his way." The bear had a direction and he knew where he was going and what he was looking for.

The reading in Psalm 37 today in verse 37 also tells us to "Mark the perfect man, and behold the upright: for the end of that man is peace." There seemed to be no distraction for the bear. What was guiding that bear? He was focused. Proverbs 11:3, "The integrity of the upright shall guide them," verse 5, "The righteousness of the perfect (do the best you can in God's eyes) shall direct his way:," verse 6, "The righteousness of the upright shall deliver them:," verse 8, "The righteous is delivered out of trouble." Ponder on these verses and you will see we have no excuse but to grow in our walk with God, please Him, honor Him, live for Him and He will be there to guide us each step. You might say it is hard or I can't stop this habit that is destroying me. The answer to that excuse is in Mark 10:27, "With men it is impossible, but not with God: for with God all things are possible."

Nothing seemed to stop or distract that bear, he just kept walking and searching. What is stopping you today from being faithful to the Lord and to His house and service for Him? I thought of the words of Job that we read in Job 16:22, "When a few years are come, then I shall go the way whence I shall not return." Life is short, time is ticking, do not live in regret. The black bear kept going. How about you today? Don't stop, keep living and serving Christ. See you on the path.

Stay focused on God and He will be there to guide each step.

August 12

Job 17-19   Psalm 38   Proverbs 12   Mark 11

Keep Your Faith Watered

Good morning! As I pulled into the drive yesterday, I mentioned to my wife how the heat and dryness has scorched the ground and yet the weeds keep growing. Just a couple of weeks ago the grass was green and thriving and some weeks we had to mow twice. That is just like so many

Christians. There was once an excitement in going to church, reading the Bible, growing in the things of the Lord and then the excitement seemed to dry up. The things that never dried up were the flesh and the temptations of the flesh. The things that were destroying us never quit being there and the things that were new and gave us life have lost their newness and the desire to keep growing has left.

As the grass in the yard appears dead and gone, a little bit of rain or water will bring life and the grass will turn green again. In Proverbs 12:3, "but the root of the righteous shall not be moved;" and in verse 7, "the house of the righteous shall stand." Job, in all his discouragement and attacks from his friends (or so-called friends), wrote in Job 17:9, "The righteous also shall hold on his way." Keep going, my Christian brother and sister, listen to the writings of Job in chapter 19 and verse 25, "For I know that my redeemer liveth, and that he shall stand at the latter day upon the earth."

As I was reading in Mark 11 this morning, three phrases drew my attention; verse 22, "Have faith in God," verse 23, "shall not doubt," verse 24, "when ye pray, believe." The beauty of the lawn will return with the nourishment from the water. Keep having faith, do not doubt. Keep praying and believing and the stirring of your spirit will be turned into a fire in your soul. Psalm 38:15, "For in thee, O Lord, do I hope: thou wilt hear, O Lord my God." The rain is coming, keep looking up. Read the first phrase of Job 19:25, and then sing with me this morning. "I will sing of my Redeemer, And His wondrous love to me; On the cruel cross He suffered, From the curse to set me free." Sing with me on the chorus, "Sing oh, sing of my Redeemer, With His blood He purchased me, On the cross He sealed my pardon, Paid the debt and made me free." Sing that chorus all day long and let the water of life flow.

Keep praying and believing and your spirit will be
turned into a fire in your soul.

Job 20-21   Psalm 39   Proverbs 13   Mark 12

Stop and Listen

Good morning! A new day is about to begin, all is quiet, the day is still dark, the birds of the sky are still asleep and nesting. The only sounds are the night sounds of those animals that were made by God to work in the night. In most places where people live, time never stops. The traffic continues to flow, many businesses are open twenty-four hours a day, those that protect us are busy watching, the nurses are busy making their rounds and checking on patients. The business of life never stops, the hurry and rush of getting things done marches on. One day life will stop and for many it will be too late.

Job's so-called friends that came to encourage him and seemed to always have a critical heart heard Job speak the words recorded in Job 21:34, "How then comfort ye me in vain, seeing in your answers there remaineth falsehood." It is hard for the world to stop, and it is hard for us that know the Lord to see the importance of taking the time to stop and be quiet before the Lord. Proverbs 13:15, "Good understanding giveth favour: but the way of transgressors is hard." We say that we love God, but we do not stop to spend time with Him. Mark 12:28-34 points us to the widow woman that gave God "all her living." She gave God her whole heart and I believe she is an example of stopping, listening, meditating and worshipping God. Jesus used her as an example for us. Psalm 39:1, the Psalmist wrote, "I will take heed to my ways." What are we doing, where are we headed, what is our life all about? Read on down to verse 4, "Lord, make me to know mine end, and the measure of my days." In verse 7 the Psalmist realized, "my hope is in thee," so he cried in verses 12-13, "Hear my prayer, give ear unto my cry, that I may recover strength." Daily our strength in the Lord must be renewed. The strength of yesterday, last month, last year is not enough for today. Stop, listen, meditate and worship the Lord today and every day. May our Lord bless you in a special way today.

It is important to learn how to stop and be quiet before the Lord.

August 14

Job 22-23   Psalm 40   Proverbs 14   Mark 13

A Psalm for Comfort

Good morning! All of us have those days that bring us to a point that we do not think we can take any more. It seems that the harder we try, the more difficult things get. We ask ourselves, can things get any worse?

I love the statement that Job made in Job 23:10, "But he knoweth the way that I take: when he hath tried me, I shall come forth as gold." If we are not careful, when we go through trials, our hearts can turn hard. Job shows us the importance of staying close to the Lord in Job 23:16, "For God maketh my heart soft."

Psalm 40 is such a comfort for us today. I encourage you to read this Psalm several times throughout the day. Let us look together at a few verses. Psalm 40:1, "I waited patiently for the Lord; and he inclined unto me, and heard my cry." Verse 5, "Many, O Lord my God, are thy wonderful works which thou hast done, they are more than can be numbered." Verse 8, "I delight to do thy will, O my God: yea, thy law is within my heart." Verse 11, "let thy lovingkindness and thy truth continually preserve me." Verse 13, Be pleased, O Lord, to deliver me: O Lord, make haste to help me." Let God be a comforter, an encourager, a strengthener. Let God today be your all. He has not forsaken us, He is there. Spend time talking with Him, walking with Him. He is our God, He is our Lord. Love Him, live for Him, serve Him. Have a blessed day.

Let God be your comforter, encourager, and strengthener.

August 15

Job 24-25   Psalm 41   Proverbs 15   Mark 14

Have You Forgotten?

Good morning! Did you ever forget where you put something? Have you ever looked at someone and you could not remember their name?

Did you ever not write something down and you tried to remember what it was that you wanted to remember? Did you ever go to the store and forget what you came to the store for? Have you ever walked into a room and you could not remember why you came into that room? Please say yes to the questions that I have asked and it will help me. I know I am getting older and I know I have not completely lost my mind. All of us, if honest, have been guilty of forgetting.

We read an interesting statement this morning in Job 24:1, "times are not hidden from the Almighty, do they that know him not see his days?" Nothing is hidden from God. In Mark 14, Jesus is speaking to His disciples in the upper room concerning betrayal and one by one the disciples say, "Is it I?." They could not believe that someone would betray the Lord Jesus that they had grown to love and serve with; their teacher, their Lord. Now we look down to verse 50 and we see this written, "And they all forsook him, and fled." Peter, "that stood by drew a sword, and smote a servant of the high priest, and cut off his ear." (verse 47). Now, Peter "followed him afar off" (verse 50). Peter, in verse 71, says, "I know not this man of whom ye speak."

Have you forgotten a promise you made to God? Have you forgotten a new commitment that you made to God? Had you forgotten that you committed to God and to others that you were going to be more faithful in church? Are you continually giving an excuse why you cannot be in church? Are we able to go to work, be at all of our appointments, do what we want to do, but when it comes time to be with God, we make excuses?

Proverbs 15:19, "the way of the righteous is made plain." I am not attacking. I am just helping us to remember the promise that we made to God and maybe we have forgotten what we said. The Psalmist wrote in 41:12, "settest me before thy face for ever." God does not forget and He will not forsake us. Maybe this morning we need to get things back in order and realize nothing is hidden from God and God never forgets. Please think about it and remember what you promised and said.

What promise or commitment have you made to God
that you've forgotten about?

August 16

Job 26-27   Psalm 42   Proverbs 16   Mark 15

Praise Him, Praise Him!

Good morning! As a young man I remember my parents teaching me a very important lesson about appreciation. They would often say, "If you can't say something good, then don't say anything." We live in a world that is never satisfied. Down the road from the little place that I lived at when I was a boy was a junk yard. You do not often hear that term "junk yard, but it was a place where wrecked vehicles or worn out vehicles were taken. Parts would be taken off to make repairs or rebuild other cars and trucks like them. My dad took me there and said, "David, many people bought these cars and thought they would be happy, but everything in life gets old, rusts, and wears out. Do not put your joy in things."

We read this morning in Job 26:14, "how little a portion is heard of him?" Job was focusing on praise to his God, not criticism of the trial he was going through. Job 27:4, "My lips shall not speak wickedness, nor my tongue utter deceit." We live in a time where there is constant complaining and little thankfulness and praise. We hear about the rights we should have or people are always talking about being offended. It is time we as God's people learn to praise Him. We will find when we praise Him, we will be thankful and not only see the bad, but rejoice in all that God is and that He will be all that we need. Job 27:8, "For what is the hope of the hypocrite, though he hath gained, when God taketh away his soul?" My folks taught me another phrase that I will never forget. "What you see is not always what you get." The world and its sin looks so good but it is not what it really is. The day they screamed out to crucify our Lord, the king said in Mark 15:14, "Why, what evil hath he done?" The centurion said as he looked up at Jesus, "Truly this man was the Son of God." Psalm 42:11, "hope thou in God: for I shall yet praise him, who is the health of my countenance, and my God."

Praise will help us to see good; praise will help us to really see things as they are. Sing with me, "Praise Him! Praise Him! Jesus our blessed

Redeemer! Sing O earth, His wonderful love proclaim! Hail Him! Hail Him! Highest archangels in glory, Strength and honor give to His holy name! Like a shepherd Jesus will guard His children, in His arms He carries them all the day long: Praise Him! Praise Him! Tell of His excellent greatness! Praise Him! Praise Him! Ever the joyful song! Take a good look at all that God has done and is doing, and you will see that He has been so good. You will praise Him!

Praise will help us see things as they really are.

August 17

Job 28-29   Psalm 43   Proverbs 17   Mark 16

What Are You Searching For?

Good morning! As I read this morning in Job 28:1, "Surely there is a vein for the silver, and a place for gold where they fine it." My mind went to the many stories that my grandfather told about the gold mines he worked at in Colorado. My grandfather was a real cowboy, born in a log cabin and left home at a very young age. His father had left the family and his mother died giving birth to his younger sister. An aunt raised my grandfather and his sister for a short time and my grandfather left home before his teen years. He was quite a man in my eyes. He told of driving the mule teams out of the gold mines day after day as the miners searched for the gold and the many minerals hidden in the mountains.

Many men have given their lives searching for something that they never found. In verse 11 we read, "the thing that is hid bringeth he forth to light." Man looks for anything and everything to make him happy and bring satisfaction, but in this world it will never be found outside of a relationship with Jesus Christ. The question is asked in verse 20, "Whence then cometh wisdom? And where is the place of understanding?" The answer comes in verse 28, "Behold, the fear of the Lord, that is wisdom; and to depart from evil is understanding." God sees beyond what we can see or understand. Do not limit God today. Even after Mary had seen the risen Saviour, men that had walked with Him did not believe and in Mark

16:14 we read, "he upbraided them with their unbelief and hardness of heart, because they believed not them which had seen him after he was risen." As I read in Job this morning how God sees beyond what man sees, my heart is challenged to trust Him more. Psalm 43:3, "O send out thy light and thy truth: let them lead me;" and in Proverbs 17:24, "Wisdom is before him that hath understanding." Miners gave their lives searching for something when God knew where it was. Man searches through the things of this world to find what he thinks will bring peace, satisfaction, joy, etc. Truly a growing relationship and a yielded life to God brings peace and joy beyond understanding. We that are saved have the light within our soul, the sweet Holy Spirit. Let God shine in you today. There is no reason to keep digging in the dirt of this world when something far more precious than gold was invited into your heart on the day of salvation. Live and walk in the Light today.

A yielded life to God brings peace and joy beyond understanding

August 18

Job 30-31   Psalm 44:1-8   Proverbs 18   Luke 1

If Only. . . .

Good morning! It is hard to imagine just a few weeks ago we were receiving heavy rains, mud was everywhere and grass was growing. Now the grass is dead, the ground is cracking and the leaves are falling before they even had a chance to turn to their beautiful fall colors. If the rains had kept coming, if the extreme heat had not arrived, and if summer would have ended in a different way, we would have had a beautiful fall. I used a little word in the last sentence three times because as we read in Job 31 this morning, the word "if" was used twenty times. I reread this chapter and looked at it this morning several times and thought, that is the way most people live their lives; living in the realm of "if." If I had, if they would have, if it had not happened, if I had been there, if I had known, if I had seen, if I had more, if I was not there, if I had not been born, if I had better parents, if I had married a different person, if I was a morning person, if I felt better, if I could sing, if I had a better car, if I had a better job, if I had more money, if I would have listened; if, if, if, if.

Down in verse 35 of chapter 31 we see this phrase, "my desire is." I ask myself, when will we stop giving excuse? Let us decide today to do right in the eyes of God. Proverbs 18:1, "Through desire a man, having separated himself, seeketh and intermeddleth with all wisdom." That verse teaches us to surround ourselves with the right people. I cannot change what I cannot change, but what I can change and need to change I should change. In Luke chapter 1, we begin our journey to read about two couples that God saw and wanted to use in a very special way - Zacharias and Elisabeth and Mary and Joseph. Neither couple had anticipated what the Lord was going to do and when the angel spoke with them, they thought it was impossible, but we read in Luke 1:37, "For with God nothing shall be impossible."

We can look at the trees that are losing their leaves, the dead grass and the cracks in the ground and get all depressed, or we can enjoy the beautiful sunrises and sunsets. We need to quit living in the realm of the "ifs" and start living in the realm of God can, God is and God will. We need to focus on having our desires to please the Lord, live for Him and always be in the place to grow in Him and to be with the people that love Him and want to serve Him. Stop living in the realm of if and live in the joy of knowing He is your God.

We need to live in the realm of God can, God is and God will.

August 19

Job 32-33   Psalm 44:9-26   Proverbs 19   Luke 2

Mechanical or Spiritual?

Good morning! Do you remember the joy, the relief, the peace, and yes, the satisfaction on that day that you trusted Christ as your personal Saviour? Oh, what a day, and then you followed the Lord in believer's baptism. I have stood at the waters' edge many times and heard many say, I feel so good now that I have been baptized. I have seen many a head raised as a sinner looks up after praying and asking God to forgive their sins and to come into their hearts, and the peace of heart brought a peace of mind and a smile on their face. But what happens next? Why were they not in church? How come they started missing Sunday School and then started missing church and now they hardly come at all or they have quit altogether? What happened?

Job 32:8, "But there is a spirit in man: and the inspiration of the Almighty giveth them understanding." We find ourselves alone in the flesh and we have not learned to walk in the Spirit. I love sending notes, teaching the Scriptures and giving and going through discipleship material, but all of us must learn how to walk in the Spirit. Can you imagine the shepherds in Luke 2, as they were watching their sheep? We read in verse 9, "And, lo, the angel of the Lord came upon them," verse 10, "And the angel said unto them," verse 26. The Spirit of God lives within the soul of every believer, but we do not work at learning to walk in the Spirit because we are not spending time living in the Spirit by spending time with God. Jesus himself as a twelve-year old boy was learning how to walk with God as recorded in Luke 2:27, "And he came by the Spirit into the temple:." A few verses later we see it is recorded that "Jesus increased in wisdom and stature, and in favour with God and man."

Too many quit their beginning walk with God because they look at the Christian life as a mechanical walk and do not understand we are to have a spiritual relationship. Too many older saints quit and become discouraged because they had learned to walk in the flesh and their walk with God was a mechanical walk, not a spiritual walk. Listen to the verse we read this morning in Proverbs 19:21, "There are many devices in a man's heart; nevertheless the counsel of the Lord, that shall stand." God understands, but He still hungers to lead us and guide us. Psalm 44:21, "for he knoweth the secrets of the heart." Think with me today. Where am I getting my strength spiritually? It is a slow process, but it is a good process and it is a must for all of us. Spend time with God, trust His Word, grow in faith in God, work on memorizing special verses that help you, stay faithful in His house with His people. Do not be an island unto yourself. I just told someone yesterday, God has not moved or changed His address. Walk with Him, stay with Him, learn from Him, be faithful to Him. A life with Christ is a life that will grow. Have a blessed day.

Our walk with God will be discouraging if
it is mechanical rather than spiritual.

August 20

Job 34-35   Psalm 45   Proverbs 20   Luke 3

School is in Session

Good morning! School has begun for another year. From kindergarten to college, the classes are filling as the students return. I thought to myself today how learning never stops. Oh, I was the one student that could not wait until school got out. I thought I was glad when I graduated from high school, then I was off to college. Life has been a constant learning process, as all of us know. I thought on the Scriptures that we have for our reading today and there was one word that I had to spend some time looking up and studying. We will look at that word in a moment, so let us look at some Scripture in our reading about learning since it is time for school to begin.

In Job 35:7, Elihu said, "What man is like Job, who drinketh up scorning like water?" The critics of Job acknowledged that all he was going through seemed to be teaching him something. In verses 10-11 it is like a teacher is challenging the students to learn everything, everywhere and at any time. "Who giveth songs in the night; who teacheth us more than the beasts of the earth, and maketh us wiser than the fowls of heaven?" That is a question that we need to ponder. All of man's learning that we receive is important, but nothing is more important to learn than the lessons that we learn from a walk with God. As John the Baptist started his ministry, we see three different walks of people having their hearts stirred by the teachings of John. Luke 3:10, "people;" What shall we do then?" Luke 3:12, "publicans;" What shall we do?" Luke 3:14, "soldiers;" what shall we do?" The gospel affects all walks of life and creates a hunger for learning.

For us as God's people, school never ends. Proverbs 20:15, "the lips of knowledge are a precious jewel."

The word that I wanted to look at is found in Psalm 45:1, "My heart is inditing a good matter:." Our hearts, lips and lives are to be "making known" and "proclaiming" the things that we learn from God. Today school is in session for all. We are to grow in Christ and that growth comes when we learn. We are not supposed to just take in but to proclaim to this world that Jesus saves. We are to be students of Christ to live a holy life in a wicked sinful world, to walk victoriously when trials come our way. Walk in newness of life today. Graduation is coming soon when we enter the portals of Heaven. Enjoy school today as we walk with our King. There will be a reward of crowns for the faithful. What a graduation that will be!

We are to be students of Christ and continually grow in Him.

August 21

Job 36-37   Psalm 46   Proverbs 21   Luke 4

God's Instruction Manual

Good morning! Have you ever said, "Well, I didn't know that." You had read something in the Bible and you said, "I didn't know that was in the Bible." As I was reading this morning in Job chapters 36 and 37, phrases kept coming out about things that we have learned but many do not know they are in the Bible. For instance, in Job 36:27-28, "For he maketh small drops of water: they pour down rain according to the vapor thereof: Which the clouds do drop and distil upon man abundantly." That is how rain is made. Look over in chapter 37 and verses 9, 13, "Out of the south cometh the whirlwind: and cold out of the north.;" "By the breath of God frost is given:." There is so much more if we would just read. Job 37:5, "Great things doeth he, which we cannot comprehend." Job 37:14, "stand still, and consider the wondrous works of God." There is so much for us to learn.

In Luke 4:4 we read, "Man shall not live by bread alone, but by every word of God." That is why it is so important to have some type of schedule to read the Bible. Each morning when I write a devotional for the day, I am taking the thoughts from the schedule that our church and my Sunday School class use. All the words in the Bible are God's Words and we must read them all even if we do not think we are getting anything from the reading. My wife bought us a new shoe rack and she asked if I would put it together. The first thing that I asked for was the directions. I wanted to read how the manufacturer made it to be put together. God created us and the Bible is God's instruction about life and everything in it, from blessings to judgments for sin, from His love to His chastisement. Proverbs 21:21, "He that followeth after righteousness and mercy findeth life, righteousness, and honor."

Take time for God and He will always have time for us. Psalm 46:1, "God is our refuge, and strength, a very present help in trouble." God has given us His Word to teach us, direct us, give us wisdom and understanding, encourage us, convict us and so on. Every word must be read and meditated upon. Let us decide today to follow the directions given in the Word of God.

God's Word is our instruction manual for every area of life.

August 22

Job 38-39   Psalm 47   Proverbs 22   Luke 5

Keep God on the Throne

Good morning! As I read in the quietness of this morning, I began to hear the wind blowing strongly and I went outside and stood in the darkness. As I looked into the sky, I saw the lightning in the distant sky and my mind went to what I read this morning. In Job chapters 38 and 39, God asked Job questions about Him and His creation and I want to ask us the same today. "Hast thou, Canst thou, Knowest thou, Who hath, Who can; Who provideth for the raven his food, Wilt thou hunt the prey for the lion, Wilt thou, Doth the?"

Over and over again, God brought the attention away from us and what we think we know, what we think we can, and what we think we do, and brought it all back to God. God does this for us to keep ourselves off the throne of our lives and keep God on the throne of leadership. Peter, in Luke 5:4, told the Lord he had fished and caught nothing. Jesus told him to "Launch out" and in verse 5 he cast the nets "at thy word." "When they had this done" (verse 6), the nets got so full they broke and they had to call another ship to help them. We then read in verse 11 how "they forsook all, and followed him."

Where is God in your life today? May we allow Him to be God every day and in every situation. Proverbs 22:19, "That thy trust may be in the Lord;" verse 21, "That I might make thee know the certainty of the words of truth." Stop today before the day begins and do as the Psalmist did in Psalm 47:6-7, "Sing praise to God, sing praises: sing praise unto our king, sing praises." "For God is the King of all the earth: sing ye praise with understanding." Look around and take a long look, and begin to see God. Let us stop and decide right now to keep Him where He needs to be in our life. Realize it is God that wants to be leading and guiding us. Let God have the leadership and guidance to do all that He desires. Have a blessed day.

We need to keep God on the throne of leadership in our life.

August 23

Job 40-42   Psalm 48   Proverbs 23   Luke 6

Doing for Others

Good morning! As I was reading this morning, I wrote so many notes of things that I am learning and observing from the Scriptures. I thank the Lord that His Word is like a well that never runs dry; it just keeps providing fresh water each time we go to it. The book of Job comes to an end and we see Job repenting, God telling Job to "Gird up thy loins now like a man:" in verse 7, and then deal with your pride in verses 8-14. The rest of chapters 40 and 41 we see God talking about the power of dinosaurs that He had put on this earth and we are taught so much by them. I like how God tells Job's friends in 42:7, "for ye have not spoken of me the thing that is right, as my servant Job hath." God told them to get right and we see God blessing Job more in the latter end than the beginning.

We learn a great principle of life from what we are taught in Luke 6:27-28 to "Love your enemies, do good to them which hate you, Bless them that curse you, pray for them which despitefully use you." The lesson of doing for others continues through the end of the chapter in Luke 6. I sat and looked at all I had written, and I remembered my mom making a plate of food for bums that used to stop at our home. My mother came from a family of twelve children and they never had very much, but I never heard my mom complain and I watched all my life until my mother passed, how she was always doing for others. We lived on a main highway going through our town and people would often stop as they were hitchhiking along the road and ask for food or if they could sleep in our front yard. I know that sounds unusual in the day and age we live, but that is how I was raised. If you have something and others need it, then share it with them. Oh, if this selfless generation could learn that lesson! I can remember my mom fixing a meal and taking it out to someone we would never see again and telling them they could eat the meal on our front porch.

As I read Psalm 48:13, "tell it to the generation following." It is time for us to learn from Job and be the Christians that God wants us to be. Keep doing for others and be faithful to God no matter the trials that you go through. Job lived to the fullness of his days. How is your life today? Is it consumed with self and all the unkindness done to you or is your life filled with doing for others and expecting nothing in return? My mother went to Heaven many years ago, but I remember at her funeral so many passing by and saying, your mother always did for others. Thanks, mom, for passing on a Bible truth to another generation.

Is your life consumed with self or filled with doing for others?

August 24

Ecclesiastes 1-2   Psalm 49   Proverbs 24   Luke 7

Is Your Head in the Right Place?

Good morning! We start today our journey through the book of Ecclesiastes in the Old Testament. I would like to ask a question, as I have been asking myself the same question this morning. What have you given your heart to? In Ecclesiastes 1:13, "I gave my heart to seek and search out by wisdom concerning all things that are done under heaven:." In chapter 2 verse 13 we read; "Then I saw that wisdom excelleth folly, as far as light excelleth darkness." What is consuming our energies? What is controlling our thoughts? So much in life consumes us and our time and yet little is accomplished. In Ecclesiastes 2:4, "The wise man's eyes are in his head; but the fool walketh in darkness:."

I remember being told, "Get your head where it is supposed to be." When I first heard that statement, I thought (but sure did not say anything), my head is on my shoulders and is where it is supposed to be. Then as I thought about it, I was being taught to think, and to think with wisdom and direction. This world lives for now and what seems to be fun and entertaining now, and does not see the destruction that is going to come in the future. Jesus said in John 7:24, "What went ye out into the wilderness for to see?" He asked the question, what did you all expect? Then Jesus went on to say in verse 27, "there is not a greater prophet than John the Baptist:." We need to be stable in our walk with God and not moved to destruction in every trial and bump that life throws at us. We need to keep our focus on lost souls and the will of God for our life. Proverbs 24:5, "A wise man is strong; yea, a man of knowledge increaseth strength." Proverbs 24:16, "For a just man falleth seven times, and riseth up again."

Keep getting up, Christian. Stay faithful. Keep your head on your shoulders and keep pressing forward for the Lord. Psalm 49:15, "My mouth shall speak of wisdom; and the meditation of my heart shall be of understanding." Glory to God, I have another day to serve the Lord and to live for Him. In this journey of life, keep your focus on the Lord and the path of His will for your life.

Keep your head on your shoulders and your focus on the Lord.

Ecclesiastes 3-4   Psalm 50   Proverbs 25   Luke 8

Seasons of Life

Good morning! I love the changing of the seasons. I walked outside this morning and the coolness is so refreshing and comforting. Ecclesiastes 3:1, "To every thing there is a season, and a time to every purpose under the heaven:." It seems like it was just yesterday the ground was being turned over to prepare the ground for planting, the seed was being sown, the fresh vegetables were being harvested, and now look at the garden. The garden looks dry and dead. Even though the weather is beginning to change there is something new in the air, another season.

That is life; there is birth, youth, teen, young adult, adult, senior seasons of life. I do not know what season of life you are in, but I do know each season is very special if lived for the Lord. God wants to do something very special in each of our seasons. Ecclesiastes 3:14, "I know that, whatsoever God doeth, it shall be for ever:;" verse 17, "God shall judge the righteous and the wicked: for there is a time there for every purpose and for every work." I can honestly say from personal experience, there is a real season change to every season of life and God has a specific purpose for each of us in every season. In Luke chapter 8 this morning I kept reading and I kept seeing "faith" challenged in each parable and each story. From Mary being saved to Jesus saying to the maid, "arise." Proverbs 25:13, "As the cold of snow in the time of harvest." Be assured the seasons will change. We must often have a great change within ourselves when the seasons of life change but be sure God has not forgotten us. Psalm 50:10, For every beast of the forest is mine, and the cattle upon a thousand hills. Verse 11, "I know all the fowls of the mountains: and the wild beasts of the field are mine." They were not created in His image, but we were. They were not died for, but we were. They do not have an eternal home, but we do. It is a must in every season of life to do as Psalm 50:15 says, "And call upon me in the day of trouble: I will deliver thee, and thou shalt glorify me." Transition and change is hard, but it is going to happen. The garden might be drying up, so look to the beauty of fall and the white snow of winter and spring will soon arrive. "To every thing there is a season, and a time to every purpose under the heaven:." The seasons will come and go, so live through the change and be what our Lord would have you to be. Have a blessed day.

God has a specific purpose for every season of our life.

August 26

Ecclesiastes 5-6   Psalm 51   Proverbs 26   Luke 9

From Bottle to Pasture

Good morning! As I rise each morning, there is a growing desire to hear from the Lord and to learn more about Him. I have been saved for many years and yet there are some days that I feel so infant in His understanding. As I read in Ecclesiastes 5:1, "be more ready to hear, than to give the sacrifice of fools;" I hunger to hear what God says to me. I remember feeding baby calves with a bottle, and how they would fight the bottle until they tasted the milk. I would put a little of the milk on my finger and let the calf taste the milk and slide the nipple from the bottle into the calf's mouth, and then when the milk was gone the calf would keep sucking on the bottle because it wanted more. When it came time for the calf to eat solid food, I would put a little in my hand and the calf would sometimes fight eating the feed and then as I would put the grain in a bucket and leave it in front of the calf, it would only be a short time before the calf would eat all of the grain.

Some of us Christians are still in the bottle stages of our walk with God. That is why we read in Luke 9:41 how Christ said to His disciples, "O faithless and perverse generation, how long shall I be with you, and suffer you?" He had done miracles before them, taught them how to pray, spent time teaching them and yet they did not get it. In verse 44 of chapter 9, it is written, "Let these sayings sink down into your ears." We need to grow in the Lord, leave the past behind, leave the milk bottle, get past the grain and head to the pasture to serve the Lord. Luke 9:62, "No man, having put his hand to the plough, and looking back, is fit for the kingdom of God." David had committed the ungodly sin with Bathsheba and paid an awful price; but he also wrote in Psalm 51:10, "Create in me a clean heart, O God; and renew a right spirit within me." Verse 12, "Restore unto me the joy of thy salvation; and uphold me with thy free spirit."

Are you still on the bottle, fighting the grain or are you still fighting the bottle? God has a plan and purpose for all of us and we will not grow until we see that He has something better for us ahead, but He is not going to force us to that growth. I knew the calves would die if they stayed on the milk, so I kept encouraging them to eat the grain and then they needed to get to the grass of the field. There will be no joy and victory over sin if we keep drinking out of the bottle. Where are you today, my Christian brother and sister in Christ? I pray I will see you in the field for Christ. Lord bless youoday.

Spiritual growth will require leaving the bottle
behind and heading to pasture.

August 27

Ecclesiastes 7-8   Psalm 52   Proverbs 27   Luke 10

Take Time for Others

Good morning! The older we get, it seems the more alone we are. I do not mean that I feel lonely because I do not. The Lord has blessed my wife and I with so many friends, at church, through the years of camp and traveling to churches and meeting people. I love my Sunday School class and those that attend. I love my church and the friends that are part of our local family. I love and miss so very much my children and grandchildren. I spend time each week on the phone with my family since they all have moved away. At my present age, there are those my age and younger that are passing on to Heaven. The older that we get the more often our friends leave this earth and go to eternity.

This morning I was reading in Ecclesiastes 7:1, "A good name is better than precious ointment; and the day of death than the day of one's birth." Then in verses 8 of the same chapter; "Better is the end of a thing than the beginning thereof: and the patient in spirit is better than the proud in spirit." When I was younger, and I am speaking of my preteen and teen years, I spent a lot of time talking with my grandparents. I loved the stories and I held on to all the words they said. In my mind I went to where they were as they were talking. Their wisdom strengthened me and their lives challenged me; I wanted to be like them. They were not perfect and they sinned, but they had a determination, character, and drive that drew me. They had a love for God that helped me. They were not preachers, deacons or even held positions in church, but they had a love for God and a respect for God that drew me.

As we read in Luke 10 this morning about the lawyer that asked Jesus, "what shall I do to inherit eternal life?" Jesus answered in verse 27, "Thou shalt love the Lord thy God with all thy heart, and with all thy soul, and with all thy strength, and with all thy mind; and thy neighbor as thyself." Do those around you that you work with, neighbors, business people that you know, family, friends see your love, and dedication to God? Do they hear from your mouth praise to our Lord? In Luke 10:30-37 is the parable of the Good Samaritan and the conclusion that we can always see is he took time, saw the need, gave what he had and made a positive impact on this man.

Be careful what kind of life you are living because the days will end sooner than you think and the end is more important than the beginning. Proverbs 27:1, "Boast not thyself of tomorrow; for thou knowest not what a day may bring forth." Psalm 52:1, "the goodness of God endureth continually." Live for God for His glory, for others, for His will. Do not pass by today what God has for you. Today might be the biggest opportunity you and I have to be the encouragement to others that God needs us to be. I have learned that selfish people, discouraged people, people that want to quit and give up; people that want to run from their situations, are always the people that only see themselves and their circumstances and do not see the opportunities that God has for them around them. You and I have only one life to live. Live for Christ and for His will and for His glory. Leave a testimony of honor to God and all that He has done and is doing in your life. Take time for others today before the others are gone. Be the encouragement for the next generation. God wants to use you today.

Take time for others before the others are gone.

August 28

Ecclesiastes 9-10   Psalm 53   Proverbs 28   Luke 11

Fight or Focus?

Good morning! The book of Ecclesiastes gives us an insight deep inside of a man. By that I mean it shows us, teaches us and warns us so often about our flesh and the need of wisdom and the lack of wisdom. As I read the Word of God, I hunger to take everything in and let my mind absorb it so that I can be a better man and a better servant for the Lord. I read this morning in chapter 9 and verse 10, "whatsoever thy hand findeth to do, do it with thy might;." I thought if you give a little boy a shovel and a bucket and point him to a pile of dirt, he will work and work and if you ask what he is doing, he will say that he is digging a tunnel or building a fort. Whatever that little boy is doing, he is doing it with his whole heart. Give a little girl some little plates, cups, spoon and some water and the tea party begins. The sand in the sand box or the dirt of the ground will turn into something very delicious. The little boy and the little girl will work hard and their imagination and energy will not stop.

In Ecclesiastes 10:10, "If the iron be blunt, and he do not whet the edge, then must he put to more strength: but wisdom is profitable to direct." It is very obvious what is being taught in this verse - that we need to work smarter than harder. That comes down to my thoughts this morning. The children have the vision and use their energy but sometimes we as adults fight so hard what we know is right and what we should be doing. It is like there is a division between us and God. Luke 11:17, "Every kingdom divided against itself is brought to desolation and a house divided against a house faileth." Look down to verse 23, "He that is not with me is against me:;" and then look at verse 28, "blessed are they that hear the word of God, and keep it."

A child will play for hours because of what they see, even though they were not told what to do; and we as adults know what is right and what we should be doing and we often fight against what we know is right . Psalm 53:2, "God looked down from heaven upon the children of men, to see if there were any that did understand, that did seek God." Let us take the admonition of Proverbs 28:20, "A faithful man shall abound with blessings." Maybe we need to sit down beside the little boy and ask him what he sees and sit down with the little girl and let her tell us what she has prepared to spark our focus on what God has for us. Have a blessed day.

May we focus on God's will rather than fight it.

August 29

Ecclesiastes 11-12   Psalm 54   Proverbs 29   Luke 12

What are You Learning?

Good morning! Our "Back to School Retreat" begins here at the camp today. This Retreat is to give the students that attend a spiritual boost for the school year. As I was reading this morning, my mind took me back to the days I attended school and then I wrote down that I never will leave school. Life is a constant learning process and there are lessons to be learned no matter our age. If we would learn many lessons in our youthful years, we as adults would have avoided many mistakes that all of us could say we made.

Ecclesiastes 12:13 begins our thoughts for the day, "Let us hear the conclusion of the whole matter: Fear God, and keep his commandments: for this is the whole duty of man." Do you remember your father or mother or grandparent asking you this question, "What did you learn in school today?" We would stop and go back through the day to give them an answer. What about us spiritually? As we read our Bible, go through situations of life, have circumstances hit us, have to make decisions, what have we learned? Living life without learning will bring us to a point of constantly repeating things and often repeating wrong things. We are going to have a test and that test is the test of life. Ecclesiastes 12:14, "For God shall bring every work into judgment, with every secret thing, whether it be good, or whether it be evil." We need to work to provide for ourselves and our families, but what is our priority of life? We are able to have the health to work because of God. We have the job we have because of God. We have the house, apartment, condo to live in, because of God. Before we were saved, we were heading in a wrong direction. Some were already saved and have made a mess of life. What are you learning in life?

Today in Luke 12:31 we read, "But rather seek ye the kingdom of God; and all these things shall be added unto you." Do we have time for everything but God? Can we go to work every morning, but are too tired to go to church on Sunday, and yet we want God to hear and answer our prayers? Luke 12:31, "For where your treasure is, there will your heart be also." Proverbs 29:25, "The fear of man bringeth a snare: but whoso putteth his trust in the Lord shall be safe." School is in session and our class today is life. How are you doing? Let us learn the lesson to put God first. Our daily assignment is to walk with God. The test will come each day and my prayer for you is that you may pass the test because you saw the importance to read, study and hide the Word of God in your heart. They often addressed the Lord Jesus as "Teacher;" He is still at the head of our classroom. Learn from Him today, listen to Him today, and walk with Him today. Class will soon be over and we will graduate to eternity. Mom would say when I would leave the house and head to the bus stop, listen to the teacher today and learn all you can. Good advice for us today.

Our daily assignment is to walk with God.

August 30

Song of Solomon   1-2 Psalm 55   Proverbs 30   Luke 13

God's Wonderful Love

Good morning! There are words in our vocabulary that are hard to describe, especially those words that express emotion. Our Bible reading today takes us to one of those words that we use daily to show expression in so many different ways. The word is love, and we first find it in the book of Song of Solomon as the expression of pure martial love as ordained of God. Chapter 2:4, "his banner over me was love;" 2:16, "My beloved is mine, and I am his:." In these two verses, we see love used as protection and ownership. If we look back to verse 4, we see "the upright love thee;" expressing those that love God and hunger to serve Him have a devotion to Him.

Early this morning I received a text from a father that his wife had just given birth to a new baby boy. We can picture the joy of both parents as this new little one will receive everything needed from clothing, food, shelter, protection, guidance, compassion, training, love, etc., so that he will grow and be the man that he should be. That is love. We read in Luke 13:34, "I have gathered thy children together, as a hen doth gather her brood under her wings, and ye would not!" Jesus is illustrating how His love has been rejected. How a heart breaks when love is rejected. Proverbs 30:5, "Every word of God is pure: he is a shield unto them that put their trust in Him." God's Word has been given to us because He loves us and wants us to have guidance, comfort and strength; but do we read it and allow His love to be there for us? Psalm 55:22, "Cast thy burden upon the Lord, and he shall sustain thee: he shall never suffer the righteous to be moved." God is our all, our everything, because He loves us. His Son was sent because He loves us. His son bore our sins because He loves us. His forgave us because He loves us. He gave us eternal life in Heaven because He loves us. He is preparing a mansion for us because He loves us. He gave us the Holy Spirit because He loves us. It is impossible to express the love of God, and yet it is rejected. Our love can be shown to God by our obedience to God.

Can you see the baby chicks running as fast as they can to their mother for protection? Can you picture the comfort of a baby being held in the arms of a mother, or a newborn baby wrapped in the little blanket to give comfort and security? Let God love you today and return the love to Him. He is there in your trial, He is there in your loneliness, He is there when we do not know what to do, He is there to meet our needs because He loves us. Let us look at those words again in Song of Solomon 2:16, "My beloved is mine, and I am his:." Love Him today and enjoy His arms around you. He is always there because He loves us. God is love.

Let God love you today and return the love to Him.

August 31

Song of Solomon 3-4   Psalm 56   Proverbs 31   Luke 14

No Excuses

Good morning! I have said to myself on many occasions, "I cannot blame anybody else but myself." That statement has helped me to get past and improve or change something in my life many times. We live in a time, and are part of a world, that does not want to take responsibility for their own actions. People want things without work. We want everyone to hear our excuse and to understand instead of facing up to the problem that is just plain old me.

As I was reading this morning in Song of Solomon 3, I kept reading the phrase, "whom my soul loveth." In chapter four and verse seven we read, "there is no spot in thee." There is not a perfect world and there is no perfect situation, but our Lord is perfect, patient, longsuffering and it is time we look to Him, hear Him and respond to what we know is right and change our lives. In our reading this morning in Luke 14, Jesus gives five different parables or illustrations that bring out the point of how excuses are not an excuse. Our problem is our lack of love toward God to do right and to face the fact that our problems can only be corrected by us. Look at verse 27, "And whosoever doth not bear his cross, and come after me, cannot be my disciple." We want to change . . . but. We know what we ought to do . . but. We know we should . . but.

As we read in Proverbs 31:31 this morning, "her own works praise her." The Godly character that the virtuous woman displayed built the relationship she had with God, husband, family and friends. We must stop and quit blaming anybody else or our circumstances. The problem is us. Now, do not get down and throw the towel in. We read in Psalm 56:9, "for God is for me." God is there to help us if we reach out to Him and if we have the character to do right. It is time we let the love that we say we have for God, rule our lives and stop our weak flesh from keeping us from doing right. We need to look at ourselves today, face ourselves and get with what we know is right and pleasing to the Lord. Get past what is keeping you from growing in the Lord and have the victory that God wants you to have. Song of Solomon 3:2, "I will seek him whom my soul loveth:." God bless you as you get the victory.

> *God is there to help us if we reach out to Him*
> *and if we have the character to do right.*

Song of Solomon 5-6   Psalm 57   Proverbs 1   Luke 15

A God That Can Be Found

Good morning! I have misplaced and lost many things in my life. My wife just purchased for me the best set of sunglasses to clip over my glasses that I have ever owned, and I have lost them. I was working out in the back part of the camp on the side of a hill and I think they slid off of the dashboard onto the ground, when I opened the door. I have looked and relooked many times and I have still not found them. Can you relate with me about losing something and you cannot find it?

What would happen if we called to God and could not find Him or hear Him? Song of Solomon 5:6, "I opened to my beloved; but my beloved had withdrawn himself, and was gone: my soul failed when he spake: I sought him, but I could not find him; I called him, but he gave me no answer." How terrible, how sad to think the bride called for the groom and there was no answer. Too many are fooling around with God and putting off getting saved and living for Him. That day might come that we cry out to Him and He does not hear. It has happened before in Scripture. Proverbs 1:28, "Then shall they call upon me, but I will not answer; they shall seek me early, but they shall not find me:." In Luke 15 there are three parables that teach us about a lost sheep, lost coin and a lost son. There is time spent in searching and there is time spent in rejoicing when found. In Luke 15:7, "I say unto you, that likewise joy shall be in heaven over one sinner that repenteth."

I thought about GPS which is part of our life today in so many applications. There are 30 main satellites orbiting the earth at an altitude of 20,000 km, and they are used to determine a ground position of an object. Wow!! But let me show you something greater than GPS; Psalm 57:5,

11,"Be thou exalted, O God, above the heavens: let thy glory be above all the earth." The Psalmist wrote in 57:7, "My heart is fixed, O God, my heart is fixed: I will sing and give praise." We better listen to God and seek Him continually while He may be found. He loves us and desires to lead us and fellowship with us. We need to take the admonition to hearken to His voice and obey Him. Greater it is to lose fellowship with God than to lose a personal item or a personal friend. Song of Solomon 5:2, "it is the voice of my beloved that knocketh, saying, Open to me." He is knocking today; listen and follow Him today. How frustrated we get when we cannot find something, but how greater it would be if there comes a day that the voice of our cry to God is not heard. He will not put up with our sin forever. He will not put up with our rejection of Him forever. He will not put up with our excuses and lack of character forever. Seek Him today. He is there and He may be found.

We better listen to God and seek Him while He may be found.

September 2

Song of Solomon 7-8   Psalm 58   Proverbs 2   Luke 16

Don't Break the Seal

Good morning! Let me challenge you to begin every day by praising and thanking God that you are His. Rejoice each morning that you are saved and know for sure that when you die, Heaven is your home. This world is full of people that wake each day and have no hope of eternal salvation. I love the words of Song of Solomon 7:10, "I am my beloved's, and his desire is toward me." God's focus and love is always on us. Oh, may we be faithful to our Lord and put Him first in everything that we do, and may His desire always be our desire! Many times promises are broken and that is sad, but we must sincerely make a commitment to God like the one that is recorded for us in Song of Solomon 8:6, "Set me as a seal upon thine heart, as a seal upon thine arm:."

I remember helping my mom can vegetables and she would have the jars in the pressure cooker. Then it would be time to take them out and set them on the counter and she would always say, "Be careful not to break the seal." If the seal was broken, we had to use the items right away or they would go bad. Luke 16:10, "He that is faithful in that which is least is faithful also in much:." God is always faithful and He sees where we have been faithful to Him and where we have not been faithful and the "seal has been broken." Luke 16:13, "No man can serve two masters: for either he will hate the one, and love the other;." We need to always put the things of God first.

I loved to go to the basement and get the canned vegetables off the shelf, because it was like getting fresh vegetables from the garden, but if the seal was broken, we could not eat them. Please listen to these phrases from Proverbs 2, verse 1, "if thou wilt receive my words, and hide my commandments with thee;" verse 9, "Then shalt thou understand," verse 11, "Discretion shall preserve thee, understanding shall keep thee;." Don't break the seal between you and God. He will always bless when we do right. Why miss a blessing from God? Psalm 58:11 "Verily there is a reward for the righteous."

I remember it like it was yesterday . . ."David, go to the basement and get a quart of apples, but make sure the seal is not broken." An apple pie was going to be made and I could taste it before it was made. My love for God and His love for me should be a seal of praise and commitment and that seal should never be broken. It is God's will for us to enjoy and grow in our relationship with Him. I can smell that fresh apple pie.

Don't break the seal between you and God.

September 3

Isaiah 1-2   Psalm 59   Proverbs 3   Luke 17

Washed Clean

Good morning! One of the very first verses I memorized was Isaiah 1:18, "Come now, and let us reason together, saith the Lord: though your sins be as scarlet, they shall be as white as snow; though they be red like crimson, they shall be as wool." My sins were and are so bad, but His love has taken my sins and washed me clean.

There is something about a Monday wash hanging on the clothesline. Monday was always a washing day and the clothes were hung on the line to dry. I often was asked to go get the laundry from the clothesline and bring it in. I loved the smell of the freshly washed and air-dried clothes; such a freshness. Religion has confused the beauty of true worship and fellowship with God. Isaiah 1:2, "To what purpose is the multitude of your sacrifices unto me?" Have we been like Israel and rebelled against God? We need to never leave the singing of Psalms and hymns and we need old fashioned preaching. Isaiah 1:16, "Wash you, make you clean; put away the evil of your doings from before mine eyes; cease to do evil;." I am afraid we look at church and reading our Bibles only as duty and not as worship and fellowship with God. Luke 17:10, "We are unprofitable servants: we have done that which was our duty to do."

Ten lepers were healed but only one returned to give glory to God. Proverbs 3:1, "forget not my law; but let thine heart keep my commandments:." The Psalmist wrote in Psalm 59:1, "Deliver me," "defend me;" and then down in verse 9, "for God is my defense," verse 11, "O Lord our shield," verse 17, "the God of my mercy." Please do not let this day begin without praising and thanking God for who He is and what He has done.

We did not hang the dirty laundry on the clothesline. The old scrub board and the ringer washer were used with the lye and ivory soap, and a lot of scrubbing was done to get the laundry clean and then hang it out on the clothesline in the sun. Greater than this is a sinner washed clean by the blood of Jesus Christ. Let us be a sweet smelling savor today for our King who has thoroughly washed us and redeemed us. Let us walk in victory today. Don't let the clean laundry drop in the dirt, I was told. Good advice for us Christians to keep from being spotted by the sin of this world. Have a blessed day.

God's love has taken our sins and washed us clean!

Isaiah 3-4   Psalm 60   Proverbs 4   Luke 18

Storms of Life

Good morning! Living over fifty years of my life in the Midwest, I grew to respect tornados and their capability of destruction. One year during family camp we were told by a storm chaser that two tornados were heading our way. The week had just started and the campers were all getting settled in. The day was beautiful and the sky did not seem to have the signs of a storm. I knew there had been sightings far away but not in our path. The weather changed so fast and soon we were in the paths of both tornados. Thank the Lord that no one was hurt and no one left, and the Lord gave us a tremendous week.

There is no tornado or hurricane that can destroy a nation and a people like sin. Our reading today in Isaiah 3:8, "Jerusalem is ruined, and Judah is fallen: because their tongue and their doings are against the Lord,;" verse 9, "their countenance doth witness against them; and they declare their sin as Sodom." It is hurricane season for many, but greater than the destruction by a storm is the sin of a people and nation. We have a protection from the destruction of sin as shown to us in our reading today in Luke 18:1, "men ought always to pray, and not to faint;" verse 7, "And shall not God avenge his own elect, which cry day and night unto him, though he bear long with them?"

The power of God through a storm can be destructive, but the power of God's destruction due to sin is beyond any storm. Let us as individuals, families and a nation humble ourselves before God. Luke 18:14, "for everyone that exalteth himself shall be abased; and he that humbleth himself shall be exalted.." We must be challenged in this sin crazed world to keep our focus and path on God and His Word. Proverbs 4:25, "Let thine eyes look right on, and let thine eyes look straight before thee."

The day that two tornados were coming in the direction of the camp, we all joined together in prayer. As the tornados came and we were pleading with our Lord, a boy had a camera and took a picture through the window

307

of a funnel as it went over the camp and settled back on the ground just outside the gate of the camp. Many times my wife and I and our family have talked about the day we were all protected and we knew it was the hand of Almighty God. Psalm 60:4, "Thou hast given a banner to them that fear thee, that it may be displayed because of the truth. Selah." I have no idea what kind of storm might come your way, but there is nothing safer than the hand of God as we stay on our faces daily before Him and seek His face in everything that we do. What banner will you be flying when the storms of life hit?

There is no place safer than the hand of God in the midst of our storms.

September 5

Isaiah 5-6   Psalm 61   Proverbs 5   Luke 19

God's Vineyard

Good morning! It has been said over and over again that what a person has to work for will be more appreciated than something that is just given and not earned. A child appreciates and takes care of a toy they had to work and save for, more than toys that are just given. Many a teen has been given a car and it is not taken care of as well as an old car that was bought with some hard- earned money and looks like a piece of junk, but is taken care of like it is brand new. My wife and I were out soul winning and we were going down a street. I eyed an old truck and I said to my wife, read the bumper sticker on that truck. It read, "Go ahead and laugh, but it is payed for."

Isaiah 5 records for us how Jehovah had a vineyard and it was planted with the choicest vine, "that it should bring forth grapes, and it brought forth wild grapes." Israel is the vineyard, and they had arrived at a point of sin that brought them to the place of God saying in Isaiah 5:20, "Woe unto them that call evil good and good evil." And in verse 24, "they have cast away the law of the Lord of hosts, and despised the word of the Holy One of Israel." In chapter 6 we read Isaiah has a vision to speak truth about the sin and there is a fire set in him. In verse 9 we read, "Go, and tell this people." God is looking for those that will hear the truth, keep the truth, live the truth and spread the truth. What a person has to work for is most often taken better care of than what we are just given.

We read in Luke 19 how God is an investor and in verse 13 he tells us to "Occupy till I come." That means we have the truth and we are to be busy about spreading the truth and winning people to Christ and living for Christ. God sees what is going on in our lives. Proverbs 5:21, "For the ways of man are before the eyes of the Lord, and he pondereth all his goings." My first car was an old 1955 Buick. It was big and the paint had bad spots in it. It was not a car that most teens would have wanted. It only cost $150, but I washed it, waxed it, bought new floor mats for it, and took care of it like it was brand new. I sanded and repaired and repainted those bad spots. I did all the maintenance because I wanted it to last. We have been given a heritage that cost people everything to preserve it. Each generation must pay a price. Psalm 61:5, "thou hast given me the heritage of those that fear thy name." God has invested in us and given us life to live and eternal life after this life. Let us be a vineyard that produces a good fruit. Psalm 61:8, "So will I sing unto thy name for ever, that I may daily perform my vows." Yes, we have a heritage that has been passed on to us, but we must do whatever must be done to preserve it for the next generation. Christ gave all. How can we do less than give our best?

God has invested in us - let us be a vineyard that produces good fruit.

September 6

Isaiah 7-8   Psalm 62   Proverbs 6   Luke 20

Butter and Honey

Good morning! We as humans make things so very hard. As I began my reading today in Isaiah, my heart was so convicted as I read the simple phrase in Isaiah 7:15, "Butter and honey shall he eat, that he may know to refuse the evil, and choose the good.." It's plain and simple so that we can know right from wrong if we will just stop, confess and ask forgiveness of sin, search the Scriptures, meditate on what we read, leave it in its context and let God speak to us. "Butter and honey shall he eat."

For many years every Saturday morning, I had the responsibility to churn the butter. It was simple, pour the cream from the top of the milk into the butter churn and turn the crank. My mom would say "soon," but to a young boy it seemed to take forever. The butter would begin to show itself forming and I would keep cranking until I could almost not crank anymore. Then I would open the churn and put the butter into a mold, and then take the butter out of the mold and put it on a piece of wax paper and put it into the cooler to get hard, and we would take it to town to sell. It was simple. I also had some beehives that would produce honey. Then in time, after the bees did all the work, the hives would be robbed so that the fresh honey could be separated and then eaten and used for so many different things.

If we would just stop and spend time each day with the Lord in reading His Word and spending time in prayer, His Word would guide us, instruct us, and convict us of sin. The time in prayer will comfort us as we pour our hearts out to Him in praise and thankfulness and then request of Him. Proverbs 6:6 today in our reading tells us to do something very simple and practical: "Go to the ant, thou sluggard; consider her ways, and be wise.." Down to verse 21 and it shows us what we are to do with the things that we learn from the Word of God: "Bind them continually upon thine heart, and tie them about thy neck.;" or simply make them part of my life. Verse 22 teaches us that what we learn will "lead thee," "keep thee," and "talk with thee." Verse 23 is our direction from what we learn: "For the commandment is a lamp; and the law is light; and reproofs of instruction are the way of life:." Let the Word of God and a walk with God be "butter and honey;" simple, practical, directional, encouraging, convicting, etc.

Psalm 62:2, 8, "He only is my rock and my salvation; he is my defense; I shall not be moved. Trust in him at all times; ye people, pour out your heart before him: God is a refuge for us. Selah." Enjoy your "Butter and Honey" today.

Let the Word of God and a walk with God be your "butter and honey."

Isaiah 9-10   Psalm 63   Proverbs 7   Luke 21

Time for Revival

Good morning! My heart yearns for revival in the time I live on this earth. The news media has chosen to only report the calamities of life. There is good news and we read it this morning in Isaiah 9:6, "For unto us a child is born, unto us a son is given." In verse 7 we read the wonderful phrase, "peace there shall be no end." Yes, in the end times there will be wars and rumors of wars, great pestilence, but I am deciding to choose the desire of God to bring revival. Isaiah 10:21, "The remnant shall return, even the remnant of Jacob, unto the mighty God." We must pray together, seek the face of God together, read His Word and be a people of Light to bring the Light to a dark world.

Luke 21:28 in our reading today challenges us to, "look up, and lift up your heads; for your redemption draweth nigh." We are seeing a turning back to God and we must increase our praying. We are seeing the Bible going back into the schools and Christians stand for truth. He is waiting on us. Proverbs 7:2, "Keep my commandments, and live; and my law as the apple of thine eye." May we stand and proclaim as the Psalmist did in Psalm 63:1, "O God, thou art my God; early will I seek thee: my soul thirsteth for thee, my flesh longeth for thee in a dry and thirsty land, where no water is."

One of our horses was out last night and when we went to put him back in, he started running up and down the fence to see where he could get back in. He had lost where the gate was partially opened where he had gotten out. As he saw us open another gate, he took off and ran to that opening. Let us open the gate of the gospel to this world that is just going here and there and not finding the truth. When the truth is shown, the peace of God will enter. Let us pray and live to see revival. Psalm 63:8, "My soul followeth hard after thee: thy right hand upholdeth me." There have been great revivals of past and we can have a great revival during our lifetime. Let us seek the Lord together and keep our eyes on Him. Have a blessed day.

We must be a people of Light to bring the Light to a dark world.

September 8

Isaiah 11-12   Psalm 64   Proverbs 8   Luke 22

A Beautiful Picture

Good morning! On the walls of most homes in the living room, den, family room or a room where a lot of time is spent, are pictures, or maybe one large picture, of something beautiful. A mountain scene, or a picture of a beautiful river or stream, or a picture of something very relaxing. It could be a drawing of something that causes you to relax or just stop and let your mind rest.

The picture drawn for us in Isaiah 11 is a picture of hope, a picture of comfort, a picture of victory; it is a picture drawn for us of our coming KING to soon rule and reign. Isaiah 11 is a picture of Christ coming to rule and reign, and the glory of the coming kingdom. It is beyond a picture because of the thought that in verse 6 we read how the "wolf also shall dwell with the lamb, and the leopard shall lie down with the kid; and the calf and the young lion and the fatling together; and a little child shall lead them." What a day that will be when all will be at peace with each other. We need to stop today and take time to look beyond our situations and circumstances of this day. We turn to Luke 11 and we read of the wonderful remembrance of when the children of Israel were in captivity and the blood was shed of the spotless lamb and the blood was put on the door post, and the death angel passed over.

May our love, hope and peace for Christ and what He is and has done for us be a comfort and peace to us today. As we look at this beautiful picture of Him and His coming, may our love for Him be more today and our service to Him be stronger today. Proverbs 8:17, "I love them that love me; and those that seek me early shall find me." Proverbs 8:32, "blessed are they that keep my ways." I have been in many homes and seen beautiful pictures hanging on a wall. I have stood on high mountain peaks way above the tree line and looked deep into the beauty of the valleys and have seen a picture that shows the beauty of God. However, nothing is more beautiful of a picture than the coming and ruling of our Lord when sin will be banished and the devil will finally be put in his place. Psalm 64:10, "The righteous shall be glad in the Lord, and shall trust in him; and all the upright in heart shall glory." Let us be part of painting a picture of hope today to a lost and dying world. Share Christ with someone today and every day. Live in victory and not in frustration or discouragement. The idea of the beautiful picture is to bring a peace and comfort. A greater peace and a greater comfort than any picture is the peace and comfort that Christ can give. Live for Him and share Him today.

God paints a beautiful picture of peace and comfort
that we need to share with others.

September 9

Isaiah 13-14   Psalm 65   Proverbs 9   Luke 23

Sound Forth

Good morning! This world seems to function very easily without God, but there will be a day when God will have His time and His judgment of sin will fall. As we read this morning in Isaiah 13:6, "Howl ye; for the day of the Lord is at hand; (verse 9) Behold the day of the Lord cometh."

Most days between 4:00- 5:30 a.m. and 9:00-10:30 p.m. we can hear the howling of the coyotes as they run in packs through the woods. This is nothing in comparison to the final coming of the Lord to judge the sins of this world, but it does set an ear on edge. The last few days as another hunting season has opened and there have been hunters out shooting, our dogs have stayed close and in a cover, away from their fear of the gun shots. We must pay heed to the words written in Isaiah 14:24, "The Lord of hosts hath sworn, saying, surely as I have thought, so shall it come to pass; and as I have purposed, so shall it stand:." God will have His day, and sin will be judged. Jesus was put on trial because the religious world did not like His message and yet as He stood before the accusers and Pilate, it was said and recorded, "I find no fault in this man" (Luke 23:4). Verses 14 and 15 of Luke 23 state the same; "have found no fault in this man touching those things whereof ye accuse him:, nothing worthy of death is done unto him." For the third time Pilate stated in verse 22, "And he said unto them the third time, Why, what evil hath he done? I have found no cause of death in him."

The hate and anger – why? Yet Jesus cried out in verse 34, "Father, forgive them; for they know not what they do." These words and many more create a desire in my heart to spread the word and to live for my King who is the way of salvation to all men. May we bow before Him and dedicate the rest of our lives to serve Him. May our lives be lived to the fullest because as is recorded in Proverbs 9:11, "For by me thy days shall be multiplied, and the years of thy life shall be increased." May we sound forth the message of redemption strong and loud to this lost world. Psalm 65:5, "O God of our salvation; who art the confidence of all the ends of the earth."

Coyotes howl to create a fear and rally the pack to catch their prey. May we cry to reach a doomed world with the message of eternal life in Christ that brings peace beyond understanding. The coyotes will seek their prey whether it is a young calf, or a rabbit, etc. just to so they can stay alive. Our message is a life eternal, forgiven of sin. May our cry be much louder and stronger than the cries of this world that offer nothing that will bring life eternal. May our Lord use you and strengthen you today. Go forth proclaiming the message of salvation.

Sound forth the message of redemption to a lost and dying world.

September 10

Isaiah 15-16   Psalm 66   Proverbs 10   Luke 24

Our Instruction Book

Good morning! The importance of daily reading the Bible can never be stressed enough. The devil wants us to not read, not understand, not apply that which we read; and especially the devil does not like us to read the promises of God that we can claim daily in our lives. As I read in Isaiah 16:2, "as a wandering bird cast out of the nest;" I immediately took time and reread chapters 15 and 16 of Isaiah this morning. It is a warning to Moab. For lack of space in writing, let me just say, Moab will soon be like a young bird that has had their nest destroyed and they are homeless.

Many a Christian becomes homeless in a relationship with Christ because we do not see the value of reading, understanding and applying the Scriptures to our daily lives. A Christian can be on fire for God, excited about being saved, faithfully attending church and without warning, turn cold to the things of God. In Luke 24:6, as we see where there was a going to the tomb of Jesus and the angels tell them, "He is not here, but is risen: remember how he spake unto you." And again in verse 16, they were walking, "and their eyes were holden that they should not know him." We get so focused on what we want to do or what we think we need to be doing and we miss the importance of what is right in front of us. As we read in Luke 24, we see "their eyes were opened, and they knew him," but look down and see in verses 32 and 44 how the Scriptures were revealed that they should have remembered. "Did not our heart burn within us, while he talked with us by the way, and while he opened to us the scriptures?" "which were written in the law of Moses, and in the prophets, and in the psalms."

We must daily read the Word of God and meditate on what we read. Luke 24:45, "Then opened he their understanding, that they might understand the scriptures." The time we spend reading, studying and memorizing the Scriptures will change so much in our lives. Proverbs 10:13, "In the lips of him that hath understanding wisdom is found:." By daily spending time in the Bible, the promises of God will become more real to us and some of the doubts that we have will grow dim and disappear. Psalm 66:20, "Blessed be God, which hath not turned away my prayer, nor his mercy from me." I received a package yesterday and when I opened it, wrapped around it were the instructions of how to put it together. The Bible is the instruction book of life and how to live it. Be thankful we have the Scriptures because there are many in this world that would give everything they have just to have a portion of the Bible. Love His Word and live His Word.

The Bible is our instruction book of life and how to live it.

September 11

Isaiah 17-18   Psalm 67   Proverbs 11   John 1

Are You on Fire?

Good morning! Reading this morning in Isaiah 17, I stopped as I read in verse 7 and I kept rereading, "At that day shall a man look to his Maker, and his eyes shall have respect to the Holy One of Israel." As I kept rereading this verse, my mind came to this world and all men and women that reject, put off, make excuse, etc. for not living for and serving God. I read on and stopped and kept rereading verse 10, "Because thou hast forgotten the God of thy salvation, and hast not been mindful of the rock of thy strength." God is going to have His day with men and women that claim to know Jesus as their Saviour, but refuse to live for Him God's way. This world wants to bring God down to their level and not come up to God's level. We see Christianity constantly trying to be like the world and we use the excuse that we have to be more like them to reach them.

John 1:29, "The next day John seeth Jesus coming unto him, and saith, Behold the Lamb of God, which taketh away the sin of the world." What did John see about the Saviour? Was Jesus looking like the world or was there so much of Him having the Spirit of God upon Him that John knew he was looking at Jesus? In verse 36 of this same chapter we see the phrase, "And looking upon Jesus," and in verse 37, "two disciples heard him speak, and they followed Jesus." In the next few verses we see people not only following, but going and getting others to listen and follow. I wrote this on my note paper; "they heard, they saw, they followed and they told others." Is that not what we are supposed to do? Proverbs 11:30, "The fruit of the righteous is a tree of life; and he that winneth souls is wise."

We are to live for God so that others may see Jesus in us. Psalm 67:5, "Let the people praise thee, O God; let all the people praise thee." May there be a fire of revival set in our soul and be burning through our lives. A fire always draws a crowd. May our lives be a burning fire for God. Driving home from church the other day, the sky was full of smoke from something burning and you could see people looking in the direction of the fire. May we be so on fire for the Lord that people want to know why we are burning, and we will tell them the story of Jesus and all that He is to us. The world does not need us to be like them, but the world needs to see a life given to Christ that has peace, joy and a desire to share what has changed their life for Christ. Let our voice, smile, attitude, work ethic, etc. shine forth the Light of salvation to a lost and dying world. May the world look and see Jesus in us and may we take the opportunity to speak and share Christ with them. Burn for Christ today.

We need to have a fire of revival burning in our heart.

September 12

Isaiah 19-21   Psalm 68:1-18   Proverbs 12   John 2

A Watchman

Good morning! Do you have a special day or time of year that you look forward to? Maybe it is a birthday, an anniversary, a vacation, a holiday, a special day that you look forward to. It has your thoughts and your preparation. You think about it often and you are excited when that day is approaching.

I look forward to a day when we can get together with our children and grandchildren. When our children are making plans for a trip to come and see us, we buy extra food, my wife works hard in getting the house ready, and we make plans of what we are going to do. The day of their travel we call them and ask the questions, where are you and when do you think you will get here?

In Isaiah 19, six times we see the phrase, "In that day." Read on to chapter 21 and we see the command to "Go, set a watchman, let him declare what he seeth." (21:6). In verse 11 of chapter 21 in Isaiah we read the words, "Watchman, what of the night? Watchman, what of the night?" Something is coming and they must be watching and ready, it is coming. Proverbs 12:11, "He that tilleth his land shall be satisfied with bread:." I asked myself this morning, what am I doing and what am I preparing for? Do we live looking for our Lord to return? Is there an urgency in our walk with God? Are we looking for His blessing? Are we living each day for His glory, with excitement and anticipation?

The farmer tills the ground because he has plans to plant a seed and reap a harvest. Should we not be living our lives in anticipation of a reward from God for serving Him and spreading His Word to a lost world that is doomed for Hell if they do not get saved? Proverbs 12:14 spoke to me in an urgent way, "The recompense of a man's hands shall be rendered unto him." I will give an account for Christ at "that day," and I need to be a "watchman" faithful to sow the Word of God, and a "watchman" to be an encourager to my brethren in Christ.

We get excited about a special day with family, vacation, a special holiday and we watch the calendar and make preparations. This is not bad and it is not wrong. Psalm 68:11, "The Lord gave the word: great was the company of those that published it." Let us be about preparing for "that day" and be a "watchman" for the cause of Christ. May we be busy reaching others, encouraging others, serving others, and be everything that we can be for Christ. Pray for others going through trials and times of testing. We need to let our hearts be moved beyond just us. "That day" will soon be "the day." May we be watching.

A faithful watchman will share the Gospel and encourage the brethren.

Isaiah 22-23   Psalm 68:19-35   Proverbs 13   John 3

Valley of Vision

Good morning! A couple of nights ago as Mrs. Smith and I were driving home from church, we looked ahead of us and saw the lights flashing of what I thought was a fire truck coming our way. As the lights kept getting brighter in the darkness of the night, I heard the siren and I said that I thought it was a fire truck. Mrs. Smith said, no I think it is an ambulance. Sure enough, she was right again. It was a larger ambulance and the siren was a little different than some of the other ambulances. About one and three-quarter miles from the camp is a fire station and at that station is a tall tower with a siren on top of it. That siren can be heard for many miles, bringing our attention to a fire or in the case of a tornado, they will warn us by turning it on. The lights and siren of the ambulance, fire truck, police car let us know there has been an emergency.

In our reading this morning, we read in Isaiah 22:1, "The burden of the valley of vision," also in verse 5, "For it is a day of trouble, and of treading down, and of perplexity by the Lord God of hosts in the valley of vision." As I read this morning and studied, I learned that the city of Jerusalem is built on the sides of two main hills and there is a valley in between. Picture buildings on both sides, built into the hills. The "valley of vision" is the announcement of the coming judgment of God. Look at verse 11, "but ye have not looked unto the maker thereof." The people were being warned, just as the siren and lights warn us. In Proverbs 13:15, "Good understanding giveth favour: but the way of transgressors is hard." We read in John 3:16 this morning that wonderful word, "whosoever." The announcement is being made that God loves all men and desires for all men to be saved, but there are those that will face the doom of Hell unless they make the decision to trust Christ. God's love is given to all men, but rejection brings judgment. God will bless those that follow Him. Psalm 68:19, "Blessed be the Lord, who daily loadeth us with benefits."

The siren is sounding, the lights are flashing, the urgency of living for Christ and serving Him is at hand. The time is short and the putting off is coming to an end. Today is the day to trust Christ and if you know Him, TODAY IS THE DAY TO SERVE HIM. There is a need and too many are standing off and not stepping forward to serve. I just read this week that only five out of one hundred young people are surrendering to missions. The fields are white unto harvest and yet where are the servants? My brother and sister, today is the day for us to look at the "valley of vision" and make a decision for Christ. Serve Him today. Step forward and be of help, reach out and be of service to our King. The emergency has sounded.

Look into the valley of vision today and make a decision for Christ.

September 14

Isaiah 24-25   Psalm 69:1-15   Proverbs 14   John 4

Beyond the Fire

Good morning! Trials, testing, fear, discouragements, disappointments, failures, heartbreaks, etc., cannot stop us when we are seeing what the Lord wants us to see. In the middle of what seemed to be close to the end for the children of Israel, Isaiah wrote in 24:15, "Wherefore glorify ye the Lord in the fires." In chapter 25 and verse 1 we read, "O Lord, thou art my God; I will exalt thee, I will praise thy name; for thou hast done wonderful things; thy counsels of old are faithfulness and truth."

Think with me about an old barn that is broken down, rotten, weeds almost covering it so that you can barely see anything remaining of the structure. At one time that barn was a place of storing fresh hay, a cover for newborn animals, a place of cover from storms, a place to store farm equipment, a place for storing grain that would soon be planted in the spring, a place to get out of the heat of the sun and you could feel a cool breeze blowing through. To some, the old barn is nothing and yet to a photographer it could be a place of beauty. To some it is of no value and to some it is a place of many wonderful memories.

How do we look through the fire, the trials, the discouragements? In John 4, we read of the woman at the well that had had five husbands and the man she was living with, she was not married to and yet this woman saw the love of Jesus, felt the love of Jesus and said in verse 29, "Come, see a man, which told me all things that ever I did: is not this the Christ?" She saw beyond the fire. In Proverbs 14 we see the word "prudent" used four different times. I looked in several different resources for an explanation for prudent and it means being wise, looking ahead, and preparing for what is ahead.

Look beyond the fire. The Psalmist wrote in Psalm 69:14, "Deliver me out of the mire, and let me not sink:." I have been told many times, quit looking at your trial and look beyond. Look up and look ahead, look beyond, look past, look far. Failure does not come because we failed; failure comes only when we quit trying. The dark clouds bring the rain that will nourish the ground. What might seem to be the end could be the greatest beginning. Proverbs 14:8, "The wisdom of the prudent is to understand his way:." Look beyond the fire.

Look beyond your trial to what God has planned for you ahead.

September 15

Isaiah 26-27   Psalm 69:16-36   Proverbs 15   John 5

From Fear to Faith

Good morning! The victory song that is recorded for us in Isaiah 26:3-4 should be a constant reminder to us about keeping ourselves focused on God. "Thou wilt keep him in perfect peace, whose mind is stayed on thee: because he trusteth in thee." "Trust ye in the Lord for ever: for in the Lord JEHOVAH is everlasting strength:." Look on down to verses 8-9, "the desire of our soul is to thy name, and to the remembrance of thee." "With my spirit within me will I seek thee early."

Life is full of distractions and the devil works overtime and our flesh is weak, but God is our source of strength and we must look to Him continually. John 5:1-14 records for us the story of the impotent man. For thirty-eight years he lay and Jesus asked him, "Wilt thou be made whole?" This statement has convicted me so many times about my faith in God, because the man gave an excuse instead of just answering the question. In verse eight, Jesus simply said, "Rise, take up thy bed, and walk." Excuses get us nowhere and do not allow us to accomplish anything. Faith in Christ always moves us toward Him and toward seeing what God can do and is doing.

Remember when you learned to ride a bicycle? How many times did all of us think, "I can't," and yet we did? We had to trust, attempt, practice and then we rode. Our voices could be heard loud and clear, "I am doing it! Look, I am riding by myself!" We must walk in faith, by faith, to see God work in our life through faith. Psalm 69:32, "The humble shall see this, and be glad: and your heart shall live that seek God." Each time we see God do things in our life, it sparks our faith in Him. Proverbs 15:14, "The heart of him that hath understanding seeketh knowledge: but the mouth of fools feedeth on foolishness."

Many a bicycle have been ridden when we decided we wanted to ride, and we got past our fears and lack of trust. Then we learned how to ride wheelies and jump ditches and that is when I began to get stitches. Let us learn to trust God and receive the perfect peace in Him by walking and trusting in Him. I still love to jump things, but I moved from a bicycle to things that are powered with a motor. Have a blessed day.

We must walk in faith, by faith, to see God work in our life through faith.

September 16

Isaiah 28-29   Psalm 70   Proverbs 16   John 6

A Living Testimony

Good morning! There are days when I am reading the Scriptures, I wish I had more time to study and meditate on what I am reading. Be careful not to start your day by reading something in the Bible just so you can say, well, I read the Bible today, or to read and just check off the list. Learn to stop, think and study the Scriptures. In Isaiah 28:10 we read, "For precept must be upon precept, precept upon precept; line upon line, line upon line; here a little, and there a little:." The word "precept" means a general rule intended to regulate behavior or thought; a command or principle intended especially as a general rule of action." We must slow down and read every word of God's Word and learn to apply the Word of God in every area of our lives. How convicting is verse 13, "For as much as this people draw near me with their mouth, and with their lips do honor me, but have removed their heart far from me, and their fear toward me is taught by the precept of men:."

Have we arrived at the point that we honor the words of men more than the words of God? Do we look to the wisdom of men more than the wisdom of God? Do we spend more time following men than following God? Do we spend more time preparing for a stable future than we spend time preparing for eternity? I asked myself these questions this morning. In John 6:26, Jesus said, "Ye seek me not because ye saw the miracles, but because ye did eat of the loaves, and were filled." Is God only good enough in times of trouble, or in times of need? In verse 66 of John 6 we read a very sad but true statement; "From that time many of his disciples went back, and walked no more with him." And then Jesus personally asks this question; "Will ye also go away?"

As we get older, there should be more Godliness in us that is coming out in every area of our life. Proverbs 16:31, "The hoary head is a crown of glory, if it be found in the way of righteousness." May we live as the Psalmist wrote in Psalm 70:4, "Let all those that seek thee rejoice and be glad in thee: and let such as love thy salvation say continually, Let God be magnified." Be a living testimony for God today.

We should have more Godliness the older we get.

September 17

Isaiah 30-31   Psalm 71:1-16   Proverbs 17   John 7

The Maze of Life

Good morning! During the fall of the year, there are corn mazes always available to walk through. The corn grows so tall and the path through the maze can sometimes be very confusing. You can turn to the left when you need to go right, or you go straight ahead and come to a dead end. The corn mazes are always fun, but sometimes life can be like a maze and we turn right when we should have gone left, or we find ourselves at a dead end and we are not sure what to do. Have you ever felt life is like a maze? Isaiah 30:21, "This is the way, walk ye in it, when ye turn to the right hand, and when ye turn to the left." Yes, life can be a maze. That is why it is so vital for a Christian to put their faith and trust in Christ and to always have His will in front of us and nothing else. Do not look at the world and all that it offers and think that will be what will help you find peace, joy and happiness. Isaiah 31:1, "Woe to them that go down to Egypt (picture of the world) for help; and stay on horses, and trust in chariots, because they are many; and in horsemen, because they are very strong; but they look not unto the Holy One of Israel, neither seek the Lord!"

Going to the world is never satisfying and it will never give us peace and understanding. John 7:37, "If any man thirst, let him come unto me, and drink." Proverbs 17:27, "a man of understanding is of an excellent spirit." Sometimes life seems like we are in a maze and we end up being in a daze and have no idea what to do. That is why our hope and trust should always be in God. When we are in confusion, it will give us a negative spirit, but walking with God and being in His will creates in us a sweet peace and confidence. Proverbs 17:27, "a man of understanding is of an excellent spirit." Psalm 71:1, "In thee, O Lord, do I put my trust: let me never be put to confusion." Psalm 71:5, "For thou art my hope, O Lord God: thou art my trust from my youth." Even as we get older and have years of understanding, be careful of that maze of life. Even in our older years God has a plan and purpose for us. Believe me, I understand how the maze of age can bring confusion as so much changes so quickly, and without warning. Listen to the Psalmist's plea, Psalm 71:9, "Cast me not off in the time of old age; forsake me not when my strength faileth." Keep on the right path with God and we will all soon make it through the maze of life.

Walking with God creates in us a sweet peace and confidence.

September 18

Isaiah 32-33   Psalm 71:17-24   Proverbs 18   John 8

He is There

Good morning! Have you ever found yourself saying, when I get this done or when I get past this, things will be better? When I get settled into a better schedule, or when I get done with this project, etc. If you will allow me to say, there will always be another project, another situation, another trial. This and many other reasons are why it is so important to stop and have a time and place every day to get alone with God and be strengthened in God before the day begins.

Isaiah 33:2, "O Lord, be gracious unto us; we have waited for thee: be thou their arm every morning, our salvation also in the time of trouble." He is there for us and we should come to Him and prepare ourselves for whatever is ahead each day. We do not know when an emergency will happen and we will need Him, or a decision needs to be made and we need His guidance. Proverbs 18:10, "The name of the Lord is a strong tower: the righteous runneth into it, and is safe." In John 8 we read of the woman caught in adultery and Jesus was there for her. The sin was ungodly, and it caught her, but Jesus was there for her. I am not excusing the sin, but it is a wonderful picture of Christ being there for her. Isaiah 33:22, "For the Lord is our judge, the Lord is our lawgiver, the Lord is our King, he will save us."

We must have that daily guidance from God and His Word, to stay away from sin and to keep going in our trials. Proverbs 18:14, "The spirit of a man will sustain his infirmity; but a wounded spirit who can bear?"

Keep seeking Him, for He is to be found. As I get older there is a hunger to show this generation and generations to come God's love, forgiveness, provision and promises. Psalm 71:18, "O God, forsake me not; until I have shewed thy strength unto this generation, and thy power to everyone that is to come." Jesus stooped down twice in John 8 and when all had been convicted of their sins, the woman was found left standing. Jesus has done all for us and left us to stand, surrender and serve Him. Let us get busy today for Him.

We need His Word daily to stay away from sin and keep going in trials.

September 19

Isaiah 34-35   Psalm 72   Proverbs 19   John 9

Let the SON Shine

Good morning! Taking the time to read the Bible each day allows the Lord to speak through His Word, guide us through His Word, teach us what we need to know, show us how we should live, explain the consequences and judgments of sin, encourage us through His promises and so much more. Just like this morning in Isaiah 34 we read of the judgment on the enemies of the Jews; and in Isaiah 35 we read of God's blessing on the Jews.

As we turn to John 9, we read how a man was born blind and the question is asked in verse 2, "who did sin, this man, or his parents, that he was born blind?" Jesus responds in verse 3, "Neither hath this man sinned, nor his parents: but that the works of God should be made manifest in him." I stopped reading and looked up the word "manifest;" it means to be clear or obvious. I draw these two thoughts to our minds. God judges sin and blesses righteousness, and there are some things that come into our lives just to glorify God. The blind man was questioned about his sight by the religious leaders trying to bring an attack upon Jesus and the man just finally said in verse 25, "whereas I was blind, now I see."

The world will never understand and the devil wants the glory taken away from God. God is and will always be for us because He loves us. Many things of life come as a distraction to draw us away from living for and serving God. Proverbs 19:21, "There are many devices in a man's heart; nevertheless the counsel of the Lord, that shall stand." Psalm 72:18, "Blessed be the Lord God, the God of Israel, who only doeth wondrous things." God loves us and we must get that first place in our lives.

Sometimes in the morning when I get up and the sun is just starting to come up, there is a mist that covers the camp. To me it is breathtakingly beautiful. As the morning sun's rays burn off the mist, the beauty of the land is revealed. The land is always there but it is covered by the mist. That is what a walk with God is like. Sometimes what we need to see is covered until the light of God reveals it to us. Let God shine in everything today. Let God lead and guide in all ways as His light shines through His Word and His Way in our life. Say along with the Psalmist in Psalm 72:19, "blessed be his glorious name for ever:." Have a very blessed day and let the SON shine through.

God is always for us because He loves us.

September 20

Isaiah 36-37   Psalm 73:1-14   Proverbs 20   John 10

Spread Out

Good morning! We often hear, read and are told to live in victory, and we should, but we all have battles that sometimes get us down and almost cause us to quit. My heart was so blessed from the Scriptures this morning, I am having trouble knowing where to begin. I was blessed and encouraged in my prayer time as I read Isaiah 37:14, "Hezekiah went up unto the house of the Lord, and spread it before the Lord." Rabshakeh had a boastful big mouth and tried to put a fear in the people of God, but be thankful we read it was all "spread" out "before the Lord." God heard and answered. In Isaiah 37:20, "that all the kingdoms of the earth may know that thou art the Lord, even thou only."

327

When God hears us have confidence in Him, He responds. In John 10:14, Jesus said, "I am the good shepherd, and know my sheep, and am known of mine." Verses 15, 17, and 18, Jesus said, "I lay down my life." He has laid down His life and conquered death and Hell for us. John 10:27, "My sheep hear my voice, and I know them, and they follow me:." With Jesus being our Shepherd, we are never alone, never lost, and can never be taken. John 20:28, He gave us "eternal life," we can "never perish" and "neither shall any man pluck them out of my hand." Glory be to our KING!

We must let God's Spirit that dwells within us guide us, encourage us, and shine forth. Proverbs 20:27, The spirit of man is the candle of the Lord." I wrote this down this morning, "To know is to understand." We are on the victory side, we cannot lose, we cannot be lost, we cannot be defeated by walking with Christ because He is our Lord, Redeemer, Saviour, Intercessor. He is our everything forever. Psalm 73:1, "Truly God is good to Israel, even to such as are of a clean heart." The day we asked Christ to forgive us of our sins because we faced them and confessed that we are a sinner and asked Him to come into our heart, was or can be the greatest day of our life. Live in victory today, fall before Him and worship Him. "Spread it before the Lord."

We cannot lose, we cannot be lost,
and we cannot be defeated by walking with Christ.

September 21

Isaiah 38-39   Psalm 73:15-28   Proverbs 21   John 11

Don't Put It Off

Good morning! The words of the prophet Isaiah must have been very haunting. In Isaiah 38:1, Hezekiah heard Isaiah say, "Set thine house in order: for thou shalt die, and not live." On my desk at the ranch house I have a lot of quotes and as I sat this morning, I looked at a card that is entitled, "Thomas Jefferson's Ten Rules." Several years ago, I purchased this little card when my wife and I visited Charlottesville, VA. The very first rule is, "Never put off until tomorrow what you can do today." The words, "Set thine house in order," should be words to guide us each day. In Proverbs 21:2 we read, "Every way of a man is right in his own eyes: but the Lord pondereth the hearts."

I reread John 11 this morning, several times. Word had gotten to Jesus about Lazarus being sick and there was the plea for Jesus to come. To those who loved him, Lazarus had died, but Jesus said that, "Lazarus sleepeth" in verse 11 and down in 14 Jesus said, "Lazarus is dead." As I read on, I noticed that "believe" and "believeth" are used 7 times in this chapter. Our faith in the Lord must be strengthened every day so that we will always believe. Psalm 73:17, "Until I went into the sanctuary of God; then understood I their end." To understand the hand of God is to have faith to believe. Psalm 73:26, "My flesh and my heart faileth: but God is the strength of my heart, and my portion for ever." Let us keep our lives in order so that God can use us as He chooses, when and where He chooses. In all our decisions, may we put God first. Do not put off today what needs to be done today. I do not want to live with a long list of "I wish I had." May we live so we can say, "I am thankful I did." God is always ready to do a great work in and through us.

Time was turned back for Hezekiah because of his plea to God in Isaiah 38:3, "Remember now, O Lord, I beseech thee, how I have walked before thee in truth and with a perfect heart, and done that which is good in thy sight." Read in verse 8 of Isaiah 38 and see how the sun was turned back "ten degrees." Let us keep our lives in order for God.

Do not put off today what needs to be done today.

September 22

Isaiah 40-41   Psalm 74:1-11   Proverbs 22   John 12

Waiting on God

Good morning! Mrs. Smith and I so look forward to the fall time of the year. We enjoy going on a drive and seeing the fall colors. As we were heading in the other day to go soul winning, she said to me, it is so dry it probably will not be a very pretty fall. It has been so long since we have had a good rain that many leaves are just drying up and falling off.

As I read in Isaiah 40:8 this morning, "The grass withereth, the flower fadeth: but the word of our God shall stand for ever." The ground where we live is so dry and hard, and the cracks in the soil are becoming so many. It is just like a Christian that does not stay in the Word of God to stay alive and grow in their walk with God. We become hard, critical and often just die spiritually. It does not have to be this way. Isaiah 40:29, "He giveth power to the faint; and to them that have no might he increaseth strength."

When I sit with a family in the hospital or when I stand at the foot of a bed and want to be an encouragement to a family, I thank God for Isaiah 40:31; "But they that wait upon the Lord shall renew their strength; they shall mount up with wings as eagles; they shall run, and not be weary; and they shall walk, and not faint." The rains will come again, and we can have victory over discouragement. When it seems like there is no hope, we need to look to our eternal help. Isaiah 41:10, "Fear thou not; for I am with thee: be not dismayed; for I am thy God: I will strengthen thee; yea, I will help thee; yea, I will uphold thee with the right hand of my righteousness." Let us focus on serving God, especially when we think He is far away or does not hear our prayers. Keep on, my Christian friend. John 12:26, "If any man serve me, let him follow me; and where I am, there shall also my servant be: if any man serve me, him will my Father honour." The rains will come, the grass will green, the flowers will blossom. Let us not lose our trust in the Lord. Proverbs 22:19, "That thy trust may be in the Lord." Let us wait upon the Lord, He is still in control, He will never forsake us. May we look to Him. Have a blessed day.

When it seems like there is no hope, we need to look to our eternal help.

Isaiah 42-44   Psalm 74:12-23   Proverbs 23   John 13

A Great God

Good morning! As I read today in the Old Testament, New Testament, Psalms and Proverbs, my heart was blessed from the comfort of God always being there, cleansing me, forgiving me and being my God. In Isaiah 43:1, "Fear not: for I have redeemed thee, I have called thee by thy name; thou art mine." Isaiah 43:3, "For I am the Lord thy God, the Holy One of Israel, thy Saviour:." Isaiah 43:11, "I, even I, am the Lord; and beside me there is no Saviour." Isaiah 43:25, "I, even I, am he that blotteth out thy transgressions for mine own sake, and will not remember thy sins."

The love that God is, has been, and will be to us and for us, should drive us to tell others about Him. Our relationship with Christ should bring us to the point of praise to Him, create a great desire to live for Him, and give us a burning desire to share Him with others. John 13:34, "That ye love one another; as I have loved you, that ye also love one another. Verse 35, "By this shall all men know that ye are my disciples, if ye have love one to another." My God is so great. Psalm 74:16-17, "The day is thine, the night also is thine: thou hast prepared the light and the sun. Thou has set all the borders of the earth: thou hast made summer and winter." Our God has created all, sustained all, and is in control of all. May we ask ourselves this morning how our heart is. Are we consumed with self or is there a great desire in our hearts to tell of the greatness of God? Proverbs 23:7, "For as he thinketh in his heart, so is he:." May our lives be totally given to God so that He can use us in the way that pleases Him. It is time for us to stop the excuses and step forth for our God. Praise Him today, live for Him today, serve Him today. May His name be praised. Have a blessed day.

Our relationship with Christ should give us a
burning desire to share Him with others.

September 24

Isaiah 45-46   Psalm 75   Proverbs 24   John 14-15

The Master Potter

Good morning! My son recently took his family on a vacation and part of their vacation was spent looking at several different kinds of crafts being made. The one that they spoke of the most was the potter. As I was reading this morning in Isaiah 45, a phrase drew my attention in verse 9, "Shall the clay say to him that fashioneth it, What maketh thou? Or thy work, He hath no hands?" We want to control every area of our lives instead of controlling our daily walk with God. God has a perfect plan for each one of us and we so often fight that plan or tell God that we can't and we make so many excuses.

In Isaiah 45:2 God promises that, "I will go before thee, and make the crooked places straight." As the potter places the clay on the potter's wheel, he has in his mind what he is about to create. Soon a beautiful piece of pottery will be created. We were created by God and for a purpose that He has for us. God's Spirit dwells in all that are saved, and we can learn His purpose for us if we will just be obedient to His Spirit's leading. John 14:17, "Even the Spirit of truth; whom the world cannot receive, because it seeth him not, neither knoweth him: but ye know him; for he dwelleth with you, and shall be in you."

The clay lets the potter work it and shape it. John 14:23, "If a man love me, he will keep my words:." The clay will sometimes be thrown down and beat and rubbed around until it is workable for the potter. The clay must be what the potter needs or the clay cannot become the vision of the potter. Proverbs 24:5, "A wise man is strong; yea, a man of knowledge increaseth strength." The more we walk with God and spend time in His Word, the stronger we get and become more like what God desires and wills for us. Let us give ourselves completely to the potter. Psalm 75:1, "Unto thee, O God, do we give thanks, unto thee do we give thanks: for that thy name is near thy wondrous works declare." God wants to do a great work in and through us. Stay on His potter's wheel and see the great vessel that God is making in and through you.

The clay must be what the potter needs or it
cannot become the vision of the potter.

September 25

Isaiah 47-48   Psalm 76   Proverbs 25   John 16

The End Result

Good morning! It is hard to watch a son, a daughter, a grandchild, a friend or a loved one go through a trial, a heartache, a testing or any type of a hard time. In Isaiah 47, judgment is going to fall on Babylon and in chapter 48:10, God says, "I have chosen thee in the furnace of affliction." In our reading in John 16:16-19 we read the phrase, "A little while" seven times and then the Lord turns our attention to verses 20-24 where He illustrates about a "woman in travail;" "but as soon as she is delivered of the child, she remembereth no more the anguish, for joy that a man is born into the world."

Life is full of hard times, discouragements, testings, etc. I wrote in my notes this morning, "Tough times build strong character." How often have we read a book or heard a story about someone that went through a very difficult time of life and came out as a living testimony for Christ? The birthing of our country, the struggle of our forefathers, the trials of the early pioneers, and yet it was necessary to bring about the end result. Proverbs 25:27, "It is not good to eat much honey: so for men to search their own glory is not glory." Honey is good, and glory earned is good but for us to only strive for the glory is like only eating the sweet foods and never eating the vegetables that bring us the nutrition that we really need. John 16:33, "These things I have spoken unto you, that in me ye might have peace. In the world ye shall have tribulation: but be of good cheer; I have overcome the world."

Keep going, my brother and sister. The mountain seems high and the valley seems so deep, but look around and see the lesson that God desires for you to learn or the patience that He is trying to help you gain. There will be a day when God will have His day and the world and all its sin will be stopped. Psalm 76:9, "When God arose to judgment, to save all the meek of the earth. Selah." What a day that will be! No mountain can be scaled without climbing the path to the top. No valley can be passed through without looking up to the greatness of God. A child going through the trials of life can be used to build the character of an adult. Let us use what God lets us go through to build our strength in Him.

Tough times build strong character.

September 26

Isaiah 49-50   Psalm 77   Proverbs 26   John 17

Remember Your Commitments

Good morning! When I first trusted Christ as my Saviour, I had no one take the time to tell me that God had a will for my life. I have purposed to tell people often who have been saved and are saved that God has a will for their lives, because He does. Isaiah 49:1, "The Lord hath called me from the womb; from the bowels of my mother hath he made mention of my name." Isaiah chapters 49 and 50 talk of the coming of Jesus and much that He will go through for us.

When we turn to our New Testament reading for today in John 17, the will of God and God's plan for us really comes into reality. So much to be said and so little space to say what needs to be said, so let us focus on verse 21. "That they all may be one; as thou, Father, art in me, and I in thee, that they also may be one in us: that the world may believe that thou hast sent me. When we got saved, we became one with God and we are to grow in Him to tell a lost world of life in Christ. John 17:26, "And I have declared unto them thy name, and will declare it: that the love wherewith thou hast loved me may be in them, and I in them." In Proverbs 26 today, our reading shows us the use of some negative words such as, fool, folly, slothful, sluggard. The words are used repeatedly eighteen times. I studied each of them and I saw how they are used as portraying laziness, instability, unwillingness, etc. So many Christians have been excited to serve God after salvation or after rededication, and yet give excuse after excuse why they can't. It has always been amazing to me how we can do what we want to do, when we want to do it, and how we want to do it, and it seems God gets left out or God gets the leftovers. Not attacking, just under conviction and hungering to be more like Christ in every area of my life.

I read on this morning in Psalm 17 and saw that the words "remember" and "remembrance" are used six times. That is where I think we need to be this morning, allowing God to stir our hearts to become stable, have direction, get busy serving and call to remembrance some commitments that we have made to our Lord. As I read Proverbs 26:11, "As a dog returneth to his vomit, so a fool returneth to his folly." We need to be heads up and forward this morning as we head into another day. Put a smile on our face, look up to Christ for victory and march forward as a soldier on the victory side. God bless you in a special way today. When the devil shows up, and he will, turn from him and let him know that you are serving Christ and His name is Jesus. We are one in Christ.

Look to Christ for victory and march forward on the victory side.

September 27

Isaiah 51-52   Psalm 78:1-20   Proverbs 27   John 18

On the Victory Side

Good morning! My prayer this morning for you is that the readings this morning will be as great an encouragement to you as they are to me. Isaiah 51 has statements such as, "Hearken to me," "my salvation shall be for ever," and "my salvation from generation to generation." Verse 11 brings us to that wonderful little chorus that I wish we could sing together this morning: "Therefore the redeemed of the Lord shall return, and come with singing unto Zion; and everlasting joy shall be upon their head: they shall obtain gladness and joy; and sorrow and mourning shall flee away."

Keep that verse with you all throughout the day. The devil knows how to attack us, and we must live on the victory side.

In John 18:2 we read how Judas "knew the place" where Jesus would be. The devil knows how to get us down, so "seek the Lord," "hearken unto" Him. Let us stand up and fight against our flesh, the world and the devil. Psalm 78:4, "shewing to the generation to come the praises of the Lord, and his strength, and his wonderful works that he hath done." Psalm 78:6, "That the generation to come might know them . . .and declare them to their children:." Psalm 78:7, "That they might set their hope in God." Step out into this day with the sight of victory in your eyes. Sing unto the Lord who is our strength. Praise Him today with all your heart. He is our God and He is our Redeemer. Let all that we have praise Him." Sing that little chorus with me, "Therefore the redeemed of the Lord......" Have a victorious day!!!

The devil knows how to attack us, and we must live on the victory side.

September 28

Isaiah 53-54   Psalm 78:21-33   Proverbs 28   John 19

He Took Our Place

Good morning! I heard yesterday that we here in this part of Kentucky have gone 31 days without any measurable rain. I looked at the cracks in the ground, the dry grass that was once very green, the rolling hills that now have turned a brown color and my mind thought as I read this morning in Isaiah 53:2, "For he shall grow up before him as a tender plant, and as a root out of a dry ground." In the dryness and hardness of mankind, God sent us our Redeemer and He is as alive today as He has ever been. Isaiah 53:6, "the Lord hath laid on him the iniquity of us all;" and in verse 12, "he hath poured out his soul unto death:." Pilate said in John 19:4, "I find no fault in him;" and yet in verse 6 they cried out, "Crucify him, crucify him. Pilate saith unto them, Take ye him and crucify him: for I find no fault in him." For you and me, and all the world, He laid down His life.

A farmer was observed kneeling by a grave and a man asked him if this was a family member. The kneeling man said, "No sir. When I was drafted to go to war, my parents were very ill and a neighbor told me that he would go to war in my place. This neighbor that went in my place was wounded in the battle of Chickamauga and taken to an army hospital where he died." The farmer looked up and said, "he died for me." Take time today to kneel and look up to Heaven and remember that He, Jesus, died for us. We live and have a busy schedule to keep us in supply of all that we think we need, and yet we do not take the time to worship the King that has done all for us.

The Psalmist asked the question in Psalm 78:19, "Can God furnish a table in the wilderness?" The answer is in verse 28 of the same Psalm, "And he let it fall in the midst of their camp, round about their habitations." May we stop and kneel and give glory to the King that "rose up" to be our Redeemer, our Lord." Take time to worship Him and praise Him. We have time for all that we want to do; is it not more important to take time for Him? He died in our place.

Take time for God – He gave His all for us.

September 29

Isaiah 55-56   Psalm 78:34-55   Proverbs 29   John 20-21

All Nature Sings

Good morning! Yesterday Mrs. Smith and I were pulling out of the camp and I noticed the tree branches moving and the tall grass in the field moving and I said to her, the weatherman said there would possibly be some high winds today. The temperature has been so hot and the weather so dry and things are so burned up, but if we stop and enjoy, the wind blowing is like a breath from heaven.

As I read this morning in Isaiah 55:12, "the hills shall break forth before you into singing, and all the trees of the field shall clap their hands." Take time today to realize that nature itself always is prepared to praise the

Lord. No tree has the gift of salvation, no flower has its name written in the Lamb's Book of Life, no bird has a mansion being prepared for it, and yet all of God's creation sings and claps their hands to our God. Listen to a river as it flows and sings to the greatness of our Lord. In John 20, the tomb is empty and in verse eleven, "Mary stood without." The disciples looked and ran on, but "Mary stood without." She looked in and the angels began to speak to her as they were sitting in the empty tomb. She heard a voice behind her and as she turned, she thought it was the gardener, and then she heard her name said by the Master, "Mary." Because Mary tarried at the tomb, saw the angels and spent time instead of running off, she was able to personally be the first to speak to our risen Saviour.

Slow down and spend time with the Saviour today. A tree does not move from where it is planted and yet its leaves clap praise to our Lord. A river continues to sing in the same path. The grass of the field does not move from field to field, and yet it waves praise to our KING. The hills stand tall and firm as a testimony of the greatness of our God. We are safe today as Proverbs 29:25 states, "whoso putteth his trust in the Lord shall be safe." Stand firm, stay stedfast, praise Him where you are, be faithful, live for Him. Thank God for the breeze that blows the greatness of our King. May our voice and life be used to bring glory to the King of Kings.

All of creation sings and claps their hands to our God.

September 30

Isaiah 57-58   Psalm 78:56-72   Proverbs 30-31   Acts 1

Fresh Water From God

Good morning! I was out by the barn and I noticed the horses standing over by the pond that has now dried up. Please do not think that I have not provided water for our horses. They have plenty of water to drink from a brand new waterer that was provided and they can have as much cool fresh water as they want, any time they want. Those horses are like us humans. They get in a habit or they will stand until they get what they want.

As I read this morning in Isaiah 58:11, "And the Lord shall guide thee continually, and satisfy thy soul in drought and make fat thy bones: and thou shalt be like a watered garden, and like a spring of water, whose waters fail not." God is leading us even in those times when we feel we are headed nowhere or we do not seem to be satisfied with where we are and what we are doing. Stay faithful, stay serving, stay praying, and He will always provide and guide us to fresh water that will sustain us and take care of us.

As Jesus had left the tomb empty, then presented himself to his disciples and those that loved Him; they stood "gazing up into heaven," in Acts 1:11. God has not left us, His promises have not failed us. We must keep serving in any way we can. His power has been given us to serve Him and our commission in Acts 1:8 to take the gospel to everyone is still just as important today as it was that day. Proverbs 30:5, "Every word of God is pure: he is a shield unto them that put their trust in him."

The pond to the horses is dry but water has been provided. God will take care of us today just like He always has. Psalm 78:72, "So he fed them according to the integrity of his heart; and guided them by the skilfulness of his hands." It only took a short time and the horses got used to the new waterer and they stand and drink. I watched as one of them put her nose down in the water and splashed it all around. It was like saying, I have found fresh cool water and I am going to play in it. Enjoy serving the Lord, He will always provide and guide us. Quit trying to make things happen and enjoy God guiding us. He will never leave us or forsake us. Let us be faithful, patient and obedient to Him. Please have a blessed day.

Enjoy serving the Lord and letting Him guide you.

October 1

Isaiah 59-60   Psalm 79   Proverbs 1   Acts 2

Christ on Display

Good morning! The last verse I read in my reading this morning is a great verse for us to begin our day with. Psalm 79:13, "So we thy people and sheep of thy pasture will give thee thanks for ever: we will shew forth thy praise to all generations."

Last night my wife and I were driving home and we saw a large American flag and it was so lit up that you could see it from a far distance. That family is proud of America and they want all to know it. They show it by the display and lighting of this great flag. Should it not be greater for us that know Christ as our Saviour to be a bright and shining light for Him? Isaiah 59:1, "Behold, the Lord's hand is not shortened, that it cannot save; neither his ear heavy, that it cannot hear:." Our God hears and cares and is there with us and for us. Many times we do not, and sometimes will never understand about some things that we go through. As I read in Acts 2:37 the words, "what shall we do?" I have asked that simple question many times and then a verse comes to mind such as Acts 2:39, "For the promise is unto you, and to your children, and to all that are afar off, even as many as the Lord our God shall call."

It is not a sin to be thankful and proud of our country, as I truly am, and we daily display an American flag at our home. My question is, do we have as great or greater display of Christ through our daily life? Isaiah 60:1, "Arise, shine for thy light is come." God has forgotten our sins of the past and we have His promise of that. Psalm 79:8, "O remember not against us former iniquities." As that great American flag was displayed with lights shining so that all could see, may we today shine beyond and more bright than anything for the glory of our Lord.

Are we displaying Christ in our daily life?

Isaiah 61-62   Psalm 80   Proverbs 2   Acts 3

Stay on the Path

Good morning! The longer I live, the more I am convinced that we need to focus on God's purpose for our lives. The world has so many distractions and it cannot be denied that we have a life in Christ because He has a purpose for our life. Isaiah 62:3 "Thou shalt be a crown of glory in the hand of the Lord, and a royal diadem in the hand of thy God." Life is a path and sometimes the path is a hard path and sometimes the path is easy to walk.

I love hiking and the main reason that I love hiking is what I see and what I get to experience, the beauty of nature and the sense of adventure. In Proverbs 2 we see the words "path" and "paths" used seven times. It is like God wants us to consider this word and in Proverbs 2:20 we read, "That thou mayest walk in the way of good men, and keep the paths of the righteous." I have been hiking and walked around a corner and I have seen a beautiful waterfall or a beautiful scene of an open majestic view. I have also been hiking and come around a corner and I have seen another steep hill to climb. There have been times that I have taken a wrong turn and I have always gone back to where I think I made that wrong turn and gotten myself back on the right path. Psalm 80 verses 3, 7, and 19 has this little but powerful statement; "Turn us again, O Lord." God desires to use us. He is there every step of life's path. Isaiah 62:2, "to comfort all that mourn;" verse 3 tells us He is "the garment of praise for the spirit of heaviness." In the very next verse He is ready to "build," "raise up," and "repair."

Sometimes the path of life is hard and discouraging but God always has a purpose greater than ours and there is always something very beautiful right around the corner or right over the next ridge. Stay on God's path today, enjoy His presence, look to Him for direction, seek Him every turn. The beauty at the end of the trail is Heaven. Many a trail has been started by a hiker because of what was at the end. Don't quit, the beauty at the end of life's path cannot be fully explained because it will be in the presence and perfectness of union with our Lord. Stay on the path. Enjoy the hike today.

Stay on God's path, look to Him for direction and seek Him at every turn.

October 3

Isaiah 63-64   Psalm 81   Proverbs 3   Acts 4

Guided by His Hand

Good morning! Yesterday I was walking, and I saw a little boy and his dad on bicycles and the dad was trying to teach the little boy. The little boy kept saying, "I know how, I can do it." I chuckled and kept walking, and thought how that is just like us Christians trying to be in full charge of our lives and the Lord is trying to lead us and guide us, but we keep telling Him, "I know how, I can do it."

Isaiah 64:4, "For since the beginning of the world men have not heard, nor perceived by the ear, neither hath the eye seen, O God, beside thee, what he hath prepared for him that waiteth for him." The little boy kept riding and the dad stayed very close. As we keep walking in this world, may our ears be open and listening for the guidance of our Lord. That little boy will fall and have an accident, but his daddy will be there. Proverbs 3:26, "For the Lord shall be thy confidence, and shall keep thy foot from being taken." Psalm 81:13, "Oh that my people had hearkened unto me, and Israel had walked in my ways!" That little boy will get a bigger bike someday. I thought as I walked, may we always have the ear of our Lord even when we grow older in Him. May we not say to God, I can, I can. I have learned that the closer I walk with God, the closer that God is with me. Stay close, listen, obey and let the Lord guide, teach and be with you. It would be great today and every day if we would just learn to reach out and let the hand of God lead us, guide us and teach us. I can hear that little voice, "I can, I can." May all of us learn to not say I can, but, "I will Lord, I will." Have a blessed day.

The closer we walk with God, the closer He is with us.

Isaiah 65-66   Psalm 82   Proverbs 4   Acts 5

A Lasting Influence

Good morning! Each morning before I begin my Bible reading, I spend time in prayer preparing myself for the Holy Spirit to speak to me. I hunger for my mind to be clear of any thoughts, my heart to be in tune and right with the Lord so that the Holy Spirit can speak to me as I read and meditate on what I have read. Every morning I take a piece of paper and write down verses that speak to me as I read. My paper is always full, and I am most of the time very afraid that I would give too much instead of focusing on one thought that we can apply for the day. Today is no different, as my paper is overflowing from thoughts. So, I just want to focus on Proverbs 4, beginning with verse 4; "He taught me also, and said unto me, Let thine heart retain my words: keep my commandments, and live."

This week Mrs. Smith and I have been together with some of our grandchildren. We long for the times that we can all be together and that is almost impossible, but we keep trying. One of our grandchildren had a birthday this week and we called them and spent time on the phone, and we spent personal time with some of the others. I noticed individual words this morning that I want to point out, such as "get," "hear," "receive," "hold," "keep," "attend," "know." Parents and grandparents, adults, and I put an emphasis on *adults* because we all teach, we will never know all the ways that we are teaching. Yesterday I was talking to a man about the Lord and His relationship with the Lord and I watched tears form in his eyes as he told me that he had lost two sons and his wife in an auto accident. He dropped his head and told me of the day of burying all three of them. We spoke of eternity and I shared Christ with him. We must spend time teaching about our Lord and living a relationship with Him and teaching our children, grandchildren and others about Him.

How is your life influencing others? What is your life, words and actions teaching others? What kind of testimony are you, and what testimony are you leaving behind? This man stuck out his hand to me and I thanked him for the privilege to talk with him and as we were looking at each other, he said it was a real privilege to speak with me. May our lives be a living and teaching example. The words that I noticed this morning are letting us know of the importance of teaching another generation and them learning how to build a walk with God and how to maintain it their entire life. Each generation must see those that learn, live, and leave Biblical principles for the next generation. Proverbs 4:27, "Turn not to the right hand nor to the left: remove thy foot from evil." Acts 5:42, "And daily in the temple, and in every house, they ceased not to teach and preach Jesus Christ." I underlined and highlighted these four words in Proverbs 4:21, "Let them not depart." Stand true to God today. Live for Him and serve Him. Today is the last day that I will get to spend with some of my grandchildren as they will head back to their home, but my life and its influences will keep living on. What influences are you leaving today with others? We will embrace and say good-bye, but our hearts will still be together. May our influences for Christ leave a lasting effect in the lives of others because our walk with God has been a life changing walk. Live for God today and be an influence for God today. We all look forward to another time to spend together, but we do not know for sure that that time will come, so make today a lasting influence for Christ.

What influences are you leaving today with others?

October 5

Jeremiah 1-2   Psalm 83   Proverbs 5   Acts 6

Broken Cisterns

Good morning! Today's reading brought back a lot of memories. When Mrs. Smith and I bought our first home, the previous owners showed us a cistern that was connected to the house. The cistern held all the rainwater that ran off the roof. The owners had connected the cistern to the new water lines in the house when they had built the house. We read today in Jeremiah 2:13, "For my people have committed two evils;

they have forsaken me the fountain of living waters, and hewed them out cisterns, broken cisterns, that can hold no water." Much of my life I lived where our water supply was a well and a couple of the wells were hand dug wells, so they were not very deep in the ground. When there would be a dry spell and the well would run dry, we could always get water from the cistern because the rainwater had been held for when the well went dry. Cistern water was not fresh water and we had to be careful to not use it for drinking. It was water that was not fresh.

God told his people that they had arrived at a point of not needing Him and what they thought they could live on was not there. Too often we do not see the importance of getting the life sustaining strength as a Christian from reading the Word of God and we neglect the importance of fellowship with God. Proverbs 5:2, "That thou mayest regard discretion, and that thy lips may keep knowledge. We were thankful for the cistern water so that we could cook, water the animals and keep clean but it was dangerous to drink the water without boiling it and making sure it was pure. With broken cisterns they did not even hold water. My brother and sister, do not forsake the fresh water from daily spending time with God in His Word and the wonderful fellowship we receive when spending time in prayer with Him. In our reading today in Acts 6, we see that "they chose Stephen, a man full of faith and of the Holy Ghost." Stephen spent time with God because that is shown in how the "Word of God increased" and people were saved and added to the church. I fear that sometimes we think we know how to live the Christian life, so we do things without the power of God and that is why discouragement sets in and we see so many quitting and giving up. We need the fresh water from God and His Word daily and we cannot live today, tomorrow or next week on what we had in days gone by. I was thankful for the cisterns, but when a cistern is cracked and holds no water, it is not good. Nothing is more refreshing than a fresh drink of cold water. Drink daily from the Word of God and enjoy that wonderful time of fellowship in a constant walk with God in prayer. See you at the well that never runs dry.

We need fresh water daily from God's Word and
spending time with Him in prayer.

October 6

Jeremiah 3-5   Psalm 84   Proverbs 6   Acts 7

Hardened Ground

Good morning! Late last evening I went and checked all the buildings of the camp and I thought how just a few months ago, we had an overabundance of rain and now everything is all dried up and the ground is very hard and cracked. As I read in Jeremiah 4:3, "Break up your fallow ground, and sow not among thorns," I thought about how hard the ground is and how it is producing nothing. The only thing that is growing is weeds.

When our heart becomes hard toward God, the things of God, and the people of God, we are like the hard ground that seems to only grow weeds. In our reading today in Acts 7, we read of the wonderful testimony of Stephen before the high priest and council, and how they sat silent until he was done. Their hearts were so hardened to the truth that they stoned him to death. May we not become hardened to the things of God. Proverbs 6:20-21 challenges us to "keep thy father's commandment, and forsake not the law of thy mother: Bind them continually upon thine heart, and tie them about thy neck." We must keep our hearts tender and not let them get hard. Love the Word of God, love to learn the Word of God, learn to daily apply the Word of God.

When the rains come, and they will come, the grass will grow again, the flowers will blossom in spring, and the new leaves will come beautifully on the limbs of the great trees. We must guard our hearts from getting hard and cold toward God. Let us today be challenged by the words of the Psalmist in Psalm 84:2, "my heart and my flesh crieth out for the living God'. God is there and He may be found, even in the most discouraging, lonely times. Psalm 84:12, "O Lord of hosts, blessed is the man that trusteth in thee." When the rain does come, it will have a sweet smell and the earth will drink it all in. My brother and sister, keep drinking the cool water of the Word of God.

We must guard our heart from getting hard and cold toward God.

Jeremiah 6-7   Psalm 85   Proverbs 7   Acts 8

Which Way?

Good morning! As I was reading this morning, another little but powerful word kept drawing my attention. That little word is "way." Let us look at it as a path that should be taken and a path that should be avoided. Do not let me lose you on a wrong path or a wrong way. Jeremiah 6:16, "Stand ye in the ways, and see, and ask for the old paths, where is the good way, and walk therein, and ye shall find rest for your souls." The Lord is telling us there is an old path, a path that has been taken, and it is a "good way" to go. At the end of the verse we read, "We will not walk therein" and in verse 17, "We will not hearken." There are decisions that we must make each day and each moment of each day, and that is what "way" we are going to take. At this time the children of Israel decided that they were not going to go the right "way," and Jeremiah 7:24 tells us they "went backward, and not forward."

God will always bless us when we walk the right "way." God will use us when we walk the right "way." God tells us His grace and strength is there for us when we walk the right "way." He will lead us to have direction for His service when we walk the right "way." In our reading in Acts 8:26, we see how Philip was led "unto the way" of the Ethiopian and Philip led this man to Christ and in verse 36, "as they went on their way," they came to water and the Ethiopian was baptized and then in verse 39, "he went on his way rejoicing." In Proverbs 7:8, the young man "went the way" of destruction to the woman of wickedness and in verse 27 we read, "Her house is the way to hell." We have a "way" to choose each moment of our life. The "way" that pleases our Lord, and the "way" that does not please Him. Psalm 85:13, "righteousness shall go before him; and shall set us in the "way" of his steps."

I pray you will choose the right "way" every moment of every day. Life is full of different paths that can be taken but there is only one "way" that pleases the Lord, for He is the "way." John 14:6, "Jesus saith unto him, I am the way, the truth, and the life: no man cometh unto the Father, but by me." See you on the "way."

God's grace and strength is there for us when we walk the right "way."

October 8

Jeremiah 8-9   Psalm 86   Proverbs 8   Acts 9

A God of Order

Good morning! Well, the rains came, the temperature dropped, and the trees have begun to turn their beautiful colors. When things are in order designed by God, there is always a beautiful result. That is the way it is with our lives. When we submit to the will of God, there is always a peace, happiness and fulfillment.

God draws our attention to nature in Jeremiah 8:7, "Yea, the stork in heaven knoweth the appointed times; and the turtle and the crane and the swallow observe the time of their coming; but my people know not the judgment of the Lord." God has a timetable about everything, including us humans and we better pay close attention. Jeremiah 8:20, "The harvest is past, the summer is ended, and we are not saved." Do we live as though we have plenty of time to do what we want and there is no fear of not doing what God wants us to do? Jeremiah 9:12, "Who is the wise man, that may understand this?" In Acts 9, Saul that brought great havoc to the Christians is now brought to his knees through blindness and God prepares Ananias to lead him to Christ, and yet there was a great fear of all the Christians because of who Saul was. They could not see what God had done in him and what God wanted to do through him. In Acts 9:15, God says, "for he is a chosen vessel unto me," and in Acts 9:27, "But Barnabas took him." God is still calling and waiting for us to hear, follow and serve. What is the excuse today? Proverbs 8:4, "I call;" Proverbs 8:6, "Hear; for I will speak;" Proverbs 8:10, "Receive my instruction;" Proverbs 8:20, "I lead in the way of righteousness."

I remember the day over 45 years ago as I was asked the question, "How long will you fight the will of God for your life?" God has not failed us nor forsaken us. Yes, there have been trials and testings and discouraging times, but God has been so good. The blessings are so many, I have no idea how to properly give praise and testimony to Him and for Him. I just want to be submitted and committed the rest of my life on this earth. Listen to Psalm 86:11, "Teach me thy way, O Lord; I will walk in thy truth: unite my heart to fear thy name." Let us give our lives completely to serve the Lord until He returns or takes us Home to be with Him. Nature listens, waits and obeys. How about you and me doing the same as nature?

When things are in order designed by God, there is always a beautiful result.

October 9

Jeremiah 10-11   Psalm 87   Proverbs 9   Acts 10

Our Source of Strength

Good morning! Yesterday morning before I headed to the church, I checked the buildings and the properties of the Ranch and spent time praying for the retreats this fall at the camp. The first one is a Sunday School "Harvest Party," then a "Couples Retreat" and then in November, the "Kentucky Shoot Out." There was a beautiful mist over the camp as I walked and prayed. I thought how only God can blanket the morning like this and then when I drove toward Lexington, the sun was coming up and revealing a beautiful blue sky that only God could paint. The cooler temperatures are bringing the beauty of color in the trees and it is like God is beginning to paint the forest. As I drove by several creeks that are flowing with a vigor and freshness from the rain, it is like they are singing a song of praise to God in Heaven.

Reading Jeremiah 10:12 this morning, "He hath made the earth by his power, he hath established the world by his wisdom, and hath stretched out the heavens by his discretion." He is God and He is everything. Let us praise Him. In Acts 10 this morning, the praying of Cornelius and Peter brought a conviction to me of the importance to set time aside during the day, maybe at dinner time or break time, to pray. Acts 10:2, Cornelius "prayed to God alway." Acts 10:9, "Peter went up upon the housetop to pray about the sixth hour." Acts 10:30, "And Cornelius said, Four days ago I was fasting until this hour; and at the ninth hour I praying in my house."

We often miss the greatness of God because of the lack of time in prayer. When I spend more time praying, I spend more time praising and less time complaining. Our strength for the battle comes from time alone with God in His Word and on our knees. Psalm 87:7, "all my springs are in thee." That word "springs" is our supply of strength from God. When you enjoy the beauty of fall, make sure you take time to PRAISE the one that gives us eyes to see, a sense to be able to smell, ears to hear the flow of a creek, feet to walk and observe the beauty God has created. As I read in Proverbs 9:11, "For by me thy days shall be multiplied, and the years of thy life shall be increased." Each day I live is because of His grace. Praise Him today! Prayer and praise are pleasing to God, so let us spend time today praying and praising our KING.

Our strength for the battle come from time alone with God.

October 10

Jeremiah 12-13   Psalm 85   Proverbs 10   Acts 11

Mine Heritage

Good morning! I love the time each morning when Mrs. Smith and I get together before a day of work begins, and we sit down and read the Bible and then spend time praying together. I also enjoy the time of reading prayer letters from missionaries. Many of the letters that we receive are from missionaries who when they were in their teen years and college age years, served on camp summer staff. I want my heart tender to the Great Commission, to take the Gospel to the world.

I read in Jeremiah 12:8-9 this morning the words, "Mine heritage is unto me." Mine heritage as a Christian is to take the Gospel to mankind. Jeremiah 12:15, "I will return, and have compassion on them, and will

350

bring them again, every man to his heritage." Just this week, by reading prayer letters, my wife and I have traveled in our minds and hearts to China, Africa, Germany, Ireland, Philippians, American Indians, Mexico, small Islands around the world, and various towns in the U.S. where new churches have been started. Our heritage of Christianity and America is to take the Gospel to a lost and dying world.

I read today in Acts 11:26, "And the disciples were called Christians first in Antioch." They were being identified as a people spreading and living Christ. In Acts 11:29, "Then the disciples, every man according to his ability, determined to send relief unto the brethren." We see the vision of missions being carried out because finances and aid were being sent to help others share the Gospel. Let us return and be renewed in our vision of our heritage to spread the Gospel around the world. May we carry a fresh burden to pray for missionaries and young families that have followed the calling of God upon their lives to take the Gospel of Jesus Christ to a lost world. It is our heritage as Christians to spread the Gospel here at home by starting new churches and to take the Gospel to the world by sending missionaries. Pray daily for missionaries and pastors starting new works here in America. Psalm 88:1, "I have cried day and night before thee:." Psalm 88:9, "Lord, I have called daily upon thee." Let us stay faithful in our community and stay with our heritage as Christians by carrying the Gospel around the world. May we make a fresh commitment to God right now. Proverbs 10:30, "The righteous shall never be removed:." Until He returns may we be faithful to the heritage from which we have come, and that is to be disciples of Jesus Christ.

Our heritage as Christians is to take the Gospel to mankind.

October 11

Jeremiah 14-15   Psalm 89:1-18   Proverbs 11   Acts 12

What Has You Chained?

Good morning! Do you ever think how the Lord feels when He looks down from Heaven and sees how this old world lives and constantly rejects Him, gives excuse why they have no time for Him or gives excuse why they cannot serve Him? As we read the Bible, we so often see the judgment of God upon people. and for some reason this world seems to think that they can escape God's judgment.

In Jeremiah 14 there was a drought so bad and so long that in verse 5 we read, "Yea, the hind also calved in the field, and forsook it, because there was no grass." What this is saying is that there were new baby calves born and the mothers left them to die because there was no grass for the female cows to eat to produce the milk needed to feed the babies. So they left them to die. I have heard many times a small calf crying for its mother and when the calves are old enough to be separated from their mothers, I have heard the cry of the cows looking for their calves. We live in a society that kills babies and commits sins that takes lives on a daily basis. Drugs, alcohol, fighting, vandalism, etc. God told the children of Israel in Jeremiah 15:6, "I am weary with repenting," and in verse 7, "I will destroy my people, since they return not from their ways." God will have His day in His time and in His way. Peter was thrown into prison in Acts 12, and the church prayed. Verse 5, "prayer was made without ceasing of the church unto God for him." As we read on, the angel came to him, the chains were removed and he walked out of prison to continue to serve God and live for Him.

What has you chained today? What has control of you today? In Acts 12:24, "But the word of God grew and multiplied." God forgives and wants us to move on, live for Him and serve Him. Proverbs 11:3, "The integrity of the upright shall guide them: but the perverseness of transgressors shall destroy them." God will bless if we stand up, let the chains of sin drop, and walk through the gate with victory ahead. All of us have things that try to keep us from living for God, but we must daily and moment by moment look to God for strength. Psalm 89:1, "I will sing of the mercies of the Lord forever: with my mouth will I make known thy faithfulness to all generations." Listen to what God said to the children of Israel in Jeremiah 15:21, "And I will deliver thee out of the hand of the wicked, and I will redeem thee out of the hand of the terrible." Live in victory today. Live in joy with God today. Praying for you.

God forgives and wants us to move on, live for Him and serve Him.

Jeremiah 16-17   Psalm 89:19-37   Proverbs 12   Acts 13

Changing of Seasons

Good morning! The temperature has dropped and the beauty of fall is quickly appearing. I so enjoy each of the four seasons and what each brings. God is faithful, no matter what man says or even thinks. God promises us the four seasons. As I was reading this morning in Jeremiah chapters 16 and 17, the words "forsake" and "forsaken" kept appearing and I thought on those words for some time. All of us have had our hearts broken because someone we loved, trusted, confided in, has now turned their back on us. I cannot let someone that has forsaken me destroy me. I must see how God must feel and what He does, to overcome the hurt that I have.

Why did the people forsake God? Jeremiah 16:12, "ye walk every one after the imagination of his evil heart, that they may not hearken unto me:." Jeremiah 17:5, "Cursed be the man that trusteth in man, and maketh flesh his arm, and whose heart departed from the Lord." There will be a forsaking, a departing, a leaving when we look to man and not to God, and when we live for the things of this world and not for pleasing the Lord. Proverbs 12:15, "The way of a fool is right in his own eyes: but he that hearkeneth unto counsel is wise." We must guard our heart. Jeremiah 17:9, "The heart is deceitful above all things, and desperately wicked: who can know it?" God has a special purpose for each of us and we must not put anything above or in front of God's purpose for our lives. Can we try to imagine how the heart of God has been broken because of the constant forsaking of His ways by people that once said they loved Him and wanted to serve Him?

We must keep our eyes on what God has for us. We must never lose our love for people but maintain a much higher love for God and serving Him. Acts 13:22, "I have found David the son of Jesse, a man after mine own heart, which shall fulfill all my will." Acts 13:2, "Separate me Barnabas and Saul for the work whereunto I have called them." You and I have a calling from God and a purpose for our lives. We must do God's will even when those that we love and have tried to help, end up quitting. Keep on because there is someone else that the Lord has for us to minister to. When a door closes and it seems like your place of service has ended, look for the next door, because God is the one that has the key to them all. Do not quit and do not forsake God and His calling and purpose for your life. No matter what science thinks or says, no matter what may be printed and in the news, God will still give us spring, summer, fall and winter. God will never forsake us. Enjoy the beauty of the day and when the seasons change and a hurt comes, remember God said He would never leave us or forsake us.

We must not put anything above or in front of God's purpose for our life.

October 13

Jeremiah 18-19   Psalm 89:38-52   Proverbs 13   Acts 14

Spread the Word

Good morning! God's Word the Bible has been preserved for us to have the Word of God. I fear that we take having a Bible so lightly and we do not realize that there are people in this world who do not have the Bible in their language. We in America have the Bible available to us in so many places and yet it is so little read.

Many years ago, I was so convicted as I came to the realization that there are people that had given their lives just because they had a copy in their possession. Still to this day, as my wife and I receive missionary letters from around the world, there are peoples of different languages that do not possess God's Word in their language. I am writing this this morning as I read the words in Acts 14:27, "And when they were come, and had gathered the church together, they rehearsed all that God had done with them, and how he had opened the door of faith unto the Gentiles." The church was under persecution and yet they were so excited to keep spreading the Word of God and the truth of salvation to all mankind.

God has a purpose for each of our lives, just like we read today about the potter in Jeremiah 18:6, "Behold, as the clay is in the potter's hand, so are ye in mine hand." Let us live today for God's purpose in our life. It is His purpose to reach a lost world. Stay right with God, live holy unto God. Proverbs 13:6, "Righteousness keepeth him that is upright in the way: but wickedness overthroweth the sinner." Life is short and the older we get, the shorter the time we have to live and serve the Lord. Psalm 89:47, "Remember how short my time is." There are people all around us that need to hear how Christ loves them, died for them, and wants to save their souls. Let us stay faithful spreading the wonderful story of Christ and His gift of salvation. Even in America there are people that have never heard the wonderful truth of salvation to all men. May we be challenged today to not only read the Bible but spread the truths of the Bible. It is God's will that all come to know Him, but how will they unless we tell them?

God's purpose for our life is to reach a lost world.

October 14

Jeremiah 20-21   Psalm 90   Proverbs 14   Acts 15

What is Your Purpose?

Good morning! Today is another new day. Do you set goals? Daily goals, short term goals, long term goals, things we must do and things we would like to do; is that part of your life? When we purpose to do things, there is more of a possibility of goals being reached or things being completed. Jeremiah was thrown in prison, put in stocks, mocked, and discouraged, and to put it bluntly, I think he faced times that he was just ready to quit. What kept him going? Jeremiah 20:9, "But his word was in mine heart as a burning fire shut up in my bones." We find that Jeremiah was yielded to God even in his trials. In Acts 15:11, "But we believe that through the grace of the Lord Jesus Christ we shall be saved, even as they." Jeremiah had a purpose from God that he knew was God's will for his life. The apostles knew God desired to have the world reached with the Gospel

355

and it did not matter if the people were Jew or Gentile. Jeremiah had a purpose for his life and the apostles had a purpose for their lives.

Do we face another day with goals and purpose or are we just going to go through the activities of work, school, tasks, projects, retirement, vacations, etc., and really have no spiritual purpose or goal? Psalm 90:12, "So teach us to number our days, that we may apply our hearts unto wisdom." Psalm 90:14, "O satisfy us early with thy mercy; that we may rejoice and be glad all our days." Too many lives are lived with no goals and no purpose. We buy things that we think will satisfy us when we really do not need these things. We spend to be happy, play to be happy, travel to be happy, retire to be happy and yet life is empty. I am not against any of the afore- mentioned things, but I am burdened for those that have no purpose in their lives and no burden for the cause of Christ. I cannot set goals for anyone else, nor can I serve Christ for anyone else, but I challenge you today to ask yourself what you are doing for Christ.

Jeremiah was burning with desire and the apostles were determined to press on to all people with the Gospel. May we be challenged this morning to look at our lives, priorities and goals and see where the cause of Christ fits in. May we number our days and be accountable with all that we do. Proverbs 14:21, "He that despiseth his neighbor sinneth: but he that hath mercy on the poor, happy is he." Let us reach the world for Christ with purpose.

When you look at your life, goals and priorities, where does Christ fit in?

October 15

Jeremiah 22-23   Psalm 91   Proverbs 15   Acts 16

Always There

Good morning! Do you ever ask yourself, what will it be today? A flat tire on the car, losing something important, someone in the family gets sick, a bill in the mail that we did not expect, trouble with a neighbor. The list could go on of troubles that could happen and often do happen to us. Jeremiah 23:23, "Am I a God at hand, saith the Lord, and not a God afar off?" God is right there, and He may be reached. Jeremiah 23:24, "Can any hide himself in secret places that I shall not see him? Do not I fill heaven and earth?" Even when we are in sin and trying to hide from God, God is there, and God knows and sees.

In Acts 16, Paul and Silas had been arrested and cast into prison. They were beaten and chained. In their captivity, suffering, and pain, they "prayed, and sang praises unto God: and the prisoners heard them." Now picture in your mind as best as you can, discouragement, confusion, suffering, question after question of why and how come. Then stop and begin to hear one voice, then two, then more of praying and singing. Remember that choir number that was such a blessing or that song sung by the quartet, or that song you were listening to that encouraged you so much you sang it all day? Listen what always happens next when we seek the face of the Lord and begin to praise Him in our weakness, discouragement, and sorrow. Acts 16:26, "And suddenly there was a great earthquake, so that the foundations of the prison were shaken: and immediately all the doors were opened, and every one's bands were loosed."

God is listening today in your fear, heartache, sickness, burden, etc. He is waiting to hear us call upon Him and begin to praise Him. By the way, we are not ever alone anyway. Psalm 91:11, "For he shall give his angels charge over thee, to keep thee in all thy ways." Just think, there are angels that have been sent by God to us. Psalm 91:15, "He shall call upon me, and I will answer him: I will be with him in trouble; I will deliver him, and honor him." Yes, today may be a day of some trials and tough times, but we are not alone; seek His face and sing like an angel and enjoy another day living and serving the KING! Let the chains of trouble and trials drop off and watch the doors of deliverance open.

Praising God in our discouragement and trials opens the doors of deliverance.

October 16

Jeremiah 24-25   Psalm 92   Proverbs 16   Acts 17

Under Construction

Good morning! Throughout the years of being in the camping ministry, there have been a lot of construction and remodeling, construction and remodeling. For Mrs. Smith and I, we have done a lot of remodeling on our homes. When our church purchased the property for Circle C Baptist Ranch, we took a three-bedroom home with a full basement and made it a camp kitchen, camp office, nurses station, camp cook housing and girls staff housing. As the Lord provided and we were able to build a place for our girls staff and the Lord provided for us to build the camp Dining Hall, it became time for Mrs. Smith and I to move into the Ranch house. For over ten years my wife has been the most patient bride as we have taken the ranch house and went from what it was to what it is today.

I read this morning in Jeremiah 24:6, "I will build them, and not pull them down; and I will plant them, and not pluck them up." God was speaking to me that we as His children are under a constant construction project. Remodeling starts with a structure, then we see the need, get the idea, save for the expense and then the project of remodeling begins. God was so fed up with the sin of His people that He was ready to fully destroy them and then He told Jeremiah, in Jeremiah 24:7, "And I will give them an heart to know me." When we began remodeling the ranch house, I tore everything out to the outside walls and we began to rebuild from the inside to the out. Walls were moved, new wiring, new plumbing, new windows and the list keeps growing. As this remodeling was and has been going on, we had to adjust to a lot of changes. Acts 17:11, "they received the word with all readiness of mind, and searched the scriptures daily." The Word of God was changing lives, just as remodeling something brings changes. Acts 17:28, "For in him we live, and move, and have our being." The house was changing and the changing was for the better. Mrs. Smith and I had to prepare ourselves and try to count the cost before we started. Psalm 92:4,

"For thou, Lord, hast made me glad through thy work: I will triumph in the works of thy hands."

As God works in our lives, and we allow Him to do what He desires, our life and walk with Him becomes so much better. Psalm 92:13, "Those that be planted in the house of the Lord shall flourish in the courts of our God." When we allow God to continually remodel us into the servant that He wants us to be and we become more faithful in our walk, our service, and in every area of our life, we become a more joyous, blessed Christian. Be patient and let the Lord continually keep remodeling your life. God has a plan and a purpose for each of us, but it is going to take some remodeling. Let the construction begin.

As we allow God to work in our lives,
we become a more joyous, blessed Christian.

October 17

Jeremiah 26-27   Psalm 93   Proverbs 17   Acts 18

You're Being Watched

Good morning! I know I am deep into being a grandpa. As we talk with our children weekly and sometimes more than once a week, I hear things that make me laugh and things that scare me. The things that scare me are, "Dad, they act just like you," or just like yesterday I heard said, "Mom, he is acting just like Papa Smith." Now nothing is alarming until you hear they were doing something wrong and it is like it is my fault. I laughed and then the Scripture this morning caused me to think. I wrote two statements as I wrote notes this morning. First, "learn from your past" and second, "What am I passing on?."

Proverbs 17:6, "Children's children are the crown of old men; and the glory of children are their fathers." What my grandchildren were doing was not bad, although there are times they get in trouble after it seems to be my fault even though I was not there. I told a story, did something, and it created an idea in a grandchild. Be guaranteed, we will reap what we sow, so we need to watch what we say and be Christ honoring in what we do, because our habits and actions will be copied.

Jeremiah constantly tried through God's strength to let the children of Israel know God's judgment will come. Jeremiah 26:13, "Therefore now amend your ways and your doings, and obey the voice of the Lord your God; and the Lord will repent him of the evil that he hath pronounced against you." Stand for truth and right and be a testimony that will be repeated in the life of someone else. If we want to see a generation coming that is living for God, then we must be the ones to set the example of living for God. Psalm 93:5, Thy testimonies are very sure: holiness becometh thine house, O Lord, for ever." We need to ask ourselves, do we want to have our hearts broken in the future because of our lack of teaching and standing for right and truth today? Proverbs 17:21, "He that begetteth a fool doeth it to his sorrow: and the father of a fool hath no joy." Proverbs 17:25, "A foolish son is a grief to his father, and bitterness to her that bare him." God is there and will always bless when we do right, teach right and live right. Paul stood even when it seemed the trouble was coming but, praise the Lord, he listened to the Lord and stood. Acts 18:9, "Then spake the Lord to Paul in the night by a vision, Be not afraid, but speak, and hold not thy peace:." I ask myself constantly, what am I passing on? What example am I setting? What will be repeated in another life because of what I have lived? Let us learn from our past and do right the rest of our lives. The example we are setting will be lived in the life of another, especially our children and grandchildren. Somebody is watching and listening to you today.

We need to watch what we say and do because
our habits and actions will be copied.

October 18

Jeremiah 28-29   Psalm 94   Proverbs 18   Acts 19

Beyond Yourself

Good morning! I was walking to my truck yesterday and a man drove by that I know and I waved at him. He stopped and got out and came over to where I was parked. I shook his hand and he proceeded to tell me how depressed he was, how he gets nothing out of church and out of his Bible reading, how he is not happy and on and on he went. He took a breath and I asked how his wife was, how his three children were, and I asked if I could show him something. I got my Bible from my truck and I opened it and asked him if he wrote notes as he read the Bible, if he prayed and asked the Lord to speak to Him before he read the Bible. I will not tell all the conversation but his problem is he is doing everything mechanical and not trying to build a relationship with God. He is only thinking about himself and he has not learned to see beyond himself.

Let us stop each day, take time to tell the Lord that we want to grow in Him, learn of Him, love Him more, trust Him more. Jeremiah 29:13, "And ye shall seek me, and find me, when ye shall search for me with all your heart." The Word of God is a comfort if we allow it to be. Psalm 94:14, "For the Lord will not cast off his people, neither will he forsake his inheritance." May I suggest that we spend more time thinking about God and dwelling on the things of God? What is it that consumes our mind? Psalm 94:19, In the multitude of my thoughts within me thy comforts delight my soul." Last night when I arrived back at the Ranch, I got out of my truck and just looked at the sunset and thought there is not an artist that can paint a picture so perfect. The colors of fall bring out beauty beyond description. The snow of winter is like a blanket of God covering the earth. The buds of spring bring the joy of a new birth. The warmth of summer is a comfort from Heaven. Proverbs 18:1 in our reading today encourages us to listen and surround ourselves with people of Godly wisdom. "Through desire a man, having separated himself seeketh and inter- meddleth with all wisdom." Proverbs 18:15, "The heart of the prudent getteth knowledge; and the ear of the wise seeketh knowledge."

I looked at my brother in Christ and I said, quit looking at yourself and thinking about yourself and learn how to see the greatness of God all around you. God is everywhere and He can be found. God hungers for a relationship with us. I asked him, does your wife love you, do your children love you, do you have a job, do you have a home to live in, do you have good health, do you have a good church, do you have a pastor that walks with God and loves his people? I just kept asking questions like that and

I said, life sounds pretty good to me. Guard your thoughts today and fill them with God and all that He is and wants to be in our lives. Enjoy the Lord today and every day.

Stop thinking about yourself and learn to see the greatness of God around you.

October 19

Jeremiah 30-31   Psalm 95   Proverbs 19   Acts 20

Yielded to the Master

Good morning! For several days now we have been working on clearing a fence row that is being moved to expand our shooting range at the Ranch and preparing for fall retreats. Yesterday I stopped working and just stood and looked across the hills and valleys at the multitude of different things that God takes care of daily. We spend little or no time looking and seeing His greatness in how He does take care of His creation. I will come back to my thought. Reading in Jeremiah 30:2, "Thus speaketh the Lord God of Israel, saying, Write thee all the words that I have spoken unto thee in a book." Just think, it is recorded for us how God spoke to men to write His Word and we hold it in our hands. Listen to God's love for us in Jeremiah 31:3, "I have loved thee with an everlasting love: therefore with loving kindness have I drawn thee."

I looked at the many different trees and different birds and thought of all the different animals that run through God's creation and get everything they need to live. The trees stand and grow and show their beauty in every storm, in the blistering heat, in the freezing cold, in the driving rains, and they continue to grow. These trees produce fruit such as walnuts that we will use in various ways, the cedars will produce beautiful wood working projects, the maples will produce beautiful cabinets, the hickories will produce strong handles and beautiful strong furniture and cabinets, and the list could go on. God takes care of it all and yet we as man cannot stand for Him and stay consistent in our walk and worship with Him and for Him. The trees will grow and be used in a multitude of ways. They will not change their location, nor do they say that they do not want to be used.

Listen to the words of the Apostle Paul in Acts 20:24, "But none of these things move me, neither count I my life dear unto myself, so that I might finish my course with joy." May we be used by God to our fullest and stay faithful until our course is finished. Proverbs 19:21 lets us know to watch out for things that can pull us away; "There are many devices in a man's heart; nevertheless the counsel of the Lord, that shall stand."

All of creation is God's and He uses it as He wishes until it comes down to man, and instead of completely yielding to God, we fight His will. Psalm 95:5, "The sea is his, and he made it: and his hands formed the dry land." I said to the Lord as I looked over the hills and valleys, Lord, use me as you see fit and help me to stand to the end of my course. As the cedar grows to be used, as the hickory grows to be used and as the creation of God is in His hands to be used, may we yield to the Master to be used as He sees fit. Grow and let the Lord use you.

May we be used by God to our fullest and
stay faithful until our course is finished

October 20

Jeremiah 32-33   Psalm 96   Proverbs 20   Acts 21

Keep on Going

Good morning! Sitting last night at a bonfire with folks from Sunday School at our "Harvest Party" activity, I looked up in the sky and noticed the overwhelming beauty in the colors. Only God in His greatness can create a picture as beautiful. Jeremiah 32:17, "there is nothing too hard for thee." Jeremiah 32:18, "the Great, the Mighty God, the Lord of hosts, is his name." Are you carrying a heavy burden today? Does it seem like life is closing in? Are there more bills than there is a month to pay them? Is loneliness, confusion, frustration, lack of understanding, closing in and it seems easier to quit, give up, or run than to stay walking forward with the Lord? Listen to God speak through Jeremiah 32:19, "Great in counsel, and mighty in work: for thine eyes are open upon all the ways of the sons of men:." Jeremiah 32:27, "Behold, I am the Lord, the God of all flesh: is there any thing too hard for me?"

God is there and He can be reached, and He will take time for us and all of our needs and burdens. Jeremiah 33:3, "Call unto me, and I will answer thee, and shew thee great and mighty things, which thou knowest not." God's will being perfected in us is not always an easy path, but with God it is the right path and the path that should be taken. The people of God kept begging Paul to leave and run away from the harm that all could see ahead of him, but he was persistent in letting all know what was in his heart to do for the Lord and the great burden he carried for the Lord and for lost people. As he said to those that wanted him to be safe and leave, Acts 21:14, "The will of the Lord be done." The path that God has for us is not the same path that Paul walked, but let God comfort and lead, and stay on the path that He has chosen for you. God will give strength. Proverbs 20:27, "The spirit of man is the candle of the Lord, searching all the inward parts of the belly." We know what is right and we must be determined to do it. Proverbs 20:5, "Counsel in the heart of man is like deep water; but a man of understanding will draw it out."

The sky can only be painted as beautiful by God, but in the heart of all painters and artists is a desire to paint a picture as beautiful. Give God the glory today and praise Him for the victory that is yours. Psalm 96:8, Give unto the Lord the glory due unto his name:." Keep going, God is there and He will not forsake you.

Let God comfort and lead, and stay on the path that He has chosen for you.

October 21

Jeremiah 34-35   Psalm 97   Proverbs 21   Acts 22

You're Not Alone

Good morning! Today begins another day to face the battles of life before us. So often I beg the Lord for words to express to others that we do not have to face the daily battles alone. I so often hear said, I am alone,

I have no one, I wish there was someone to help, I wish I could just talk with someone to show me what to do. We do have that Someone. Jeremiah wrote these words in Jeremiah 35:13, "Will ye not receive instruction to hearken to my words? Saith the Lord." Also, down in Jeremiah 35:17, "I have spoken unto them, but they have not heard; and I have called unto them, but they have not answered." God is there and waiting to speak with us and direct us. Make it a daily purpose in your life to take time to talk with, listen to and get directions from the Lord.

The apostle Paul was giving his testimony in Acts 22:8 and he told of how the Lord struck him blind to get his attention and Paul said, "Who art thou Lord?" He was trying to destroy those that followed Christ and the teachings of Christ, and yet in his hate and anger God did what he needed to do to get Paul's attention. Then in blindness he said in Acts 22:10, "What shall I do, Lord?" Do not wait for a time of heartbreak, a catastrophe, moment of despair to call upon the Lord. God has chosen you and me for a purpose and our life's goal should be to live that purpose of God for God. Acts 22:14, "The God of our fathers hath chosen thee, that thou shouldest know his will." Let God use you today and ask Him for His strength to be used. Acts 22:15, "For thou shalt be his witness unto all men of what thou hast seen and heard."

Do not live like you know better than God. Do not allow yourself to march into this day without God and His strength. Do not harden yourself to think that you can make it without God or you can handle matters in your way. Proverbs 21:2, "Every way of a man is right in his own eyes: but the Lord pondereth the hearts." Proverbs 21:29, "A wicked man hardeneth his face: but as for the upright, he directeth his way." God loves us and it is time for us to show our love to Him by listening, following and leaning on Him every moment of every day. Psalm 97:10, "Ye that love the Lord, hate evil: he preserveth the souls of his saints; he delivereth them out of the hand of the wicked." He is there for us, so let us allow Him to lead us. What a joy and comfort to know this day that the Lord is with us every step of the day.

God has a purpose for us and our life's goal
should be to live that purpose for Him.

October 22

Jeremiah 36-37   Psalm 98   Proverbs 22   Acts 23

Special Words

Good morning! Think of someone special of whom you would like to hear their voice. Think of something that they said that meant so very much to you. Think of something that this special person in your life said that helped you so very much. Do you ever find yourself dwelling on this person in a special way? All of us have someone that is this special to us. Without a doubt this person in my life is my wife. I have saved the cards and letters she has gotten for me and sent to me. I love to hear her voice and I love the times we are alone together and when there are no interruptions.

As I read in Jeremiah 36 and 37 this morning, I kept reading the phrase, "the words of the Lord." Jeremiah 36:1, "this word came unto Jeremiah from the Lord saying." A roll was taken, and the words of God were written. The "words of the Lord" were written, preserved, and read, and conviction came. The king tried to destroy the "words of the Lord" by burning them. They were written and again preserved. In Acts 23, there is a conspiracy to kill Paul because of his preaching about the resurrection of Christ, that is truth from the "words of the Lord." In our reading today in Proverbs 22:12, we read, "The eyes of the Lord preserve knowledge, and he overthroweth the words of the transgressor." Proverbs 22:20, "Have not I written to thee excellent things in counsels and knowledge." Proverbs 22:21, "That I might make thee know the certainty of the words of truth;." God's Word has been preserved for all mankind.

May we love it more each day. May we read it each day. May we learn and grow from it each day. Psalm 98:2, "The Lord hath made known his salvation: his righteousness hath he openly shewed in the sight of the heathen." This happened through the "words of the Lord." May there be a new commitment to read, study, memorize and love the "words of the Lord" today. Begin every day with the "words of the Lord." Hide the "words of the Lord," in your heart. More precious than hearing the words of the one or ones I love on this earth, is hearing "the words of the Lord."

Love your Bible afresh and anew this morning and every morning, all day and every day.

May we make a new commitment to read,
study, and memorize God's Word today.

October 23

Jeremiah 38-39   Psalm 99   Proverbs 23   Acts 24-25

Tie Another Knot

Good morning! There are days that we think we have problems and we cannot see the end. It seems everything is going wrong and everything is falling apart. Before we quit and before we give up, let us look to the Scriptures. The Scriptures record stories of real people and real-life situations. God does not justify all the sin that man does, but He does let us see man in his real state of being and how God deals with man.

Today we look at a faithful prophet Jeremiah in the depths of a dungeon where there is no water and he is sunken in the mire; Jeremiah 38. We see Jeremiah drawn out of the dungeon and in verse 20 we read his words, "Obey, I beseech thee, the voice of the Lord, which I speak unto thee: so it shall be well unto thee, and thy soul shall live." In Acts 24 and 25, Paul is captive and going through a trial , being accused, and he gives this testimony in Acts 24:14, "But this I confess unto thee, that after the way which they call heresy, so worship I the God of my fathers, believing all things which are written in the law and the prophets." Listen how his testimony affected Felix in verse 25, "And as he reasoned of righteousness, temperance, and judgment to come, Felix trembled." Felix then testified in Acts 25:27, "For it seemeth to me unreasonable to send a prisoner, and not withal to signify the crimes laid against him."

Do not let the devil get you down today. Set your eyes on God and look to Him for strength and let the situation and trial be used to glorify God. Proverbs 23:5 "Wilt thou set thine eyes upon that which is not?" God has a purpose, so may we allow Him to work His purpose through us.

Only God knows how He is going to work through us and through our trials. Felix trembled, the king listened to Jeremiah and God wants to use us. Psalm 99:1, "The Lord reigneth; let the people tremble:." Today might seem to be the end, but with God all things are possible. You might be at the end of your rope; tie another knot and hang on. God has a purpose greater than you and me.

Let your situation and trial be used to glorify God.

October 24

Jeremiah 40-41   Psalm 100   Proverbs 24   Acts 26

Don't Pull Back

Good morning! As a young fellow and as an older fellow, I enjoy teasing. I can remember it being said to me often as a young fellow, "you better be able to take what you put out." In plain English, if you tease someone else you better be able to receive it back. We reap what we sow. It will return to us what we give out. Jeremiah 40:3, "Now the Lord hath brought it, and done according as he hath said:."

The truth is, we have things that come into our lives where we ask the question, what have I done wrong to deserve this? It is good for us to constantly be evaluating our relationship to Christ, our commitments to Christ, our promises that we made to Christ, etc. I am saying that I have seen many young people and adults walk an aisle, give their heart to God for whatever His will is, and then pull back and take their life back and do what they want and not what God wants. In Acts 26:16, Paul is giving his testimony before king Agrippa, and Paul is telling how he is now what he is because God had a "purpose" for him. Jeremiah prophesied over and over again, warning of following wrong and not following God, and the children of Israel received the judgment of God for a purpose. In Acts. 26:16, Paul testifies that he was saved to be sent "to open their eyes, and to turn them from darkness to light, and from the power of Satan unto God." King Agrippa listened and said in verse 28, "Almost thou persuadeth me to be a Christian."

Christian, today is the day and every day after, we must arrive at a point of putting Christ first and quit holding back any area of our life for Christ. Proverbs 24:11, If thou forbear to deliver them that are drawn unto death." I stopped and looked up the word "forbear," which means to hold oneself back. Each day and each moment of every day should be a time of surrender to Christ and His will. Have you given your life to Christ and pulled back? Have you made a commitment to do the will of God and pulled back? Are you going through a time in your life because of a decision or several decisions that have brought you to a dead end? There is no dead end with God. He forgives when we see the need to forsake and return to Him. Proverbs 24:21, "meddle not with them that are given to change:." God blesses a consistent walk with Him. Don't give up. Don't let yourself be defeated. Listen to Psalm 100:5, "his truth endureth to all generations." God has a "purpose" for each of us. I do not want to miss what God has for me. Listen to those words of Jeremiah 40:3, "Now the Lord hath brought it, and done according as he hath said:." Each of us must face where we are and look at the face of our Creator and say, "here am I, Lord," show me and use me, I know you have a "purpose" for me. Live for God's "purpose" in your life.

Each day should be a time of surrender to Christ and His will.

October 25

Jeremiah 42-43   Psalm 101   Proverbs 25   Acts 27

Time with God

Good morning! This morning is different from other mornings for me. I so hunger and need to hear from my God. I hunger to hear, and I listen each day, but have you ever just stopped and said, Lord, I need you to guide me so carefully today? I fear we are in such a rush in our lives that we often miss that important leading that we so need. We have been saved so long or we think we have figured everything out in the Christian life that we can go on without hearing clearly what the Lord is saying. STOP, LISTEN, MEDITATE! Jeremiah 42:3, "That the Lord thy God may shew us the way wherein we may walk, and the thing that we may do." When he speaks, and He will, "we will obey the voice of the Lord our God," Jeremiah 42:6.

Paul was one of 276 people on a ship that was in a very severe storm, and after he prayed and fasted he said this to all on the ship; "For there stood by me this night the angel of God, whose I am, and who I serve." He let them know that they were going to be alright and he told them in verse 25, "for I believe God." He stopped, prayed and listened. Proverbs 25:8 says, "Go not forth hastily to strive, lest thou know not what to do in the end thereof." I wrote a note in my Bible by this that said, "Do not overreact, be patient with the situation." I hunger to hear, listen and obey the Lord in every way. Psalm 101:2, "I will behave myself wisely in a perfect way, I will walk within my house with a perfect heart." God is watching us today and every day. Psalm 101:6, "Mine eyes shall be upon the faithful of the land, that they may dwell with me: he that walketh in a perfect way, he shall serve me." STOP, LISTEN, MEDITATE! Do not just rush into this day. Take time and enjoy the fellowship with the Lord in His Word and in a time in prayer to Him. Let His Word speak each time we open and look in. Have a very blessed day.

We should not be in such a rush that we miss God's leading for the day.

October 26

Jeremiah 44-46   Psalm 102:1-10   Proverbs 26   Acts 28

Always There

Good morning! It is raining as I begin to type, and my mind goes to the farmers that are trying to bring in their harvest. To some the rain is a comfort, to some it is a discouragement. The lakes and ponds are way down because of the drought and yet so much rain has come in the last few weeks that farmers cannot get their crops in. What is positive for one is negative for the other.

As I read in Jeremiah, Acts, Proverbs and the Psalms this morning, I kept seeing things tie together. In Jeremiah 46:14, "Stand fast," Jeremiah 46:28, "for I am with thee;" Acts 28:6 "and saw no harm come to him;" Proverbs 26:10 "The great God that formed all things;" Psalm 102:1 "Hear my prayer, O Lord." As some look at the rain today as a positive, some will look at the rain as a negative. Some today will have a good day and some today will go through some trial. What I am trying to say is that God is always there and He will always hear our plea.

In the time of judgment in Jeremiah, it was also a time of standing fast and seeing God's preservation. When Paul in Acts was bitten by a serpent, all that saw thought he was being judged and they watched and saw the protection and provision of God. In Proverbs, God teaches us how to identify the fool and yet how to be wise. In Psalms, God tells us He is there in a time of trouble. My heart is blessed just to think, no matter if it is rain or sunshine, God is there and He is in control. As you begin this day and take every turn that this day brings forth, "stand fast" and see our "great God." He is there and wants to be our joy, our comfort in joy and in sorrow. Have a blessed day.

Whether sunshine or rain, God is always there and always in control.

October 27

Jeremiah 47-48   Psalm 102:11-17   Proverbs 27   Romans 1-2

Can Others See Christ in You?

Good morning! I watched as a horse stuck his head through the barbed wire fence to eat the grass on the other side of the fence. I walked over and the horse pulled his head back through the fence, and if anybody was standing close, they would have heard me talking in English to a horse that does not understand English. I know it sounds like I am losing my mind to talk to a horse like that, but I wonder how many times the Lord has looked at us and asked, why are you so stubborn and rebellious?

My heart breaks as I read another two chapters in Jeremiah and see the rebellion of the people toward God. Jeremiah 48:10, "Cursed be he that doeth the work of the Lord deceitfully." The people thought they were so strong. Jeremiah 48:10, "How is the strong staff broken, and the beautiful rod!" We begin reading in the book of Romans today and see that man becomes so rebellious without God that in Romans 1:25 we read, "Who changed the truth of God into a lie, and worshipped and served the creature more than the Creator, who is blessed for ever." We do not have to look very far in our world today to see total rebellion toward God. Just as I stood at a fence and looked at a horse for which I try to provide everything that it needs, and it seems it is never enough. Oh, that we would keep a heart for souls and telling them of the love and forgiveness of God. Romans 2:4, "the goodness of God leadeth thee to repentance."

Maybe it is we Christians that spend so much time bragging on ourselves and our accomplishments instead of bragging on God and His accomplishments, that has brought a distraction so that the lost world does not see God through us and in us. Proverbs 27:2, "Let another man praise thee, and not thine own mouth; a stranger, and not thine own lips." May this world filled with sin see Christ in all areas of our lives. May we let the world see Jesus in how we speak, how we dress, how we treat others, how we work, how we pay our bills on time, how we reach out to others, etc. Psalm 102:12, "But thou, O Lord, shalt endure for ever; and thy remembrance unto all generations." May Jesus be seen in us, by a sin blackened world. As God's people, we see the results of rejection of God and a life filled with sin, but may they see, hear and receive from us the wonderful story of salvation to all mankind.

Live so that others can see Christ in every area of your life.

October 28

Jeremiah 49-50   Psalm 102:18-28   Proverbs 28   Romans 3-4

Stay in the Lane

Good morning! As I was leaving church last night and shaking hands to those I passed, a man said to me, be careful going home, that road is dangerous. I stopped and we visited for a moment and then I said, to those that live in the area the road is straight and has no curves. If you have never traveled the road to the camp, it is truly a beautiful drive but the road is very winding with many curves. It is true, those that live in the area cross the center line often and they seem to try and make the curves straight.

I thought about the road as I read this morning in Jeremiah 50:2, "set up a standard." There is a standard in everything that we do in life. The road to the camp has a white line on the outside edge to let you know where the edge is and even some of the road has a rumble strip to let you know when you are getting too close to the edge. There are yellow stripes to let a person know when it is not safe to pass and there is a stripe going down the middle of the road so that a person can stay safely in their lane of travel. All of the road markings and signs are to keep us safe that travel on the road, but when the markings are ignored there is the possibility of danger. A higher authority than all of us who live in the area where the road is, decided when they built the road to mark it to make it safe for all who travel on this road. When the markings are ignored, even though a higher authority decided they needed to be there, there will be danger in travel.

Jeremiah 49:7, "is counsel perished from the prudent? Is their wisdom vanished?" As we turn to the book of Romans 3:3, "For what if some did not believe? Shall their unbelief make the faith of God without effect?" The answer is that unbelief does not change God. Romans 3:4, "let God be true, but every man a liar;." Man does not like to face the reality of sin. Man, by nature, wants to do what he wants to do, no matter what God or any authority has to say. The road is safe when the markings are obeyed, but when ignored, the road can be a possible danger. No, the road is not a danger, the people traveling on the road are the problem. Such is life. Romans 3:10, "There is none righteous, no, not one:." Man is a sinner and that must be admitted. Romans 3:23, "For all have sinned, and come short of the glory of God;." We only want to see our side and when the yellow line is crossed on a crooked road, it is for us to have to turn less or so we can go faster and that causes us to break the law. We can never justify sin and that is why we are all sinners. Proverbs 28:13, "He that covereth his sins shall not prosper: but whoso confesseth and forsaketh them shall have mercy." Daily life lived for God has boundaries that if lived, will give us a life blessed in Christ. When the boundaries of God are crossed, there is sin committed and it must be confessed and forsaken. When man is born, we were born sinners and the truth must be told. Psalm 102:18, "This shall be written for the generation to come." "For all have sinned!" The road of life must be lived straight and narrow, so that we can live a blessed life in Christ. When the curves come, stay within the boundaries marked by God. The road of life will end someday and may it be said that we made it safely to the arms of God because of our trust in Christ by faith through the confession of our sins and His forgiveness of those sins, and by faith in Him through His grace to us. Drive safely today. The road might have some curves, but make sure you stay within the lines that God established. Have a great trip and enjoy the journey.

God's boundaries are in place to keep us safe.

October 29

Jeremiah 51-52   Psalm 103   Proverbs 29   Romans 5-6

Praise Him

Good morning! Yesterday morning as well as today the mist is covering the ground and the valleys are a beautiful picture. To one it is beautiful and to another that is driving to work it is dangerous. Even though the mist creates a beautiful scene, the same mist creates a danger for one driving.

When God looks from Heaven, He is able to see the whole picture and when we look from where we are at the picture, it sometimes seems so unclear. As our reading in Jeremiah came to the end of the book, captivity had come and God's judgment had fallen. In Romans 5 and 6 we read of God's love, forgiveness, and grace toward us. Sin brings death and yet God's gift of salvation brings eternal life to all who accept Jesus Christ. In Proverbs 29:25, we find safety in the Lord; "whoso putteth his trust in the Lord shall be safe."

I was so blessed as I turned to Psalm 103 for our reading in the Psalms today and observed six times the statement, "Bless the Lord." He forgiveth,

He healeth, He redeemeth, He crowneth, He satisfieth, and He renews. Proverbs 103:12, He casts my sins far away so that they are gone. "As far as the east is from the west, so far hath he removed our transgressions from us." Take time to praise the Lord today. In a trial, praise Him! Going through a battle, praise Him! Have more bills than money, praise Him! Under attack, praise Him! In sickness, praise Him! Psalm 103:22, "Bless the Lord, all his works in all places of his dominion: bless the Lord, O my soul.." Have a blessed day praising the Lord!!

God is able to see the whole picture even when we cannot.

October 30

Lamentations 1-2   Psalm 104:1-17   Proverbs 30   Romans 7-8

Taken for Granted

Good morning! I look up from my desk and there is a calendar showing the month of October and a beautiful fall picture. The month of October is almost gone, and the beauty of the fall colors is quickly leaving us. Why is it that what we often love the most we take for granted and it is gone before we know it?

We begin our Old Testament reading today in the book of Lamentations. Lamentations expresses the heart of God's love for Israel and His brokenness, grieving and sorrow for the very people whom He is chastening. Lamentations 1:8, "Jerusalem hath grievously sinned; therefore she is removed:." Lamentations 1:16, "because the comforter that should relieve my soul is far from me:." As we read the first two chapters, we can sense the brokenness of God and His love for His people. Romans 7:18, "For I know that in me (that is, in my flesh,) dwelleth no good thing:."

I fear the separation of God because of sin. I fear the separation of that love that God has for me. I am continually thankful for God's forgiveness and forgetfulness and yet the flesh is a daily fight. May our focus be on Him and not consumed of our flesh. Romans 8:5, "For they that are after the flesh do mind the things of the flesh; but they that are after the Spirit the things of the Spirit." Romans 8:6, "For to be carnally minded is death; but to be spiritually minded is life and peace." This is why it is so important to spend time with the Lord in reading His Word, praying, attending a church for fellowship, preaching, singing and serving. Life is not all about trying to find what satisfies the flesh but what controls and fills our spirit. Proverbs 30:5, "Every word of God is pure: he is a shield unto them that put their trust in him." I must have read Psalm 104:1-17 a dozen times this morning. May I suggest you read and meditate on those verses? "Who coverest, Who layeth, Who maketh, Who laid the foundations; He sendeth the springs into the valleys, He watereth the hills, He causeth the grass to grow, The trees of the Lord are full of sap." God's love for us is beyond description. Our praise to Him should be our prime focus. Stop now and just praise Him for who He is! May we see the depths of His love for us today. If you have lost that sweet relationship with God, just stop and get it back beginning right now. He is there, He is patient, He hears our pleas. Let everything that hath breath praise the Lord!

> *Life is not about satisfying the flesh,*
> *but finding what controls and fills the spirit.*

October 31

Lamentations 3-5   Psalm 104:18-35   Proverbs 31   Romans 9-10

Whosoever Means Me

Good morning! I love the word "whosoever." Every time I read "whosoever" in the Bible, I know that means me. We read and see and hear about the athletes that are great, the politicians that are great, the people of the world that are rich, those that seem to have success in everything and every area of their life.

With God, I am the "whosoever." I am first with God and the most important today and every day. As I read in Lamentations 3:22, "his compassions fail not;" verse 23, "They are new every morning: great is thy faithfulness." Those promises are for me and for you; we are first place in the eyes of God. He knows me and cares for me. Romans 10:13, "For whosoever shall call upon the name of the Lord shall be saved." That "whosoever" is me and you. All the promises of God, His grace, His mercy, His love, His forgiveness is mine and yours. As we read in Proverbs 31 and verse 31, "let her own works praise her." My praise to God is just as important to God as the richest man in the world. As a matter of fact, it does not matter if I am rich or poor, I am important to God and I must praise Him. Lamentations 3:41, "Let us lift up our heart with our hands unto God in the heavens." Psalm 104:34, "I will be glad in the Lord." Stand up, step forward, look up and praise the Lord. Thank the Lord today that we are the "whosoever's." God loves me and salvation is to all who trust Him. I am His and He is mine. He loves me and I cannot be taken from Him. I feel like shouting today. Let us sing praise to Him. Lift your head high.

As I was cleaning a cabin yesterday, I was listening to a story of a man being burned at the stake in years gone by and as the fire was beginning to burn, this man began to sing unto the Lord and as his hands and arms caught on fire, witnesses recorded that his arms were raised as praise unto His God. Walk in victory today because you and I are the "whosoever's." "I will praise Him! I will praise Him! Praise the Lamb for sinners slain; Give Him glory, all ye people, For His blood can wash away each stain." PRAISE HIM!!!

It does not matter if we are rich or poor, we are important to God.

November 1

Ezekiel 1-3   Psalm 105:1-15   Proverbs 1   Romans 11-12

Fruit Producers

Good morning! Well, winter, or at least the cold and wind of winter, has arrived. As we have been preparing for another retreat at the camp, I often stop and just enjoy the blessings of the Lord. As I looked yesterday, I saw the fruit of two trees laying on the ground. One tree produces a fruit of no value and right next to it is a tree that produces a fruit of great value. We will keep you wondering for a moment. We have begun our reading today in Ezekiel, a prophet that is speaking boldly of the sins of Israel. In Ezekiel 3:7, he uses the word "impudent," which means lack of holy shame, and then we read, "hard hearted," meaning stubbornness of heart. Along with the sins of the people were a people that I believe wanted to live for God and wanted to see and experience the promises of God.

In our reading today in Romans 11, Paul writes and talks of grafting. We are to be reproducing in the Christian life. Paul wrote in Romans 11:14, "If by any means I may provoke to emulation them which are my flesh, and might save some of them." The word "emulation" means to match or to resemble. We are to be reproducers. We are grafted to Christ when we received Him as our Saviour. Proverbs 1 starts out with the importance of attaining wisdom and then turns to the destruction of sin. Proverbs 1:10, "My son, if sinners entice thee, consent thou not." Proverbs 1:33, "But whoso hearkeneth unto me shall dwell safely, and shall be quiet from fear of evil." In Christ, walking with Christ, and in desiring to please Christ in everything, we become grafted in Him.

There are two trees that are beside each other and they both reproduce but their fruit is so different. A hedge tree produces hedge apples and they are of no value. They cannot be eaten, there is no use other than they go

378

to seed and produce other hedge trees. Hedge wood is hard and can be used as fence posts but there is no food value in the apples. The other tree I observed right next to the hedge tree is the great, tall, strong walnut tree. The walnuts are all over the ground and can be gleaned and used for many purposes. The wood of the tree can be used to make beautiful furniture. The walnut grows tall and straight, the hedge grows wild and bent with stickers on the branches. In life we can reproduce with beautiful fruit that grows for Christ or live for sin and reproduce nothing of any value. May I ask, what are you producing in your life? As I was writing this morning, I was eating some walnuts. Delicious fruit, healthy fruit, strengthening fruit. The hedge apple can be used for fall decorations but not for health or strength purposes. I hunger for my life to produce a good fruit. May we be strong and fruitful in Christ for His Glory. Have a fruitful day.

What kind of fruit are you producing?

November 2

Ezekiel 4-5   Psalm 105:16-45   Proverbs 2   Romans 13-14

Under God's Ownership

Good morning! Have you ever spoken to someone and they ignored you on purpose? You knew this person heard you and they still ignored you. I wonder how God feels when He is trying to speak to us and we ignore him. That is exactly what happens so often to us and we always get ourselves into some type of trouble. Ezekiel 5:13, "they shall know that I the Lord have spoken it in my zeal."

A little child will hear a parent and choose to go on and not listen. A parent can say "no" and yet the child goes ahead. Is that just like us when our hearts are not in tune with the Lord or we just want something even though we know it is probably not what the Lord wants for us? We must teach a child the respect of authority and the honor of authority. Romans 13:1, "Let every soul be subject unto the higher powers. For there is no power but of God: the powers that be are ordained of God." I have often said, "if we do not obey whom we can see, how will we ever hear and obey whom we cannot see?." We need to be under conviction when we read in Romans 13:13, "Let us walk honestly, as in the day." The word "day" refers to the Lord's return. The ownership of us is the Lord and His Word tells us that in Romans 4:8, "For whether we live, we live unto the Lord; and whether we die, we die unto the Lord: whether we live therefore, or die, we are the Lord's." We will give account for our lives and that is a fact to always remember. Romans 4:12, "So then every one of us shall give account of himself to God."

Oh, that we would learn to walk in a way that pleases the Lord and realize that our associations on this earth do affect us. Proverbs 2:20, "That thou mayest walk in the way of good men, and keep the paths of the righteous." God will not forget, and He is in control no matter what man does or thinks. May we live to please the Lord and honor Him. Psalm 105:42, "For he remembered his holy promise, and Abraham his servant." Listen, learn, live and love the Lord with your life. There are eternal rewards for a life lived for Christ and there are judgments for the life lived for self and this world. In that "day," may we desire to hear "well done, thou good and faithful servant." Live for Him today.

God owns us and someday we will give an account to Him of our life.

November 3

Ezekiel 6-7   Psalm 106:1-16   Proverbs 3   Romans 15

The Faithful Remnant

Good morning! What a joy to hold the Word of God in our hands and to read God's very words. Do not take what I just said for granted. Could there come a day that the Word of God will be illegal to hold in our hands here in America? Never in my life, and I was born in 1951, would I have ever dreamed that there would be so much hatred toward God, His principles and His servants. Around the world the church is being persecuted. The hatred for God is growing and yet you and I have so many promises of God for standing true and faithful to God.

As I read this morning in Ezekiel chapters six and seven, this phrase jumped out seven times; "they shall know that I am the Lord." What a powerful statement told to the children of Israel, preserved for us, that we can be faithful because God is going to powerfully show Himself, and He has. What spoke powerfully to me this morning in Ezekiel is the phrase, "yet will I leave a remnant," Ezekiel 6:8. God promises there will be those that remain faithful. Why not step up today and be that remnant for this generation? Romans 15:4, "For whatsoever things were written aforetime were written for our learning." Proverbs 3:1, "My son, forget not my law; but let thine heart keep my commandments:." Proverbs 3:21, "Keep sound wisdom and discretion." God is giving us the opportunity to be the remnant for now to keep going and standing for Him. It is not in our strength that we will stand. Listen to the words recorded in Proverbs 3:26, "For the Lord shall be thy confidence." Stand and keep standing, be faithful and keep being faithful, win souls and keep winning souls, serve and keep serving, tithe and keep tithing, walk with God and keep walking with God. Psalm 106:3, "Blessed are they that keep judgment, and he that doeth righteousness at all times." Ezekiel 6:8, "yet will I leave a remnant." Stand true, stand tall, stand till we go home to Heaven.

Why not step up and be the remnant for this generation?

November 4

Ezekiel 8-9   Psalm 106:17-33   Proverbs 4   Romans 16

Sin Never Satisfies

Good morning! It is time, and way past time, for those of us that know Christ as our Saviour, to open our eyes to what is truly around us. As I was reading this morning in Ezekiel 8:5, "lift up thine eyes," I thought about a world blinded to sin and I thought about Christians that are blinded to sin. I asked myself, do we accept too much, do we ignore sin, do we not turn from what we know our Lord would not approve, do we try to hide from the fact that we enjoy sin and do not want to admit it? I asked myself the above-mentioned thoughts and more as I continued reading and meditating.

Ezekiel 8:6, "turn thee yet again, and thou shalt see greater abominations." Ezekiel 8:12, "hast thou seen," "for they say, The Lord seeth us not;." Ezekiel 8:13 and verse 15, have the phrase, "turn thee yet again." Ezekiel is writing for the Lord a justification for sending His people into captivity because of their lack of facing and forsaking sin. Paul writes in Romans 16:17, "Now I beseech you, brethren, mark them which cause divisions and offenses contrary to the doctrine which ye have learned; and avoid them." Romans 16:18, "For they that are such serve not our Lord Jesus Christ." We must face sin in our lives and in the world and reject it, turn from it, deal with it, forsake it. Proverbs 4:2, "For I give you good doctrine, forsake ye not my law." We do not have to live in sin. We should not enjoy sin. We should learn from walking with God how to turn from sin. Proverbs 4:4, "He taught me also, and said unto me, Let thine heart retain my words: keep my commandments, and live." There is joy, peace, satisfaction, and so much more in living a life that is pleasing to the Lord. Sin never satisfies. Sin will never bring peace. Sin has no hope. How God's heart must break when He sees us turning from Him and living for self, sin and this world! We read in Psalm 106:21, "They forgat God their Saviour, which had done great things in Egypt." Stop, "lift up thine eyes," "turn thee yet again," see that God will bless a life that is yielded, surrendered and dedicated to Him.

I watched as a bird sat on a branch and was constantly moving its small little head, staying aware of what was going on. May we as the redeemed of God be constantly aware of the sins of this world. Live to please HIM today.

God will bless a life that is yielded, surrendered and dedicated to Him.

Ezekiel 10-11   Psalm 106:34-48   Proverbs 5   1 Corinthians 1-2

Seeing Through God's Eyes

Good morning! Another day is before us, and in this day we will be constantly making decisions about authority. Now that is a different way to start a morning devotional thought! As I was reading this morning and making notes, the word "authority" kept coming up in my mind. Authority of every kind affects each of us daily. Reading His Word and obeying what is written, driving and obeying the speed limit as well as not messing with our cellular phones, doing the work that has been given to us by our employer without complaint or question, getting along with family members and friends without argument or attacks, facing the temptations of the flesh and the attacks of the devil without yielding and sinning.

In Ezekiel 11 we see the phrase "ye shall know that I am the Lord," several times. We read in Ezekiel 11:12, "ye shall know that I am the Lord: for ye have not walked in my statutes, neither executed my judgments, but have done after the manners of the heathen that are round about you." In I Corinthians 1 we read the word "foolish" several times and in I Corinthians 1:18, "For the preaching of the cross is to them that perish foolishness; but unto us which are saved it is the power of God." I hunger to see and understand through God's eyes and not mine. I know I cannot see what God sees, and I want to learn how to wait on God and have patience with God. Many wrong directions and decisions have been made because we look at things through our eyes and our timing and do not ask God to let us see what He sees and what His timing is. Families have moved, jobs have been changed, marriages have been destroyed and many have missed the will of God for their lives because what we see is not what God wants us to see and we are so "foolish" in our decisions. I Corinthians 1:27, "But God hath chosen the foolish things of the world to confound the wise;."

It is the heart of God for us to grow spiritually. I Corinthians 2:14, "But the natural man receiveth not the things of the Spirit of God: for they are foolishness unto him: neither can he know them, because they are spiritually discerned." Proverbs seals it this morning. Proverbs 5:12, "How have I hated instruction, and my heart despised reproof;." Proverbs 5:13, And have not obeyed the voice of my teachers, nor inclined mine ear to them that instructed me!" God will bring judgment on us when we rebel, resist or refuse to allow Him to guide us. Psalm 106:43, "Many times did he deliver them; but they provoked him with their counsel, and were brought low for their iniquity." God loves us. Listen to Him today. Be patient with Him. Learn to go to Him in prayer and pour out your heart to Him and then patiently wait for Him to speak. May this day be a day of joy walking with the Lord and a day of peace because you have listened and allowed the Lord to lead you. May you be blessed in a special way today.

We ought to hunger to see and understand through
God's eyes rather than our own.

November 6

Ezekiel 12-13   Psalm 107:1-22   Proverbs 6   1 Corinthians 3-4

God's Good News

Good morning! For well over forty years each, my father and father-in-law were in the newspaper industry. They did not know each other until my wife and I began to date, but each one of them worked their lives in the newspaper industry. As a twelve-year old boy, I began an apprenticeship learning the printing trade at a weekly newspaper. Being a small town that only had a weekly paper, we did other printing as well. I can remember Tuesdays as being the busiest day of the week for both a daily paper and a weekly paper, because of the grocery store ads for the week. The editor/owner for the weekly paper that I worked at would work very late attending meetings and finishing editorials. I can remember how stressed, and sometimes depressed, he would get over the news that was to be printed. My wife and I to this day receive a weekly paper from the town that we live at by the camp. The headlines and the front-page stories are almost 100% bad news. That is why I love reading "The Sword of The Lord" and "Revival Fires" newspapers. I wanted your mind to be thinking about what we most listen to or read, which is mostly negative reading, seeing and listening.

In Ezekiel 12:2 this morning I read, "thou dwellest in the midst of a rebellious house, which have eyes to see, and see not; they have ears to hear, and hear not: for they are a rebellious house." Is that not the world today? The world does not even see the course of destruction that is ahead. Also, in Ezekiel 13:9, 14, 21, 23, I read some GREAT news; "ye shall know that I am the Lord." Wow, in a time of rebellion God says, I am going to let you know who is in charge. We see man getting puffed up in about every aspect of our lives and God says in I Corinthians 3:6 and 7, that He is the one "that giveth the increase" that lasts or really matters. We read in chapters 3 and 4 of I Corinthians about pride amongst the Christians and in chapter 4 verse 6 we read, "that no one of you be puffed up for one against another."

It is time we look, learn and live what we read in the Scriptures and get our focus off the news that is printed, seen or heard. Yes, I want to keep up with what is going on, but it is not pleasing to the Lord to live in the news. We are challenged to live the truths of the Bible and in Proverbs 6:21, "Bind them continually upon thine heart, and tie them about thy neck." God is still in charge and control. It is we that must continually trust, learn and live the promises in the Word of God. Psalm 107:8, 15 and 21, "Oh that men would praise the Lord for his goodness, and for his wonderful works to the children of men!" Live in reality with God today. Praise Him today! Live knowing that Jesus is coming again and a home is being prepared for all those that know Him as their personal Saviour. He is our KING, our LORD; let us praise Him today. Quit living the headlines of the local, national and world news and live in what will change the news, God's will of salvation to all mankind. Glory to His name. Read the right news; Jesus is coming again!

We must focus on the Scriptures and not the headlines.

November 7

Ezekiel 14-15   Psalm 107:23-43   Proverbs 7   1 Corinthians 5-6

Testimony or Stumblingblock?

Good morning! It has been many years since I lived at my parent's home. I graduated at seventeen years of age in 1969 and was married in 1971. Boy, life has flown! I have a brother and sister that are younger than me. My sister is three years younger and my brother is six years younger. As I read from the Old Testament to the New Testament readings this morning, and on to Proverbs and then to Psalms, I kept thinking about what kind of an example I have set with my life for the Lord. I have grown a lot in my relationship and walk with the Lord. I find myself hungering more now to walk closer to the Lord than I have ever in my life.

As I read Ezekiel 14: 3, 4, and 7, "these men have set up their idols in their heart, and put the stumblingblock of their iniquity before their face:." I asked myself and the Lord, am I a testimony for Christ or am I personally a stumblingblock to a fellow brother or sister in Christ? As I look back (and I know I cannot go back), I was not a very good example to my brother and sister. As I thought about my wife and our children, and the example that I have been and am being to them, I asked myself, am I a stumblingblock to them? Is my life being an example for Christ that would encourage others to have a walk with God? I Corinthians 6:12, "All things are lawful unto me, but all things are not expedient: all things are lawful for me, but I will not be brought under the power of any." We have the freewill to do whatever we want with our lives, but we need to ask ourselves, is my life a stumblingblock or is my life and the example that I am setting encouraging others to live for Christ?

Proverbs 7:7, "And beheld among the simple ones, I discerned among the youths, a young man void of understanding." We are being watched. What testimony for Christ or the devil are we living? A generation behind us is looking at us. Psalm 107:31, "Oh that men would praise the Lord for his goodness, and for his wonderful works to the children of men!" Eyes of all ages are watching. Eyes of those we know and do not know are watching. Eyes of friends and eyes of those that are not our friends are watching. Do we praise or complain? Are we kind or unkind? Are we patient or impatient? Are we an example for Christ, or are we an example for the things of this world? Are we really what we say we are? Are we the same at home as we are at work, or as we are at church? Do we say what we think others want us to say, or do we speak the truth? Do we speak with patience or with frustration? I Corinthians 6:20, "For ye are bought with a price: therefore glorify God in your body, and in your spirit, which are God's." I cannot return to yesterday, last week, last month or last year; but I can sure bring glory to Christ today and not be a stumblingblock. The story of our life has not yet come to the end, so may we today decide that we will not be a stumblingblock to others.

We cannot go back, but we can bring glory to
Christ today and not be a stumblingblock.

November 8

Ezekiel 16-17   Psalm 108   Proverbs 8   1 Corinthians 7

God's Longsuffering

Good morning! Our reading today in Ezekiel 16 and 17 caused my heart to more appreciate the patience of God. In Ezekiel 16:30, "How weak is thine heart;" God's longsuffering is beyond my understanding. God talks throughout the chapter about their abominations and yet in Ezekiel 16:60 we read, "Nevertheless I will remember my covenant with thee in the days of thy youth, and I will establish unto thee an everlasting covenant." Keep in mind, God will judge sin, but God will forgive and forget when there is a repenting of sin.

Picture today in your mind, two children arguing over a toy and the parent coming in and asking, what is going on? The patient parent listens and then says, each of you say, I am sorry. The parent leaves the room or play area and the looks that each child gives the other! Can you picture their faces? Why we allow the devil to get a hold on us, and why we allow our flesh to become so weak is a battle that we will have the rest of our lives.

I Corinthians 7:5, "that Satan tempt you not for your incontinency." The word incontinency is defined as lack of self-control or being undisciplined. We need to grow and develop discipline in our walk with God and in our fight against the flesh. As I read this morning in Proverbs 8:1, 5, 9, 14, we see the word *understand* and its different forms used five times. It is like a parent telling the children to quit fighting and saying, "Do you both understand?" or looking at them and plainly saying, "Are you getting what I am saying?"

Sin will destroy our joy, our peace, our desire to live and serve the Lord. As I read on in Psalm 108:1, "O God, my heart is fixed; I will sing and give praise, even with my glory." May our hearts get fixed or fastened to do what is right and pleasing to the Lord. In Psalm 108:13, "Through God we shall do valiantly: for he it is that shall tread down our enemies." Look to God for strength today, look to God in trials and temptations today, look to God for joy and peace today. Let us walk hand in hand with Him today.

May our hearts get fixed and fastened on doing
what is right and pleasing to the Lord.

November 9

Ezekiel 18-19   Psalm 109:1-13   Proverbs 9   1 Corinthians 8-9

To Reach a Soul

Good morning! My heart is heavy today, thinking about those that I have come across this week that are marked by sin. I am not being judgmental; I am sharing my broken heart for those that reject Christ. They are all around us and we need to do everything that we can to reach them with the gospel. Ezekiel 18:4, 20, "The soul that sinneth, it shall die." Verse after verse in the book of Ezekiel is God's judgment on people that He loved. The question is always asked, how can God judge someone? It is not His judgment that destroys a life; it is the rejection of God's love and the love of sin more than accepting the love of God.

Ezekiel 18:32, "For I have no pleasure in the death of him that dieth, saith the Lord God: wherefore turn yourselves and live ye." There are deaths beyond our understanding, but sin is what has always brought death. I am afraid we are just like the children of Israel and have idols in our lives. The idol that I am speaking of is anything that we put before God. So often a person is too tired to go to church, but they can go to work. Friends come and visit, and instead of taking them to church with us, we stay home. The first activity for all of us, and the greatest priority, should be pleasing God and doing that which pleases Him. I Corinthians 8:6, "But to us there is but one God, the Father, of whom are all things, and we in him; and one Lord Jesus Christ, by whom are all things, and we by him." I believe that if the lost world is going to be reached with the Gospel, we must do everything that we can. I Corinthians 9:22, "To the weak became I as weak, that I might gain the weak: I am made all things to all men, that I might by all means save some."

I read this phrase in Psalm 109:8, "Let his days be few;" meaning those that have rejected God and become attackers to the things of God. Living for God and serving God in any way we can to reach the lost will bring the favor of God. Proverbs 9:11, "For by me thy days shall be multiplied, and the years of thy life shall be increased." I am not living to live a certain number of years. I am living to reach souls however many years that I have left to live. Yesterday my wife and I read missionary letters, as we do on almost a daily basis, and my heart was stirred to focus on reaching every soul everywhere that we can. God is going to lead someone across your path today that He desires for you to share Christ with. Do not miss the meeting that God has planned for you. Live to bring eternal life to others.

We must do everything we can to reach the world with the Gospel.

November 10

Ezekiel 20-21   Psalm 109:14-31   Proverbs 10   1 Corinthians 10

No Comparison

Good morning! I have been blowing out plumbing lines this week of different buildings and RV's at the camp and as I have been working,

I have been comparing this fall to other falls. With a coming anticipation of winter, we tend to compare this year, the trees, the rainfall, the temperature to other years. I remember it often said in my youth as men would talk at the barbershop, the corner drug store, the service station, or wherever men would sit around and talk, they would say, "I remember back in the drought of the 30's."

What we remember spiritually is very important. Ezekiel 20:4, "cause them to know the abominations of their fathers." Ezekiel was writing the words of the Lord and he was stressing the importance of remembering the sins and rejection of the fathers. Ezekiel 20:13, 16, 20, 21, 24, have the statement; "polluted my sabbaths." I remember when Sunday was a holy day, businesses were closed, families ate at home, afternoons were for resting. Now it seems that Sunday is just another day. Ezekiel 20:11, "And I gave them my statutes, and shewed them my judgments, which if a man do, he shall even live in them." Our flesh has taken control, our priorities are not giving God what God deserves, and so much more. I Corinthians 10:3, "For though we walk in the flesh, we do not war after the flesh." I am afraid we in human flesh look and compare with others to justify what we want to do. I Corinthians 10:5, "Casting down imaginations, and every high thing that exalted itself against the knowledge of God, and bringing into captivity every thought to the obedience of Christ." God will have His day, and it will come sooner than we realize. How long will God allow sin to reign and control man? Proverbs 10:25, As the whirlwind passeth, so is the wicked no more: but the righteous is an everlasting foundation." David cried unto the Lord in Psalm 109:27, "That they may know that this is thy hand; that thou, Lord, hast done it."

We need to do right and quit comparing ourselves and our situations to others and live for God, God's way. I Corinthians 10:12, "they measuring themselves by themselves, and comparing themselves among themselves, are not wise." I have heard it said hundreds of times, "Do right, do right, until the stars fall." Do right today and every day.

We must quit comparing ourselves to others and live for God.

Ezekiel 22-23   Psalm 110   Proverbs 11   1 Corinthians 11

Self-Examination

Good morning! As I read this morning continuing in the book of Ezekiel, I just do not understand why the people were continually so rebellious, and then I read chapter 22 over several times. As I reread and reread Ezekiel 22:6-12, "In thee;" I began to see the problem is me. We must be under a constant evaluation of our lives before the Lord. The children of Israel were now being called "dross" (Ezekiel 22:18) and they were going to be melted. Ezekiel 22:22, "As silver is melted in the midst of the furnace, so shall ye be melted in the midst thereof; and ye shall know that I the Lord have poured out my fury upon you." This is why the Lord was bringing judgment and this is still the reason the Lord brings judgment.

Ezekiel 22:26, "they have put no difference between the holy and profane, neither have they shewed difference between the unclean and the clean." In I Corinthians 11:28, we are challenged to take a real look at ourselves; "But let a man examine himself." We need to continually examine our actions and attitudes under the authority of God. The blessings of living right in the eyes of God were pointed out in our reading in Proverbs 11:6, "The righteousness of the upright shall deliver them." God will bless a life lived right in His eyes. Proverbs 11:5, "direct his way," verse 6, "deliver them," verse 8, "delivered out of trouble," verse 10, "city rejoiceth," verse 18, "shall be a sure reward," verse 28, "flourish as a branch."

God loves us and wants to bless us and use us, but we must arrive at a point of allowing Him to be first place and foremost in our lives. Psalm 110:3, "Thy people shall be willing in the day of thy power." God will show Himself in blessing or chastisement. I do not know about you, but I enjoy the blessings of God more than the chastisement of God. The life of a Christian given to Christ is a life filled with peace and joy. Even in those times of testings and trials, there is a peace and comfort. Those two words,

"In thee," spoke to me this morning that I cannot ever point my finger at anybody else. The problem with all of us in found "In thee."

We need to continually examine our actions
and attitudes under the authority of God.

November 12

Ezekiel 24-25   Psalm 111   Proverbs 12   1 Corinthians 12-13

Mark the Day

Good morning! As I awoke this morning and looked outside, the ground is covered with our first snow. Yesterday I was working and doing final preparations on some of the camp buildings and RVs, getting things ready for the dropping temperatures so that we will not have broken, frozen water lines. I thought back to previous years and days that were cold. It seems as though this year we hit the teens in cold temperature a little earlier than usual.

I read in Ezekiel 24:2, "write thee the name of the day, even of this same day:." Yesterday was Veterans Day, a day set aside to remember the sacrifice of those that have served our great country to give us the freedom we enjoy and so much more. As Ezekiel was told by God to "name the day," I thought about the special days we observe, such as birthdays, anniversaries, Christmas, Thanksgiving, Veterans Day, Memorial Day or as I call it, Decoration Day, etc. What about special days that we have made spiritual decisions? Could it not help us in our walk with God to remember special days of special decisions that we have made? I think we need to remember these special spiritual days.

Many soldiers have worn dog tags and had an important task to do. Every soldier is important when it comes to an army functioning. Every Christian soldier is important in the family of God. I Corinthians 12:11, "But all these worketh that one and the selfsame Spirit." I Corinthians 12:14, "For the body is not one member but many." The strength of an army is not in just a few, but in all doing their part. The strength of a church family is not just in one or two, but each is vital to the whole. Do not let the devil get on your shoulder and say you are not important and that you do not do anything. Mark the day you were saved and became part of the family of God. Mark the day you were obedient and got baptized. Mark the day you began to see the obedience of tithing. Mark the day you began to pass out tracts and went soul winning. Our days and places of service in the Lord's army are vital. Our love for God and others is where our strength is. II Corinthians 13:13, "And now abideth faith, hope, charity, these three; but the greatest of these is charity." There are days in our life that we need to remember, as these days can encourage us and keep us going. Psalm 111:4, "He hath made his wonderful works to be remembered: the Lord is gracious and full of compassion." Do not forget the day you were saved and do not forget that your position in the family of God is important. The true joy of the Christian life is serving others and that is "charity," love in action. Make today a special day for someone else because you went out of your way to be a Christian soldier and give an act of "charity." Show kindness to someone. Be the Christian soldier that God wants you to be. Look beyond you. Mark this day as the day you began to take a good look at the needs of others.

Remembering special spiritual days will help us in our walk with God.

November 13

Ezekiel 26-27   Psalm 112   Proverbs 13   1 Corinthians 14

Right Associations

Good morning! I have seen many people get excited about a walk with God and reading their Bible, but their walk and reading seems to end very soon. One of the reasons I feel this happens is we do not take the time to understand the passage of Scripture and we get the attitude of not understanding what is being said.

For example, today in Ezekiel chapters 26 and 27, we see the judgment of God upon a great city that was once a friend, helper, supplier, etc. to Israel, but her ungodliness and worldliness had led Israel into sin. God was going to bring judgment to this once great city. The city of Tyre was a great supplier of many construction materials and dry goods to Israel and the world. Ezekiel 27:17, "Judah, and the land of Israel, they were thy merchants: they traders in thy market." Now because of the wickedness, God says, "thou shalt be a terror, and never shalt be any more," Ezekiel 27:36. God is patient, longsuffering, forgiving, full of compassion, but there is a point that God will say, that is enough.

Let us think about our associations. Are my friends and acquaintances strengthening my relationship with Christ or am I becoming more like them and less like Christ? I Corinthians 14:26, "Let all things be done unto edifying." God desires for us to grow in Him and not be confused or drawn away from a closer walk with Him. I Corinthians 14:33, "For God is not the author of confusion, but of peace, as in all churches of the saints." What things are you reading, listening to and participating in? Do these things bring you closer to Christ or do they draw you away from those things that you have known are right? Proverbs 13:6, "Righteousness keepeth him that is upright in the way: but wickedness overthroweth the sinner." We must be around those that help us to walk with the Lord, help us build a strong relationship with Christ, and stand firm on the Word of God. Proverbs 13:20, "He that walketh with wise men shall be wise: but a companion of fools shall be destroyed." Let us hunger and work toward having a firm relationship with Christ and His Word, unwavering, even in times of trials and temptations. May our hearts be fixed as the Psalmist writes, Psalm 112:7, "his heart is fixed, trusting in the Lord." Stand firm, stand right, stand for Christ.

We must be around those who help us build a strong relationship with Christ.

November 14

Ezekiel 28-30   Psalm 113   Proverbs 14   1 Corinthians 15

God in First Place

Good morning! God has given us another day. Stop and think for a moment, we have nothing to do with us having another day. It is

God's will that we have another day and He has a purpose for us in this day. Man has allowed His flesh to supersede the power of God, and man so often thinks that He is in control and more powerful than God. As we read this morning in Ezekiel 28:6, "Because thou hast set thine heart as the heart of God." In Ezekiel 28, God reveals the beauty of Satan; verse 13, he was covered by every precious stone, verse 14, he was the "anointed cherub," verse 15, "wast perfect," "till iniquity was found in thee" and in verse 17, "thine heart was lifted up because of thy beauty." Twelve times in chapters 28-30, I read, "they shall know that I am the Lord God."

I do not know what God will have to do to each one of us to get us to acknowledge the power of Almighty God. As written in I Corinthians 15:31 by the apostle Paul, "I die daily." I am afraid that we as the human race think that we know more than God and we will seek the approval of man more than the approval of God. Man is unstable in all his ways. Man is constantly changing. There is a fight in our flesh every moment of every day and that fight is for who is going to be in charge. There is only peace in a walk with God. There is only peace in a surrendered life to do the will of God. Proverbs 14:26, "In the fear of the Lord is strong confidence:." Proverbs 14:27, "The fear of the Lord is a fountain of life, to depart from the snares of death."

Stop today and just put the Lord first place, right on top of every decision, every thought. When the battle begins to rage, stop and put God up front and ask for His wisdom and His direction. When we praise Him, there is a comfort, peace, and direction. Psalm 113:2, "Blessed be the name of the Lord from this time forth and for evermore." May I ask the simple question as we begin this day, who will be our guide, our leadership, our stability, our encourager today? Let it be and let the world know what was written twelve times in Ezekiel 27-30, "they shall know that I am the Lord God." Put God first today.

Stop today and put the Lord on top of every decision and every thought.

November 15

Ezekiel 31-32   Psalm 114   Proverbs 15   1 Corinthians 16 & 2 Cor. 1

Beyond Ourselves

Good morning! Mrs. Smith says that I have a mind that never shuts off. Most of the time I feel I have a mind that never turns on. I awoke several times during the night thinking about those that I love and pray for, those that I have seen accept Christ as their Saviour and were growing in the Lord and something stopped the growth. I thought about those that I love that have been saved for a long period of time and seem to be content where they are, and are not desiring to step up to the next level of service for the Lord. I thought about those that are making decisions without counsel, those that make excuse without excuse. I stopped and decided it is time to just praise the Lord.

The news media thrives on the negative and the drama of life. In our reading in Ezekiel 31 and 32, we read how the greatness of wickedness shall be destroyed. Ezekiel 32:31, "Pharaoh and all his army slain by the sword, saith the Lord God." Paul wrote to the Corinthians in chapter 16, verse 9, "For a great door and effectual is opened unto me, and there are many adversaries." He was telling the church that there will be many that will quit and try to stop what God is doing but I love what was written in 16:13-14, "Watch ye, stand fast in the faith, quit you like men, be strong. Let all your things be done with charity."

It is time for us to stand firm and look beyond ourselves and see things that we can do to be an encouragement to others. Paul ended his writings in I Corinthians 16:18, by writing, "For they have refreshed my spirit and yours:." He was speaking of brothers in the Lord that were standing faithful and serving. Reading on in II Corinthians 1:3, "the God of all comfort and in verse 4, "Who comforteth us in all our tribulation, that we may be able to comfort them which are in any trouble, by the comfort wherewith we ourselves are comforted of God." I love the song, "The Son Is Coming Up in The Morning." Just think, we have another day to see God's hand in our lives. Let us live for Him, stand for Him and look to Him for all our decisions. Proverbs 15:19, "the way of the righteous is made plain." Psalm 114:7, "Tremble, thou earth, at the presence of the Lord, at the presence of the God of Jacob;." The news media, the government, nor any group are not in charge. My God is real, and He is going to let this world know that He is God and I want to shout, He is my Lord! Stand tall, brother and sister in Christ. Stand true and faithful. Be an encourager today even if you do not feel like it. You will be pleasantly surprised how serving others brings a joy beyond ourselves.

It is time for us to look beyond ourselves and
see things we can do to encourage others.

November 16

Ezekiel 33-34   Psalm 115   Proverbs 16   2 Corinthians 2-3

Stir Your Spiritual Coals

Good morning! The chill of the late fall and early winter is here this morning. I went to the wood stove to stir the coals left over from when I stoked the fire before we called it a day. As I knelt down and stirred the coals, I thought about the campers that come to camp and have made decisions for Christ. I wish there was a way that I could stir the spiritual coals in the lives of all that come to camp but are now gone home. As I read in Ezekiel 33, verse after verse kept speaking to me as word after word kept coming alive just like the stirring of the coals. "Watchman," "sound the trumpet," "warn them," "thou shalt hear the word at my mouth, and warn them from me." Ezekiel 33:11, "Say unto them, As I live, saith the Lord God, I have no pleasure in the death of the wicked; but that the wicked turn from his way and live: turn ye, turn ye, from your evil ways; for why will ye die."

I went to the chapel area and I thought how God has blessed throughout the years and how many have come, and many decisions have been made. Praise the Lord, but we need continually to have our spiritual coals stirred and fresh wood put on the fire or the fire will go out. Oh, that we would keep our spiritual coals stirred constantly as we read the Word of God, pray and hear our pastors preach and teach the Bible. Live a victorious life in Christ. II Corinthians 2:14, "Now thanks be unto God, which always causeth us to triumph in Christ." II Corinthians 3:5, "but our sufficiency is of God." As I looked into the wood stove, it looked as if the fire was out, but when I stirred the ashes, the coals came alive and I put wood on the coals and opened the dampener and the fire came alive. Psalm 115:13, "He will bless them that fear the Lord, both small and great." Do not let anything put a dampener on your fire for the Lord. Proverbs 16:7, "When a man's ways please the Lord, he maketh even his enemies to be at peace with him." Let God stir your ashes, read His Word and get some air on the coals, go to Sunday School and get some fresh wood for the fire, listen to the preaching from your pastor and let the fire burn for God. The chill of a cold life will soon be warmed by the fire for God. Stay warm spiritually.

We need to continually have our spiritual coals stirred or the fire will go out.

November 17

Ezekiel 35-36   Psalm 116   Proverbs 17   2 Corinthians 4-5

Love in Action

Good morning! I am thankful for the daily promises of God, the reassurance that He is there, the comfort knowing that I can go to Him in prayer anyplace and anytime. I am thankful His Word is a guide even in a darkened world. This morning I read in Ezekiel 36:5, "Surely in the fire of my jealousy have I spoken against the residue of the heathen." God was, is and always will be jealous for His people, especially when the devil and his demons come to lure us away from living for God.

II Corinthians 4:8-9 explains life the real way it is many days, "We are troubled on every side, yet not distressed; we are perplexed, but not in despair, Persecuted, but not forsaken; cast down, but not destroyed;." I read on down in the same chapter to verse 16, "though our outward man perish, yet the inward man is renewed day by day." I cannot return to yesterday and I do not want to return, but I have the strength from God to go another day. Rejoice that we can be renewed each and every day. II

Corinthians 5:17, "Therefore if any man be in Christ, he is a new creature: old things are passed away; behold, all things are become new." Rejoice today, my brother and sister. Proverbs 17:22, "A merry heart doeth good like a medicine: but a broken spirit drieth the bones."

As my wife and I were out soul winning yesterday and we went from door to door, my heart broke for those that have no desire to leave this world behind and walk in a new life with Christ. My heart breaks for Christians that have new life but have stopped the growth of Christ because of a lack of spiritual character to go to the next level in their walk with Christ. Check how your love for the Lord is today. How is your desire to fellowship with other Christians? When is the last time you gave someone a tract? My love for the Lord in action is the true meaning in my heart. Psalm 116:1-2, "I love the Lord, because he hath heard my voice and my supplications. Because he hath inclined his ear unto me, therefore will I call upon him as long as I live." Let us focus on those words we read in Ezekiel 36:26, "A new heart also will I give you and a new spirit will I put within you:." The Lord bless your day, let Him know you love Him.

Our love for the Lord in action is the true meaning in our heart.

November 18

Ezekiel 37-38   Psalm 117   Proverbs 18   2 Corinthians 6-7

Something Out of Nothing

Good morning! Do you remember hearing the phrase, "What is one man's junk is another man's treasure"? All of us have things that we think are important and we save them, and then often just throw them away. Our reading this morning takes us to Ezekiel 37 to the vision that God has for His people. Ezekiel is asked the question, "Can these bones live"? He answered in verse 3, "O Lord God, thou knowest." There is a vision of a valley of dry bones and as the Lord speaks, life is given to these bones. God goes on and says that the people feel there is no hope, but as we read on, we see that the dry bones become an army and God then talks of David being the one shepherd (37:24).

There are several places at the camp that summer staff have helped me clear out the brush, mow the weeds, build benches, make a beautiful trail. What seemed to be just an area of woods and brush turned into a beautiful spot for many uses. If we would allow the Lord to have every part of our life, God could do some great things beyond what we can see or ever dream. II Corinthians 6:16, "as God hath said, I will dwell in them, and walk in them; and I will be their God, and they shall be my people." II Corinthians 7:1, "Having therefore these promises, dearly beloved, let us cleanse ourselves from all filthiness of the flesh and spirit, perfecting holiness in the fear of God."

As we see our life, we may see a mess, but let God today perfect what He sees. A weedy side of a hill or an area of brush in a valley could turn into a beautiful spot. We must have a willingness to separate ourselves unto God and allow Him to be our God as He desires. Proverbs 18:1, "Through desire a man, having separated himself, seeketh and intermeddleth with all wisdom." The truth is, God sees something very special in each of us. Psalm 117:2, "the truth of the Lord endureth for ever." You might look at yourself as nothing, but let God have the nothing and let Him develop a something for His glory. An old stump can turn into a beautiful table, an old twisted limb can turn into a beautiful lamp, and an old sinner can be used as a lighthouse for Christ.

God sees something very special in each of us.

November 19

Ezekiel 39-40   Psalm 118:1-14   Proverbs 19   2 Corinthians 8-9

Stand True

Good morning! I have always enjoyed history. If you would come to my office at the church or at the house, you would see a large amount of my books are about history and events that are about our country. From the very beginning of our country's existence, there has always been a struggle and a struggle for direction. America has always had a segment of those willing to stand for principles that have brought us this far, holding true to the principles of the Word of God and our founding fathers. Until we leave this earth, there will be battles to stand true to Biblical principles. About the time we think an organization or business is standing true, they seem to change.

Ezekiel 39:7, "So will I make my holy name known in the midst of my people Israel; and I will not let them pollute my holy name any more: and the heathen shall know that I am the Lord, the Holy One in Israel." That makes things very clear how God feels about His name. Paul wrote powerful words to the churches at Corinth about the churches of Macedonia. II Corinthians 8:3, "For to their power, I bear record, yea, and beyond their power they were willing of themselves." On down in the same chapter and verse 5, "And this they did, not as we hoped, but first gave their own selves to the Lord, and unto us by the will of God." The world is constantly tugging on us and words were so wisely written in Proverbs 19:21, "There are many devices in a man's heart; nevertheless the counsel of the Lord, that shall stand."

When we stand true to Biblical principles, we are going to always upset someone and we will be attacked, but listen to the Psalmist in Psalm 118:2, 3, 4, "his mercy endureth for ever." Psalm 118:6, "The Lord is on my side; I will not fear: what can man do unto me?" Psalm 118:8, "It is better to trust in the Lord than to put confidence in man." Stand today for God. Be true and faithful to Him. Be unashamed to live and stand by Biblical principles. Love God's Word and let it be your guide in all decisions. Claim this verse today throughout the day, Psalm 118:14, "The Lord is my strength and song, and is become my salvation." Stand true, stand faithful.

Be unashamed to live and stand by Biblical principles.

November 20

Ezekiel 41-42   Psalm 118:15-29   Proverbs 20   2 Corinthians 10

A Holy Place

Good morning! I read this morning in Ezekiel 41-42 about the description of the temple. As I read, I imagined Ezekiel trying to picture what he was writing. For the last thirty-eight years that my wife and

401

I have been serving in the camping ministry, we have had to have a vision for something that was not seen and first picture it in our hearts, then our minds, and then pray, have faith and go to work. To Mrs. Smith and I and to many summer staff members, each project, each building, and each area that we build something, it has become a special place. All of us have special places that the Lord has put in our lives.

In Ezekiel 42:13-14, we read some statements, "holy chambers," "holy things," "for the place is holy," "for they are holy." As I read this morning, I thought about so many places that the Lord has used that have become very special to me because of what He did in my life at that spot, at that place. In II Corinthians 10:3, "For though we walk in the flesh, we do not war after the flesh:." Yes, we do live each day in the flesh, but it is so important to have the "holy place" where you meet with the Lord. We have possessions that we value; homes, cars, etc., in which we have invested money and time, but how about a "holy place" where we meet with God and spend time with Him? Each time I go to church, it is more than going to a building. It is going to hear God speak to me. We are not to worship things, but we should respect, honor and develop a spirit about honoring a "holy place." Proverbs 20:27, "The spirit of man is the candle of the Lord, searching all the inward parts of the belly." Be faithful to the "holy place" so that God can keep the candle inside shining.

Psalm 118:24, "This is the day which the Lord hath made; we will rejoice and be glad in it." Psalm 118:28, "Thou art my God, and I will praise thee: thou art my God, I will exalt thee." I do not know where you are when you are reading this little devotional, but wherever it is, take time and make it a "holy place," meeting with the Lord. Look forward to getting each day started in a "holy place" by getting alone and reading God's Word and spending time in prayer with Him. Make that place a "holy place" so that you can work on being "holy" to honor our God. Sing with me the little hymn, "Take time to be holy, Speak oft with thy Lord; Abide in Him always, And feed on His Word. Make friends of God's children; Help those who are weak, Forgetting in nothing His blessing to seek." "Take Time To Be Holy."

Look forward to getting each day started in a holy place with God.

Ezekiel 43-44   Psalm 119:1-16   Proverbs 21   2 Corinthians 11

Stay Inside the Fence

Good morning! For most of my life I have had the daily responsibility of taking care of some type of animal; horses, cattle, hogs, chickens, ducks, goats, dogs, cats, etc., and it seems that each brings their problems. By problems, I mean you can provide them water, grain, feed, housing and they all seem to find that weak spot in the fence or pen and get out. You can daily make sure their water supply is okay, there is grain for them, and you have put out the hay that was needed and they will still find the new hole in the fence or the gate that was left open.

As I read in Ezekiel 43 and 44, I read the final description of the temple and then the altar and the priests' qualifications. We read about the eastern gate being shut, for only God was to enter there. As we came to verse 18 through the end of the chapter, we read the guidelines for the priests, how God wants to bless us and gives us guidelines to live by. In our reading in II Corinthians 11:3, "But I fear, lest by any means, as the serpent beguiled Eve through his subtility, so your minds should be corrupted from the simplicity that is in Christ." The devil is constantly trying to lure us away from a life in Christ. He is trying to distract us from serving God and living a life that will please the Lord. Proverbs 21:30, "There is no wisdom nor understanding nor counsel against the Lord." Psalm 119:16, "I will delight myself in thy statutes: I will not forget thy word." Living within boundaries and guidelines set by the Lord is a safe, secure, blessed place.

For an animal to stay within the fence line is a place they will be fed, watered and taken care of. So much more could be learned from our Scripture reading today, but let me say the coyotes and other animals that run free in the wild know that when an animal gets out away from the herd or the safety of the pen, they are an easy prey. My brother and sister in Christ, stay in the safety of the Lord, His Word and the strength of being part of a local church. God has given us everything we need to live a victorious life in Christ. Stay where you need to stay. Be fed, strengthened and grow in the Lord.

Stay in the safety of the Lord, His Word and the
strength of being part of a local church.

November 22

Ezekiel 45-46   Psalm 119:17-32   Proverbs 22   2 Corinthians 12-13

Cover from the Storm

Good morning! As I awoke this morning, I could hear the rain hitting the window. I do not know why but my mind went to the animals having a covering to get out of the storm. It is always interesting to me how the animals of the wild all have a place they go to get away from a storm. A hole in a tree or the ground, a small cave around some rocks, a large tree with many branches, the depth of a valley to get away from the driving wind. For an animal to go to safety is an instinct given them by God. What about man? What do we do when the storms of life come? Where do we run to? Are we prepared for the storms?

In Ezekiel 45 and 46 we read about guidelines for worship. Ezekiel 46:13, "Thou shalt daily prepare," also a little further in the same verse, "thou shalt prepare it every morning." Ezekiel 46:14, "And thou shalt prepare a meat offering for it every morning." Ezekiel 46:15, "Thus shall they prepare the lamb, and the meat-offering, and the oil, every morning for a continual burnt-offering." It is so important to have a time with God every morning. The storms of life will come and daily devotions, spending time reading the Word of God, spending time in prayer will strengthen us and prepare us for the storms of life. Paul wrote to the Corinthian churches in II Corinthians 12:10, "for when I am weak, then am I strong," and in 13:4, "For though he was crucified through weakness, yet he liveth by the power of God." The power of God comes from spending time with God. Proverbs 22:20-21, "Have not I written to thee excellent things in counsels and knowledge, That I might make thee know the certainty of the words of truth;."

Animals have the sense to prepare. We need our eyes opened to the importance of daily spending time in the beginning of the day with God. Psalm 119:25, "quicken thou me according to thy word," verse 27, "Make me to understand the way of thy precepts," verse 28, "strengthen thou me according unto thy word." Does a fox, coyote, squirrel, deer, rabbit, skunk, owl, hawk, crow, cardinal, etc. have more God given sense to prepare for the storm than we that have been bought by the blood of the Lamb? Let us make a fresh commitment to the importance of daily preparing, by daily spending time alone with God in the morning, reading every word and fellowshipping with God in prayer. Think about it.

We prepare for the storms of life by daily spending time with God.

November 23

Ezekiel 47-48   Psalm 119:33-48   Proverbs 23   Galatians 1-2

Pleasing God or Man?

Good morning! The longer I live, the more I remember the things I was taught by my parents and grandparents. There are days I long to hear their voices again, but I do live with the promise that I will see them in Heaven someday. As I read this morning in Ezekiel 47 and 48, I read of the river of God's provision, the borders, divisions and portions. As I sat and pondered on what I had read before I turned to the New Testament, it came back to my mind sitting along a creek bank with my grandfather. We had just set bank lines and we sat and talked. It was late fall and the first snow had not fallen. Those days and times will never return. My grandfather worked for the city and drove a road grader to smooth the gravel roads, keep the ditches cleaned out and of course, move snow in the winter. When the roads would get plowed there would be driveways that would get snow pushed back in them and people would always call and complain. He was to keep the roads clear and as he did this, some snow would come back into some drives and lanes.

I turned to Galatians 1 and read down to verse 10, "for if I yet pleased men, I should not be the servant of Christ." Too many live their lives to please others rather than living to please the Lord. Galatians 1:15-16, "But when it pleased God, who separated me from my mother's womb, and called me by his grace, To reveal his Son in me, that I might preach him among the heathen; immediately I conferred not with flesh and blood." My grandfather cleared the roads and by doing his job he upset some. We must live to please God and not live to be accepted by or to please this world. Proverbs 23:19, "Hear thou, my son, and be wise, and guide thine heart in the way." Psalm 119:33-34, "Teach me," "Give me understanding," "Make me to go in the path of thy commandments." Psalm 119:45, "And I will walk at liberty: for I seek thy precepts."

I saw the stress of my grandfather to do his job and yet even before the first snow fell to clean the roads, he knew there were those that would be upset. As I read about the borders and divisions and portions in Ezekiel, I thought of the fighting this day that is going on in Israel. May our lives be lived with a Christ-like attitude and spirit, but most of all be lived to please the Lord. Be kind and patient with others.

We must live to please God and not to be accepted by or to please this world.

November 24

Daniel 1-2   Psalm 119:49-64   Proverbs 24   Galatians 3-4

A Life of Purpose

Good morning! When I was in basic training in the army, there were days that were more difficult than others. Some days the training was all new and other days it was a repeat and practice of what we had already be taught. The idea was to keep pushing us to learn more and to develop as a soldier. There were principles of discipline that had to be learned and had to be maintained. The push was always there to go farther so the training became more intense.

As we began our reading in the book of Daniel today, the four Hebrew brothers really had no idea what was ahead because they were captives. These men were captives in Babylon. From the beginning they were set apart. You and I have been set apart by God for a purpose and God knows what He has planned for us. As a soldier, I was set apart from civilian life. My training taught me new things and took me to a place and point of pressure that I had not experienced before. We read in Daniel 1:17, "God gave them knowledge and skill in all learning and wisdom: and Daniel had understanding." God had a purpose beyond them, beyond their ability, beyond their understanding. Each time I begin reading in the book of Daniel, the word "purpose" jumps out. I need to purpose to prepare, to be submitted to God, to be open to His leading, to be wise in God's knowledge and understanding. As we looked on in Galatians 3:11, "The just shall live by faith." Oh, that our lives would be lives yielded to whatever God has for us. We must stay stable and consistent in our walk with God in times that are changing so fast and not changing for the right. Proverbs 24:21, "My son, fear thou the Lord and the king: and meddle not with them that are given to change:." We need to stay in the Word of God, learn the principles of God, and walk in the ways of God. Psalm 119:50, "This is my comfort in my affliction: for thy word hath quickened me." Psalm 119:59, "I thought on my ways, and turned my feet unto thy testimonies."

A good soldier must listen, learn, and be ready to lead. Too many Christians are satisfied where they are spiritually, and under attack of the devil they fold and sin. Let God "prove" Himself in you today by deciding you will "purpose" to live for Him. The four Hebrew brothers stayed prepared for what was ahead even when they had no idea what was ahead for them. Stay ready today, because you live by and for purpose.

Decide today you will purpose to live for God.

November 25

Daniel 3-4   Psalm 119:65-80   Proverbs 25   Galatians 5-6

Just Do Right

Good morning! As I began to read in Daniel this morning, there is so much to write about. We see faithfulness tested. We see jealousy try to destroy. We see pride stick up its wicked head. We see authority questioned.

We see courage displayed. I prayed about where to start and then my mind fell on 3:29, "there is no other God that can deliver after this sort." Sin and its destructive power is everywhere. Sin controls, sin destroys, sin cripples, sin deceives, sin blinds, sin lies, sin separates.

I read the words of the king in Daniel 3:15, "who is that God that shall deliver you out of my hand?" It is always God's will that we conquer the flesh because it is the flesh that always grows weak. Galatians 5:16, "Walk in the Spirit, and ye shall not fulfil the lust of the flesh." We must continually strengthen our spirit and our walk with the Lord. Galatians 5:17, "For the flesh lusteth against the Spirit, and the Spirit against the flesh: and these are contrary the one to the other: so that ye cannot do the things that ye would." We can have victory. Galatians 5:25, "If we live in the Spirit, let us also walk in the Spirit." It is the spirit that must be strengthened; and that comes from a continual walk with God in His Word, in prayer, doing what is right in the eyes of God. Galatians 6:9, "And let us not be weary in well doing: for in due season we shall reap, if we faint not." Take one day at a time. Proverbs 25:8, "Go not forth hastily to strive, lest thou know not what to do in the end thereof." Look to God, look to Him every step of the way. Psalm 119:69, "The proud have forged a lie against me: but I will keep thy precepts with my whole heart." Do right and right will prevail. The Hebrew brothers were thrown into the furnace and they came forth because they did not lose their faith in God and they did not weaken under testing. I am sure there was doubt and fear, but there was faith and victory. Daniel 3:18, "be it known unto thee, O king, that we will not serve thy gods." Do right today.

Do right every step of the way and God will give victory.

November 26

Daniel 5-6   Psalm 119:81-96   Proverbs 26   Ephesians 1-2

Stay Faithful

Good morning! As I began our reading today in Daniel chapters 5 and 6, I kept asking myself, what kind of testimony am I to those around me and especially those that are the closest? Daniel has an unstained testimony of faithfulness to God. Listen to the testimony of others; Daniel 5:11, "There is a man in thy kingdom, in whom is the spirit of the holy gods." That testimony got to the king and we read his statement in Daniel 5:14 as Daniel is before him; "I have heard of thee, that the spirit of the gods is in thee, and that light of understanding and excellent wisdom is found in thee."

Jealousy and envy always stick their head up. They did in the life of Daniel and he faced being thrown into the lion's den and yet the king wanted to see the God that Daniel served deliver him. Daniel's life was a testimony of faith and faithfulness. When testing and trials came, Daniel was seen praying, not to the gods, but was found faithful praying three times a day before the Lord. We know he was condemned to be thrown into the lion's den and he came out unharmed. Listen to the king's testimony in Daniel 6:16, "Thy God whom thou servest continually, he will deliver thee."

Do others see us faithful to God? Ephesians 1:4, "that we should be holy and without blame before him in love." Be careful about self-exaltation and being prideful. Proverbs 26:28, "a flattering mouth worketh ruin." Do not let the ways, things and attitudes of this world lure you away from being faithful to the Lord. Psalm 119:87, "They had almost consumed me upon earth; but I forsook not thy precepts." May it be said today and every day about us that; "they could find none occasion nor fault; forasmuch as he was faithful, neither was there any error or fault found in him." Stay faithful to God.

May it be said of us that we have stayed faithful to God.

November 27

Daniel 7-8   Psalm 119:97-112   Proverbs 27   Ephesians 3-4

Sharpen Your Axe

Good morning! As we read this morning about the visions of Daniel and the kings of nations that will be of great power and have great control, we also read in Daniel 8:25, "but he shall be broken without hand." This old world offers nothing of lasting strength, lasting peace, lasting joy. As Paul wrote to the Ephesians while in prison in Rome; "That Christ may dwell in your hearts by faith; that ye, being rooted and grounded in love," Ephesians 3:17.

I have cleaned out many a fence row and the toughest part is always getting the roots out of the ground of the trees that grew and had to be removed. Several winters ago, we lost a beautiful tree at the Ranch due to an ice storm. I cleaned up all the limbs and cut up and split all the wood that could be used for heat in the stove. All that was left was the stump. Even though all that could be seen was just the stump, the roots below ground that gave the tree its strength and stability were still strongly attached. That is why it is so important for us to heed the words of Ephesians 3:16, "to be strengthened with might by his Spirit in the inner man." Ephesians 4:23, "And be renewed in the spirit of your mind." The tree that grew the roots so deep and so strong withstood every storm, the heat of the sun, the cold of the winter and the driving rains.

This is why it is so important for us to have the strong influences that will keep us strong in the Lord. Proverbs 27:17, "Iron sharpeneth iron; so a man sharpeneth the countenance of his friend." Reading, meditation and applying God's Word to our daily life will keep us strong. It takes a very hard file to keep the edge of the axe sharp. Psalm 119:97, "O how love I thy law! It is my meditation all the day." Psalm 119:99, "thy testimonies are my meditation." The sharpness of the axe is determined by the strength of the steel in the file. We must be continually sharpened by the Word of God which will be the strength to convict us, correct us and continue us. The strength of this world seems so strong but the power of God through a life grounded in Christ will have victory. We must let our roots grow deep into the daily relationship with God. Stand true, stand strong, stand for God today. The mighty axe of God's judgment will fall, and God will clear out all the brush.

We must be continually sharpened by the Word of God,
which will strengthen us.

Daniel 9-10   Psalm 119:113-128   Proverbs 28   Ephesians 5

A Day of Thanksgiving

Good morning! I do not know where you are or what day it is for you when you read this devotional, but today is Thanksgiving Day as I write, and I would like to wish you Happy Thanksgiving. As I read this morning in the books of Daniel, Ephesians, Proverbs and Psalms according to our schedule, I kept reading verses of worship to God. I have grown to love my Lord in a way I never knew could be possible for me, and I hunger to grow much more. I love my God, my Lord, my Saviour. I want to grow to understand how to greater worship and present myself before the Lord as Daniel did. Daniel 9:3, "And I set my face unto the Lord God, to seek by prayer and supplications, with fasting, and sackcloth, and ashes." Daniel 9:18, "for we do not present our supplications before thee for our righteousnesses, but for thy great mercies." Daniel 9:19, "O Lord, hear; O Lord, forgive; O Lord, hearken and do." May we always stop and prepare and present ourselves in a humble way before our God.

As I then turned to Paul's writing to the Ephesians, I read in Ephesians 5:18-20, "but be filled with the Spirit; Speaking to yourselves in psalms and hymns and spiritual songs, singing and making melody in your heart to the Lord; Giving thanks always for all things unto God and the Father in the name of our Lord Jesus Christ." I thought of the many generations that have gone on before us and read the same Scriptures about thanking and praising God and have enjoyed the blessings of God and took time to show God their love for Him. Proverbs 28:20, "A faithful man shall abound with blessings," Proverbs 28:25, "he that putteth his trust in the Lord shall be made fat."

Do not just take time today to eat, play games and do things with family and friends; but take time to love, thank, and give praise to God. Psalm 119:114, "I hope in thy word," verse 115, "I will keep the commandments of my God," verse 119, "I love thy testimonies," verse 127, "I love thy commandments," verse 128, "I esteem all thy precepts."

411

Make Thanksgiving today a time of thanksgiving and praise to our God that has made this day possible for us. HAPPY THANKSGIVING to you and yours.

Take time today to love, thank and give praise to God.

November 29

Daniel 11-12 Psalm 119:129-144 Proverbs 29 Eph. 6 & Phil. 1

No More Good-Byes

Good morning! As I was reading the last two chapters of Daniel this morning, it was like reading the wonderful ending of a book. When I say a wonderful ending, I mean a wonderful ending for all those that know Christ as their Saviour. Daniel 11:32, "but the people that do know their God shall be strong."

We have just enjoyed time with family. Mrs. Smith and I have to say good-bye and begin our travels back home today but, praise the Lord, there will be a day that we do not have to say good- bye ever again. Daniel 12:1 gives us the chain of events, "And at that time shall Michael stand up;" he will sound the "Trump of God" and all saved will be raptured or caught away from this earth and the Tribulation will begin. Daniel 12:1, "and there shall be a time of trouble." This world wants to keep living for the satisfaction of the flesh, but true joy comes from yielding in our spirit and putting Christ first place and knowing Him personally as our Saviour. Daniel 12:1 ends with "at that time thy people shall be delivered, every one that shall be found written in the book." The book is the "Book of Life," referred to in Revelation 20:12-15.

We are challenged today in Ephesians 6:10 to be strong, "Finally, my brethren, be strong in the Lord and in the power of his might." Ephesians 6:11 admonishes us to "Put on the whole armour of God, that ye may be able to stand against the wiles of the devil." Our spiritual armour is to protect us and the Sword, the Word of God, is our weapon. What a comfort as those that have to say good-bye to family can still stand miles apart in one spirit. Philippians 1:27, "that ye stand fast in one spirit, with one mind striving together for the faith of the gospel." Stand fast, my brother and sister. Proverbs 29:25, "The fear of man bringeth a snare: but whoso putteth his trust in the Lord shall be safe." Oh, the tears have flowed down my cheek and there is that large lump in the throat, but my strength must be in the Lord. Psalm 119:144, "give me understanding, and I shall live." What a day that will be when all the saved, born again, will be together in Heaven. There will be no more parting up there. Stay faithful, stay true to God, stay walking with God. Miles might separate us but unity in serving the Lord will keep us together.

Praise the Lord, there will be a day that we
will never have to say good-bye again.

November 30

Hosea 1-2   Psalm 119:145-160   Proverbs 30-31   Philippians 2-3

Others First

Good morning! Can you imagine getting a letter from a loved one and never opening it? While I was gone in active duty for the army, Mrs. Smith and I would send letters back and forth to each other. Can you imagine if we never opened the letters up and read them? We would break each other's hearts and we would not keep up with what was happening in our lives as we were apart.

God has preserved His Word for us and it is vital that we read it, study it and meditate upon it. Israel had sinned over and over again and as we began today in the book of Hosea, the statement found in Hosea 1:2 says, "for the land hath committed great whoredom, departing from the Lord." The picture is of a husband who has a wife that is not faithful. Each time I read this book my heart is grieved, especially as I read 2:19, "And I will betroth thee unto me for ever." The word "betroth" means to promise to marry. As I was away from my wife in a physical way, I had made a commitment to her on the day we were married to be faithful to her until

413

death. The people of God had not been faithful to God and that is the picture as we begin in Hosea.

Philippians 2:3, "Let nothing be done through strife or vainglory; but in lowliness of mind let each esteem other better than themselves." We live in a world of selfish pride and the attitude of "look and see what I am doing." Proverbs 30:8, "Remove far from me vanity and lies." Proverbs 30:32, "If thou hast done foolishly in lifting up thyself, or if thou hast thought evil, lay thine hand upon thy mouth." Our attitude toward each other in marriage and outside of marriage toward others should always be "others first." The wife of Hosea was not faithful. We need to ask ourselves, are we faithful to our Lord, His Word, His commands? Do we spend much of our time boasting about ourselves or praising the Lord and lifting up His name? Psalm 119: 145-146, "I cried with my whole heart; hear me, O Lord: I will keep thy statutes. I cried unto thee; save me, and I shall keep thy testimonies." Peace in a marriage, peace in a friendship and peace with God comes when the other is always put first. We read in Philippians 2 this morning about avoiding strife and vainglory, and looking to esteem or respect with a higher admiration than ourselves. Who is first place in your life, your thoughts, your priorities of goals? Let us stop today and take a long look at who is first place.

Our attitude toward each other should always be "others first."

Hosea 3-4   Psalm 119:161-176   Proverbs 1   Phil. 4 & Col. 1

A Shelter in the Storm

Good morning! Last evening in the rain and the wind I went out to check buildings and the property here at Circle C, and I am always amazed at the wisdom of animals and their ability to seek shelter in storms. An animal was not created in the image of God as we were. An animal does not have the Holy Spirit that dwells inside after we ask Christ to be our Saviour. An animal does not have the Bible to teach it, and yet the wisdom they have from their Creator!

How sad as I read in Hosea 4:6, "My people are destroyed for lack of knowledge: because thou hast rejected knowledge." Today the average Christian is constantly seeking new ways, easier methods, and drifting from the old paths. What Paul wrote is so important for us today. Philippians 4:1, "stand fast in the Lord." The world lives in such a hatred and sadness and yet there can be joy for the Christian. Philippians 4:4, "Rejoice in the Lord alway: and again I say, Rejoice." Philippians 4:19, "But my God shall supply all your need according to his riches in glory by Christ Jesus." The Lord has blessed us so very much, and yet it does not seem to be enough for so many. Proverbs 1:10, "My son, if sinners entice thee, consent thou not." Proverbs 1:15, "My son, walk not thou in the way with them; refrain thy foot from their path."

The animals of the field and woods that have only the wisdom that God gave them, seem to have more sense and contentment than a human with a heart that can be touched by God. I challenge each of us to spend time reading, learning and applying the truths preserved for us in the Word of God. Psalm 119:168, "I have kept thy precepts and thy testimonies; and I love them exceedingly." When the storms come, run to God for shelter.

He will always be the protection and comfort that we need. Think about the song, "A Shelter in the Time of Storm."

God is always our shelter in the storms of life.

December 2

Hosea 5-6   Psalm 120   Proverbs 2   Colossians 2-3

Open Communication

Good morning! The other day my wife and I were out soul winning and making some visits. One of the stops that I wanted to make was in a care center. We had never met this individual; all we had was a name. As the nurse took us into the room, the individual that we were looking for was not there but there was a lady sharing the room and I attempted to talk with her. Her eyes were so kind and she attempted to communicate with me but there was not the ability that I am sure she once had. My heart sank, as here was a life that has come to a point that they cannot communicate or interact with another person. They just sit or lie and just stare. As we walked down the hallway to go find the individual we were looking for, we were silent as both of our hearts ached for the person we had tried to talk with.

In Hosea 5:15, God said He was going to pull back until Israel came to a place of acknowledging their sin. Read these words with me; "I will go and return to my place, till they acknowledge their offense, and seek my face: in their affliction they will seek me early." Age and disease had brought the lady in the care center to the place that she can no longer communicate as she once did. Sin will draw us away from God to an empty, lonely, desperate place. We were challenged this morning in Colossians 2:6, "As ye have therefore received Christ Jesus the Lord, so walk ye in him:." That individual in that bed wanted to communicate and they could not; sin will cloud our relationship with Christ and make it seem as though we cannot communicate with God. We need to put anything away that draws us away from the Lord. Colossians 3:2, "Set your affection on things above, not on things on the earth." You might seem all alone today, at a confusing time, not sure what to do next and just plain frustrated. God is there and He can be found. We just need the wisdom of God, and it will give us direction and understanding. Proverbs 2:4-5, "If thou seekest her as silver, and searchest for her as for hid treasures; then shalt thou understand the fear of the Lord, and find the knowledge of God." God is there and He can hear our plea. Psalm 120:1, "In my distress I cried unto the Lord, and he heard me."

Do not be a Christian that is empty, no direction, no joy, no purpose. Look to the Lord today. He may be found, He is our comforter. We have life, let us live it for God. Reach out to someone hurting today and be an encourager. Do not be a Christian that is just sitting there and acting like life has stopped. As we read this morning in Colossians 3:9, "seeing that ye have put off the old man with his deeds," I have life in Christ. I have purpose in Christ. There is a new day awaiting and there is someone out there to whom you can be a blessing. Go find them and smile with a heart for God. Share Christ today and have the privilege to lead a soul bound for Hell to new life in Christ.

Reach out to someone hurting today and be an encourager.

December 3

Hosea 7-8   Psalm 121   Proverbs 3   Col. 4 & 1 Thess. 1

The Little Details

Good morning! Most of my life I have been a breakfast person. I love getting up early and smelling breakfast being prepared. Now at almost seventy years old, my eating habits have changed drastically but my love for breakfast has not changed. I can eat breakfast three meals a day, just ask Mrs. Smith. Breakfast being prepared brings a beautiful aroma that just starts the day right.

As I read this morning in Hosea 7:4, "as an oven heated by the baker, who ceaseth from raising after he hath kneaded the dough, until it be leavened." Also read down to verse 8, "Ephraim is a cake not turned." As a young boy, I loved to learn how to cook and I learned right away you have to pay close attention to what is being prepared. You have to prepare the dough for the biscuits exactly right and the oven has to be just right, or you can cook the biscuits too fast and burn them and they can still be doughy on the inside. I can remember my grandad teaching me how to watch the bubbles on a pancake and know the exact time to flip them over.

Our Scripture reading for today is showing us the importance of paying attention to even the smallest sins in our lives. We must pay close attention to every area of our lives. Be careful especially this time of year of some of the Christmas music that is being played. Be careful of your speech; some slang words are nothing more than cussing. Colossians 4:6, "Let your speech be alway with grace, seasoned with salt, that ye may know how ye ought to answer every man." A good cook pays close attention to what they are preparing, and we must pay close attention to the details of our lives. Proverbs 3:6, "In all thy ways acknowledge him, and he shall direct thy paths." A great biscuit with a little burned on the bottom can ruin the taste of the whole biscuit. Bacon too done can ruin a good piece of meat. Let the Lord show you the little details of sin and deal with that sin. Psalm 121:7-8, "The Lord shall preserve thee from all evil: he shall preserve thy soul. The Lord shall preserve thy going out and thy coming in from this time forth, and even for evermore." A good cook will closely watch every detail in preparing a good meal. Let us watch every detail in our lives to enjoy the blessings of God. Have a great breakfast.

> *We must pay close attention to even the smallest sin*
> *in our lives and deal with that sin.*

December 4

Hosea 9-10   Psalm 122   Proverbs 4   1 Thessalonians 2-3

Teamwork

Good morning! There are nights that I cannot sleep because of eating too late, or I cannot get my mind to stop and I keep thinking about a project I am working on, or things that I did not get done. Then there are those nights that the dogs are howling at something. We have two dogs at the camp and they are quite the pair. One is twelve at this writing and the other one is between three and four years old. It is fun to watch them play together. The older one is the wiser, more patient, more settled. The younger one is a very smart dog, but she is also very high energy and quite impatient. The older one is a much better hunter than the younger one and when the horses or cows get out, the older one is better help in getting the horses and cows back in than the younger.

As I read this morning in Hosea 10:2, "their heart is divided," and then on down to Hosea 10:12, "break up your fallow ground: for it is time to seek the Lord." My mind went to thinking about a younger generation coming and an older generation leaving. Before I go any farther, I want to say that God wants to use all of us until we leave this earth. How He uses us is His choice but what I see as the situation is that some of us older ones have a lack of patience to teach and some of the younger ones coming up have a lack of patience to learn. It takes time to teach and it takes time to learn. The phrase, "break up your fallow ground," has often been preached on. "Fallow ground" is ground that was once used and brought forth fruit and now it is laying idle and not being used. God wants to use you no matter your age. I Thessalonians 2:12, "That ye would walk worthy of God, who hath called you unto his kingdom and glory." As Paul wrote to the church in I Thessalonians 3:8, "For now we live, if ye stand fast in the Lord." Do not quit, older generation, and younger generation, do not run on ahead without the wisdom and aid of the seniors. The Lord wants us all to keep going forward, but as a team. Proverbs 4:25, "Let thine eyes look right on, and let thine eyelids look straight before thee."

Each summer I am blessed to serve with teens and some in their early twenty's. We need each other and we need to be patient and learn together. That is what has brought us through all these years. As I get older, I see the importance of having the younger around to help, learn, and keep the pace going as I know I am getting just a little slower. There is some pride in that statement. Reach out today to someone in a different generation. Psalm 122:6, "they shall prosper that love thee." When I was younger, I did not always understand my parents, and now that I am older and my parents are gone, I do not always understand the young ones coming up. That does not prevent us from working and serving together. Our older dog was barking the other night, but it was a different bark. It was like the older dog was crying for the younger dog. You know, when they got together, the barking stopped and they curled up beside each other and that is where they were when I went out in the morning to water and feed them. The younger generation coming up has ideas, energy and enthusiasm; and the older generation has wisdom, experience and steadfastness. Work together for the glory of God. Our service is about Him and not us. Serve as a team today.

The Lord wants all of us to keep going forward as a team.

December 5

Hosea 11-12   Psalm 123   Proverbs 5   1 Thessalonians 4-5

Guidelines

Good morning! I watched as the lineman from the power company slipped on the long rubber protective gear over his arms as he checked his safety equipment before he raised himself to the new power pole. The power company installed a new pole and brought power to a new building, and I observed their safety procedures. From the engineer coming and deciding where the pole would be installed, where the power would come from, where I would install the meter base to the exact gauge of pipe I would use, how far it is to be buried underground, to how much pipe will go up the side of the pole. All this and much more just to get power to a building.

Hosea 12:6, "turn thou to thy God: keep mercy and judgment, and wait on thy God continually." Guidelines! I Thessalonians 4:7, "For God hath not called us unto uncleanness, but unto holiness." I Thessalonians 5:22, "Abstain from all appearance of evil." Guidelines! Proverbs 5:2, "That thou mayest regard discretion." Guidelines! All around us are "guidelines," not to hurt us or harm us, but for safety. Speed limits, yellow caution signs, stop signs, yield signs, etc. are all for everyone's safety. Guidelines! Psalm

123:2, "Behold, as the eyes of servants look unto the hand of their masters, so our eyes wait upon the Lord our God."

Do not be frustrated today because things are not going exactly the way you think they should be. God could be protecting you from something. Do not hurry up the plan of God, the will of God or the ways of God. Walk with Him and enjoy the safety of God. Live in those boundaries that are pleasing unto Him. Guidelines! As we read in Hosea 12:6 this morning, "keep mercy and judgment, and wait on thy God continually." God's guidelines are secure, safe guidelines.

Walk with God and enjoy the safety of His boundaries.

December 6

Hosea 13-14   Psalm 124   Proverbs 6   2 Thessalonians 1-2

Escape and Evasion

Good morning! Daily life for a Christian is a life that must stand against the constant attacks of the devil. Around every corner there is some trap set to try and lure us away from a walk with God. Even just sitting down and attempting to have a quiet time with God in the morning, there is some kind of distraction. Hosea 13:4, "thou shalt know no God but me: for there is no Saviour beside me." Hosea 14:9, "for the ways of the Lord are right, and the just shall walk in them:." All of us have tried many times to begin again, to start over, to have a clean slate, to make a promise to ourselves of quitting a bad habit, to have victory in some area and the distraction comes and we fail again.

I remember having several weeks of training in the army called "escape and evasion." Training to teach soldiers how to escape being captured and how to escape if ever captured. Some of that training was very intense. Spiritually speaking, we must constantly be aware that the devil will never be happy until he wins, and he never will. He and his workers are on the move to trip us up, turn us away from a relationship with God, tempt us to sin. II Thessalonians 2:7, "For the mystery of iniquity doth already work:." The path for the antichrist is already in place, the work and plans of the devil have been set in motion since the devil was kicked out of Heaven. We must determine to escape and evade any of the devil's traps and tricks. II Thessalonians 2:15, "Therefore, brethren, stand fast, and hold the traditions which ye have been taught, whether by word, or our epistle." We were challenged in Proverbs 6:5 this morning, "Deliver thyself as a roe from the hand of the hunter, and as a bird from the hand of the fowler." Many a trap and bait have been set to catch an animal and they have escaped capture. May we be on guard, may we be alert, may we be wise in the Lord. Psalm 124:7, "Our soul is escaped as a bird out of the snare of the fowler's: the snare is broken, and we are escaped."

The devil cannot get the soul of a Christian, but he can distract us from serving and living a holy life unto the Lord. In the army, I camouflaged myself and moved slowly to escape being captured. I listened, watched and was patient. Listen to the voice of the Holy Spirit, be wise and watch for the leading of God, be patient to wait upon Him." Proverbs 6:23, "For the commandment is a lamp; and the law is light; and reproofs of instruction are the way of life:." Stay away from the traps of the devil. Escape the temptations that have trapped you before. Be wise and walk with God.

The devil is trying to trap and lure us away from a walk with God.

December 7

Joel 1-3   Psalm 125   Proverbs 7   2 Thess. 3 & 1 Tim. 1

Press Forward

Good morning! Today and every December 7th since 1941, must be remembered. That was the day of the attack on Pearl Harbor by Japan. For us as God's people, we must never forget the words of Joel 1:2-3, "Hear this, ye old men, and give ear, all ye inhabitants of the land. Tell ye your children of it, and let your children tell their children, and their children another generation." These are powerful words telling how God judges sin and blesses righteousness. God had brought His judgment on His people and yet we read on in Joel 2:25, "I will restore." Joel 2:28, "I will pour out my spirit upon all flesh." Joel 2:32, "whosoever shall call on the name of the Lord shall be delivered."

Today is a day to be remembered for a time that our country drew together because of a devastating attack not only on our country, but our principles, our way of life. May this day also drive us to stand up against the devil as He attacks with his demons our Saviour and all that salvation and a forgiven life stands for. As soldiers stood, may we as God's people stand. II Thessalonians 3:3, "But the Lord is faithful, who shall stablish you, and keep you from evil." II Thessalonians 3:13, "be not weary in well doing." As we remember the attack upon our country, may we press forward for our Lord, remembering what He did and what has been provided by all men. Proverbs 7:24, "Hearken unto me now therefore, O ye children, and attend to the words of my mouth."

Men and women of our armed forces fought for victory. May we today and the rest of our lives fight for souls of men. Psalm 125:1, "They that trust in the Lord shall be as mount Zion, which cannot be removed, but abideth for ever." The victory is ours.

May we press forward for the Lord as we stand up against the devil.

December 8

Amos 1-2   Psalm 126   Proverbs 8   1 Timothy 2-3

Empty Promises

Good morning! As I was reading today, I asked myself a question - how many empty promises has God received? Many a parent has heard from a child, "I will not do it again." Many a person has bowed at an altar and told God that they will do right. How often has our Lord heard the statement, "Lord, I am through with this sin"? Through many a trials there have been those that have cried out to God and said, "I will do right."

As I read this morning in Amos chapters 1 and 2, I counted 19 times the words, "I will." These "I wills," are God saying I am bringing judgment and I have been patient long enough. In the same chapters, the phrase,

"I will not turn away the punishment thereof," is mentioned 8 times. It sounds like God has been patient long enough. We read in I Timothy 2 of the qualifications or, may I say, proper order and behavior for men and women, and then in chapter 3 we read the qualifications for pastors and deacons, but let us focus on I Timothy 2:15, "that thou mayest know how thou oughtest to behave thyself in the house of God, which is the church of the living God, the pillar and ground of the truth." May our promises to God not be empty. May we follow the guidelines to holiness given in the Scriptures. Where is our love for God? His love for us is always there, and especially shown when we desire to walk with Him. Proverbs 8:17, "I love them that love me; and those that seek me early shall find me." May our promises to God not be empty. Are you keeping your commitments to God, your promises? Does God see us faithful? Does He see us serving as we promised? Psalm 126:3, "The Lord hath done great things for us; whereof we are glad." Promises kept are promise blessed. Let us not forget what we promised God we would do.

Our commitments to God should be kept promises, not empty promises.

December 9

Amos 3-4   Psalm 127   Proverbs 9   1 Timothy 4-5

Stay at It

Good morning! Often, I find myself wishing I would have learned something earlier in life instead of having to learn it now. I hunger to keep learning everything that I can about everything I can and sometimes I frustrate myself, because I know that I cannot go back one step and I must always be going forward. Psalm 127:1, "Except the Lord build the house, they labour in vain that build it." This verse is not talking about a physical house, but our lives; learning principles from God that will lead us to build a Godly life. Proverbs 9:10, "The fear of the Lord is the beginning of wisdom: and the knowledge of the holy is understanding."

Each week at camp and every retreat at camp, we see the Lord working in lives and then we see those same lives harden to what the Lord spoke to them about, or they try to make excuse why their decision was not the Lord's will. As I read today in I Timothy 4:7-8, "exercise thyself rather unto godliness. For bodily exercise profiteth little: but godliness is profitable unto all things, having promise of the life that now is, and of that which is to come." May I stop and ask you a question this morning? Are you living, preparing, seeking the will of God and following the Holy Spirit in the way He has led you, or are you wandering in a direction to please you? As a man, I cannot live in defeat of failures of the past or wrong decisions of the past. I must press on to walk with God and live in His will daily. Amos 3:3, "Can two walk together, except they be agreed?" In verse twelve of the same chapter Amos writes, "prepare to meet thy God."

I often meet someone that says, "Bro. Dave, I sure remember those days of how God worked in my heart at camp." My prayer is that God is still working in their heart and the decisions that they made at camp were a direction for them to continue to grow in the Lord. I Timothy 4:13, "Till I come, give attendance to reading, to exhortation, to doctrine." It is God's will for us to keep growing, no matter our age and no matter what wrong decisions we have made. Get right with God, go forward in the will of God, seek God daily and every moment of each day. Live to please God, serve God, and go on for God. Leave the past in the past, understand we cannot change circumstances of today, but we can live to please God and to grow in a relationship with Him for our strength and guidance in the days ahead. He will come soon. Let us stay in His Word, in His will, about His work. Lord bless you.

It is God's will for us to keep growing,
no matter our age or wrong decisions in the past.

December 10

Amos 5-6   Psalm 128   Proverbs 10   1 Tim. 6 & 2 Tim. 1

Seek Him

Good morning! The days are getting shorter, the temperature is dropping again, and the forecast is for snow mixed with rain. As I looked at the weather forecast on my phone, I read that there would be possible ground cover of snow. As the winter cold progresses, there is a need for hay for the horses. I will get a large round bale of hay today for the horses so that they will have food. It is amazing to me how I do not have to make an announcement or go get the horses to let them know there is fresh hay. They spend their time looking for food to sustain their lives.

Amos wrote, "Seek ye men, and ye shall live," Amos 5:4. Amos 5:6, "Seek the Lord, and ye shall live." Amos 5:8, "Seek him," "The Lord is his name." Amos 5:14, "Seek good, and not evil, that ye may live." All the animals of the forest and field will seek food and water to sustain life. Oh, that man would take the animal world as an example and realize there is blessing upon blessing in seeking the Lord and serving Him. We read this morning in I Timothy 6:6-8, "But godliness with contentment is great gain. For we brought nothing into this world, and it is certain we can carry nothing out. And having food and raiment let us be therewith content." Animals will seek to live, yet man will have little or nothing to do with what will give eternal life and God's blessing. May we proclaim with our lives the truth of life to a lost world. Proverbs 10:11, "The mouth of a righteous man is a well of life." Proverbs 10:31, "The mouth of the just bringeth forth wisdom:."

Somehow those horses will find that new bale of hay today and they will be fed. They will keep seeking and somehow they know that I will provide it for them. May we as God's people that He saved by the blood of His Son, know the fact that He will provide and bless when we seek Him and serve Him. Psalm 128:4, "Behold, that thus shall the man be blessed that feareth the Lord." He is there today. Seek Him and He shall be found. Have a blessed day.

There is blessing upon blessing in seeking the Lord and serving Him.

Amos 7-8   Psalm 129   Proverbs 11   2 Timothy 2-3

Stand in the Storm

Good morning! Think with me as we drive down an old country road. Look with me through the tall grass and the trees that have grown around the old barn and the old house that is still standing. I have often said to my wife, if that house could speak, just think of the memories and stories that could be told.

From generations past to generations of the future there will be those that will faithfully stand the tests of temptations, trials and discouragements, and will be found faithful when they stand before the King of kings. As we read in Amos 7:8, "Then said the Lord, Behold I will set a plumb line in the midst of my people." God is looking for those that are willing and ready to stand for truth and stand for Him. Amos 7:14-15, "I was no prophet, neither was I a prophet's son; but I was an herdsman, and a gatherer of sycamore fruit: And the Lord took me as I followed the flock." God is not looking for those of special talent, or of special abilities. God is looking for everybody that loves Him and hungers to serve Him. Amos was not of royalty, he was a herdman. He was not of special ability, he was a gatherer of sycamore fruit. God took him and God used him. As we read in II Timothy 2:2, "And the things that thou hast heard of me among many witnesses, the same commit thou to faithful men, who shall be able to teach others also."

As the old barn and the weathered house at one time were built with care, built to be used, built to last; they have passed the test of time and the old weathered boards and the still standing walls testify of a strong, stable building. As we grow in the Lord, may we focus on II Timothy 2:15, "Study to shew thyself approved unto God, a workman that needeth not to be ashamed, rightly dividing the word of truth." May we be students of the Word of God to stand in the storms of life, to be used to be a plumbline for the Lord. Proverbs 11:3, "The integrity of the upright shall guide them:." Be honest before the Lord, be Godly before the Lord and stand through the storms. Psalm 129:2, "Many a time have they afflicted me from my youth, yet they have not prevailed against me."

I remember a day I stopped and asked a farmer if I could walk back upon a hillside to look at an old house that was once built to be a mission house. It is now empty and forsaken, but as I stood there, I could hear the boards, the window frames, the old interior walls tell the story of days gone by. May we stand, be used, be faithful for our Lord.

God is looking for those who love Him and hunger to serve Him.

December 12

Amos 9 & Obadiah 1   Psalm 130   Proverbs 12   2 Tim. 4 & Titus 1-3

That Day

Good morning! Hurry, hurry, hurry; that seems to be the theme this time of the year. Hurry to that sale, hurry to this party, hurry to go visit this one and that one. Hurry, hurry, hurry! And yet as I read this morning in Psalm 130:5, "I wait for the Lord, my soul doth wait, and in his word do I hope." Psalm 130:6, "My soul waiteth for the Lord more than they that watch for the morning: I say, more than they that watch for the morning."

All of us get excited this time of year about seeing family, spending time together, parties, fellowships, Christmas programs and cantatas, etc. But as I read this morning, I had to stop and get back on my knees and ask the Lord to help me understand more about waiting on Him. It seems there is more of an urgency about the season than there is an urgency about pleasing the reason for the season. In Amos 9:1, I want to point out two phrases; "I will sift the house of Israel," and "yet shall not the least grain fall upon the earth." As you and I look at not only America, but the entire world, there is a shaking by God going on. In some areas there is revival of people being saved and new churches being established, and in other areas there is a greater denial of truth than this world has ever seen. As I read in

Obadiah 1:3, "The pride of thine heart hath deceived thee;" and as I read on there is a little phrase mentioned eleven times; "in that day."

We all need to be looking for "the day of the Lord." In II Timothy 4:7, we read the words that the apostle Paul wrote as he was preparing for "that day" in his life. "I have fought a good fight, I have finished my course, I have kept the faith." Paul was focused on being faithful until "that day" that the Lord took him Home. "That day" can be a day of judgment or a day of rejoicing to meet our Saviour and to hear those words, "well done, thou good and faithful servant." Or "that day" can be a day that some will hear, "depart from me, for I never knew you." Proverbs 12:28, "In the way of righteousness is life; and in the pathway thereof there is no death." Be looking and be prepared for "that day." I am looking forward to seeing family and spending time with friends, enjoying delicious food, playing games and having some good Christian fellowship, but may I live, serve and be looking for "that day." Have a blessed day.

We need to focus on being faithful until
"that day" when the Lord takes us Home.

December 13

Jonah 1-2   Psalm 131   Proverbs 13   Philemon 1 & Hebrews 1-2

Have You Hit Bottom?

Good morning! I am so thankful and humbled to think that God wants to use each of us, considering the sinners that we are. It is we that limit the Lord. I have said, and I am sure you have said, I can't do that, I could never go there, I could not learn that language, and on and on. We make excuses why we cannot instead of just saying, yes, Lord, I will. Jonah heard the Lord say in Jonah 1:1, "Arise, go to; but in verse 3 we read, "But Jonah rose up to flee." The storm came, the ship was tossed, and the men feared so greatly they cried out in every way and to every god they knew. The question was asked in verse 8, "for whose cause this evil is upon us." The world even knows when a Christian is out of fellowship with God. In Jonah 2:7 is a cry that many have cried, "When my soul fainted within me

I remembered the Lord." Jonah hit bottom, he had run from God, was not obedient to God and God let him hit bottom.

Many have come to God in need but not all have stayed right with God. I do not know where you are today, but if you have hit bottom and come back to God, please stay in your place doing what is right, because each time a person falls away, they always fall further than they did before. Hebrews 2:1, "Therefore we ought to give the more earnest heed to the things which we have heard, lest at any time we should let them slip." Throughout the years serving God, I have heard many say a sad statement; God took everything I had. Proverbs 13:15, "Good understanding giveth favour: but the way of transgressors is hard." We have read how God's people kept rebelling against God until He brought them to their knees and David wrote these words in Psalm 131:3, "Let Israel hope in the Lord from henceforth and for ever." May we stop today and check what we are doing, where we are and where we are heading spiritually. Are we being faithful to God? Are we seeking what we can do to serve God? Are we staying in fellowship with God? Jonah did do what God told him to do, but he sure went the rough way. There is no better place to be than in the perfect will of God, doing the will of God. Have a blessed day.

Each time a person falls away, they always fall further than they did before.

December 14

Jonah 3-4   Psalm 132   Proverbs 14   Hebrews 3-5

Stay in the Saddle

Good morning! I read this morning in Jonah 3:1, "And the word of the Lord came unto Jonah the second time, saying." I am so thankful we serve a God of the second chances. God wanted to see the city of Nineveh turned from their wickedness to Him and He wanted to use Jonah. God wants to use each of us no matter our age, our abilities, our location or anything that we might think would hinder the hand of God.

As I was reading this morning, I thought of how many times I have been bucked off a horse or how many times I have tried to ride a steer. I can even remember the first time, as a little fellow, I tried to get on the back of sheep and, to my surprise, I fell off. I learned quickly that what I think I can do and what I can do are often not the same. Hebrews 3:12-13, "Take heed brethren, lest there be in any of you an evil heart of unbelief, in departing from the living God. But exhort one another daily, while it is called To day; lest any of you be hardened through the deceitfulness of sin." The Lord wants to use us, but it is through His strength and not ours. As a little boy I rode a little toy horse that was on a metal frame with springs and I would dream how one day I would ride bucking horses. That day came for me to get on a horse and I remember the first time a horse bucked, and I was not ready, and I got bucked off. The more I rode the more I saw the need to stay alert to what the horse might do. A horse could get startled from the smallest thing and if I was not alert, I could get bucked off or just fall off.

Proverbs 14:16, "A wise man feareth, and departeth from evil: but the fool rageth, and is confident." We as God's people must stay alert to the deceitfulness of sin. We must put God first place in every decision and we must live by principles that will help us to stay right with God. Psalm 132:4-5, "I will not give sleep to mine eyes, or slumber to mine eyelids, until I find out a place for the Lord, an habitation for the mighty God of Jacob." It is relaxing to me to ride a horse, but I still need to stay alert. I love serving the Lord, and the devil would like nothing more than to take a Christian from walking with God into a life of sin. Live your life in God's will and make sure God's will is your will. Make sure you always seek God first and then make sure you do not let flesh take over what God wants. I have a great saddle but if I do not stay alert, that good saddle is not enough to keep me on the horse. Stay alert today and enjoy the ride. God's way is always the right way. If you get off the trail, get back on as soon as possible. My grandad often said, if you get thrown, get back on. Have a blessed day.

Live your life in God's will and make sure His will is your will.

December 15

Micah 1-2   Psalm 133-134   Proverbs 15   Hebrews 6-8

Stand Tall

Good morning! As Mrs. Smith and I were driving to town yesterday to go soul winning, she asked me to stop by a creek that we were crossing. I stopped and we looked at the beauty of the little stream. The leaves are all gone and the forest looks so dark, but along the creek are the tall white birch trees. Mrs. Smith brought to my attention how many there are and how tall they stand. As we drove on, we kept seeing more beautiful white birch trees that were adding a beauty to the forest, even though all the leaves are gone and the trees have gone dormant for the winter season.

As I read Micah 2:7, "do not my words do good to him that walketh uprightly." In a sin darkened world, we need to stand tall and alive for God and His glory. Those white birch trees brought life to the forest. You and I need to bring life eternal to a sin darkened world. Hebrews 6:12, "That ye be not slothful, but followers of them who through faith and patience inherit the promises." It may seem to us that there is no hope for this world, but there is through Christ. Hebrews 7:25, "Wherefore he is able also to save them to the uttermost that come unto God by him, seeing he ever liveth to make intercession for them." What a beautiful picture to look through the forest and see those tall, strong, stable, beautiful white barked trees coming up in the middle of a darkened forest! Proverbs 15:3, "The eyes of the Lord are in every place, beholding the evil and the good." God sees what we do not see, and that is why we must be busy about bringing the light of the gospel to this darkened world.

Psalm 134:1" Behold, bless ye the Lord, all ye servants of the Lord." As I read those two simple phrases, I thought how God can use all of us to bring joy, peace, and happiness to lives that are darkened with sin. The lights of the season are all around us, and they will soon go out; but the light of Christ will keep shining just like those tall white birch trees in the forest with no leaves. Take a look at the forest of men before us and bring the bright white of a sinner washed clean by the blood of Jesus. Stand tall today and stand as that sinner washed clean and be a living testimony for Christ.

*In a sin darkened world, we need to stand tall
and alive for God and His glory.*

December 16

Micah 3-4   Psalm 135   Proverbs 16   Hebrews 9-11

Just Praise Him

Good morning! As I read this morning, I have found my heart and mind so very full. There are days I feel we just need to stop and say nothing, but just bring praise to the Lord. God's love, patience and longsuffering to us is beyond what can be written or expressed in word or action, other than continued praise to God. Micah 4:5, "we will walk in the name of the Lord our God for ever and ever." The children of Israel continually sinned against God and His love for them never failed, even in times of His judgment.

No more lambs have to be sacrificed for the forgiveness of sin because as is recorded in Hebrews 9:12, "Neither by the blood of goats and calves, but by his own blood he entered in once into the holy place, having obtained eternal redemption for us." Look on down to verse 14, "How much more shall the blood of Christ, who through the eternal Spirit offered himself without spot to God, purge your conscience from dead works to serve the living God?" The question is asked, what more does Christ need to do? The answer is, NOTHING. Hebrews 10:12, "But this man, after he had offered one sacrifice for sins for ever, sat down on the right hand of God." Jesus is continually interceding for us that know Him as our Saviour. Praise Him today that our sins are forgiven and remembered no more. Hebrews 10:17, "And their sins and iniquities will I remember no more." As we read in Hebrews 11 and 12, may our faith be strengthened by the testimonies of those that have gone before us. Hebrews 10:23, "Let us hold fast the profession of our faith without wavering; (for he is faithful that promised)."

Stop and evaluate your heart and the priorities of your heart. Proverbs 16:9, "A man's heart deviseth his way: but the Lord directeth his steps." Let us take time not only this day, but every day for the rest of our lives, to spend time praising the Lord. Psalm 135:1, "Praise ye the Lord. Praise ye the name of the Lord; praise him, O ye servants of the Lord." Psalm 135:13, "Thy name, O Lord, endureth for ever; and thy memorial, O Lord, throughout all generations." Praise Him today!!

Sometimes we just need to stop what we are doing
and spend time praising the Lord.

December 17

Micah 5-6   Psalm 136   Proverbs 17   Hebrews 12-13

The Greatest Gift

Good morning! Micah 5:2, "But thou, Bethlehem Ephratah, though thou be little among the thousands of Judah, yet out of thee shall he come forth unto me that is to be ruler in Israel; whose goings forth have been from old, from everlasting." This verse and others will be part of many Christmas plays during the month of December and rightfully so. My thought for us to ponder this morning is, something big coming from something small, or something growing to be something of which we could not dream.

At this time, I have the privilege to serve the Lord with my granddaughter. She has been the camp secretary for nearly five years. I have also had the privilege to serve the Lord a summer with one of my grandsons. Looking ahead, this coming summer there is a possibility that three of our six grandchildren will serve with us on summer camp staff. As I look back, we had the joy to serve the Lord for over twenty-five years with our children, and all of our grandchildren have spent time with us working at the camp. Even though they were not on staff, they worked and did some type of labor. Now our children and grandchildren have moved on but, praise the Lord, they are all serving the Lord in their local churches. Proverbs 17:6, "Children's children are the crown of old men; and the glory of children are their fathers." Proverbs 17:21, "He that begetteth a fool doeth it to his sorrow: and the father of a fool hath no joy." Verse 6 tells of the joy of our children living for the Lord and verse 21 speaks of the sorrow of a child not living for the Lord. Do you pray daily for your children and grandchildren? If you are not married yet, and even if you are, are you living to bring joy to the Lord and blessings to your parents? Proverbs 17:25, "A foolish son is a grief to his father, and bitterness to her that bare him." If you are a son or a daughter, a mom or a dad struggling to live for God, listen to the words of Hebrews 12:1, "let us lay aside every weight, and the sin which doth so easily beset us, and let us run with patience the race that is set before us." As we read in Psalm 136 this morning, all 26 verses end with, "for his mercy endureth for ever." Quit living in past failures and live for and with the joy of the Lord, living and serving the Lord.

Those children and grandchildren have grown up right in front of Mrs. Smith and me. What greater gift can I give them this Christmas than to live for Christ and bring honor and glory to Him? He came as a child, He grew into a man and He died as our Saviour. Live for Him.

There's no better gift we can give our children
and grandchildren than to live for Christ.

December 18

Micah 7 & Nahum 1   Psalm 137   Proverbs 18   James 1-4

Piece by Piece

Good morning! I have heard many Christians, young and old, say the Christian life is so hard. I want to go on record and say it is a decision that must be continually made. Think with me about a little child given their first puzzle. Someone helped them to understand how to take the puzzle apart and put one piece in its place and then the next and the next until all the pieces were in place. The child would then turn it over and put it back together. As the child would grow, the puzzles kept getting harder and each puzzle had more pieces. How frustrating it is to try to put a puzzle together and to think there is a piece missing. If we only could find that one piece, the puzzle could be complete. As the child grew, the principle of putting the pieces in place was the same, there were just more pieces.

We must hunger to make sure all the pieces of our walk with God are put in their place. Micah 7:18, "Who is a God like unto thee, that pardoneth iniquity, and passeth by the transgression of the remnant of his heritage? He retaineth not his anger for ever, because he delighteth in mercy." There is no God as patient, forgiving, and understanding as our God. Micah 7:19, "thou wilt cast all their sins into the depths of the sea." Our sins are gone when we ask Him to forgive us. Nahum 1:7, "The Lord is good, a strong hold in the day of trouble; and he knoweth them that trust in him." We told the child to look at the picture on the box so they would know what the puzzle was to look like. As an adult, we looked at the picture on the box so we could put the puzzle together correctly. As a Christian, we need to keep our eyes on Christ to know what a Christian life is to be like. James 1:3, "Knowing this, that the trying of your faith worketh patience." The picture was the key; keeping our eyes on Christ and living a life pleasing to Him by walking with Him daily and daily being in His Word. James 3:7-8, "Submit yourselves to God, Resist the devil and he will flee from you. Draw nigh to God, and he will draw nigh to you. Cleanse your hands, ye sinners; and purify your hearts, ye double minded."

Can you hear the child saying, "I did it, I did it!"? The child was able to do it piece by piece and we need to walk the Christian life step by step. Proverbs 18:10, "The name of the Lord is a strong tower: the righteous runneth into it, and is safe." Each day we walk with God, let us take the time and do as Psalm 137:3 says, "Sing us one of the songs of Zion." Songs of praise need to be sung as we walk and grow in our walk with God. A puzzle is completed by putting each piece in its place. The Christian life is walked step by step.

We need to keep our eyes on Christ to know
what the Christian life is to be like.

Nahum 2-3   Psalm 138   Proverbs 19   James 5 & I Pet. 1-3

Spiritual Ghost Town

Good morning! Have you ever been to a ghost town where at one time it was a thriving town and now all that stands are empty buildings? Many a story have been told about buildings that were once used and now they stand vacant. You can now drive through many small communities and see a school building that once was full of children and a playground that would have heard the laughter of children playing, and now the building and the playground stand empty.

Nahum was the prophet of God that told of the destruction of Nineveh, a great city that Jonah was sent to and if you remember, it was several days journey just to go around this great city. Nahum now writes that they of this great city cry, "Stand, stand, shall they cry; but none shall look back," Nahum 2:8. It was once a great city with size, power and authority. Now in Nahum 2:13 and 3:5, it is recorded that God said, "Behold, I am against thee, saith the Lord of hosts." What once was is now gone. Many a Christian once was excited about church, about winning souls, about running a bus route to pick up children, about revival meetings and missions conference and now there is only a spark left spiritually. At one time it was a priority of going to church when the doors were open and now they have excuses. Proverbs 19:21, "There are many devices in a man's heart; nevertheless the counsel of the Lord, that shall stand." May we not be like an old ghost town that was once and now is not. I Peter 1:13, "Wherefore gird up the loins of your mind, be sober, and hope to the end."

During this time of year when the pressures of life press so hard, keep on keeping on. When you give excuse, it is kicking the door open to quitting. Make church a priority, make soul winning a priority, make tithing a priority, make serving God a priority. Psalm 138:3, "In the day when I cried thou answeredst me, and strengthenedst me with strength in my soul." As it has been said many a time, "when you feel like you are at the end of your rope, tie another knot in the end and hang on. See you in church.

When you give excuses, it is kicking the door open to quitting.

December 20

Habakkuk 1-3   Psalm 139   Proverbs 20   1 Pet. 4-5 & 2 Pet. 1-2

Keep the Fire Burning

Good morning! As I was loading wood last night to bring to the house for our wood stove, I stopped and looked at the different wood that is stacked in the pile. For most of our married life, Mrs. Smith and I have heated our home with a wood burning stove. No, I am not Daniel Boone or Davy Crockett, although I have thought many times of what it would have been like to live during that time. Back to the wood pile. If you would pass by the stacks of wood, it just looks like wood but there are many different types of wood in the pile. I do not burn green wood; I try to let all the wood dry for a season, but even at that the different woods burn differently.

As our reading today took us to the book of Habakkuk for the Old Testament, I read in 1:13, "Thou art of purer eyes than to behold evil, and canst not look on iniquity." Habakkuk was giving testimony of the holiness and patience of our God. Some of the wood in the wood pile burns very hot and for a long time. Some of the wood in the wood pile will not burn as long and will not make as hot of a fire. I thought of the harder the wood, the longer it burns. The closer we walk with God, the more we resist sin. The softer the type of wood, the less heat it provides. The weaker we are to fighting sin, the farther our walk is away from God. I Peter 4:17, "For the time is come that judgment must begin at the house of God: and if it first begin at us, what shall the end be of them that obey not the gospel of God." In burning wood and especially keeping a fire going during the night, I use a good hard wood such as oak, hickory or hedge. I burn all kinds of wood but the wood that lasts the longest is the wood that it took the longest for the tree to grow.

Reading, studying and meditating on God's Word takes time but builds a solid life in Christ and when the devil attacks, we win the fight and last the longest in serving God. Proverbs 20:5, "Counsel in the heart of man is like deep water; but a man of understanding will draw it out." Live in the Word of God and the Word of God will live in you. Psalm 139:23, "Search me, O God, and know my heart: try me, and know my thoughts." When the temperatures dip down cold at night, I want a wood in the stove that will last through the night. Walk with God and you and I can live through the test of time. Do not be hardhearted, but be hard against sin. For me, I will burn the hard wood because it produces a hot long-lasting fire. Stay warm.

When the devil attacks, we win the fight
and last the longest when we are serving God.

December 21

Zephaniah 1-3   Psalm 140   Proverbs 21   2 Pet. 3 & I John 1-3

Faithful No Matter What

Good morning! I am so very thankful for the many things that my father and mother lived and that they taught by their lives. I will try to say it another way. My parents were not perfect, but they were a generation that lived what they said they were, and what they said they were is what they lived. If they said they were going to pay a bill on time, they paid that bill on time. If they said they were going to be a certain place at a said time, they were there. A man's handshake was a promise that was going to be kept. I ask myself and I ask you today, are you who and what you say you are?

The little book of Zephaniah was written during a time when there was outwardly a form of Godliness but it was truly a wicked time. Zephaniah 1:2, "I will utterly consume all things from off the land, saith the Lord." I think God is saying very plainly that He has had enough of the wickedness. The cry of the prophet is recorded in Zephaniah 2:3, "Seek ye the Lord, all ye meek of the earth, which have wrought his judgment; seek righteousness, seek meekness: it may be ye shall be hid in the day of the Lord's anger." The same cry for holiness needs to be heard in our day. The sadness of sin is that it has such a hold on our lives that we turn a deaf ear to God. Zephaniah 3:2, "She obeyed not the voice; she received not correction; she trusted not in the Lord; she drew not near her God." It is time for us that are saved to get right and stay right, to be what we know we should be and to live what we know we should live. II Peter 3:2 says it best, "That ye may be mindful of the words which were spoken before by the holy prophets, and of the commandment of us the apostles of the Lord and Saviour."

I remember the first job I had, when the boss hired me, he stood up behind his desk and shook my hand and told me when to show up. You know I was thankful, excited, and in my heart I wanted to do my very best. How about our life in Christ? I John 2:6, "He that saith he abideth in him ought himself also so to walk, even as he walked." We will always have excuses and we must conquer those excuses. Proverbs 21:2, "Every way of a man is right in his own eyes: but the Lord pondereth the hearts." As I looked into the eyes of my first boss and told him I would be there and I thanked him for the job; I thought of the words of my dad, "You better do what you told your boss you would do." As I finished reading this morning in Psalm 140, I thought on two words, "deliver me." I am my own worst enemy and if I am going to please God in everything, I must do what is always right in the eyes of God and be what I say I am. I must be a Christian that hungers to please God in every area of my life. Can you look in the eyes of God today and make a fresh commitment that you will be faithful no matter the circumstances, trials or testings? May we live what we say we are.

We must conquer our excuses and stay faithfully committed to God.

Haggai 1-2 Psalm 141 Proverbs 22 1 John 4-5, 2 John, 3 John

Go for the Pin

Good morning! One of the many joys that I have had, and still have as a grandfather, is wrestling with my grandsons. I love high school and college level wrestling, where two meet on a mat in the same weight category and the bout begins. II John verse 8, "Look to yourselves, that we lose not those things which we wrought, but that we receive a full reward." A young man will work hard in learning wrestling moves, making weight, physically working to strengthen himself for that time he will meet his opponent on the mat.

As we read this morning in Haggai 1:4, "Is it time," verse 7, "Consider your ways," verse 14, "And the Lord stirred up the spirit." The people of God were being restored and they needed to rebuild the temple. The temple was unfinished and he was trying to encourage them to finish the work. Haggai 2:14, "be strong," "and work," "for I am with you, saith the Lord of hosts." I have been on a wrestling mat and facing my opponent and the coach has often said, you know what to do, just do it. It often depended on how badly I wanted the win. I John 4:4, "greater is he that is in you, than he that is in the world." A wrestler might have a special move and I needed to watch and be ready to counter that move or I could lose the match. Victory is ours in the Christian life and we need to live for victory. I John 5:13, "These things have I written unto you that believe on the name of the Son of God; that ye may know that ye have eternal life, and that ye may believe on the name of the Son of God." We need to focus on what brings victory. I could not dwell on how good another wrestler was, I needed to be my best. Proverbs 22:17, "Bow down thine ear, and hear the words of the wise, and apply thine heart unto my knowledge."

As I was wrestling, I needed to stay alert and listen to what the coach was telling me that maybe I did not see. Often, I would use the move of the other wrestler to my advantage. Psalm 141:8, "But mine eyes are unto thee, O God the Lord: in thee is my trust; leave not my soul destitute." We must listen continually to the voice of God and keep our focus on having victory in the Christian life. We need to quit seeing only the negative and look for the blessings of God. A wrestler could defeat himself by dwelling on how good the wrestler was that he was facing. III John 11, "Beloved, follow not that which is evil, but that which is good. He that doeth good is of God: but he that doeth evil hath not seen God." Victory is ours today. As a good coach would say, go for the pin. Live for Christ today, live for victory. Quit letting the negatives of life and the circumstances determine your joy. Live in and for victory.

Victory is ours and we need to focus on what brings victory.

December 23

Zechariah 1-2   Psalm 142   Proverbs 23   Jude & Rev. 1-3

Jesus is Coming

Good morning! During this time of the year as we draw closer to Christmas and the meals are being planned, the excitement of family and friends getting together seems to be the forefront of all that is consuming us. As I read in Revelation 1:3, "Blessed is he that readeth, and they that hear the words of this prophecy, and keep those things which are written therein: for the time is at hand." Many parents, many commercials, many songs will echo over and again, "you better watch out, you better not cry, because Santa Claus is coming to town." Yes, we will hear it over and again. I have said that phrase myself years ago. I have even made mention of Zechariah 2:6 as a proof text for Santa Claus; "Ho, ho, come forth, and flee from the land of the north." Truth is, it is not a laughing matter. Santa Claus is not coming to town, but the truth is Christ is returning and our reading today is proof that it can be today.

Zechariah 1:3, "Turn ye unto me, saith the Lord of hosts, and I will turn unto you, saith the Lord of hosts." Zechariah 1:14, "I am jealous for Jerusalem and for Zion with a great jealousy." More than any song and more than an advertisement to sell things, may our prayer and actions this year be to spread the tidings of great joy that Christ our Redeemer is coming and we need to be ready. Revelation 1:4, 8, "I am," "which is, and which was, and which is to come." God says in Revelation 2:2, "I know thy works," and in Revelation 3:22, "He that hath an ear, let him hear what the Spirit saith unto the churches." I am excited to sit down, read the Bible, open some gifts, eat a fine meal, but may our focus be on pleasing the Lord in all that we do. May our joy be because of the Lord our Lord, our Redeemer, our Saviour. Jude 14, "Behold, the Lord cometh with ten thousands of his saints." There is coming a day that total victory in this world of sin will be when Jesus returns with His saints, bought with His precious blood. He is wonderful, counselor, mighty God. Proverbs 23:11, "For their redeemer is mighty." Psalm 142:5, "I cried unto thee, O Lord: I said, Thou art my refuge and my portion in the land of the living." I want to enjoy all the joys of the season, and I know you do too.

Put Christ first in all that you do, say and express this season. I loved those words we read this morning in Zechariah 2:10, "Sing and rejoice, O daughter of Zion: for, lo, I come, and I will dwell in the midst of thee, saith the Lord." Have a joyous day, Jesus is coming soon.

May our prayer and actions this year be to spread the tidings of great joy.

December 24

Zechariah 3-4   Psalm 143   Proverbs 24   Revelation 4-7

Remember the True Meaning

Good morning! Today is Christmas Eve and the push is on to be ready for Christmas Day. Christmas has changed throughout the years, but the true meaning of Christmas has become more real and special to me. I can remember as a young boy the excitement of waking up and seeing gifts in the front room, waking our parents, excited to begin the day. Then came the day of spending the time buying and wrapping gifts and hoping folks would be happy with what was purchased for them. I can remember my grandparents coming and staying with us from Christmas Eve to the day after Christmas. As I stood in the living room this morning and turned on the lights and decorations, I stopped and thought back of the first

Christmas that Mrs. Smith and I spent together, then our daughter came along, then our son. Now our children have their families and how our grandchildren are growing, and they will soon have their own Christmas days. Many years have come and gone, but the true meaning of Christmas is the same, and praise God, it is still the same.

Zechariah 3:8, that we read this morning, "I will bring forth my servant the BRANCH." That was the prophecy of Jesus coming to this earth. He came that day into this world in a lowly manger with two parents handpicked by God. Listen again to the words written by Zechariah in 4:6, "Not by might, nor by power, but by my spirit, saith the Lord of hosts." What a sound to hear the heavenly host singing that day! We read in Revelation 4:8 about the singing and praising that is going on in Heaven, "they rest not day and night, saying Holy, Holy, Holy, Lord God Almighty, which was, and is, and is to come." Glory! Our KING is the God of the past, the God of the present and the God of the future. He is my King and His name is Jesus.

Today, in the rush of preparation for the family getting together tomorrow, do not let the changes of this world affect the true meaning of Christmas. Proverbs 24:21, "My son, fear thou the Lord and the King: and meddle not with them that are given to change." All of us have the special memories of Christmases past. Keep reading the Christmas story, praying as a family, singing a song of praise to our King. Psalm 143:5, "I remember the days of old; I meditate on all thy works; I muse on the work of thy hands." The word "muse" is to take time and dwell or think on. Keep Christ in Christmas. Enjoy the family coming to be with you or enjoy that special time with the Lord. Just make sure you never forget the true meaning of Christmas.

Many years have come and gone but the true
meaning of Christmas is still the same.

Zechariah 5-6   Psalm 144   Proverbs 25   Revelation 8-11

Merry Christmas

Merry Christmas!! This is the day of remembering the birth of our Lord and Saviour Jesus Christ. As I got up this morning to go have my private time with the Lord and to write this devotional, I stopped and went back in my mind to many Christmas mornings. The songs have been sung over and again, the plays have been practiced and presented, the presents wrapped and now waiting under the tree, the food of all kinds have been prepared and the children will soon awaken with excitement as only a child can have. Grandpas and grandmas will arrive or be awakened to the sounds of, "come and see!" Moms and dads will be attacked in their bedrooms by children wanting to know if they can open their presents now. A smile comes to my face as I type and yet there is also a quietness as I stop and pray for those that will be alone this morning, some for the first time and for others it has been several Christmas mornings.

As I began to read, I read in Zechariah 6:12, "Behold the man whose name is The BRANCH; and he shall grow up out of his place." Christmas Day and every day for a Christian is a day about Jesus. In Revelation 11:15, "The kingdoms of this world are become the kingdoms of our Lord, and of his Christ; and he shall reign for ever and ever." Do not forget the most important part of this day and that is to exalt our KING and his name is Jesus. Revelation 11:17, "We give thanks, O Lord God Almighty, which art, and wast, and art to come; because thou hast taken to thee thy great power, and hast reigned." He has not returned to rule and reign this world yet, but in our hearts and in our lives, He is our KING and he does reign. In Proverbs 25:1, I am so thankful for two small words that I read this morning; "copied out." We can read the very words of God today and every day because they were "copied out" for us. Psalm 144:1, "Blessed be the Lord my strength." Psalm 144:2, "My goodness, and my fortress; my high tower, and my deliverer; my shield."

Rejoice today, my brother and sister. Enjoy the time with family and friends. Please take the time together, or if you are alone, and read that beautiful story of the birth of our Saviour. Listen once again to the heavenly host, picture the shepherds kneeling before our KING. Psalm 144:15, "happy is that people, whose God is the Lord." He came to this world that all men may be saved. Trust Him today, live for Him today, serve Him today and the rest of your life. Merry Christmas to all.

Take time today to read that beautiful story of the birth of our Saviour.

December 26

Zechariah 7-8   Psalm 145   Proverbs 26   Revelation 12-13

Fasting and Prayer

Good morning! Do you ever find yourself trying to do everything that you think you are supposed to be doing to please the Lord, and there seems to be a void, or something is just not right? Do you ever find yourself praying and it does not seem like the prayers are being answered or the prayers are not getting any higher than the ceiling? I am sure that every one of us at times finds ourselves in these circumstances. Why, and what do we need to do more?

As we read this morning in Zechariah 7:5, "did ye at all fast unto me, even to me?" Those words "did ye at all fast," kept coming to my attention as I read on. Fasting is not very often spoken of outside of losing weight or going through a physical cleanse, but fasting is throughout the Scriptures for many reasons. As I read on in Zechariah 7:12, "Yea, they made their hearts as an adamant stone, lest they should hear the law, and the words which the Lord of hosts hath sent in his spirit by the former prophets." Fasting spiritually brings a cleanse spiritually. It is spending extra time praying and reading the Word of God instead of eating. Allowing ourselves to come before God, cleansed spiritually, can reveal an area of our lives that needs to be cleansed and revived. Our Lord might just be wanting to spend extra time with us and fasting allows this time. Revelation 12:11, "And they overcame him by the blood of the Lamb, and by the word of their testimony:." I praise the Lord daily, and many times a day, for His blood that was shed for my sins, but I feel there are times I need to go the extra mile to show the Lord that I mean business in my relationship with Him, and there is no better way than to deny myself and spend that time with Him in prayer and fasting. Proverbs 26:22, "The words of a tale bearer are as wounds, and they go down into the innermost parts of the belly." The belly is an area of our body that affects all other areas, and there may be something that we do not even know is in our lives. To be clean before God is to be clean for God. To be cleansed from sin is to be ready to be used. To be cleansed is to be ready to receive what we spiritually need in our lives. To be cleansed and open with God could bring a spiritual revival that is needed in our lives.

Psalm 145:18, "The Lord is nigh unto all them that call upon him, to all that call upon him in truth." Let us think about a spiritual time of cleansing before God to get right down to the truth that we need about answered prayer, direction for the next step, guidance in a decision. I think we need to consider fasting a meal, a day or whatever length of time God needs for us to cleanse ourselves before Him. Zechariah 7:5, "did ye at all fast unto me, even to me?." Spend some time studying fasting and see how God used this time to bring about greater works for Him.

To be cleansed and open with God could bring a spiritual revival in our lives.

December 27

Zechariah 9-10   Psalm 146   Proverbs 27   Revelation 14-15

Focus on Jesus

Good morning! I can only imagine what excitement it was the day Jesus rode into Jerusalem on the colt, the foal of an ass, as Zechariah 9:9 states for us; "Rejoice greatly, O daughter of Zion; shout, O daughter of Jerusalem: behold, thy King cometh unto thee: he is just, and having salvation; lowly, and riding upon an ass, and upon a colt the foal of an ass." What a day that must have been! Then we read this morning about what John saw in Revelation 14:1, "And I looked, and, lo, a Lamb stood on the mount Sion." When John looked, He saw Jesus standing. Oh, that we would keep our focus on Jesus every day, and that our worship would be on Him. Revelation 14:7, "worship him that made heaven, and earth, and the sea, and the fountains of waters."

This world has become so confident in itself and what it can do and what it can produce. In our reading today in Proverbs 27:1, we are warned, "Boast not thyself of tomorrow; for thou knowest not what a day may bring forth." As this year will end in just a few days, may we keep our focus on Jesus, and all that He has done and is going to do. Psalm 146:2, "While I live will I praise the Lord: I will sing praises unto my God while I have any being." When all of life is done, what will last forever is a relationship with Jesus Christ. Psalm 146:5, "Happy is he that hath the God of Jacob for his help, whose hope is in the Lord his God." May we as born again believers keep the focus of Christ first every day and in everything that we say and do. May all decisions that we make be a decision because we have sought the Lord and His will and guidance.

Just a couple of days have passed since we sang songs of praise and adoration to and about our King. Should not every day be about a focus on Jesus? Should not we be more faithful when the church doors are open? Should we not show our love for Christ through our giving to Him and His work? As I reread Zechariah chapters 9-10, I noticed thirteen times the two little words "I will." Those two words "I will," is God's promise to His people. How about today our will, will be His will, so He can fullfil "His will" in our lives. Since God said, "I will," do you not think it would be great for us to say to Him, "I will"? As He rode into Jerusalem that day, He will soon come again to take us to Heaven as He said, "I will."

When all of life is done, what will last forever
is a relationship with Jesus Christ.

Zechariah 11-12   Psalm 147   Proverbs 28   Revelation 16-17

Hope in Jesus

Good morning! The Psalms are so beautiful to read. I often wish I could hear each one put to music. I love to read the history behind the hymns that we sing. As I read this morning in Psalm 147, I noticed that I had marked a thought throughout the years in every verse. As I read, I noticed a word that I had marked eighteen times, and that is the word "He." I then noticed how many times I had marked the word "his." I hunger to learn how to love God more and more. Psalm 147:11, "The Lord taketh pleasure in them that fear him, in those that hope in his mercy."

As I drove yesterday, I was captivated by the multitudes going everywhere as fast as they could go. People honking at each other, impatience everywhere you looked. Hurry, hurry, hurry; everyone has their priorities. Man thinks he is so powerful, so full of answers and yet has so little knowledge about his Creator. Proverbs 28:26, "He that trusteth in his own heart is a fool: but whoso walketh wisely, he shall be delivered." God will have His day soon, and very soon it will be time for the redeemed to leave this earth. As I read in Revelation 16:17, "It is done," I thought about God saying to the angel Gabriel, it is time to sound the "Trump of God," and God will have His day. As we read in Zechariah 12, five different times we find the phrase, "In that day." There is coming a day that every knee will bow and every tongue will confess that Jesus Christ is Lord. May our focus today be in taking the time to enjoy time with the Lord and make it a priority of every day. Love Him, praise Him, talk with Him, serve Him, learn more of Him. Listen to the words again of Psalm 147:11, "The Lord taketh pleasure in them that fear him, in those that hope in his mercy." Let your hope be in Jesus. He is always there waiting for us to spend time with Him. Stop right now and just tell Him how much you love Him.

May our focus today be in taking time to enjoy time with the Lord.

December 29

Zechariah 13-14   Psalm 148   Proverbs 29   Revelation 18-19

Captivated by God

Good morning! As I was reading this morning, my mind went to many years back at a week of deaf camp. It was late and all the campers had been sent to their cabins and I was making my rounds to make sure everything was okay. As I approached the boys cabins, I noticed a group of campers outside, just standing and looking up into the sky. I flashed my flashlight so as not to startle them and as I approached, I asked a counselor what was going on. Most of the deaf campers were from intercity churches and they had never seen a clear sky full of stars like they saw that night. They asked me what the sound of the stars was like. I told them the stars did not make any sound, they just glimmered. As I read this morning in Psalm 148:5, "Let them praise the name of the Lord: for he commanded, and they were created."

That night, as the deaf that could not hear nor speak looked into God's creation, they were captivated by stars that were created by God and yet nothing was said or heard. Oh, that we could be so captivated by God, and all that He is. This world captures most all of our attention and creates a distraction from the wonderful hand of God. Proverbs 29:25, "The fear of man bringeth a snare: but whoso putteth his trust in the Lord shall be safe." We should stop and take time to be captivated by the greatness of God. The riches of this world, the fame of this world, the power of this world, controls the mind and heart of so many. My heart grieves when I get around some and it is like bragging time has come. My mind always goes to a missionary that is unknown or a preacher that will never be heard of until we get to Heaven. May I throw out a challenge for us today to look and offer praise unto our God that is so often never recognized for His greatness. Zechariah 14:9, "And the Lord shall be King over all the earth: in that day shall there be one Lord, and his name one." Revelation 19:6, "Alleluia: for the Lord God omnipotent reigneth."

You should have been with me many a night throughout all the years, as I stood in the middle of darkness with deaf campers looking at the stars of Heaven, and watching the tears trickle down their cheeks as they were captivated by the greatness of God and His creation. Revelation 19:16, "And he hath on his vesture and on his thigh a name written "KING OF KINGS, AND LORD OF LORDS.""

We should stop and take time to be captivated by the greatness of God.

December 30

Malachi 1-2   Psalm 149   Proverbs 30   Revelation 20-21

Be Real

Good morning! We are just about to the end of this year and I am spending time looking back and looking ahead. Looking back at the blessings of God and looking forward to what will be done for Him in the new year. Each day it is important for us to be under the microscope of looking at our heart and life and keeping it right with God. Malachi 2:15-16, "take heed to your spirit." The words and actions of the children of Israel were not the same. I stopped reading and I asked myself the same question. Am I living what I say I am? Does my life back up what I say I am?

Some time back I was to be at a certain location and the time was running close. I was to meet with three other men, and one of the men said, I hope Bro. Smith has not forgotten. I was told later that one of the other men said, if Bro Smith said he is going to be here, he will be here. Boy, was I glad that I was where I said I would be! This world thinks the good that they do will help them get to Heaven. You and I have learned that the Bible teaches and shows us that it is not our works that get us to Heaven, but it is through the gift of salvation and faith in Jesus Christ. As we read in Revelation 20:12-13, "judged every man according to their works" but Revelation 20:15 says, "And whosoever was not found written in the book of life was cast into the lake of fire." God's Word is true and what it says is what it means. Let us ask ourselves again, am I what I say that I am? Am I living the life of a Christian or am I living a lie? As we read the word of God and grow in the teachings of the Bible, our lives can be transformed to be more like Christ in every way. This world wants to change the meaning of what God says to satisfy their lifestyle but God says in Proverbs 30:6, "Add thou not unto his words, lest he reprove thee, and thou be found a liar."

My dad put great emphasis in teaching us the importance of being what you say you are, and be who you are all the time. Our Lord takes pleasure when we are truthful and obedient unto Him. Psalm 149:4, "For the Lord taketh pleasure in his people." Be real with yourself and with others and most of all with God. He saved us and is preparing a home for eternity, so live a life that brings honor to Him. I am thankful that day that I kept my appointment as I said I would. Our lives speak louder than our words.

Be real with yourself, with others and most of all with God.

December 31

Malachi 3-4   Psalm 150   Proverbs 31   Revelation 22

Ever Flowing Praise

Good morning! As I finished reading my Bible this morning and looked at its pages, I thought of all that is contained within; it is a neverending fountain. Mrs. Smith and I stopped recently along the side of a road and watched as a stream flowed so swiftly and strongly. That picture has not left my mind as I have asked the Lord to let my life be a flow of Christlikeness every day. We must spend time each day in the Word of God to keep the flow of God and His Word coming through us. The rain was falling and running down the hillside to the creek below and that is what keeps the streams flowing.

Even though this is the last day of a year, may we face the new year with a renewed hunger to keep feeding on God's Word. Life changes as we get older and it seems each year the world gets farther away from God, but how I praise His name that our Lord stays the same. Malachi 3:6, "For I am the Lord, I change not." We should not be separating ourselves from God and His service but drawing closer every day. As the water falls from the sky and keeps the creeks flowing, so should we be drawing from the Word of God and growing stronger in Him. His return for us is soon. Revelation 22:7, "Behold, I come quickly: blessed is he that keepeth the sayings of the prophecy of this book." The word "blessed" should be so important to each of us. Revelation 22:14, "Blessed are they that do his commandments." May the daily reading and meditating on the Word of God bring a life growing in Christ. As the woman of Proverbs 31 was praised by her family, the chapter is concluded with "let her own works praise her." Psalm 150:6 should be heard at the end of this year and the beginning of next; "Let every thing that hath breath praise the Lord. Praise ye the Lord."

As my wife and I watched the water flow, there was the sound of the falling rain and the flowing water. May today not just be the last day of a year, but may it be a day to praise Him forever and ever.

Daily reading and meditating on the Word of God
brings a life growing in Christ.

CPSIA information can be obtained
at www.ICGtesting.com
Printed in the USA
JSHW021933131122
33103JS00002B/3